THE MARQUESS OF QUEENSBERRY

THE MARQUESS OF QUEENSBERRY

OF

WILDE'S NEMESIS

LINDA STRATMANN

YALE UNIVERSITY PRESS
NEW HAVEN AND LONDON

For information about this and other Yale University Press publications, please contact:
U.S. Office: sales.press@yale.edu   www.yalebooks.com
Europe Office: sales @yaleup.co.uk   www.yalebooks.co.uk

Set in Adobe Garamond Pro by IDSUK (DataConnection) Ltd
Printed in Great Britain by TJ International Ltd, Padstow, Cornwall

Library of Congress Cataloging-in-Publication Data

Stratmann, Linda.
  The Marquess of Queensberry: Wilde's nemesis / Linda Stratmann.
    pages. cm.
  ISBN 978-0-300-17380-2 (cl: alk. paper)
1. Queensberry, John Sholto Douglas, Marquis of, 1844–1900.
2. Nobility—Scotland—Biography. 3. Queensberry, John Sholto Douglas, Marquis of,
1844–1900—Trials, litigation, etc. 4. Wilde, Oscar, 1854–1900—Trials, litigation, etc.
5. Douglas, Alfred Bruce, 1870–1945. 6. Great Britain—History—19th century. I. Title.
  DA816.Q44S77 2013
  941.081092–dc23
  [B]
                                                                              2012043030

A catalogue record for this book is available from the British Library.

10 9 8 7 6 5 4 3 2 1

This book is dedicated with great fondness to Teddy and Tom

. . . his family has always been noted for an eccentricity which has led to some strange romances, to some extremely dramatic episodes, and to a large number of tragedies.

'Obituary of Percy Douglas, tenth Marquess of Queensberry',
Johannesburg Star, 2 Aug. 1920, p. 4

Contents

Illustrations

Author's Note

A BIOGRAPHY is only as good as the validity of its prime sources, and in writing about John Sholto Douglas, Marquess of Queensberry there are tripwires to avoid and minefields to cross. Where there are contrasting versions of the same events, the biographer has to look at the weight of evidence, and assess the veracity, beliefs and memory of witnesses. The violent antipathy towards homosexuality in the 1890s which led many to conceal or reject the truth about relationships, the attitude to mental illness at a time when it was still possible to get someone committed to an asylum for flouting the rules of polite society, and the powerful emotions experienced by so many of the leading personalities in this story must all be taken into account.

The semi-autobiographical writing and correspondence of Queensberry's sister Lady Florence Dixie should be treated with some caution. Florence had a tendency to embellish and romanticise the truth, to describe events not as they were but as she would like them to have been, often placing herself at the centre of the action, and even inventing incidents outright.

The political diaries of Lewis Harcourt are, in his references to Lord Rosebery, compromised by his strong antagonism to the man he felt had prevented his father from becoming Prime Minister. Frank Harris's *Oscar Wilde: His Life and Confessions* is regarded by many Wilde biographers as unreliable; littered with exaggerations and inaccuracies.

The most dubious source is Sir Edmund Trelawny Backhouse, parts of whose memoirs have been denounced as fraudulent, some demonstrably so, making it impossible, especially concerning sexual encounters, to disentangle truth and half-truth from fantasy.

In the conflicted triangle of Queensberry, his son Lord Alfred Douglas (Bosie) and Oscar Wilde, emotions ran high, and allegations were flung and assumptions made many of which do not stand up to critical examination. Both Bosie and Queensberry had a tendency to write in an angry, pained and accusatory manner, which makes identifying the true situation extremely difficult. Though Queensberry was volatile in his moods, it is, however, hard to point to anything he declared as a fact which is both flagrantly untrue and which he knew to be untrue at the time of writing. The best known letters of Queensberry are those in which, pushed to the limits of endurance, he poured out his fury, grief and frustration. His calmer writings, many of which are published here for the first time, give a more balanced view of events and of the man.

A great deal of what is stated as fact about Queensberry has as its only source the self-justifying memoirs of Bosie, or letters he wrote in passionate defence of Oscar Wilde in which a major theme was attacks upon his father. Where allegations made by Bosie about his father can be checked against documentary sources or the evidence of those who were present at incidents where he was not, they can be shown to be untrue. Bosie also tended to contradict himself, sometimes in the same book, and retract statements he made in earlier publications. Bosie's niece Violet Wyndham was to comment 'Alfred Douglas is not always reliable in his statements'.[1]

I agree with Merlin Holland who in his introduction to *The Complete Letters of Oscar Wilde* states: 'no fact, date or statement given by Frank Harris or Lord Alfred Douglas can be accepted without reliable corroborative evidence'.[2]

By contrast, Wilde's long letter to Bosie, later published as *De Profundis*, his style shorn of all literary affectation, was not written in the heat of anger but over a period of months after almost two years of bitter introspection and is a considered and deeply sad document, although Wilde's perception of Queensberry and his motives was undoubtedly and understandably coloured by his own catastrophe.

During his lifetime John Sholto Douglas was designated eighth Marquess of Queensberry. This numbering was revised in the twentieth century with the restoration to the line of his distant cousin James as third marquess. James, born in 1697, had severe mental disabilities; violent and uncontrollable, he was kept permanently under lock and key from an early age. He was removed from the succession by a charter of novodamus in 1706. In 1707 he escaped from his confinement and, looking for something to eat, encountered a young scullion in the kitchen, killed him, and roasted him on a spit. When discovered, he had started devouring the corpse. He died in 1715. I have chosen to use the numbering after James's restoration, in which John Sholto is ninth marquess, but the reader should note that contemporary references use the earlier numbering.

The Scottish title is correctly spelled 'marquess' although it is frequently, as on Queensberry's notorious calling card, found spelled French fashion, 'marquis'. 'Marquess' will be used here except where 'marquis' is part of a quotation.

Acknowledgements

I WOULD like to thank the very many people and organisations that have assisted me in the compilation of this book, and my apologies to any whom I may have inadvertently missed from this list.

The many staff of what almost seem to me to be my alternative 'homes' the British Library, Colindale Newspaper Library and the National Archives Kew, have, as always, been wonderfully helpful. Special thanks are due to the cheerful young men who, when I turned up at Kew hobbling on a painful foot, happily fetched and carried boxes and files for me.

I am greatly indebted to Pamela Clark and Angeline Barker of the Royal Archives Windsor, for a wonderful and fascinating visit, and to Julie Crocker for assistance with the papers. My grateful thanks are due to Her Majesty Queen Elizabeth II for granting permission for the use of the material quoted in this book. I would also love to thank the lady researcher whose name I didn't get who generously left her own work to help me transcribe the handwriting of Edward Prince of Wales (the future King Edward VII).

I would like to thank Professor C. M. Woolgar and his colleagues at the University of Southampton for granting access to the Palmerston Papers. My thanks are also due to the National Archives of Scotland, the East Sussex Record Office and the Bishopsgate Institute, for all their help.

Lord Gawain Douglas, great-grandson of John Sholto Douglas Marquess of Queensberry, has very kindly made family documents and photographs available.

Marie Castrillo, manuscripts curator of the National Library of Scotland and the many staff who assisted me on my visit have given invaluable help in accessing the Rosebery Papers. I am grateful to the Trustees of the National Library of Scotland for granting permission to quote from the Rosebery collection. I am indebted to the family of the fifth Earl of Rosebery for granting permission to quote from his unpublished letters and manuscripts.

My thanks are also due to Satu Haase-Webb who carried out researches for me at the Library of Congress, Washington, Andy Manns, Crime Scene Investigator with the Avon and Somerset Constabulary for his illuminating observations on the scene at the Quantock Estate, Jennifer Squires who kindly provided a tour of the Queensberry burial ground Cummertrees, Linda Hahn, a cousin of Margaret Mooney aka Loretta Addis, for details of the Mooney family history, Ashley Schoppe, University of Tulsa, Colin Harris, Helen Langley and Rebecca Wall of the Bodleian Library Oxford, Senate House Library for access to the Herbert Spencer Papers, Penny Hatfield, College archivist of Eton College, Jacqueline Cox of Cambridge University Archives, Dr C. J. R. Thorne of Cambridge University, Heather Johnson of the Royal Naval Museum Portsmouth, Cathy Broad of the Humanist Reference Library London, the Family History Centre London, the Principal Probate Registry London, and Visit Scotland, Dumfries Information Centre.

Especial thanks are due to Heather McCallum of Yale University Press for giving me the opportunity to undertake a project that has been dear to my heart for many years.

I am grateful always for the unfailing help and support of my husband, Gary, who for the last two years has referred to the Marquess of Queensberry as 'the other man'.

Ancestry of John Sholto Douglas, 9th Marquess of Queensberry

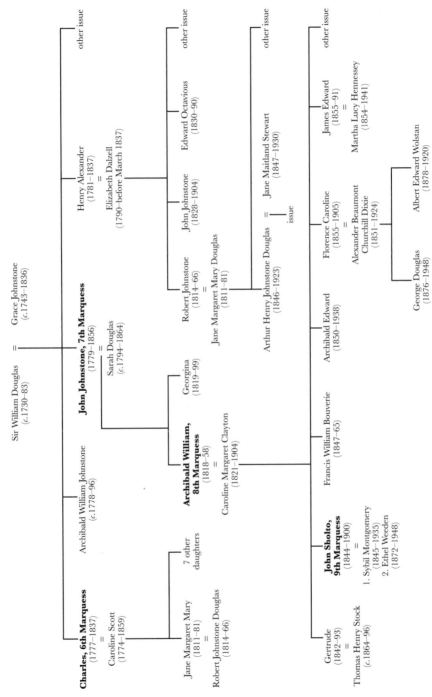

John Sholto Douglas, Marquess of Queensberry and his descendants

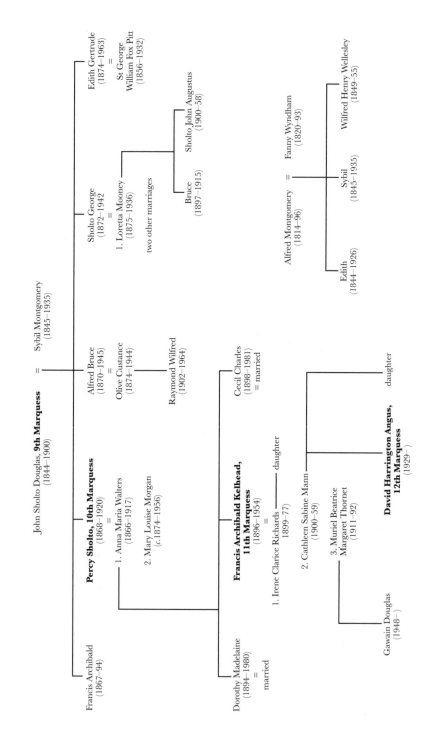

Introduction: The Card

A t 4.30 p.m., on 18 February 1895 John Sholto Douglas, ninth Marquess
of Queensberry entered the Albemarle Club, near London's fashionable
Piccadilly. He had never felt more alone, or more desperate. For the last two
weeks he had been trying unsuccessfully to arrange a confrontation with
Oscar Wilde, whose relationship with his son Lord Alfred (Bosie) Douglas,
was the talk of London society.

Queensberry had known for some time that Bosie had been blackmailed
over homosexual liaisons at Oxford University but had kept this distressing
information secret. It was galling enough that Bosie had failed to take his
degree and made no effort to enter a profession, yet was content to live a life
of pleasure funded by allowances from his parents and the hospitality of
friends, but now his son was plunging recklessly down the road to certain
ruin, possible exile, or a miserable death. Unlike the Oxford problem, which
had been quickly hushed up, the Wilde affair was a public scandal, talked of
in clubs, restaurants and theatres, satirised in a *Punch* cartoon and a novel.
Despite this, when Bosie told his mother and brother Percy that there was no
truth in the rumours, they had believed him. Queensberry, said Bosie, was
suffering from delusions; not only were the stories about him and Oscar
Wilde false, but his insane father had made them all up.

With his family ranged against him, Queensberry had unwillingly taken a
desperate step to convince Percy that he was telling the truth by revealing the
Oxford blackmail, but to no avail. Percy's belief in his brother was unshaken,
and there had been a terrible quarrel in which Percy had challenged his father
to bring matters to a head. Now, with the challenge ringing in his ears,
Queensberry decided to do just that.

He knew that Wilde was in London where his new play *The Importance of Being Earnest* had just opened to the rapturous approval of theatregoers, but he did not know where Wilde was staying. The Albemarle was Wilde's London club, and Queensberry had been keeping a watch on it for several days. In the club's hallway he took out a card, quickly scribbled a few words and handed it to the porter asking him to give it to Oscar Wilde, then he left.

The words on the card were 'For Oscar Wilde, posing somdomite [*sic*]' Even Queensberry, whose intention may well have been to sting his quarry into a meeting, or at least a correspondence, cannot have anticipated the destructive effect those few words would have.

CHAPTER 1

Son and Heir

———————•———————

JOHN Sholto Douglas, ninth Marquess of Queensberry has a unique and unfortunate place in the history of literature: he is almost universally reviled as the man who precipitated the tragic downfall of Oscar Wilde. The ultimate though not exclusive responsibility for Wilde's downfall must be borne by Wilde, who committed a criminal offence, had the man who exposed him put on trial for libel, and then lied in the witness box, but Wilde's well-deserved rehabilitation as a literary genius and a good if not flawless human being has led to the demonising of his accuser. Queensberry, denounced by biographers as eccentric to the point of clinical insanity, a homophobic, anti-Semitic, militant atheist, described by his own son as 'the perfect type of evil, cruelty, ferocity and brutality',[1] is usually portrayed rampaging through his narrow-minded world like a grotesque pantomime villain, spitting hatred and threatening to horsewhip anyone who disagreed with his twisted obsessive views.

His kindest critics suggest that he might not have been wholly responsible for his actions, the victim of a tainted inheritance from his Douglas forebears, 'the mad, bad line,'[2] as Wilde put it; the notorious family peculiarities, like the Douglas surname presumably passing down only through the male. Extracting the real Queensberry from this cascade of vilification reveals a man who was neither mad nor bad, nor was he an atheist: his prejudices, however we may view them today, were those of the society and the time in which he lived. He was not, admittedly, always an easy man to know or to like. Volatile, self-willed and aggressive, he was formed from the passions of two hardy nations and damaged early and often by tragedy, labouring for much of his life under acute grief and crushing misery. While famed for a quick, hot temper and an eagerness to settle disputes with his fists, his greatest conflicts lay within, for beneath the bombastic exterior was a craving for the happiness, truth and love that would forever elude him.

The idea that the Douglases were, as a family, not only highly unbalanced but had always been so is a confection of the popular press that did not arise until the 1870s and was largely, although not entirely, due to the turbulent and troubled career of John Sholto Douglas. With the exception of the unfortunate third marquess,[3] no Douglas prior to that decade appears to have suffered from any mental incapacity. Before John Sholto made an impact on the public consciousness, the Douglases had a very different standing: that of a noble line with a long and battle-scarred history that had played a vital role in the making of Scotland. As feudal lords they were Barons Drumlanrig from the fifteenth century, and Earls, Dukes and Marquesses of Queensberry from the seventeenth, serving their country in a succession of high-ranking public appointments. The Douglas family, declared the *Dumfries Standard* in 1858, 'while not one of the wealthiest, occupies a distinguished place on the roll of the Scottish peerage,'[4] and when a youthful John Sholto entered the navy the *Leeds Mercury* commented: 'The navy is looking up.'[5] In the 1860s if the Douglases had an unfortunate public reputation, it was not for eccentricity but fatal bad luck. 'The noble house of Queensberry,' commented the *Illustrated London News* in 1865, 'has been at various periods, strangely subject to mortal mischances.'[6] The mere fact that John Sholto became marquess at all was the culmination of a series of unlikely events and occasional bizarre accidents.

When John Sholto's grandfather, John Douglas of Lockerby (the eighteenth-century spelling of Lockerbie) was born in 1779 the likelihood that he would become Marquess of Queensberry must have seemed remote. The marquessate was in the hands of his fourth cousin once removed, William, fourth Duke of Queensberry, a libidinous bachelor of fifty-three with a taste for opera girls and teenage ballerinas, who could, had he been so inclined, have surprised everyone by taking a young bride. Even if William died without a legitimate son, the next heirs to the peerage were John Douglas's two older brothers, Charles and Archibald.

William had not anticipated acquiring the Queensberry peerages, but on 19 October 1754 thirty-two-year-old Lord Henry Douglas, Earl of Drumlanrig, three months married and son and heir of the third Duke and fourth Marquess of Queensberry, inaugurated what later came to be thought

2

of as the 'Drumlanrig curse'. Riding over a ploughed field, he drew and cocked his gun for the purpose, it was thought, of shooting crows or pigeons, when his horse stumbled, the gun discharged, and he shot himself dead. The next Earl of Drumlanrig, Henry's younger brother Charles, suffered from a weak constitution and was sent to Lisbon for his health, where he managed to avoid being killed in the 1755 earthquake. He returned home to die of consumption in the following year, aged thirty, leaving William as heir to both the dukedom and the marquessate.

'Old Q', as Duke William came to be known, the relative with whom John Sholto is most often compared, was a devotee of the racecourse and a keen gambler. Although aristocratic sportsmen had been patrons of the prize ring, as professional boxing was then known, since the early eighteenth century, organising championships, giving financial backing to fighters and laying enormous wagers, the one sport in which Old Q seems never to have taken any interest was pugilism. In their strenuous efforts to discover the ninth marquess's eccentric ancestors newspapers often declared him to be a direct descendant of Old Q – John Sholto was a fourth cousin three times removed on his grandfather's side and four times removed on his grandmother's – but aside from a tendency to risk life and limb by riding their own racehorses, the two had little in common apart from recreational tastes they would have shared with many another aristocrat of their time. Certainly William had none of John Sholto's chaotic, sometimes misguided, but occasionally prescient crusading spirit; nor did he suffer the succession of bitter disappointments, frustrations, family conflicts and personal tragedies that made so much of John Sholto's life an unhappy pandemonium; neither did William share his distant cousin's restless wandering nature, being content to divide his time between the turf at Newmarket and his boudoir in Piccadilly, to the neglect of his Scottish estates. His one foray into estate management was cutting down ancient woodlands to finance the marriage portion of his illegitimate daughter, stimulating the rage of his tenants and a poem by Wordsworth. William's supposed 'eccentricities' were no more than one might have expected of a wealthy man who had decided to devote his time and money to the pursuit of pleasure.

When William succeeded to the Queensberry titles in 1778 his predecessor's British peerage, the Dukedom of Dover, became extinct. It is unlikely that the lack of a British peerage was a sore point with William, as it was to be with both John Sholto and his father. Under a ruling which was to echo destructively down the Douglas line, Scottish peerages created before the Act of Union of 1707 did not automatically entitle the holder to a seat in the House of Lords, and Scottish peers were required to elect sixteen of their number to represent them in the Lords for the duration of each parliament. In 1786 William became a British peer as Baron Douglas of Amesbury. William never married, and when he died on 23 December 1810 the Dukedom of Queensberry and the family seat Drumlanrig Castle passed to his cousin the Duke of Buccleuch who was known thereafter as the Duke of Buccleuch and Queensberry. Charles Douglas, John Sholto's great-uncle, succeeded to most of the Scottish titles as sixth Marquess of Queensberry, Viscount of Drumlanrig and Baron Douglas of Hawick and Tibbers, but not the English barony. For a second time in the Douglas family a British title died with its holder.

With the accession of Charles the marquessate enjoyed a long period of stability and worthy public service. Of the notorious Douglas eccentricities, which were to be a subject of public comment from the 1870s, there was no sign. Charles had married Caroline Scott in August 1803, and by 1810 the union had produced four daughters, with another child due the following year. Hopes must have been high for a son and heir, but although Caroline was to bear eight children they were all girls.

With the title of marquess came lands that had been in the Douglas family since 1733, Tinwald and Torthorwald, lying east of Dumfries, and the great estate of Kinmount just north of the Solway Firth. The original mansion, Kelhead House had burned down in the eighteenth century, and in 1812 Charles directed the building of a new one at a cost of £40,000. Its architect, Sir Robert Smirke, favoured simplicity of outline, and was scathingly critical of excessive ornament. The severe, almost fortress-like mansion house with its lofty stone portico (the decorative balustrades and urns seen today were not added until 1899) still overlooks the parkland, woods and waters of the estate which lies just over a mile north of the village of Cummertrees. An 1823 engraving shows the three-storey house with its central four-storey tower, not without a stately grim beauty of its own, rising like a grey ziggurat from an ocean of Scotch firs and copper beeches.

Charles was elected as a representative peer in 1812 and served in that capacity for the next twenty years. Described as 'that truly popular nobleman',[7] he was well liked not only by friends and relatives but the public and his tenants. The one picture we have of him shows a jolly, plump fellow, rather red in the face, enjoying himself at a ball.

Scottish representative peers were usually re-elected without question at each parliament, but as both Charles and, later, John Sholto were to discover, exceptions could be made for any man who decided to rock the boat. Whiggish Charles was one of the few Scottish peers to support the Reform Act of 1832, and for this impertinence his fellow Tory peers refused to re-elect him in 1833. Within days, however, it was rumoured that he would receive a British peerage, and later that year he was created Baron Solway of Kinmount. Charles did not enjoy his barony for long. After a period of precarious health he died on 3 December 1837. His younger brother Archibald had died unmarried in 1796, one of the hundreds of men lost when HMS *Courageux* slipped its moorings and was wrecked off the Barbary Coast. The marquessate passed to Charles's second brother John, but the title Baron Solway died with him.

John Douglas, seventh Marquess of Queensberry failed, like his brother, to exhibit any eccentricities. His main interest was agriculture, and he preferred the life of a 'quiet, useful, respected country gentleman'.[8] After the necessary attendances at court following his accession, he returned to his previous modest habits. He stood as a representative peer for Scotland in August 1841, came a miserable last in the poll, and never stood again. The only slightly disreputable incident in his history occurred in 1822 when he acted as a second to Sir Alexander Boswell in a duel, called over an alleged libel, which ended fatally for his friend.

In 1817 John married Sarah Douglas, a first cousin once removed. There was a strong military flavour to this side of the family. Sarah's father was Major James Sholto Douglas and her brothers served in the Peninsular War. Their only son, Archibald William (the future father of John Sholto Douglas) was born in Edinburgh on 18 April 1818, and took after the vigorous Douglases on his mother's side rather than his quiet father. His sister Georgina was born in 1819.

Archibald went up to Eton in January 1832. The English public school of the period was noted for its harsh regime: poor and inadequate food, frequent corporal punishment, bullying, and lack of organised recreation. Boys settled disputes with their fists and it must have been here that Archibald developed an early enthusiasm for pugilism; thereafter he was 'renowned for the alacrity with which he took to his fists, and for the dexterity with which he used them'.[9] Eton may have coloured Archibald's view of public schools, since he did not choose one for the education of John Sholto. He left Eton between the summer of 1834 and Easter 1835. What he did in the next two years is unknown, but by 1837 he had settled on a military career, and joined the 92nd Foot as an ensign. Pugilism remained a lifelong interest, but he also swam, rowed, played cricket, and was a bold if inelegant horseman. Following the accession of his father as marquess, Archibald took the courtesy title of Viscount Drumlanrig, soon shortened to 'Drum' or 'Drummy' by his friends. In March 1838 he accompanied his parents and sister to London, and was plunged into a dazzling round of dinner parties, balls and fashionable assemblies. At the Queen's levee at St James's Palace on 21 March the new marquess and viscount were formally presented to Her Majesty. Some two thousand people might attend such an event, all resplendent in silks, velvets and jewels, with orders, decorations and chains of office on display and, after kissing the Queen's hand, there would be lavish banqueting, followed by games and music. It was a world away from the more modest delights of Dumfriesshire. There is no surviving portrait of Archibald, who was described as above average height with 'a firmly knit and well set up frame'; his face 'inclining to ruddiness and essentially good-tempered'.[10] In *Nature's Nursling*, a novel written by his daughter Gertrude which has strong autobiographical elements, 'Lord Cyril Camion', who is undoubtedly based on Archibald, is 'a young handsome man, with beautiful, sad blue eyes, and wavy hair and beard of amber-gold'.[11]

With his new rank came promotion. In July 1838 Archibald left the 92nd Foot for the 2nd Life Guards, as cornet (standard-bearer) and sub-lieutenant. Several of his fellow officers were followers of the prize ring, and Archibald joined this group of enthusiasts who met regularly at Limmer's Hotel, at the corner of Conduit Street and George Street near Hanover Square. There, 'in a little tunnelled recess at the bottom of the dark, low-browed coffee-room',[12] 'the rich squirearchy, who visited London during the sporting season'[13] ate plain English dinners, drank port and gin-punch, and arranged fights. He became a patron of Johnny Walker, who went on to become the lightweight bare-knuckle champion of England.

The young viscount's sporting activities were characterised by a physical courage and daring amounting sometimes to recklessness. It was the heyday of fox hunting as the favoured sport of the gentry, and long, fast, exhilarating rides with hedges to jump offered the thrill of danger that Archibald craved. Said to be 'one of the hardest riders across country that these islands contained',[14] he took the most formidable fences without fear. 'No exposure ever seemed to affect his fine hardy frame, and fatigue could not touch it.'[15] On 14 September 1838 Drumlanrig and another young officer made an ascent in the Royal Nassau Balloon, a popular spectacle, but a mode of transport still in its experimental stages and in the following year he took part in a grand tournament at Eglinton Castle. He also, as did other young officers, rode his own horses in steeplechases.

Archibald was a risk-taker with a need to prove himself and nowhere was this more evident than in his gambling habits. His friends were often concerned at his 'fatal propensity to select one horse in a big race for whom he had conceived an often baseless antipathy' and lay a sum against it which 'it would have sorely crippled him to pay, if indeed he was able to pay it at all', claiming that 'the escapes often by the skin of his teeth from which [he] . . . emerged with impunity, would have shattered the nerve of an ordinary man'.[16]

But Archibald also had more serious things on his mind – he was ambitious to create a position for himself in public life, and the royal court, once he had tasted its glamour, was an irresistible lure. Although he was only twenty, his political views were well known. In August 1838 *The Satirist* suggested why Prime Minister Lord Melbourne had not awarded Archibald's father a British peerage. 'If I raise Queensberry to the peerage,' Melbourne is supposed to have said, 'and he should die, which is not improbable, I add another Tory to the House in his son.' *The Satirist* agreed, 'particularly when it is known that the son is one of those upstart popinjays who look upon Toryism as proof of good taste'.[17]

In March 1839 Archibald was again formally presented to the Queen, this time in his new role and uniform. The following August when Her Majesty arrived at Windsor Castle escorted by a detachment of the 2nd Regiment of Life Guards, Viscount Drumlanrig was in command, and he was to perform this duty on other occasions. Archibald had just reached his majority, and was an eligible young man; handsome, active, pleasant to all and with a peerage (albeit a Scottish one) in the offing. His parents must have hoped for an advantageous marriage, perhaps to a bride selected from the glittering company at the royal court, but any plans were abruptly thwarted in May

1840. Earlier that month Archibald had attended a regimental ball, and here he met Caroline Margaret Clayton, the daughter of Sir William Clayton, a baronet of Harleyford Manor in Buckinghamshire.

Lieutenant Colonel (later General) Sir William Clayton was Member of Parliament for Great Marlow, and a magistrate and Deputy Lieutenant of Buckinghamshire. In 1817 he married Irish-born Alice Hugh Massey O'Donnell, daughter of Colonel Hugh O'Donnell. The couple were divorced in 1830. Four of their five children had been born at Harleyford, but Caroline was born in Bantry, Cork on 13 July 1820. Although she lived there for just the first two years of her life, she always regarded herself as Irish, and possessed a strong sympathy for and identity with the people of Ireland that were to shape much of her later life and exert a lasting influence on her children. Caroline at nineteen was a petite, pretty girl with fashionably long dark ringlets, although she had also, from the evidence of family portraits, inherited the prominent Clayton nose. However, it must above all have been her personality which Archibald found compelling. Caroline Clayton was a woman of passionate beliefs and unquenchable spirit, 'at once gentle and daring. With her to see the truth and embrace it were one and the same act.'[18] Dynamic, outspoken, and with a towering force of will, Caroline nevertheless saw the role of women solely as an inspiration and a support to men, and in that capacity she was fearless. Her only weapons were her voice and her pen. The attraction between these two bold and impetuous young people must have been almost instantaneous.

Sir William had no objection to Archibald paying court to his daughter but the marquess was not to be won over. There was only one thing the young couple could do. Three weeks after their first meeting they eloped to Gretna Green. The marquess was said to have pursued the pair, but he failed to catch up with them, and Archibald and Caroline were married on 28 May 1840. On their return to Windsor, Archibald, who had gone absent from his regiment without leave, went to face the music and was promptly arrested. He was confined only for an afternoon; when the commander, Colonel Reid, learned the reason for Archibald's absence the love-struck young viscount was freed and went to join his bride. Both families accepted the *fait accompli*, but ensured that the couple were married at St Mary's Church Marylebone, on 2 June. The escapade touched the Queen's youthful romantic heart, and she set her seal of approval on the match by inviting the viscountess to dinner prior to receiving her at court. Her influence did a great deal to soothe the marquess's hurt feelings. In the following month Archibald was appointed Deputy Lieutenant of Dumfriesshire.

Archibald now had his eyes firmly set on a career in public life, and on 26 August, less than two weeks after his father's failure to be elected as representative peer for Scotland, he wrote to Sir James Robert George Graham, a friend of the marquess, who had recently been elected Conservative member of parliament for Dorchester. ' I am very anxious to obtain some appointment in Her Majesty's household,' wrote Archibald, 'and have therefore ventured to illicit [sic] your assistance in recommending me to those who may have it in their power to further my views.'[19] He was unsuccessful.

Caroline took a keen interest in politics, and she and her sister canvassed for their father in the 1841 general election; however, the next few years saw her concentrating her considerable energies on home, children and her husband's career. The couple's first child, Gertrude Georgina was born at Clewer House, Windsor, on 21 August 1842.

Marriage and fatherhood did not quell the young viscount's passion for racing and gambling, and he was a prominent figure at all the major race meetings, where he was less interested in mingling with the fashionable crowds than negotiating with the betting fraternity. His first really heavy loss was in the 1843 Epsom Derby, when he could meet his debts only through the generosity of his sister who lent him the whole of her personal fortune of £10,000. Thereafter he paid her 5 per cent per annum on the loan and insured his life in her favour for the capital.* Sometimes he escaped financial disaster by the narrowest of margins, revealing not a flicker of emotion to his racing friends and earning a reputation as a man of iron nerve. Archibald was no nearer to achieving his ambition when early in 1844, with Caroline three months pregnant, he resigned from the Life Guards and took his family to live abroad. Gambling debts may have prompted this decision. In *Nature's Nursling*, his fictional counterpart Lord Cyril Camion is a penniless exile in Italy. Camion had entered a regiment against the wishes of his father, who described his career in the military as 'one long scene of disgrace'[20] and accused his son of living 'an idle, useless life'.[21]

After spending time in the South of France the Drumlanrigs moved to

* Georgina's life is little documented. She died unmarried in 1899.

Florence where on 20 July a son and heir was born, John Sholto Douglas, the future ninth Marquess of Queensberry. There are few records of the Drumlanrigs' activities abroad, although Archibald ensured that he received the newspaper *Bell's Life in London and Sporting Chronicle* to which he wrote letters, principally concerning the prize ring, and occasionally rode in races. A letter written by him from Florence on 23 October 1845 begins, tantalisingly, 'On my return from the East a few days ago'.[22] They were still in Florence in November 1845 when Caroline was in the Parco delle Cascine, riding a racehorse which ran away and threw her against a tree, knocking her unconscious and flattening her prominent nose. As *The Satirist* commented: 'had the accident happened to Drummy, considering thickness of his skull, the tree would have had the worst of it'.[23] Clearly the sporting lord did not have a reputation as a thinker.

In the summer of 1846, they returned to England and their third child, Francis William Bouverie Douglas, was born at Harleyford on 8 February 1847. Archibald appeared at the usual races and regattas, but, undoubtedly with the support and encouragement of his wife, he had serious business in hand. He had decided to stand for parliament for the constituency of Dumfriesshire at the forthcoming general election. With no more than a courtesy title, Archibald was not eligible to stand for election as a representative peer for Scotland, but he did qualify to sit in the House of Commons during the lifetime of his father. A term in the Commons could be a stepping stone to that elusive seat in the Lords, and a much-coveted appointment at the royal court. Canvassing began in earnest in July 1847. On 4 August at the Dumfries hustings, Sir William Jardine, a Dumfriesshire baronet proposed Archibald as 'a fit and proper person to represent the county'.[24] Archibald's speech was interrupted by heckling and hisses from those who remembered his previous pursuits; however, as the only candidate for Dumfriesshire he was duly returned. He took his place as one of the Peelites, a breakaway arm of the Conservative Party, which supported Free Trade. The Prime Minister at the time was Lord John Russell, a Whig.

Archibald made a good start, demonstrating that he intended to take an active part in government. Although still appearing at major race meetings, he attended parliament regularly, took part in debates, served on at least one subcommittee and corresponded on political subjects. Two of his wider concerns resonate curiously with critical events in the life of John Sholto.

Archibald's strong Protestant ideals led him to adopt beliefs considered reactionary even by his contemporaries. While claiming to favour religious tolerance, he believed 'Protestantism to be the only real truth'[25] and was determined that parliament should remain Christian. He voted against the Jewish Disabilities Bill of 1848, which proposed amending the oath of allegiance sworn by members of parliament to enable Jews to take the oath, claiming that the Bill was anti-Christian and its supporters actuated by financial considerations. He also opposed state endowments to the Roman Catholic Church, and headed a committee that deplored the increasing influence of Roman Catholics in public life, although his was one of the more moderate voices, some of the attendees still being in favour of the firebrand and the stake.

Archibald's tendency to view the world from astride a rigidly moral high horse was making him unpopular in political circles, but he was well liked both by his tenants, who found him fair and generous, and his sporting friends, who appreciated his open friendliness and good-hearted courage. Whatever stresses Archibald may have endured he largely kept hidden, although as he was fond of a pipe he often returned from the hunt with the stem bitten through. There was a streak of obstinacy and quarrelsomeness about him, and tempers could run high where large bets were concerned. John Kent, in his memoirs of Lord Cavendish Bentinck, relates that on one occasion Archibald was with some difficulty persuaded not to horsewhip leading turfite Charles Greville, a gouty gentleman twenty-four years his senior.

For Archibald, sport remained an interest and a healthy outlet. 'It was his habit to relieve the weary hours of hanging about the House of Commons' by escaping to the 'more congenial atmosphere' of the back parlours of well known pugilists, and putting on the gloves to spar 'with some aspiring novice'.[26] There was real skill in those fists; Nat Langham, one of the most admired middleweight bare-knuckle prizefighters of the day, was often heard to say that 'a rare pugilist was spoilt when Lord Drumlanrig was born to a peerage'.[27] He still swam when he could and in July 1848 was nearly drowned while bathing in the Thames with some friends from the Life Guards. In the following year he became vice president of the Scottish Society of London whose object was to promote Scottish sports and games. In 1849, his attendance record in parliament shows him ranked eighteenth out of fifty-four Scottish MPs; however, the lure of sport – and perhaps extramarital liaisons

– led to a gradual decline in his appearances in the Commons. 'Fox-hunting, steeplechasing, pugilism, the fair sex, and – last but not least – the Turf, claimed him, however, for their own, and prevented him from bestowing that time and attention upon politics, without which no man, however gifted, can hold his own in the House of Commons.'[28] There was another addition to the family on 17 June 1850 when Archibald Edward Douglas was born at Glen Stuart, a family house on the Kinmount estate.

In August, following the resignation of his father as Lieutenant and Sheriff Principal of Dumfriesshire, Archibald was appointed in his place. His duties in Scotland and London required regular travel between the two locations, and Caroline, who often supported charitable bazaars in London, must have accompanied her husband at least some of the time. The census of 1851 taken on the night of 30–31 March, shows that Archibald, Caroline and baby Archibald Edward were at Glen Stuart, while Gertrude, John Sholto and Francis were with their grandparents and aunt at Kinmount.

An active, sports-loving, outdoor boy like John Sholto could hardly have had a better childhood. There were ponies to ride over the Solway sands and wild tracks of moorland heather, hills to climb, rivers to swim, the sea to bathe in, rock pools to explore, sports such as football, racquets and rounders, paperchases, and every kind of hearty, noisy game. The duties and cares of the marquessate must have seemed far distant. John Sholto was his mother in miniature, with dark hair and grey eyes; his brother Francis was fairer and taller. The two boys were keen rivals in their games. Francis was more easy-going and less combative; John Sholto, the smaller, always had something to prove. No one, however, could doubt the brothers' genuine affection for each other.

The stately pile of Kinmount had its own charms, with its flower garden, conservatories, and a stone terrace that sloped down to a lawn by the banks of a lake, surrounded by flowering shrubs. Parkland and woods stretched into the distance, and from the upper windows of the castle could be seen the silver gleam of the Solway, with a backdrop of the Westmorland mountains. Even Gertrude was later to admit that the climate was 'not on the whole desirable',[29] yet many of the Douglas children, including John Sholto, enjoyed the bracing outdoor life, the 'serene and cloudlessly blue' skies, the rain which 'left the face of nature deliciously fresh and green',[30] the 'exhilarating breezes from the Solway' carrying the scent of heather and salt water. The scenery, 'everywhere pretty', gave 'a sense of infinite repose'.[31] It was a landscape to which John Sholto was often to retreat in his troubled later life in a vain attempt to escape his growing unhappiness.

The interior of the castle was furnished in grand style, the red drawing room as described by Gertrude in *Nature's Nursling* with crimson damask curtains and cushions, ebony furniture, gilded ceilings and Turkey carpets, the fire blazing in a grate of burnished steel, and paintings in heavy gilded frames. The food was nourishing plain traditional Scottish fare: home-made bread and local butter, game pie, fried eggs and ham. The day began with morning prayers, and on Sundays after breakfast the family walked in procession to the village kirk at Cummertrees with its bare whitewashed walls, and sat in the family gallery where they could see the gravestones through the windows and listen to the minister preach about hellfire. Even in John Sholto's young, unclouded days, he was a seeker after universal truth, and willingly embraced the teachings of his kirk. 'I, ever since I was a child have been deeply religious,' he wrote. 'Until I was twenty years of age I was a most sincere Christian.'[32] The children were educated by governesses in a schoolroom with maps, pictures, rugs and a cosy fire, the windows affording a view of the green park and distant woods and mountains.

Although remote from London, Kinmount was accessible by a fast overnight express train, and there was a little station at Cummertrees where slow trains stopped and fast ones would do so when required by the marquess's family. From Cummertrees a road between cornfields led to a lane at the back of the castle and a green gate opening on an avenue flanked by beech trees. The family often visited Harleyford, where Sir William Clayton's handsome Georgian manor house stood near the banks of the Thames surrounded by gardens and parkland, but if the children had a favourite playground in Scotland, it was Glen Stuart, a long, two-storey cottage nestling in picturesque woodland which they preferred to the stately grey castle.

In the November 1852 general election, Archibald was re-elected and traditional Conservative Lord Derby became Prime Minister but when this government collapsed in December Derby was replaced by Lord Aberdeen, a Peelite, and Archibald saw his chance. Once again he wrote to Sir James Graham (now First Lord of the Admiralty) expressing his desire for an appointment in Her Majesty's household and asking for a recommendation: 'My position in life has always been a difficult one and unless I succeed in getting office in all probability I may be compelled to leave Parliament and to retire more completely than ever into private life. Since ever I have had a seat in the House of Commons my desire has been to bring matters to their present position.'[33]

On 29 December Archibald was appointed Comptroller of Her Majesty's Household and arrived in Windsor on the following day for an audience with the Queen. The new administration required re-elections, and in January 1853 Archibald was back in Dumfriesshire for the hustings. Here he encountered unexpected opposition, possibly because of his heavy gambling. His original proposer, Sir William Jardine, had withdrawn his support, and a party of Dumfriesshire gentlemen, dissatisfied with Archibald's conduct, had asked another man to stand in opposition. The difficulties were soon smoothed over and Archibald was again returned to parliament. His victory was tempered by a personal sorrow. On 1 January at Glen Stuart, Caroline gave birth prematurely to a son who died on the following day.

Archibald's new role brought him into direct and frequent contact with the Queen. He was one of her closest attendants at levees, investitures and 'drawing-rooms', and a member of the Privy Council. He was the official liaison between the Queen and parliament, carrying ministers' questions to Her Majesty and addressing the House with her responses. Dinners at the palace, state balls and royal concerts became regular events. On 28 June 1853 he was second only to the royal heralds in the procession at the christening of Prince Leopold at Buckingham Palace, and he rode in a carriage as part of the Queen's entourage at both the state opening and closing of parliament. His new prominence made him sought after by financial concerns, and he became director of the Deposit and General Life Assurance Company and chairman of the Central Australian Gold Mining Company. This starry career cannot have been lost on young John Sholto, who must have been proud of his distinguished father. The Drumlanrigs and their three eldest children were all invited to the May Ball at the palace in 1854 but were prevented from attending by the death of the Dowager Marchioness Caroline; however, they were invited in the following year and probably attended.

The two sporting interests that were to dominate John Sholto's life, pugilism and the turf, were developed in his carefree boyhood. One can imagine Archibald teaching his son to ride and to box, delighted at the boy's aptitude and enthusiasm. It is tempting to see John Sholto very much as the son of his father, but while he had inherited Archibald's sporting tastes, boldness and quick temper he also shared many of his mother's more controversial qualities. There was a fierce tenacity in both John Sholto and Caroline; they shared an obsessive will to find a burning truth and the determination not only to hold on to that truth against every counter-argument but also to convert others to their way of thinking. The reckless espousal of great causes was to lead in both their cases to accusations of eccentricity and even madness. So wide did they cast their net that they often made themselves appear foolish or even ridiculous. Sometimes, they were many years ahead of their time.

CHAPTER 2

The Queensberry
Inheritance

I N January 1855 Lord Aberdeen resigned, and in the following month Lord
Palmerston was asked to form a government. Palmerston was everything
Archibald was not: a long-serving dedicated statesman, a Whig, an old opponent of Peel and an advocate of religious tolerance. Court appointments
remained unchanged, but Archibald, with his seventy-five-year-old father's
health giving cause for concern, knew that his time in the Commons was
running out. Archibald desperately wanted to remain in politics and the only
certain way he could do so after his father's death was to be awarded a British
peerage. He asked for his uncle's old title Baron Solway to be revived but, to
his dismay, Lord Palmerston refused. Palmerston, quite apart from his
concerns about Archibald's political and religious beliefs, regarded him, not
without good reason, as a man who craved the glittering prizes without being
willing to work for them. Whether or not this related specifically to
Drumlanrig's claims, in 1855 Her Majesty had, in Palmerston's opinion,
made 'very just remarks as to the inconvenience of making additions to the
Peerage in the cases of persons who have not an adequate fortune to support
their dignity'.[1] Archibald, who had employed charm, good looks and persist-
ence to obtain the long-coveted court posting, would find that these could
only take him so far in the Queen's estimation.

On 25 May, at 26 Wilton Crescent, the Drumlanrigs' London home,
Caroline gave birth to twins, Florence Caroline and James Edward Sholto. As
the children grew it must have become apparent that there were several
distinct characters in the family. Gertrude and Archibald Jnr were quiet and
serious, Francis was handsome, dependable and amiable, while John Sholto,
full of bouncing high spirits, revelled in physical activity. Florence, like John

Sholto was fearless, dynamic and opinionated. A small, trim yet deceptively strong girl with 'a sunny face and sparkling eyes'[2] and a mass of wavy auburn hair, she loved horses, dogs and hunting, and adored her less demonstrative twin James, who was her devoted shadow, calling him 'Dearest' while his pet name for her was 'Darling'.

Caroline was a redoubtable political wife who both supported her husband and managed the Drumlanrig home and family, and was, said Florence, 'one of the kindest and gentlest of women, and devoted to her children . . . good to the poor and a friend to all in need'.[3] Caroline held strong views on politics and religion, many of which conflicted directly with Archibald's, but to what extent she voiced these thoughts or tried to influence him is unknown. However passionate her personal convictions, she must have realised that while her husband was in parliament and the royal court, with the ever-present hope of a British peerage, there were ideas it would be unwise for her to pursue. On domestic issues, however, she exercised a gentle firmness over her spouse. When the couple's coachman took one of Archibald's hunters so that he could elope with a maid and returned the horse lame, Drumlanrig was furious and dismissed both servants. Caroline, to calm his anger, said 'Oh, Archie, would you have minded how many horses were lamed when you eloped with me?' and he relented.[4]

On 28 December 1855 the six children of Archibald and Caroline were christened at Cummertrees, Caroline presenting the church with a silver christening bowl. Caroline's interest in the welfare of her servants and tenants included their religious observance. Through her 'energetic and well-directed patronage' of the small church at Cummertrees the parishioners were 'favoured with a Wednesday evening service, sermons being preached by ministers of various denominations to crowded audiences'.[5] In April 1856 eleven-year-old John Sholto had another taste of the royal court when the viscount, his four eldest children and sister Georgina, wearing Highland dress for the occasion, attended a 'juvenile ball' for sons and daughters of the nobility and gentry at Buckingham Palace. The children were treated to a supper in the state dining room, and enjoyed dancing to Her Majesty's band.

Archibald may have thought this life of pleasure and privilege would always be his and his family's to enjoy, but from the summer of 1856 there were signs that the dream was fading, and it would end more catastrophically and tragically than anyone could imagine. The Deposit and General Life

Assurance Company collapsed with debts of £12,000, and investors who had bought shares in Australian gold mines on the strength of the viscount's royal appointment were aggrieved to find they had lost their money. These were unhappy experiences for Archibald, but he continued his parliamentary and social duties with no hint that anything was amiss, until, without warning, it was announced that he had resigned his post as Comptroller of the Queen's Household. The news appeared in the press on 15 July.

There was considerable speculation as to his motives, but no answers were forthcoming. The *Morning Chronicle* suggested that he was aspiring to 'a higher place in the legislature'.[6] More recently it has been suggested that he resigned in a 'fit of petulance'[7] due to Palmerston's continued refusal to recommend him for a peerage. The truth, however, was that Archibald had not resigned at all. His increasing neglect of parliamentary duties had come under the keen scrutiny of Lord Palmerston, who examined the weekly lists of those who attended divisions. Archibald had been largely absent and his careless attitude had rubbed off on others. With the ammunition he needed to get rid of him, on 8 July Palmerston wrote to the Queen:

> Viscount Palmerston submits a Return shewing the number of government divisions in which each member of the government, and of Your Majesty's Household have been present. These returns are made out weekly. Your Majesty will see how seldom Lord Drumlanrig has been in divisions during the session, and his example is pleaded as an excuse for those who absent themselves. Viscount Palmerston would beg to submit to your Majesty that Lord Drumlanrig should cease to hold the office which he has in your Majesty's Household.[8]

Archibald's charm had long worn thin, and he must also have suffered under the disapproving gaze of Prince Albert, who expected high moral standards from men in public life. The Queen responded briefly in a letter the following day, the last day on which Archibald was to take part in a parliamentary division, 'the Queen entirely agrees in Lord Drumlanrig's being dismissed from his Office'.[9] It is unlikely that a triumphant Palmerston lost much time in giving Archibald the news. The public was unaware of Drumlanrig's downfall when he attended a cricket match at Lords on 14 July, but he must already have been preparing to leave London.

Parliament was prorogued on 28 July, and on 6 August society was shocked by an announcement in the press that Archibald had died suddenly at his London residence, casting 'a pallid hue . . . over the fashionable world',[10] but soon afterwards, to the delight of his sporting friends, this was revealed to be a hoax. On 5 August, in perfect health, Archibald had left London on the mail train to Scotland. The source of the story was never identified but it may have been a gleeful satire by his political enemies.

In the next few months Archibald attended race meetings, and probably spent time with his family, especially his ailing father, from whom he may have been able to conceal his disgrace.

On 19 December 1856 John Douglas, Marquess of Queensberry died in Edinburgh. He was interred at the family vault in Cummertrees, where the memorial plaque describes him as 'A man in whom there was no guile. One truly unselfish.' Archibald now became eighth marquess, but twelve-year-old John Sholto did not take the courtesy title of Viscount Drumlanrig. Instead he was formally known as Baron Douglas of Hawick and Tibbers; informally as Lord John Douglas.

The new peer made every effort to stay in parliament. Heartened by the fact that there was no statute prohibiting his remaining as MP, Archibald wrote to the Speaker of the House of Commons and also sought an opinion from Sir James Graham. Graham had to disappoint him. 'I shall be very sorry to lose you from the House of Commons: but, being a Scotch Peer by undisputed title of descent, you can no longer sit there,' he wrote on 3 January 1857. Archibald may even have hinted at the possibility of renouncing his peerage for Graham added, 'All these privileges are incalculable and inherent in you by birth: you cannot descend from your high estate and denude yourself at pleasure of them.' Worse was to follow. Although Archibald was eligible to stand for election as one of the sixteen representative Scottish peers, Graham advised him that 'The Minister of the Day greatly influences the return of the Sixteen: & a Scotch Peer in Opposition is generally excluded from the House of Lords.'[11] Since the 'Minister of the Day' was Palmerston, that avenue was currently closed.

By the end of January 1857 Archibald was obliged to admit defeat and resigned from parliament. As time passed, the contrast between overseeing his Scottish estates and his position at the heart of the royal court and government no doubt told upon him. Another man was attending the Queen in his place, and yet another was MP for Dumfriesshire, and he, through no fault of his own, was without occupation. Archibald, as his racing friends had observed, was adept at putting on a bold and unflinching front in adversity but after almost ten years of a political career he felt suddenly like a hollow man. In private, with his family, his pain may have been more apparent. Gertrude, certainly, was aware of it. Early in *Nature's Nursling* Lord Cyril's 'dark deep rich blue' eyes have in 'their clear depths . . . a vague melancholy, which told of severe mental suffering', and his general expression was 'woefully sad'.[12] Later he looks drawn, ill and depressed.

Archibald was now, on paper at least, a wealthy man, but the bulk of his wealth was in the form of entailed estates, which he was able neither to sell nor mortgage. The lands did however produce a rental income, which might have been sufficient for any gentleman who did not have an extravagant gambling habit. Archibald did not entirely withdraw from public life. He was at a royal levee on 12 March, when, as the new marquess, he was presented to the Queen. On 16 April, at Buckingham Palace, he presented his congratulations on the birth of the Queen's ninth child, Princess Beatrice. If he had hoped for a rekindling of his career at court, he was disappointed. Two days earlier the Scottish peers had held an election for their sixteen representative members in which there were no vacancies. On a happier note, the Queensberrys were looking forward to an addition to their family, but on 26 May the marchioness was staying at St Leonards on Sea when she was delivered prematurely of twin girls, who were stillborn. Archibald must have thought deeply about the future of his family, for on 6 June he made a will which hinted at some anxiety about his differences of political and religious opinion with Caroline.

On 19 February 1858 after losing a vote in the Commons, Palmerston was obliged to resign. His place was taken by Lord Derby at the head of a Conservative minority government, a change fatal to any possibility of Archibald obtaining a peerage. When a place fell vacant amongst the Scottish peers in April 1858 Archibald did not stand for election. He must have known he stood no chance of success, and the disappointment may have plunged him further into depression. The only outlet for this man who had just turned forty and was already realising that his best years were behind him, was sport and gambling, and he was seen at the Derby and at Ascot. He continued to hunt with his pack of hounds in Dumfriesshire, where he remained a popular figure, and his hunting friends gave a banquet in his honour in Dumfries.

In 1858 John Sholto was thirteen, the age at which his father had gone to Eton, but if Caroline favoured a public school education for the future marquess, Archibald must have overruled her. The young lord was nominated for the Royal Navy as an officer cadet. There was some history of naval service in the Douglas family; Admiral John Erskine Douglas who died in 1847 was a distant cousin, and John Sholto's parents may have recognised a restlessness in him, which exhibited itself as a passion for travel. Another factor that may have influenced the decision was that the navy had recently become more attractive as a career following the introduction of a new and rigorous system of training for officer cadets in May 1857.[13] The candidates, who had to be aged thirteen to fifteen and in good health, were required to pass an examination at the Royal Naval College, Portsmouth. John Sholto would have had to satisfy the examiners that he could write English legibly from dictation, could read and translate a page in either French or Latin, and knew the leading facts of Scripture, English history, geography, arithmetic, algebra, and the first book of Euclid. On 5 June 1858 he joined HMS *Illustrious*, launched in 1803 and now lying at anchor at Portsmouth for use as a training ship. The only drawback from the point of view of a youth with a burning desire to see the world was that the first year of his naval service would take place on a vessel that would never leave harbour.

There are no pictures of naval cadet Lord John Sholto Douglas, so one has to imagine him at this time based on later portraits – wiry dark hair combed smooth, intense grey eyes, short body trim as a whippet in his dark blue uniform with gilt buttons. Travel, adventure, comradeship and the opportunity to prove himself lay invitingly ahead. He would have boarded the *Illustrious* with a sea chest crammed with clothing and study materials: a French grammar, a dictionary of nautical terms, and books on navigation, geometry, geography, algebra, trigonometry, the steam engine, and the use of mathematical and nautical instruments. The new cadet was also expected to have his own set of instruments and a spyglass. After eighteen months, provided he had a good record of study and behaviour, he would be eligible to sit an examination for promotion to midshipman. As an education intended to fit a young man for a career at sea it was ideal, but for a youth who probably did not intend to make the navy his life, it was too narrowly defined. Men who did their training at this time were later to comment that they had grown up ignorant of general subjects. In this company of young men, some of them away from parental supervision for the first time, boisterous high spirits, practical jokes and dangerous exploits were the order of the day. The fresh face and new uniform of a cadet would mark him out as the butt for merciless 'ragging' by more senior students. Such pranks and jokes all had to be taken in good part.

Shortly after settling John Sholto's career, Archibald entered the public house owned by pugilist Owen Swift, a much-frequented haunt of racing men. There he encountered Norman Buchanan, a friend of wealthy ironmaster James Merry, owner of Saunterer, favourite for the Goodwood Cup. Buchanan 'in a swaggering half-inebriated manner'[14] offered to take a very substantial bet against Saunterer. Accounts vary as to whether the odds were £8,000 to £300 or £10,000 to £500. Either way it was a ridiculous bet but Archibald, who was certain that Saunterer could not stay the distance, offered to take it, and no entreaties by his friends, or assurances from Saunterer's trainer that the horse could not lose, could sway him from that decision.

On 29 July Saunterer won at a canter.

Archibald, it was said, 'treated his loss with the utmost *nonchalance*'.[15] According to the *Sporting Times* the first thing he did after watching the race was to go to Portsmouth to see his son. If he did, John Sholto never publicly revealed what passed between him and his father at that meeting. The cadets were then on leave, and did not return to the ship until 31 July, so it is not certain that John Sholto was in Portsmouth; he may have been with his parents. At the start of August, Archibald was in London where he enjoyed a swim in the Thames below Greenwich. On Wednesday the 4th he left London by the night train to Scotland, and his friends assumed that he was going there to raise funds to pay the debt. He arrived in Dumfries the following morning, and reached Kinmount in the afternoon, in excellent health and apparently good spirits. On Thursday he gave evidence at a lawsuit in the Sheriff's Court at Dumfries and was back at Kinmount the same afternoon, where he amused himself shooting rabbits. He was planning to shoot better game and engaged rooms at Lockerby, near to the moors, for himself and a cousin in a week's time.

If Archibald had reviewed his finances he would have learned that his total available cash including money held in the house and by his factors, together with small amounts of rent and debts that were due and payable, was less than £1,000. The contents of his house and farm stock would have raised another £2,000. His total worth, excluding the entailed estates, was just over £22,000 but the bulk of that was in the form of life insurance policies and rents accrued but not yet payable. Merry had allowed him time to pay his debt, but the position was hopeless. Archibald was worth more dead than alive. Kinmount was unusually quiet. Gertrude, just days from her sixteenth birthday, was staying there, but Caroline, her younger children, the Dowager Marchioness Sarah, and Lady Georgina had been away for some time staying at Moffat, while Glen Stuart was occupied by two cousins, John Johnstone Douglas of Lockerby (a future premier of Queensland) and his brother Edward, sons of the seventh marquess's younger brother Henry. On 6 August Archibald ate his lunch and wrote a number of business letters, as well as one to John Sholto and one, according to the *Sporting Times*, addressed to a lady who was never named. It 'told its own tale'[16] and was later shown to the lady's and Archibald's friends. That afternoon he took a double-barrelled shotgun and said he was going out to shoot rabbits. He asked Gertrude if she would accompany him, but she declined as her mother was returning and she was to meet her at Ecclefechan railway station. At two o' clock, Archibald went out alone, his manner being 'particularly cheerful, and even jocular'.[17] Some men who were working the land saw him shoot a crow, and disappear behind a high knoll to pick it up. At about half past three they heard a second shot. At four the Johnstone Douglases asked the workmen if they had seen his lord-ship and they pointed to where he had last been seen.

Archibald was found lying in a field close to the carriage approach, hidden from sight of the labourers only by the high knoll. His clothing was saturated with blood, a shotgun wound just above the left breast slanting upwards to exit from his back, through which part of a lung, studded with small shot, was protruding. His hat, undented, was still on his head and his expression was peaceful. Death would have been instantaneous. A dead crow lay a few yards away, and his shot belt, ramrod and powder flask were beside him, which suggested that he must have been, as was his habit, sitting on the ground watching for rabbits. Only one gun barrel had been discharged. The news was rushed back to Kinmount, where the family had just returned, and horror and grief overwhelmed the household. As the cloaked body was carried in, Gertrude stood in the hallway weeping, Francis lay face down on an ottoman and sobbed, while nearby, Caroline and Archibald Jnr were dazed with shock.

A telegram was sent to Portsmouth where the terrible news would have been broken to the fourteen-year-old John Sholto by his captain. The new marquess was sent home on leave. What a devastating loss this must have been to the adolescent, the son of an affectionate father and admired sportsman whose career was an example of high achievement. The eminent public man who had waited on Queen Victoria, processed in royal splendour, addressed parliament, and taken his family to Buckingham Palace, was suddenly and cruelly gone at the age of forty. John Sholto was undoubtedly told that it was an accident, but in time he would have heard grim rumours of suicide. Death can sometimes be felt as abandonment, all the more so when it is a voluntary act. In the rest of John Sholto's life there is no record of a speech or conversation in which he makes any allusion to his father and only one brief mention in a letter written in 1893 referring to the entailed estate. Whatever his feelings were, he buried them deep, but feeding on the inheritance of his mother's firebrand temperament and his father's impetuosity, this loss at a crucial point in his development, the transition from child to man, may have formed the root of his later unhappy and permanently dissatisfied personality.

The racing fraternity, recalling the 1856 hoax, refused at first to believe that Archibald was dead. London newspapermen called at Archibald's last known addresses in the capital and found that he had not lived there for two years. Once the news was confirmed, 'in sporting circles a belief is expressed that the death was not accidental'.[18] Archibald's gambling losses 'which have involved him in pecuniary embarrassments, which have reduced him for a time to abstain from any close connection with London society'[19] became a matter of public debate.

A move was soon made to protect the family from the distressing and dishonourable notion that Archibald had committed suicide. Archibald, it was conjectured, must have been sitting watching the rabbits and, having discharged one barrel in shooting the crow, had been reloading his gun when it accidentally went off. Another theory was that he had been lying in wait for the rabbits and was drawing the gun towards him, barrel first. Friends and the sporting papers were quick to comment that Archibald had always been careless when handling firearms. The obituaries did not stint on praise: Archibald had been 'possessed of superior natural endowments . . . the head of a loved and loving family . . . frank in his bearing, and social by temperament, and had much besides that was loveable in his character';[20] 'many – very many,' said *Bell's Life*, 'both rich and poor, have lost a friend, whose noble and generous heart and kindly disposition endeared him to all who knew him.'[21] The only flaw that anyone would countenance was that the marquess's devotion to sport, and the turf in particular, had prevented him from achieving eminence in his career. Archibald had been 'one of the most universal sportsmen, as far as his small means permitted, that the three kingdoms possessed'.[22]

A few days later, the press announced, with a huge sense of relief, that 'as a result of the most careful enquiry' there was no truth at all in the 'perfectly gratuitous' insinuation that the Marquess of Queensberry had committed suicide.[23] Privately, Archibald's family suspected the truth. Gertrude with her fictionalised Lord Cyril Camion hinted at her father's stress: 'half maddened by his disgrace and the heavy burden of his financial affairs, Cyril had seemed to be on the verge of some desperate act.'[24] The overwhelming conclusion is that Archibald, suffering a massive loss of self-esteem at the failure of his court and political career, and the humiliating outcome of his reckless gambling, saw only one honourable way to pay his debts, and took his own life.

The funeral of Archibald Douglas, eighth Marquess of Queensberry took place at 2 p.m. on Thursday 12 August 1858, with the whole of the tenantry of his estates, as well as family, friends and the neighbourhood gentry, assembling at Kinmount for prayers. The hearse then moved through the grounds of the estate, followed by a procession of sorrowful mourners some three-quarters of a mile in length to Cummertrees church where the coffin was deposited in the family vault.

John Sholto, as the eldest son, inherited the entailed landed estates. The residue of Archibald's personal and moveable effects after small bequests to his executors was bequeathed to 'my faithful and beloved wife Caroline Marchioness of Queensberry having perfect confidence that she will deal with the same solely in our children's benefit and that if the proceeds of said Estate are not required for the younger children's education she will when my eldest son comes of age make over to him all or whatever proportion of said estate and effects she does not positively require for her own use'.[25] Anticipating that the children would live with their mother, Archibald, who must have been anxious that Caroline would not educate them as he might have wished, had appointed five additional guardians, his sister Georgina, John and Edward his two Douglas cousins, and friends Edward Heron Maxwell and William Carruthers of Dormont, 'earnestly and confidently' entreating his wife to 'consult with and be constantly advised by' them.[26]

The new marquess rejoined his ship on 24 August. From then onwards his signature consisted of only one word – 'Queensberry'.

CHAPTER 3

The Young Gentleman

THE primary task of a naval cadet was study and training to fit him as an officer destined for command. As one of the 113 cadets on the *Illustrious* Queensberry would have received lessons every day except Sunday, and a monthly allowance of £3 16s. A substantial part of his education consisted of mathematics and navigation with additional classes in French and drawing. There were four instructors although occasionally the boys were treated to a lecture from Captain Harris on subjects such as the construction of ships and the currents of the ocean. Menial duties – the daily cleaning, frequent painting, repairs, taking on of supplies and making and mending of clothes – were carried out by trainee seamen called 'novices' of whom there were 145, and there were forty-five marines who, in addition to their military duties acted as servants to the cadets.

Queensberry's day on the *Illustrious* started at about 5 a.m. when the novices were roused from their hammocks and sent to scrub the decks, while cadets had to wash and dress quickly. Ablutions took the form of a salt water bath, followed by a basin of fresh soapy water, which mischievous boys would sometimes tip on to the heads of unsuspecting juniors. After mustering for the first inspection of the day, cadets spent an hour preparing for lessons. Breakfast was at 6.30 and there were prayers every morning at 8.30, after which formal classes began, the quiet studies of the cadets in one part of the ship often disturbed by the vigorous and noisy drills of the novices.

The cadets and their officers took a daily walk through Portsmouth dockyard, inspecting the ships, learning about rigging and fitting out and stowing supplies in the hold. There were practical exercises in managing the sails – the younger cadets on deck, hauling on ropes while the older boys went aloft – lifeboat practice, signalling, working anchors and cables, knotting and splicing, and the use of nautical instruments. Queensberry's first experience of ceremonial duties was on 31 August when the young crew dressed the ship and manned the yards to cheer Her Majesty as she passed by in HMS *Elfin*. The day ended with prayers at 9.15 p.m.

Living conditions were basic but clean. There was a common room known as the 'gunroom' where cadets could do their preparation, read, reply to letters from home, and plan mischief. Food was nourishing, but plain. The stores included beef, both salt and fresh, and vegetables, as well as salt pork, cooking oil, ship's biscuit, oatmeal and split peas. This bland fare was enlivened by pepper, vinegar and mustard. Flour, suet, sugar and raisins would have been used to make puddings, and there was also cocoa, tea and rum. Cadets were allowed substantial periods of leave, including six weeks over Christmas and New Year, and every so often some of their number were taken ashore for recreation or to attend a service at the dockyard church. There were no purpose-built sports facilities, but the boys may have played cricket or football, or gone swimming.

The success of the new training scheme soon necessitated a transfer to a larger vessel, the three-decker *Britannia* built in 1820. Here the cadets, who now numbered 130, had a large mess room, which was also used for study, inspections and prayers and as a general common room. There was still no formal recreation so boys with energy to spare after an active day would take advantage of the more spacious *Britannia* for races around the mess room, mock battles on deck, and a game called 'Sling the Monkey' in which a cadet swung from a bowline while his messmates tried to hit him with knotted ropes.

Thus far Queensberry's naval experience was limited to instruction on board a moored ship, which must have been frustrating for a youth who was eager to travel, but on 24 June 1859 he joined the *Aboukir*, a ninety-gun ship of the line, which was due to go to sea with a complement of over 800. The young marquess had already begun to show an interest in the kind of charitable donations expected of a gentleman, and appropriately that summer he responded to an appeal from the Royal National Lifeboat Institution of Scotland by making an annual donation of 2 guineas. On 21 August the *Aboukir* left Portland Harbour to join the Channel Fleet under the flagship *Royal Albert*, and there were two additional subjects to study: gunnery and the steam engine. After weeks of preparation, the fleet finally headed out under sail on 28 October, the cadets no doubt looking forward to their first real experience of the open sea.

On the morning of 1 November the fleet was engaged in routine gunnery practice in calm weather, but that afternoon it was unexpectedly struck by the heaviest deluge of hail and sleet that had hit the English coast for many years. The storm continued all night, and efforts were made to get to Plymouth, but with poor visibility and winds increasing to a fury followed by torrents of rain this proved impossible. Matters were complicated by the arrival of a fleet of trawlers, and it required careful handling of the larger vessels not to run them down. The fleet tried a new tack, the ships turning to face into the gale, and this enabled them to set a course around the Eddystone Lighthouse round which they 'darted like dolphins'.[1] After a long night of storms, which had strewn the coast with wrecks, the gale finally lifted and the Channel Fleet steamed triumphantly into Portland in good order and without loss.

Aboukir returned to Plymouth on 1 February 1860 and Queensberry joined a new berth. This time he would see a great deal more than the south coast of England. His itinerary for the next two years reads like the stuff of boys' adventure stories. His new appointment was the recently constructed screw steam frigate *Forte*, which was lying at Sheerness, due for departure to the Cape of Good Hope as the flagship of Admiral Sir Henry Keppel.

While the *Forte* was being made ready, Queensberry enjoyed some leave with his mother, brothers and sisters who were staying at Harleyford for a few weeks. Florence later described a swimming contest between her eldest brother and thirteen-year-old Francis, whom Caroline had had no qualms about educating at Eton. Since Florence was only four at the time, her account may owe a great deal to the recall of others who were present. The brothers were on a punt, which had been moored midstream, playing with sacks filled with some buoyant material. The sacks were flung overboard and allowed to float downstream then the boys would plunge in, seize a sack and swim back to the punt. The active and high-spirited boys were fiercely yet amiably competitive. Queensberry 'strained every nerve to reach the punt first'[2] but the taller and more powerful Francis, 'a generous lad' who 'loved his brother dearly',[3] was the better swimmer. Florence believed that Francis could have won easily but deliberately held back to spare his brother's feelings, and the race ended in a dead heat.

Although Queensberry hated to lose any kind of race, he accepted fair defeat gracefully and always gave credit where it was due. After the swimming contest a log of wood came floating down the river and James, with a stick in his hand, said he could get it before his twin did. Florence was not to be beaten and jumped into the river. James and the twins' nursemaid screamed in terror and Queensberry and Francis leaped in after their adventurous sister and hauled her on to the bank. 'Thank the Lord Jesus she was saved', Florence recalled Queensberry exclaiming, but he freely admitted that it was his brother's swimming that had saved her, saying 'I could not have got to her in time.'[4]

Soon afterwards Francis was due back at Eton and the young marquess received orders to rejoin his ship. On 28 April, the *Forte* under Captain Turnour left Spithead by The Needles en route for the Cape. On 9 May it was at Funchal Harbour in Madeira, to take on fresh provisions. Officers and cadets, permitted generous shore leave, were often involved in boisterous and sometimes destructive, selfish and frankly criminal behaviour onshore. Queensberry, full of youthful exuberance, ready for any challenge and careless of his own safety, would have been in the thick of any such adventure. That May, Queensberry and four other cadets including Henry Stephenson, (nephew of Admiral Sir Henry Keppel and later Admiral Sir Henry Stephenson) indulged in a typically wild escapade: they 'attempted to gallop through the town against orders, were set upon by the Portuguese, fifteen policemen and sixty or seventy inhabitants, and defied capture until the Guard was turned out. After three hours in gaol they were secretly released after dark on payment of a fine through the intervention of the Admiral, whose only regret was that his nephew's party '"had not marked them a little more".'[5] Many a senior commander included fond recollections of similar youthful excursions in his memoirs, one observing that offences committed by young officers 'were principally the outcome of high-spirits, mischievousness, thoughtlessness, or lack of experience. Frequently they showed a spirit of devilry that was all to the good, provided that it was not carried to excess.'[6] Discipline was firm and midshipmen caught out in minor offences could expect to stand extra watches, do extra drill, or lose leave privileges and pocket money. There were more sedate entertainments ashore, however, when good behaviour was expected, and the young officers were afforded generous hospitality.

On 3 June the *Forte* called at Rio de Janeiro for coaling and refitting, where the cadets were permitted to go ashore and sail small boats in the spacious harbour, and on 5 July the fleet reached Simon's Bay on the Cape for an extended stay. On 17 August sixteen-year-old Queensberry was promoted to midshipman. In his examination for that rank he would have shown that he could use mathematical tables and instruments, demonstrated a good knowledge of steering and managing a boat under oars and sail, as well as knotting, splicing, rigging, and the 'Simple Exercise of the Great Guns'.[7] The logbooks he had kept from his time of entry in a seagoing ship and certificates of good conduct would have been presented for inspection. The new midshipman continued to study but also played an essential part in the running of the ship by keeping watches and supervising the cleaning of the decks; he was also responsible for handling the ship's boats and the management of small parties of seamen. Every day he calculated the ship's position and noted it in a book to be seen by the captain. The 'young gentlemen', as midshipmen were known, also practised regular drills with cutlass and rifle and the ship's guns. In eighteen months Queensberry was due to take further examinations, in which he would have to demonstrate more detailed knowledge of seamanship, familiarity with the parts of a steam engine, proficiency in French, and skill as a practical observer, and again present his logbooks and certificates of good conduct for inspection.

Prince Alfred, second son of Queen Victoria, was also visiting the Cape Colony, serving as a midshipman aboard HMS *Euryalus* and a grand ball was held in his honour, which Queensberry attended. 'It is not often that England's great nobility is so well represented at a Cape ball,' enthused the *Cape Monthly Magazine*. 'There goes the Most Noble the Marquis of Queensberry. "Where? where?" is asked. One pictures a tall, grave, stately personage, in star and garter, supporting the weight of such sounding titles. We collapse entirely on being told *that* is his lordship – the bright, handsome, blythe middy – dancing so unweariedly.'[8]

The *Forte* left the Cape in January 1861, and headed east, calling at Ascension Island, Sierra Leone, Accra, Lagos and Luanda, before returning to Rio. Here the HMS *Emerald*, a fifty-one-gun frigate, steamed into harbour and Admiral Keppel and his officers, including Queensberry, joined its complement. There were several other young aristocrats on board, and the *Emerald* was sometimes called the 'House of Lords'.[9] The *Emerald* visited Bahia, St Vincent and Fayal before returning to Spithead where it anchored on 6 August 1861 and Queensberry attended the Royal Victoria Yacht Club regatta at Ryde. His maternal grandfather Sir William was amongst the fashionable gathering, and Caroline, who had been on the Continent with her family, arrived at the Portland Hotel, Southsea to see her eldest son.

In the three years since her husband's death Caroline had been constantly on the move. Some of her time was spent at Kinmount, and some at Glen Stuart, but she also visited London, St Leonards, Southsea and Harleyford. The 1861 census records her living at Warriston House, Edinburgh with Gertrude, Francis, Archibald Jnr and the twins. Soon afterwards she and all her children apart from her eldest departed on an extended tour of Switzerland, Germany, Italy and France, where they were enthralled by the beauty of the scenery, especially the 'towering ice-clad mountains of the Alps, which had recently become a source of fascination for the British sportsman'.[10]

In the previous decade, faster travel to the Continent by rail and steamship had made the Alps more accessible to British tourists, and when writer Albert Smith published an account of his 1851 ascent of Mont Blanc a surge of interest ushered in what became known as the Golden Age of Alpinism. The new sport of mountaineering fused effortlessly with a growing public preoccupation with health, and the importance of exercise both for fitness and the development of manly character. To the sportsman who longed for a heroic adventure, the Alps held the additional attractions of travel, danger and patriotic achievement. The Alpine Club of Great Britain was formed in 1857 with the object of ensuring that British climbers were the first to climb the unconquered Alps, and its members included a young barrister and future High Court judge Alfred Wills, whose ascent of the Wetterhorn in 1854 and subsequent book of his experiences had further popularised the sport, and the artist and explorer Edward Whymper. Fourteen-year-old Francis, who loved a sporting challenge, was captivated by the glamour of the icy peaks.

The next voyage of the *Emerald* was to Halifax, Nova Scotia. April 1861 had seen the first hostilities in the American Civil War, and the start of the Union naval blockade of Southern ports. Britain was largely in favour of the separation of the Confederate States from the Union, but stayed out of the conflict, although the Royal Navy continued to patrol the eastern seaboard of North America and the West Indies. In October, with the threat of a possible rupture of relations between Britain and America, it was decided to transport some of the new breech-loading Armstrong guns to the Royal Navy squadron on the North American station.

On 5 October the *Emerald*, heavily laden with guns, ammunition and stores, sailed under the command of Captain Arthur Cumming, but five days later and still 900 miles from its destination it ran into heavy gales. From the first stormy day the ship leaked so heavily that at times there were 10–12 inches of water on the lower decks. As the ship laboured in a heavy sea, the weight of armaments on board made it roll dangerously, breaking cabin furniture and causing massive damage to sails, spars and yards; one marine suffered a broken leg from shot falling off the storage racks. Several times the ship tilted over so perilously that it seemed as though it would never come back up again. Heavy squalls and the constantly changing wind direction made progress impossible. Three quarter boats that had hung at the vessel's side were lost in the storm, the topsails were carried away, and it was too dangerous to send men aloft. Attempts were made to get the ship under steam, but the engines and machinery were so badly damaged that it was hard to make any headway. The storm was still raging on 22 October when another ship came into view, and the *Emerald* had to fire its guns to attract its attention and avoid a collision. Two days later the mission was abandoned and the *Emerald* turned back for home. The crew, it was later observed with approval, remained well disciplined throughout the ordeal. It took eleven days for the *Emerald* to limp back to Plymouth through 'thick and dirty weather'[11] for much-needed repairs. On 9 December the *Emerald*, loaded with more guns, set sail again but encountered fresh gales of such severity that no progress could be made either by sail or steam. The boats were damaged, and the steering wheel yoke broke in two and was carried away. Worrying news was received in Boston that the *Emerald* was overdue, and a sloop of war, *Daring* was sent out in search of the missing vessel. For the second time, however, the *Emerald* had abandoned its voyage, and made it back to Plymouth on 14 December, to hear that the dispute with America was at an end.

Later that month the *Emerald* sailed for a less challenging destination – Liverpool. The voyage through misty weather via Anglesey was completed without incident and the *Emerald* returned to Plymouth to be fitted with new guns. The seventeen-year-old marquess had now been away from home for almost two years, and was permitted to take some leave with his family. Queensberry brought a number of 'his brother middies' to stay at Kinmount where, recalled Florence 'they managed to make everything extremely lively and pleasant'.[12] The six-year-old twins were natural riders, having been taught to ride bareback on Shetland ponies by Queensberry and Francis, and 'often participated in some of the young officers' rollicking pastimes, one of these being paperchases on horseback, a very lively game indeed, which produced some keen riding and a good many falls!'[13]

Of all the Douglas siblings, Queensberry's sister Florence was most like him. Fiercely independent from her youth, she resented the fact that boys and girls were educated separately, and shared her brother's love of vigorous outdoor sports and zest for adventure. Florence and Queensberry, like their mother, had a taste for travel, and all three, on seeing a wrong, felt it was their duty to put it right. Francis, who was studying for the army, and Archibald Jnr who was at preparatory school in the south of England were also on leave, and the days were filled with walks along the seashore, picnics in the woods, 'aquatic festivities'[14] on the lake and a host of other amusements which made the times fly by. The only solemn day was Sunday, when romping games were strictly forbidden and dull morning prayers were intoned around the dining room table, followed by a dreary sermon at the kirk. According to Florence, however, Queensberry was already having doubts about stern Presbyterianism; later she recalled one of the 'middies' walking back from the service commenting that it was 'precious dull work',[15] to which Queensberry agreed with a laugh. His fellow midshipman, Byng (possibly the future Captain Robert Lowther Byng), asked Queensberry if he believed in the minister's 'vindictive God and those impossible angels'.[16] Queensberry paused a minute for thought then replied, in a low voice, 'Yes, I *think* so, Byng.' Noticing that the twins were listening he added hastily, 'Shut up, Byng; don't let us talk about these things before those children. No, honestly, I can't answer you.'[17]

All too soon he and his brother 'mids' received their orders to return to the *Emerald*, which was to take up duties in the Channel. The 'young gentlemen' were kept busy with Armstrong gun drill, target practice, cutlass exercises, mizen topsail drill, and knotting and splicing. On 4 May the *Emerald* arrived at Portland Roads near Weymouth.

Thus far Queensberry's naval career was, apart from some high-spirited escapades winked at by authority, without blemish. However on 21 May 1862, with the *Emerald* preparing for sea, Admiral Robert Smart, commander-in-chief of the Channel Squadron, whose flagship *Revenge* was anchored off Portland, asked the captain of the *Emerald*, 'To report under what circumstances Marquis of Queensberry went on leave, my sanction not having been given'. Being absent without leave was a serious matter, and Queensberry cannot have been unaware of this.

On 22 May at 9.05 a.m. *Revenge* signalled the *Emerald*, 'Has Lord Queensberry returned?' receiving a reply five minutes later: 'No.' At 9.25 the *Revenge* signalled 'Was Lord Queensberry recalled by telegraph yesterday?' to which the reply at 9.30 was, rather worryingly given the events of 1858, 'Yes.' Queensberry cannot have gone far, and at 8.30 p.m. that same day he must have been back on board, for the *Revenge* signalled 'Send immediately Lord Queensberry'. Whether Queensberry complied is unknown, but the following morning at 9 a.m. *Revenge* signalled 'Send explanation called for concerning Lord Queensberry's leave'.[18]

The reasons for Queensberry's absence from duty are unknown but it is probable that there were family matters that he felt demanded his immediate attention as they were more important than his obligations to the Royal Navy. There is no record of any disciplinary action being taken, and while his title would have had a great deal to do with this, it may have been appreciated that he had not gone off on a selfish spree but had serious issues to address. Steps were taken to remove him from further temptation. Admiral Smart wrote a letter to the Admiralty reporting the 'misconduct',[19] and the anxious midshipman was ordered to report to the *Victory* to await passage to his new ship the *Nile*. Queensberry was not so easily diverted, and wrote to Smart applying for a month's leave. This was refused and he was directed to join the *Victory* at once.

Queensberry's sudden departure may have been connected with a family upheaval that was about to become public. If the young marquess was having doubts about the religion of the Scottish Kirk, his mother was undergoing her own crisis of belief and was about to take a step which would have consequences for her children no less dramatic than the death of her husband. Caroline, a steadfast believer in heaven, hell, angels and the devil, had taught her children to believe the same, with varying degrees of success. She was said to be 'a patroness of Christian revivalism and the evangelist preacher Richard Weaver, the "converted collier"'.[20] Weaver had preached in Edinburgh in 1860 and Caroline may have heard him. With Gertrude a grown woman and her two eldest sons settled in their education, Caroline felt able to do what her heart had dictated for a long time, and what her husband must have feared. She converted to Roman Catholicism. Learning that the guardians of her youngest children were meeting to discuss her actions, and afraid that Archibald Jnr and the twins would be removed from her care, she determined on a secret flight to the Continent. In late August, she carried out her plan.

Accounts of this event vary. Florence's colourful memoir described a dramatic escape starting at Kinmount at night, the seven-year-old twins and their nurse, fortified by mugs of hot cocoa, travelling by carriage to meet the train, and being met by their mother for the journey to Folkestone, where they were joined by Archibald Jnr. Press reports, however, state that the flight started at 11 a.m. from Weybridge where Caroline was then living with her children. In another version Caroline first went to France alone to establish a place of refuge, asking Gertrude to arrange for a nursemaid to take the children to a safe meeting place, and on her return from France she collected the children and all made their way across the Channel. Initially the fugitives settled in Boulogne, where Caroline engaged a Catholic tutor for her children, M. L'Abbé Bonamy.

The Douglas guardians and relatives were empowered 'through the strong arm of English law to rescue the children and make them wards in chancery',[21] although this applied only to Archibald Jnr and the twins as under Scottish law they could choose their own guardians on reaching the age of fourteen. Detectives were sent to find them, and the abbé, concerned that the children would be removed from their mother's care, advised her to go to Nantes where a Breton family called de Kersabiec might help her. In Nantes Caroline was introduced to Mrs Eleanor Leslie, a widow and devout Catholic known for her charitable work, and came to rely on the good counsel and comforting presence of her new friend. Mrs Leslie found Caroline an apartment, but no sooner did the fugitives begin to feel safe than they heard disturbing news. Mrs Leslie's brother, Falconer Atlee, British Consul at Nantes, learned that Caroline was still being pursued. According to press reports a detective had traced Caroline to Nantes in November. A retired police officer, Superintendent Thomson, later claimed to be the man who had discovered Lady Queensberry.[22] Atlee's house had an entrance and a staircase at each end and, realising that this would be very useful for anyone who might have to make a quick escape, he invited Caroline to make her home there as long as she wished. This offer was gratefully accepted.

Emperor Napoleon III who, during his exile in England had been a friend of Caroline's father, Sir William Clayton, granted Caroline his protection, and she was allowed to retain custody of her children and educate them as she wished. In November 1862 Lord Archibald, who was 'religiously inclined' and 'a gentle, kindly, quiet lad, very different in temperament to the twins, or his two elder brothers',[23] took his first communion and in December he was confirmed. Gertrude, who had also converted to Catholicism, came out to join them, and Francis, who had declined to convert, was able to visit.

When the news of his mother's flight reached Queensberry he was in no position to do anything about it; he had been transferred to the *Rinaldo*, a screw-driven sloop of war with seventeen guns and a complement of 170, which was appointed to the North American station. On 8 October he arrived at New Orleans.

The youthful Queensberry had strong political opinions, and – a trend that would continue for the rest of his life – he was unafraid not only to go against the current of public opinion, but to freely express himself. 'I was always a Radical and a Home Ruler,' he commented later.[24] During the American Civil War he had believed in 'preserving the integrity of the Union',[25] and in October and November 1862 Queensberry discovered he was 'about the only Union man in the ship . . . our men used to sing nightly on the forecastle, laying [*sic*] off New-Orleans, and surrounded by half-a-dozen Federal ships, "The Bonny Blue Flag," the Southern Rebels' song.'[26]

In February, when the *Rinaldo* was at Hamilton, Bermuda, Queensberry was anxious to see his family, and wrote to Admiral Milne his commander-in-chief for permission to return to England. This was granted and he took passage across the Atlantic, arriving at Spithead. In April he was permitted to go to London to visit his grandmother, and it was probably at this time that he visited his family in Nantes, where according to Florence, 'both he and [Francis] became great favourites amongst the "royalist" community'.[27]

On 7 May he was back aboard the *Emerald*, which was with the Channel Fleet at Portsmouth Harbour off the Isle of Wight. Under Queensberry's influence the main recreation of the young gentlemen was boxing. 'Queensberry was a beautiful boxer,' recalled Rear-Admiral Sir Sydney M. Eardley-Wilmot, who served as a midshipman with Queensberry on the *Emerald*. 'As a senior midshipman he instructed the youngsters in this art. . . . He was absolutely fearless, and would fight the biggest man he met on shore with little or no provocation. Sometimes he got the worst of it. On one occasion he could not return that day to the ship owing to two conspicuous black eyes. He kept himself in condition by running with the coaches in the Isle of Wight, the railway not being built then.'[28]

The fleet headed north and its appearance at Sunderland on 23 July sent the town into holiday fever, with flags fluttering, church bells pealing and crowds of visitors pouring in, eager to inspect the ships. A grand ball was given on Friday for Fleet Admiral Dacres and his officers, to which the young midshipman was invited, and he was also at a banquet on Saturday night. On 4 August the *Emerald* was at Edinburgh where a dinner was given by the Lord Provost, magistrates and council to Admiral Dacres and the officers of the fleet at the music hall following a pleasure excursion to the Bass Rock. Queensberry was one of the eleven officers representing the *Emerald*. In September he was in Liverpool, where over a thousand men were entertained to a beef, mutton, grog and ale banquet, and nautical songs were sung lustily.

In October the *Emerald* returned to Plymouth, where Queensberry, presumably having time on his hands, was game for another risky challenge. There were no signs that his temporary disgrace had had any effect on his ebullient high spirits:

> One daring deed of his is worth recording. In Plymouth Sound about a quarter of a mile from us lay our chummy ship the *Defence*, one of the new ironclads. One boisterous autumnal evening Queensberry went on deck, swore the officer of the watch – a brother midshipman – to secrecy, and told him he was going to swim to the *Defence*. Remonstrance was unavailing. Queensberry went down the accommodation ladder and plunged in. Owing to the current he missed the gangway of the *Defence*, but fortunately our Captain had gone aboard to dine, and his galley was made fast astern. Queensberry managed to get into the boat, and appeared all dripping on the quarter deck. He was provided with dry clothes, and our Captain brought him back in his galley. Of course, we younger mids looked upon him as a hero, and indeed, he was a fine character, always ready to take the blame in any escapade with others, but something in later years seemed to warp his nature, which spoiled his career.[29]

Shortly afterwards the *Emerald* returned to Sheerness to be taken out of commission, and Queensberry, now nineteen years old and with over five years of service, was transferred to the *Edgar*, one of the last of the old two-decked battleships, while continuing his studies aboard the training ship *Excellent* moored in Portsmouth Harbour to take the examination for the rank of lieutenant. The examinations were held at the Royal Naval College and included gunnery, navigation and the steam engine. He would also have had to produce good conduct certificates from all the captains he had served under.

Queensberry sailed in the *Edgar* for what was to be his last tour of duty in the Royal Navy in December 1863, visiting Madeira, Tenerife, Gibraltar and Lisbon. On 15 February 1864 he was promoted to sub lieutenant. One of his fellow officers was the future Admiral Sir Robert Hastings Harris. The *Edgar*, wrote Harris, 'was not a happy ship'.[30] The young officers, comparing it with the newer design of armoured vessels, thought it a potential deathtrap in any conflict, its construction and drills obsolete and the bullying discipline outmoded, unjust and useless for producing an efficient fighting force. 'Our wardroom mess was composed of the most genial and excellent fellows,' added Harris, 'and among ourselves we were as happy as we could be, and all of us were ready to do our best for the ship. Yet we one and all detested the system under which we were governed, and in our mess we occasionally and, I am afraid, rather too freely, expressed aloud our indignation at the often entirely undeserved abuse that it had been our fate to receive at drill or exercise.'[31]

In March 1864 there was a curious echo of the Liverpool visit. The *Court Journal* announced that a marriage had been arranged between Queensberry who was 'highly respected by his brother officers' and a Miss Casey, daughter of a Mrs W. Somerford Casey, the widow of a 'wealthy merchant of Liverpool' whom he had met during the Channel Fleet's brief stay in 'the modern Tyre'. The prospective bride was said to be in her twenty-fourth year with a fortune of £20,000.[32] The story was retracted as untrue a few days later. Whether it arose from a misunderstanding, a youthful peccadillo, wishful thinking or even complete invention cannot be determined, but Queensberry's marriage choice was clearly a matter of public interest.

The *Edgar* was back at Portland in April, and Queensberry had the opportunity for recreation ashore. On the 22nd he attended a ball at Willis's, a suite of assembly rooms in King Street, close to St James's Theatre. The large, elegant ballroom with its classical columns and pilasters was decorated with new draperies and a profusion of flowers, and the company was entertained by a band, with supper being served at one o' clock. A notable guest was Alfred Montgomery, a popular society dandy, gentleman usher to Her Majesty and Commissioner of the Inland Revenue, who was accompanied by his two daughters, Sybil, almost nineteen, and Edith, a year older. The Montgomery sisters were said to be so lovely that when they went out driving together people stood on chairs to see them. Golden-haired Sybil with her turquoise blue eyes, rosebud mouth and creamy complexion, was slender and graceful, had a gentle sweet-toned voice, and cannot have failed to come to the attention of the young marquess.

In June the Channel Fleet was at Spithead under orders for the next cruise and the fleet fielded a cricket team against the officers of the Royal Marine Light Infantry in which Queensberry both batted and bowled. Perhaps the onshore relaxation gave him the opportunity to consider his future. In little more than a year he would reach his majority and take charge of his landed estates. The navy, its studies, its comradeship and world travel must always been intended as an education and a broadening of experience, rather than a career. While the newspapers speculated that Queensberry was about to take another appointment, his unhappy time on the *Edgar* may have soured his enthusiasm for the naval life, and from a practical point of view it would be unwise to start a new tour of duty. A recent development would also have prompted his desire to remain on land. His mother had come to a compromise with the guardians of the younger children, and having received their assurance that she could retain sole charge of Archibald Jnr, now fourteen, and the twins who were almost nine, had ended her exile. That May, she arrived in London and she and the three children travelled to Scotland, where Gertrude joined them. Francis was travelling on the Continent, where, something of a risk-taker like his father, he swam the Hellespont.

Gertrude was now almost twenty-two. 'A beautiful child and girl, she had grown into a beautiful woman.'[33] She had many admirers, but had fallen in love with one of Queensberry's brother officers, and they were engaged to be married. At the time of the engagement Gertrude had been a Protestant, as was her fiancé, but when he returned from service abroad he discovered that she had become a Roman Catholic. Dispensation to marry could be granted only if the children were brought up in the Catholic faith and to this he could not agree. With considerable sorrow on both sides, the engagement was broken off. A few weeks later Gertrude donned a bridal gown of white satin with a bouquet in her hand, and after a ceremony she retired briefly to reappear in a dress of white serge. Gertrude had renounced the vanities of the world and become a nun. She entered a convent at Hammersmith.

Francis was studying for his army exams, and Archibald's education proceeded without incident but Caroline's defiant, rebellious and restless younger daughter was a source of despair to her governess. Caroline – defiant, rebellious and restless herself – was unable to appreciate those qualities in her own child and so to their considerable distress the twins were separated, Florence being sent to a convent school near London and James to a Catholic boarding school for boys.

On 11 July Queensberry wrote to Admiral Dacres resigning from the Royal Navy, and Dacres forwarded his letter to the Admiralty. He was formally discharged on 15 July. 'What was it then,' asked his grandson, the eleventh marquess, 'that turned this healthy, ordinary young man into the soured unhappy misanthrope he became in later years?'[34]

CHAPTER 4

Night on a Mountain

A FTER leaving the navy Queensberry spent a few months visiting family and friends, then on 9 November 1864 he formally enrolled at Magdalen College, Cambridge University, where almost certainly his intention was not to study for a degree but to mark time until he reached the age of twenty-one and gained control of his inheritance. No records remain to show what he studied, but an article in *Bailey's Monthly Magazine* suggests classics and mathematics.[1] His chief interest however would have been sport, which from the middle of the nineteenth century was a central part of the education of the elite. Cambridge offered cricket, rowing, athletics, fencing and boxing, to develop the manly virtues of physical health, courage and endurance while ensuring that youthful energies were directed towards wholesome pursuits. Queensberry was a successful amateur athlete at college level, although he never represented the university. At the Magdalen College sports in 1865 held at Fenner's sports ground he won the quarter-mile in 56 seconds and the mile in 5 minutes 24 seconds and came third in the hurdles.

A few days later an unusual contest took place, in which the Marquess of Queensberry matched himself against his greatest opponent – the clock. A wager may have been involved. He undertook to run five miles in 33 minutes and an interested crowd assembled at Fenner's to watch the attempt. He completed the distance in 32 minutes and 16 seconds. At the Oxford and Cambridge sports on 25 March crowds at the university gymnasium saw contests of boxing (a gentlemanly exercise far removed from the brutality of prize fighting) for silver cups, with Queensberry 'cleverly winning that for light weights'.[2] An all-round sportsman like his father, in the following month he rode in the Scottish National Hunt steeplechase, and in May played cricket for Magdalen against Jesus College, Oxford.

At Cambridge Queensberry formed a close friendship that was, for a time, to supply a much-needed focus to his life. John Graham Chambers was born in Llanelly on 12 February 1843, had been educated at Eton and entered Trinity College, Cambridge in 1861. He was a fine sportsman who excelled at rowing, putting the shot, throwing the hammer and the cricket ball and walking, although his 'heavy build and powerful frame'[3] did not make him an ideal runner. Known for his integrity and loyalty to his friends, Chambers was a firm believer in the value of physical education, and was admired and respected by his fellow sportsmen.

By the summer of 1865 Queensberry's university days were over. On 7 June he attended the wedding of Baron Ferdinand de Rothschild where the lovely Sybil Montgomery and her sister were bridesmaids. Soon, he was back in Scotland for his coming of age on 20 July. The twenty-first birthday of an eldest son was a major event in a noble family. Weeks of planning and preparation, and substantial expenditure, were required to entertain large numbers of guests of every rank over the course of several days. Since Queensberry was already a marquess the event was of even greater significance. Stepping over the legal divide from boy to man would give him control of his lands and fortune, which until then had been managed by his guardians. In the midst of the bustling arrangements for the most important party of his life, he must have thought of his future with pleasurable anticipation: the enjoyment of his estates; being surrounded by family, friends and loyal tenants; involvement in local, even national, affairs; perhaps at last gaining that elusive British peerage, and all very possibly with the beautiful Sybil at his side. Queensberry's twenty-first birthday was to shape the rest of his life, but in a way that no one could have anticipated.

Eighteen-year-old Francis, now 'a tall, strapping young fellow'[4] of considerable promise, was abroad, but had promised to be home two days before the start of festivities. If he resembled Gertrude's fictionalised version of him – Archie in *Nature's Nursling* – he was a cheerful soul, friendly and pleasant to all. He had taken his army entrance examinations in April, coming first out of 119 competitors, and having accepted a commission in the Black Watch decided to holiday in Switzerland before joining his regiment. For the bold and adventurous youth, Switzerland, which he had already visited on several occasions, meant only one thing – the Alps. He was a member of the Alpine

Club, and had, for his age, considerable experience of mountaineering. In 1865 two great prizes still awaited the serious alpinist: the as yet unconquered Ober Gabelhorn, and the larger, almost pyramidal Matterhorn, at 14,692 feet one of the highest peaks in the Alps, its four great sheer faces towering 5,000 feet above the glaciers that surrounded its base. There had been unsuccessful attempts to scale the Matterhorn since 1858, and many of the most experienced Alpine guides believed it to be unclimbable. British alpinists, however, remained confident. It was still the golden age, full of opportunities and optimism. On 7 July, Francis was one of a party that reached the summit of the Ober Gabelhorn. Although later they discovered that another party had been successful only the day before by another route, it was nevertheless a remarkable achievement for an eighteen-year-old. There was almost a tragedy when Francis and his guide Peter Taugwalder the Younger were swept from the summit by an avalanche but they were roped to another member of the team, and the rope held. Francis may have omitted that alarming detail when sending a telegram to his family announcing his success.

Four days later Francis and his party arrived at Breuil, where they met Edward Whymper, an illustrator who on his first tour of the Alps in 1860 had 'acquired the passion for mountain-scrambling'.[5] He first attempted to scale the Matterhorn in 1861, using the southern route, then considered to be the best. He failed, but the mountain had come to exert a fascination over him and he returned to it again and again, each time being forced to give up. In June 1865 he abandoned his seventh attempt after a rockfall, but by then had made a breakthrough discovery: that the unpromising-looking north-east ridge starting from Zermatt was the easiest route. In his opinion, 'Up to the height of nearly 13,000 feet there were no extraordinary difficulties; the way so far might even become a "matter of amusement."'[6] The remaining 1,700 feet presented obstacles which no lone climber could overcome. An Italian expedition had just arrived, determined to be the first to conquer the mountain and, spurred on by this challenge, Whymper started to prepare for another attempt.

He was impressed by the 'nimble young Englishman'[7] whose recent ascent of the Ober Gabelhorn – a peak he had decided not to attempt because of its difficulty – had already excited his admiration. Francis told Whymper that Old Peter Taugwalder, 'hard as nails, brown as a pet meerschaum . . . head and shoulders like a Highland bull'[8] thought that an ascent of the Matterhorn was possible from the north.

It was soon agreed that Francis, who was keen to attempt the climb, would join Whymper, and Old Peter was engaged as a guide. The party moved off to Zermatt with their stores, which included three ropes: two stout strong ones and a weaker reserve. They stayed at the Monte Rosa hotel, which, like Zermatt, had benefited from the fashion for visiting the Alps and was the chosen destination of the gentleman mountaineer. Here Whymper encountered an old comrade, Michel Croz, a guide of great experience, energy and reliability. Croz had been engaged by the Revd Charles Hudson the vicar of Skillington, thought to be the best amateur mountaineer of his time, in yet another rival attempt on the Matterhorn on the following day. There was a consultation, and the two parties joined forces. Whymper had a high opinion of Hudson, who was accompanied by nineteen-year-old Douglas Robert Hadow. It was Hadow's first season in the Alps, but Hudson readily vouched for his friend's abilities so he was admitted to the party.

They started out from Zermatt at 5.30 a.m. on 13 July, 'a brilliant and perfectly cloudless morning',[9] and proceeded to the base of the peak, camping at a height of 11,000 feet. The next morning was again bright and clear, and they set out for the summit at dawn. It was on this final ascent that Hadow's inexperience became apparent, and while the rest of the party was able to scale a difficult section of the rock face, he needed continual assistance. At 1.40 that afternoon they stood on the summit, overcome with delight to find the snow untrodden by their rivals. Below, they saw the Italian team still toiling up the slope, and the victorious party cheerfully pelted them with stones until they turned back. After an hour on the summit preparations were made to descend, and the first five men were roped together, Croz leading the way, then Hadow, Hudson, Francis and Old Peter. Young Peter and Whymper who were tied together followed. Francis, concerned that Old Peter would not be able to hold the others if there was a slip, asked Whymper to tie to Old Peter, too, which he did. A suggestion was made that rope should be attached to rocks for extra security but this was not done, and the party moved down cautiously, the members relying on each other. Hadow once again experienced some difficulty and the party was obliged to pause while Croz laid aside his axe and took hold of Hadow's legs, putting his feet in the proper positions. He had turned and was about to move off when disaster struck.

Hadow slipped and fell backwards; his feet hit the unsuspecting Croz in the small of the back and knocked him over. Whymper heard Croz's startled exclamation, and saw him and Hadow flying downwards. The shock jerked both Hudson and Francis from their footing, and they too fell. Whymper and Old Peter planted their feet as firmly as they could, and since the rope between them was taut, the jerk came upon them as one man and they managed to hold on, but to their horror the rope between Old Peter and Francis snapped. In the next few seconds they saw their four companions slide helplessly down on their backs, spreading out their hands to save themselves. One by one they disappeared from view, and 'fell from precipice to precipice on to the Matterhorngletscher below, a distance of nearly 4,000 feet'.[10] For half an hour Whymper and the two guides, who were sobbing in distress, were unable to move from the spot. When Whymper finally examined the broken rope he saw to his astonishment and dismay that it was the weakest, never intended for the purpose for which it had been used. It was 6 p.m. before the shocked and grieving alpinists reached safety and began to make their way towards Zermatt. Of their fallen comrades they saw no sign. The finally reached Zermatt at daybreak, and a team of men was mustered to look for the bodies. Six hours later they returned to say that they had seen the remains through telescopes. Whymper, despite his exhaustion, decided to go out again the following day and a team of volunteers including the chaplain of Zermatt joined him for a 2a.m. start. At 8.30 they reached a ridge above the glacier and were able to confirm that all hope was gone. The bodies of Croz, Hadow and Hudson, 'shapeless remnants of humanity'[11] identifiable only by their personal possessions, were found, but no trace was discovered of Lord Francis, apart from a pair of gloves, a belt and a boot. A later party discovered a sleeve. The fallen men had been tied together with the stronger rope so only that between Old Peter and Lord Francis had been the weaker one. Why this had been used was a mystery that was never resolved. The fragments of the mangled bodies were collected together in a heap on the glacier, surrounded by heavy stones, and prayers said over them.

At Kinmount, the castle and Glen Stuart were packed with guests. There was to be a week of open house; dinners and balls for rich and poor, and special entertainments for the schools and the tenantry, with ample leisure and freedom for everyone to amuse themselves informally. Caroline was in London preparing to travel to Scotland, and anxious about her second son. Francis had informed her that he was due to make an attempt on the

Matterhorn on 14 July but three days later there was still no word from him. She sent telegrams to her father at Harleyford and to Queensberry at Kinmount, asking if they had any news. Neither had, but Queensberry replied, saying that they expected him home in a day or two. On the 17th Caroline and Florence took the train to Kinmount where Queensberry met them at the station. He had still heard nothing but was not expecting a message as he had been told that Francis would come to Kinmount immediately after his ascent of the Matterhorn, and the dog cart was to be sent to meet the evening train.

When it returned empty, and – uncharacteristically, since Francis was a thoughtful boy – there was no telegram to say that he was delayed, the family, with some annoyance which cannot have been unmixed with anxiety, assumed he had caught the night train and would arrive early next morning.

The morning of 18 July dawned bright and warm with clear blue skies. The dog cart went to the station again and once again returned empty. Queensberry spent a restless and irritable day. According to Florence he sent a telegram to Zermatt asking if Francis had left for England and despatched a servant on horseback to await a reply. The next train was not due until evening. In Gertrude's fictionalised account, the family went out to meet it but instead of Francis, a telegraph messenger stepped out and handed Queensberry an orange envelope. Florence, however, who loved to give herself the central role in any drama, later described a servant galloping up the carriage drive to the castle and handing her the envelope, which she took in to the family.

The telegram read: 'Terrible accident on the [Matterhorn]. Four of the climbing party killed Lord [Francis Douglas] one of them. No trace of the body can be found.'[12]

Caroline, white and rigid with grief, went to her room and locked the door, but Queensberry, after the first moments of paralysing shock, determined to take immediate action: he would go to Zermatt and find his brother's body. He rang for the butler and ordered him to bring the dog cart and his portmanteau. Then the young marquess finally gave way to distress. Florence comforted him until he took his leave, saying that he would wire as soon as possible. The guests were out at the time, but as they returned and were given the terrible news, one by one, their carriages were brought to the door and they departed in silence.

On 19 July while Queensberry was on his way, a party of twenty-one men of Zermatt recovered the bodies of Hudson, Hadow and Croz and brought them back for formal burial. It was concluded that the body of Lord Francis lay up on the rocks above the glacier.

Queensberry was never to write about his journey, which must have been two to three days of grief and frustration. With no information on what was happening at Zermatt he may have tormented himself with a faint spectre of hope that Francis might be found alive. His probable route was by train to London and Folkestone, by steamer across the Channel to France, and then train to Paris, where the Paris, Lyons and Mediterranean Railway left at 8.40 p.m., reaching Zermatt at 3.25 the following afternoon. He may even have arrived in time to spend the last hours of his twenty-first birthday in the shadow of the Matterhorn.

When Queensberry learned that Francis had still not been found, all hope vanished. He offered a large sum of money to anyone who could recover the body and despite having no experience in mountaineering decided to join the search party due to go out on the following day. Alone in his hotel room, impatient to make a start, frustration got the better of him and, unable to wait, he determined to set out alone. 'I was half mad with misery,' he later wrote to Florence, 'or I don't suppose I should have tried to do such a thing, and how I managed to get as far as I did, all alone and without a guide, beats me entirely, as it has others.'[13]

He started by moonlight and walked up the valley leaving the pastures and drifts of alpine flowers for the bare stony slopes, and beds of snow. The summit of the great mountain seemed almost to hang over his head, its ridges too steep and forbidding for any man to conquer. He reached the plateau of the Matterhorngletscher, its surface pitted with the rocks that from time to time fell with thunderous roars from the cliffs above to shatter into fragments. He was, he admitted, 'not dressed for the work I had undertaken'[14] and had only a pair of 'ordinary thick walking boots'.[15] Thus clad he struggled on, almost struck several times by pieces of stone and rock that 'came bounding down from above'.[16] After crossing the plateau he reached the base of the mountain at dawn, but from here the way became increasingly steep. At last he arrived at a point which he later learned was called the Hut. In 1865 it was no more than a rocky ledge suitable for pitching a tent. After several fruitless and exhausting attempts, he found not only that he was unable to go any further up the mountain, but that he could not get down again. He had probably been walking and climbing for about six hours, and may have reached around 11,000 feet.

There he remained, half frozen, trying his best to keep warm, listening to the rumble of avalanches above, the realisation dawning that he had set himself an impossible task and that it was hopeless to try and find his brother's body that way. 'And, as I stood up there all alone, [Florence], I thought and thought where he was, and called him, and wondered if I should ever see him again. I was half mad with misery, [Florence] and I could not help it.'[17] Although he had left a note at the hotel and felt sure that someone would come and look for him, it was a matter of chance whether they would arrive before he died of cold.

Most people come to the mountains in a spirit of adventure, to meet a physical challenge, to test themselves against nature in its most extreme forms, and find experiences they can have nowhere else: the smell of the crisp cold air, the beauty of Alpine landscapes, the dazzle of sunlight on sculptured snow, and seas of glacial ice, the great silences broken only by the thunder of distant and sometimes not so distant avalanches, to see rare plants and mineral strata and fossils that speak of time past almost beyond imagination. The sheer size and age of the mountains move visitors as though they are contemplating the vastness of space, granting them an insight into their own insignificance, vulnerability and fleeting existence. The Victorian traveller was obsessed with mountains, with the challenge of the unclimbed, and the thrill of fear and wonder which made them feel more alive. Danger gave them a wrench of terror followed by the sublime pleasure of relief and a certainty of the presence of God. Conquering danger made one a better person, physically and mentally. Risk could be addictive. Small wonder that many experienced spiritual elation in the mountains.

For Queensberry, it was different. He came to the Matterhorn out of grief and helpless desperation, saw none of its beauty and found only the deep and enduring bitterness of failure. If he had found Francis's body, been able to bury the remains and say farewell, and reassure his family that those offices had been carried out with dignity, then he might have found some peace. Instead, the Matterhorn opened a wound that would never heal. Abandoning the search for his brother's body he commenced a search for his soul, but unlike many who have undertaken this quest was unable to comfort himself with the concept of his brother's continued individual existence in heaven. Until then, Queensberry had believed in the God of the Bible, but his belief died that night. He did not, as is frequently asserted, reject God, or embrace atheism; what came to him was an altogether less defined concept of the divine. 'And then I had some wonderful thoughts when I wondered where he was. They came to me like a flash of lightning. It was about the relation of the body and soul of man . . . these thoughts brought me a lot of comfort in my misery.'[18] When he and Florence later talked about his search for Francis he said that if there was a God he did not think of Him as a being, as he had been taught. He could not, and never attempted to, define the nature of God but referred to Him thereafter as 'The Inscrutable'. He had thought about the soul, and believed that 'when we die our soul becomes part of an undying force, that which creates everything, and must live, being itself Creation'.[19] It was some years before Queensberry was able to put these thoughts into words, and when he did he was misunderstood, but that night on the mountain was a crucial turning point in his life, one which was to have a profound effect both on how he perceived society and on how society perceived him.

Several hours later two guides found him, numb with cold and no longer caring what happened to him. Had the weather turned stormy as it often did on the Matterhorn, with strong bitter winds and further falls of snow, he would not have survived.

News of the disaster caused a sensation when it reached London and speculation about its causes filled the papers for several weeks, some commentators openly questioning whether it was sensible or reasonable to try and climb mountains at all. The incident marked the end of the golden age of Alpinism: now all major Alpine peaks had been scaled, and the playground of the gentleman amateur had finally shown its merciless power. The *Illustrated London News*, recognising the tragedy on a more personal level, commented on the fatal misfortunes that had afflicted the Douglases, recalling the first Drumlanrig tragedies and the 'accidental' death of Archibald senior.[20]

It was three days before Caroline felt able to leave her room and eventually Kinmount was closed up and she made Glen Stuart her home. Gertrude emerged from the convent to be with her mother, and Florence observed that religion had proved to be little comfort to her sad-eyed sister for the loss of her love. There had already been plans to build a church in Zermatt to hold services in English, and in August it was suggested that it should be a memorial to those who had died. The funds were swelled by donations from the Alpine Club and friends and relatives of the deceased, Queensberry sending £50. On 29 June 1869 the foundation stone of St Peter's church was laid, and it opened a year later. A plaque in the Queensberry enclosure at Cummertrees church also commemorates Francis.

The twenty-one-year-old marquess now commanded an enviable estate estimated at 30,000 acres of valuable farmland yielding an annual rent roll of £20,000. The entire fortune handed down from father to son for seven centuries was thought to be worth about £780,000.[21] Queensberry spent some of his time in Scotland, attending to his estates. Despite his youth he was already well regarded in the racing world, and stewarded the Royal Caledonian Hunt meeting in October. He was also starting to move in London society, his eye on an altogether different quarry, the enchanting twenty-year-old Sybil Montgomery. Queensberry was undoubtedly an ardent wooer, and a wooer moreover with land and a title.

Sybil Montgomery and Queensberry could not have been more different. Sybil was a stay at home girl who liked a quiet life and refined amusements. Queensberry liked travel, conflict, sport and broad entertainment. Sybil and her sister were 'brought up in an aesthetic atmosphere. Painting, music, poetry and literature were to them what hunting, shooting, skating, racing, indeed all sport, were to [Queensberry].'[22] Sybil's chief interest was reading, and her taste was for Greek and Roman history, English literature and poetry. Queensberry, while he did undoubtedly read, did so – judging from the works he mentioned – more for information than pleasure. Bosie's claim that his father 'never read a whole book, except a novel, in his life'[23] is one of his many anger-driven exaggerations. Bosie worshipped his mother without reserve and described her as 'the most unselfish, the most incredibly good and sweet and kind and patient, and also the most valiant and loyal woman that ever drew the breath of life'.[24] Since he was her adored and on his own admission 'frightfully spoilt'[25] favourite, he was undoubtedly biased. The eleventh Marquess by contrast, thought Sybil 'cold' by nature. 'My grandfather was madly in love with her,' he said, 'and there is no doubt that the response on her side was very much less ardent.'[26]

As Queensberry pursued and won his heart's desire he could not have known that his association with the Montgomery family would cruelly fashion the course of the rest of his life, the union with Sybil a turning point no less critical than his night of anguish and enlightenment on the slopes of the Matterhorn.

CHAPTER 5

'He Thought He Loved'

SYBIL Montgomery's father, Alfred was born on 13 April 1814, the fourth son of Sir Henry Conyngham Montgomery of Donegal who had served in India as a cavalry officer, and later as a member of parliament. The opportunities for even such a well-connected fourth son being limited, Alfred, who was educated at Charterhouse, became a clerk in the Admiralty, and soon demonstrated a capacity for reliability, trustworthiness, and a meticulous attention to duty. He was also well dressed, well read, amusing company, and very handsome. Even his faults were attractive. A lisp and a stammer which for another man might have been regarded as a social impediment became in Alfred Montgomery a pleasing fashion accessory.

He was very young – Bosie said sixteen, but certainly under twenty – when he was appointed private secretary to Richard Colley Wellesley, first Marquess Wellesley, Lord Lieutenant of Ireland and brother of the Duke of Wellington. Alfred's youth gave rise to rumours that he was Wellesley's illegitimate son. When Wellesley gave up the viceroyalty of Ireland in 1834 Alfred was granted a pension of £300 a year. In 1838 he was appointed one of the gentleman ushers to Her Majesty and at functions such as drawing rooms, levees, state balls and concerts cut an elegant figure under the approving eye of the young Queen. It was a capacity in which he was to serve for almost fifty-eight years.

Montgomery's faultless dress sense made him in time one of the most noted dandies in London, but it was his intelligence and wit, the wide range of subjects in which he took an interest and about which he could talk entertainingly, and accurate knowledge of 'the secret social history of his times'[1] that ensured his enduring popularity at society gatherings: 'After a very little conversation one discovers that he combines with a thorough knowledge of the world a comprehensive acquaintance with English literature as well as a vast repertory of stories.'[2] Not that his was always a gentle humour; his 'thoughtful, refined wit, just tinged with sarcasm'[3] was particularly relished at refined dinner tables. Since he 'always gave some quaint turn to everything he said,'[4] it can only be regretted that Alfred never seems to have recorded his many stories, written a memoir or turned his hand to the writing of light comedy. Few of his witticisms are recounted by his friends although one has an interesting Wildean pre-echo: 'Alfred Montgomery said there was only one thing that he could not resist, and that was temptation.'[5]

Society hostesses must have been disappointed to find that he was not inclined to court their daughters. Alfred Montgomery was notoriously averse to the mere idea of marriage and, 'a confirmed bachelor, was wont to declare that, in his estimation, to marry was to enter Inferno'.[6]

In September 1842 the Marquess of Wellesley died, leaving his secretary some important papers, and £1,000 'in regard of his affectionate, dutiful and zealous services'.[7] The sum of £1,000 was a handsome one, but wholly insufficient for a gentleman of fashion, so it was time for another career move. Despite every indication that Alfred Montgomery was fated always to be single, on 12 October 1842 he married twenty-one-year-old Fanny Charlotte Wyndham. The reasons for the match, on Alfred's side at least, may well have been financial. Fanny Wyndham was a serious, introspective and deeply religious girl, who published poetry, essays and novels deploring the evils of fashion and vanity, hoping to guide her erring readers to the path of virtue which she believed was chiefly achievable through self-denial and prayer. Fanny's novel, *Mine Own Familiar Friend* (1871) described a marriage in which a plain wife admires her handsome husband but finds he has married her in the hope of inheriting an estate and having a son and heir, and may have been inspired by her own story.

Fanny was born on 30 May 1820. Her father, George, was the eldest natural son of George O'Brien Wyndham, third Earl of Egremont, a wealthy and energetic peer who had numerous mistresses and sired more than forty illegitimate children. The earldom became extinct in 1845, but George Wyndham inherited substantial estates including the magnificent Petworth House in Sussex. In 1859 he was elevated to the peerage as first Baron Leconfield.

The Montgomerys' first child was a daughter, Edith, born on 9 May 1844. Although the granddaughter of a peer, her birth was unregistered. When

Sybil was born on 28 May 1845 at Hampton Court Palace, she is mentioned in the registers simply as 'female'. The Montgomery finances must have been strained, for in June 1846 when Prime Minister Sir Robert Peel appointed Alfred a Commissioner of Stamps and Taxes at a salary of £1,000, a grateful and relieved Fanny wrote to Peel to thank him, saying that the appointment 'has made us all very happy'.[8] Although Montgomery never achieved great distinction in his profession, 'He was one of the old school of officials, who never failed to brighten and illuminate all the dull details of routine work.'[9]

The lack of fanfare for the birth of two girls suggests that their arrival may have been a disappointment to Alfred, but the birth of a son was an altogether different matter. Wilfred Henry Wellesley Montgomery was born on 7 April 1849. In the same year Alfred was appointed Commissioner of Inland Revenue, a post he held until his retirement in 1882.

Soon after the birth of Wilfred it was apparent that the marriage was in difficulties. At census day 1851 Fanny was living in Somerset while Alfred resided in Mayfair with his mother and sister. The location of the three children remains a mystery. In the early years the couple had attended social functions together, but a joint visit to the theatre in July 1851 seems to have been the couple's last public outing. The reason, according to Bosie, was his grandmother's conversion to Catholicism, as a result of which she was separated from her children. On 23 August 1855 Wilfred Montgomery died at the aged of six, having suffered from congestion of the liver and brain for forty-eight hours.

Dapper, old-fashioned Alfred, unencumbered by his serious wife was a constant and welcome presence at society events. In time, he would take his beautiful daughters to fashionable gatherings in London where they were much admired. In an age where character was thought to be visible in face and form, the ideal male was muscular, vigorous and glowing with health. A mannered, aesthetic man, while not necessarily suspected of homosexuality, was deemed to be weak, effeminate and ineffectual, unsuited to the exclusively male world of commerce or the exercise of authority. To small dark pugnacious Queensberry, manliness both in character and physicality was of supreme importance, but in his relationships with women he was moved by a graceful blonde beauty, which he saw as the essence of the feminine. In time Queensberry came to abhor the waspish wit and dandified manners of Alfred Montgomery, and could not tolerate the Montgomery good looks and artistic refinement in his sons, especially Bosie, whom he sometimes found it difficult to think of as his own. All this lay in the future as he admired the pink and white loveliness of Sybil Montgomery.

Queensberry and Sybil formally announced their engagement in November 1865 and were married on Monday 26 February 1866 at St George, Hanover Square. The best man was Henry Stephenson RN, he of the Portuguese escapade, and the celebrant was the Reverend Grantham Munton Yorke, husband of Sybil's aunt Marian. There were ten bridesmaids, including Gertrude and Florence, and Sybil's sister Edith. Sybil wore white satin trimmed with Brussels lace and the bridesmaids were dressed in white and mauve. The reception was held at the Montgomery home at 8 Chesterfield Street, Mayfair, where the bride's father presided over a wedding breakfast served to a large and distinguished company, including the 2nd Duke and Duchess of Wellington, and the Duchess of Marlborough. The list of guests supplied by the newspapers did not include the bride's mother. 'Modern Babylon feasted and made merry, and talked vapid nothings,'[10] observed Florence who did not like the submissive vows that Sybil had just made, and said so. 'You are as bad as your brother,' exclaimed a shocked duchess. 'He's a terrible fellow for calling a spade a spade.'[11] The Marquess and his bride then departed to spend their wedding night at Braxted Park, Essex the seat of Mr Charles Du Cane, MP.

In her autobiographical novel *The Story of Ijain* Florence was later to comment

> Poor [Queensberry]! He thought he loved because he saw a beautiful face. It had been no part of his religious education to regard the marriage tie as one not to be entered upon without serious consideration. . . . A man should be sure of a woman's love for him before he marries her. A girl should not be urged by her parents, nay, almost forced, to marry a man she does not care about, merely to obtain wealth, or title or position. . . . It is an act hateful to Nature, and bound to bring its revenge. . . . the crime becomes all the greater when children are born of such a marriage; for the sins of the parents are visited upon the luckless offspring, who never asked to be born.[12]

More apparently ill-assorted matches have succeeded as the couple have either complemented each other or managed to compromise, but this was not to be the case with the Queensberry marriage. It was 'disastrous for both of them'.[13] In hindsight it would have been better if Queensberry had married a girl like Florence, a high-spirited, outspoken, active, sporty type, fond of dogs and horses, but at the same time a passionate and introspective seeker of truth. He might have sired a line of rebellious girls and combative sons to instruct in pugilism. There would have been fireworks, but it would have been fun.

The besotted groom afforded every consideration to his enchanting bride. After the honeymoon they travelled to Kinmount, and in deference to Sybil's artistic nature Queensberry chose not to alight at the 'unattractive and desolate'[14] local railway station at Cummertrees, taking her instead to Annan eight miles away.

To a young woman who liked her personal comfort and had been used to overwintering in Italy, the cold and austerity of a Dumfriesshire castle in February must have been a shock and an ordeal. It is unlikely that the great grey pile of Kinmount had sophisticated plumbing, lighting and heating systems, and the large rooms were difficult to keep warm. London, the home of high society, fashion and taste, was very far away. It was not long before the new marchioness began to regret her marriage and all that came with it. Queensberry as Master of the Dumfriesshire Foxhounds was up at dawn, while Sybil was rarely out of bed before midday. As mistress of Kinmount she was expected to direct the work of the servants and organise the entertainment of visitors, but she preferred to spend her time reading, and took no interest in the running of the house. Sybil's grandson observed: 'many a time when my grandfather had invited a number of his friends to lunch, nothing was ordered, which naturally annoyed him intensely'.[15]

In Gertrude's *Nature's Nursling*, 'graceful, golden-haired' Lady Dune is undoubtedly based on Sybil. Lady Dune spoke softly with a 'characteristic coolness' and a 'little light laugh' that could grate on the nerves of an impatient man. 'She was one of those imperturbable beings who never allow themselves to be flurried, or, if they can possibly avoid it, *bored* about any of the vulgar details of existence.'[16] Kind, good tempered and placid, Lady Dune's indolence could sometimes rouse her family to indignation, and since she was careless and forgetful she was a poor housekeeper. She had good qualities, however. 'Though neither very warm nor tender-hearted, she was an eminently charitable woman, and, provided she was not called upon to exert herself to procure it, delighted in the happiness of others.'[17]

There were society events to alleviate the boredom and discomfort of Sybil's new life, and one can imagine the pride with which Queensberry introduced his exquisite bride. In May they were presented to the Queen at a royal levee and in June they were again at a royal 'drawing-room'. Queensberry was still pursuing his love of racing, which Sybil did not share, but he was rarely far from home, and although the new and still adoring husband often stewarded or rode in races he remained largely in Scotland. He continued his interest in competitive foot-racing, and at a contest which took place at Crystal Palace on 8 October John Graham Chambers was one of the stewards and Queensberry was there to present the prizes.

On 3 February 1867 Sybil gave birth to a son and heir, Francis Archibald Douglas, at her father's house in Chesterfield Street, and the event was marked by a revival of the courtesy title Viscount Drumlanrig. Thus far the lives of the Queensberrys had been, if not contented, without serious friction. All that was to end with the arrival of a son. 'Almost immediately after my uncle Drumlanrig was born,' said the eleventh marquess, 'husband and wife began to disagree. They had absolutely nothing in common, and as years went on, things became worse and worse.'[18] The cause of the rapidly widening divide between husband and wife was their conflicting beliefs on the upbringing of children. 'Easy-going and indolent by nature,' commented Gertrude about Sybil's fictional counterpart, Lady Dune, 'she inclined to the opinion that, as much as possible, young people should have their own way. She had no special theories on education, no very strong religious principles, few prejudices, and a vast amount of good nature.'[19] Queensberry was neither a cruel nor an overbearing father, but, like his mother, he believed in educating his children for a useful and independent future.

Fatherhood would not stop Queensberry being a risk-taker and early that year he was riding in a steeplechase when he fell and broke his leg. Helped back into the saddle, he went on to win the race. Once he was able to get about on crutches, his surgeon suggested that he try sea bathing to strengthen the limb and recommended Ventnor on the Isle of Wight. That May, Queensberry visited Ventnor with Sybil, Florence and James. Florence, who loved a drama, wrote in *The Story of Ijain* how Queensberry went swimming in a choppy sea and had to be rescued by a boatman when, according to her account, the weather turned rapidly from a lovely summer's day to a shrieking storm with heavy snow.

The youthful Queensberry's stamina and courage on horseback became legendary. 'After hunting all day with Lord Wemyss' hounds, he started off across the Cheviots for Kinmount on the Solway, *a distance of one hundred and two miles* riding most of the way on the sorriest of posters [hired horse], and finally, having arrived home at 2 a.m., hunted his hounds the same day.'[20] For the first thirty-five miles he rode the horses he had hunted, then hired hacks from the tenants of the Duke of Buccleuch and rode on to Kinmount, 'where they had to cut off his boots and breeches'.[21] Bosie later speculated as to whether his father's erratic moods could have been 'due to one or other of the terrible falls he got steeplechasing and hunting. At different times he broke all his limbs, and his collar-bone two or three times, and more than once my mother told me he was brought home on a hurdle unconscious from concussion.'[22]

On 15 July 1867 a fateful family connection was forged when Fanny Montgomery's brother Henry married Constance Evelyn Primrose, sister of Archibald Primrose, the future fifth Earl of Rosebery. Meanwhile events were afoot that would raise the public profile of the Queensberrys, irritate John Sholto and cause Sybil some embarrassment. These were the first rumblings of what would later become, in press accounts, the notorious eccentricities of the Douglas family, but the origins lay not with any Douglas by descent, but with the outspoken Dowager Marchioness Caroline. Caroline openly supported the Fenians, an organisation which demanded the establishment of an independent Irish Republic, and opposed Home Rule, which would have kept Ireland within the Union with Great Britain. On 18 September two Fenians were included in a group of prisoners being transported to Manchester city gaol in a van. A gang of armed men made a sudden rush on the van, and in the conflict all the prisoners escaped and the court officer Charles Brett was shot dead. When three men were tried and sentenced to hang for the murder of Brett, Caroline's fiery spirit was thoroughly roused. Writing from Ventnor, she sent a cheque for £100 for support of the prisoners' families, with a letter of comfort saying 'we have daily mass for you here'.[23]

Press and public reaction to Caroline's intervention was sharply divided. Some praised her Christian and humane act, stating that for the marchioness 'to provide for the widow and fatherless foundlings of an executed man is an act of sublime generosity that will carry her name down to posterity',[24] but 'A Lancashire Man' called her 'a silly old lady'[25] and the *Preston Guardian* drily suggested that if she had so much money to spare 'we would recommend, as suitable objects of her bounty, the widow and children of police-sergeant Brett'.[26]

The execution of the men on 23 November only gave strength to Caroline's new-found voice. Over the next few years she would become even more outspoken, inundating the press with long, exhortatory letters, assisting prisoners' families and joining the campaign for an amnesty for Fenian prisoners. She regularly denounced Home Rule, and sent cheques to support the campaigns of political candidates. In 1870 she wrote to the *Limerick Chronicle* ordering the editor to 'lose no time' in advocating the co-operation of Protestants and Roman Catholics to seek a repeal of the 1800 Act of Union between Great Britain and Ireland.[27] To Fenian supporters she became a heroine.

She had, said *The Examiner*, 'made herself conspicuous';[28] so much so that someone spread the rumour that she had married an Italian courier. Some of her most powerful, stirring and certainly longest letters were sent to *The Irishman* and were addressed 'To Irishmen', urging true-hearted patriots to unite and free Ireland from the slavery of foreign rule. Oft-repeated words like 'truth', 'glorious', 'noble hearts' and 'invincible' drove the message home. She made it clear, however, that her role was purely passive: 'if voices from sympathetic hearts will inspire the noble men engaged in their country's battle to fresh vigour, certainly mine cannot remain silent, for surely it *is* the woman's mission to cheer on and encourage the men in all their great works of patriotism and charity'.[29]

While his mother was becoming politically notorious, Queensberry was establishing himself as a prominent supporter of all things sporting – chiefly racing, but also athletics, boxing and cricket. He was not active in coursing, but permitted it on his land. He also, as was commonly expected of the nobility, became a figurehead of companies, such as the Scottish Union Insurance Company of which he was deputy governor, and was for a short period Lieutenant Colonel of the Dumfriesshire Rifles.

In April 1868 he suffered another of his numerous injuries. The hunting season in Dumfriesshire was usually wound up with steeplechases in which he took part. On this occasion his horse fell taking a fence, and he fractured his right leg. Typically, the 'bold and fearless rider'[30] scrambled back up into the saddle and went on with the race, coming in second. He had to call for a pony carriage to take him to Kinmount. Fortunately only small bones were broken and he made a speedy recovery. A year later he was fit enough to undertake a gruelling race on foot over the Bogside Steeplechase course, the private racecourse of the Earl of Eglinton. It was exactly the kind of challenge Queensberry liked, bold, audacious and something that few men would even contemplate, let alone attempt. He was matched against Fred Cotton, author and composer of the hunting song 'The Meynell Hunt' and once described as 'the most perfect specimen of an athlete',[31] although neither man had undertaken any training 'beyond a round of balls in the neighbourhood'.[32] The course was about four miles, and there were 'several stiffish obstacles'[33] including a brook with twelve feet of water and a fence on the take-off. A number of heavy bets depended on the result. Both men got round the course, and the contest was so tight in the final yards that Lord Eglinton and his brother held the ends of a driving whip as a finishing tape. Cotton put on a spurt and won by six yards in 24 minutes 15 seconds, and promptly collapsed a few paces further on. Queensberry collapsed with exhaustion just short of the tape. He took the defeat in good part, but characteristically felt he had won in at least one respect: 'Never mind, I came to before old Fred!'[34] Fred Cotton and Queensberry also hunted together when, one suspects, there was some friendly rivalry. On one occasion with the Croome hounds only Queensberry and Cotton succeeded in following the hounds across the Severn. The water made Queensberry's breeches so slippery that he later said he had fallen off at every fence until he killed his fox, adding with typical bravado, 'The swim cured me of a bad cold.'[35]

'Lord Queensberry might always be relied upon to do original things,' commented a friend, Amy Menzies. Having dined with Lord Coventry and driving home in his phaeton, Queensberry decided to save his horses three or four miles by taking a short cut via a ferry. The hour was late, the ferry was on the other side of the river and the ferryman nowhere to be seen. Queensberry was not to be deterred. He undressed, swam the river, walked half a mile up the street to the ferryman's house, found him in bed and woke him up. It then 'became necessary to convince the man . . . that [Queensberry] . . . was not a raving lunatic'.[36] He eventually succeeded and they returned to the boat and made the crossing. The 'dumbfounded ferryman' watched Queensberry dress himself again and drive off. Suitable remuneration was surely involved. 'At all times Lord Queensberry was liberal and generous,' said Mrs Menzies. 'He was an amiable man and loved a fair fight.'[37]

In August 1868 Fanny Montgomery wrote to Conservative Prime Minister Benjamin Disraeli on behalf of her son-in-law, though whether at Queensberry's instigation or even with his knowledge is unknown. Alleging that Archibald had been promised the title Baron Solway she asked Disraeli if he could use his influence to 'obtain for the son the realisation of the promise made to the Father' as the honour would give her son-in-law an 'occupation and interest and a path open to public usefulness'. As an unsubtle inducement she suggested that if granted the peerage Queensberry would remain '"a good man and true" and would not in his youth and inexperience be cajoled by the other party'. In particular, 'his father-in-law is always working to draw him from the Conservative allegiance'.[38] Fanny's letter was ostensibly motivated by an urge to assist her daughter by advancing her son-in-law, but she may have relished exposing her estranged husband's Liberal leanings. The chance of a peerage by that route, if there ever had been one, vanished when the Conservatives lost the general election in December.

On 13 October that year Sybil gave birth to her second son, Percy Sholto at Kinmount, and the relationship between husband and wife deteriorated further. Sybil became 'not only indifferent to her husband – she was beginning to dislike him actively, and this dislike turned to hatred as the years went on. . . . On every possible occasion she opposed him in his attitude toward the children, and in consequence he absented himself more and more from the family.'[39] The eleventh Marquess later said: 'Had my grandmother been kinder, more considerate, she could have done anything she liked with him. But instead she mocked him for his lack of culture and his passion for the sports she detested, and incited her children to despise him and set at naught his authority.'[40] Sybil, while a loving mother, had favourites amongst her children. Initially her entire affection was centred on her firstborn, Francis, and was to remain so for the first twelve years of his life. Percy was an especial concern since he contracted polio and was obliged to wear leg irons but he eventually made a full recovery.[41]

These desperate fissures in the Queensberry marriage were not apparent outside the family, and publicly Queensberry was a popular figure. In November 1868 *Bailey's Monthly Magazine of Sports and Pastimes* devoted a feature article to the youthful and energetic 'Marquis', extolling him as 'a young nobleman who gives every promise of filling up the niche in the gallery of Northern Sportsmen'. The Douglases were not yet regarded as a line of eccentrics. 'There are few families in the Peerage of Great Britain that can boast a more distinguished ancestry than the subject of our Memoir. . . . The present Marquis of Queensberry comes of a truly sporting family,' the article noted, his father being 'an active encourager of all manly sports'. He 'speedily showed he was the son of his father . . . for he gave his active patronage to all those games which serve to develop manliness of character, self-reliance under difficulties and vigour of constitution among his tenantry, . . . it is impossible not to observe how truly he inherits the tastes of his ancestor, the late Duke of Queensberry, for sport of every description, while his disposition is free from those blemishes which unfortunately disfigured the career of his great ancestor.'[42]

Caroline had turned her attention to the future of her two youngest sons, eighteen-year-old Archibald Jnr, and James, thirteen. She rented a property at Drayton Hall, Norfolk with the idea of giving the boys 'an insight into the mysteries of farming, cattle and sheep rearing, and agriculture generally'.[43] Neither of them took to it, Archibald having already decided that he wanted to be a priest, and James being opposed 'to the study of the haunches and hams of the fat and the lean kine of Norfolk'.[44] Archibald was sent to St Mary's College, Oscott, to study for the priesthood while Florence and James, their mother hoping to progress their education by appointing a tutor and a governess, spent as much time as they could 'playing pranks and committing juvenile escapades'.[45] Gertrude meanwhile had completed her novitiate and in 1867 became a Sister of the Black Veil. However, after five years of convent life she asked to be released from her vows for reasons she described as 'personal, grave and important' but which had nothing to do with either the convent or the nuns, for whom she still felt a warm attachment.[46] She went to live in Boulogne.

In 1870 Queensberry relocated his family to Ham Hill House, a two-storey, eight-bedroom hunting lodge in Ham Lane, Powick, Worcestershire. It was a pleasant spot three miles from Worcester and overlooking the Teme valley. There were ornamental and kitchen gardens, a few acres of orchard land, and stabling for seven horses. The move may have been at the wishes of Sybil, who was disenchanted with both the amenities and the social and cultural life of Kinmount.

Ham Hill was a fresh start, enabling the couple to put on the brave front of a contented marriage. In April Queensberry became Master of the

Worcestershire Hunt. He was made an honorary member of the Gentleman's Club, judged horses at an agricultural show, was toasted enthusiastically at the annual hunt dinner, sang at a charitable concert, rode in steeplechases and played cricket. Sybil became the patroness of charitable bazaars, distributed prizes at flower shows, and attended fashionable costume balls where a glittering assembly danced the Marchioness of Queensberry's quadrille. Together, the Queensberrys attended services at Worcester Cathedral, and supported local theatres. In August they accompanied the visiting Prince and Princess Christian of Schleswig-Holstein on a visit to the Lord Lieutenant of Worcestershire at Hagley Hall.

Queensberry had always intended to hunt the county from season to season, and efforts were made to persuade him to stay on for a second year, a request he briefly considered, but in April 1871 his horses were put up for auction with the comment that he was 'giving up the country'.[47] In June, Ham Hill was sold. Mrs Menzies, who was presumably told this by Sybil, commented that there were some difficulties about his position as master of the hunt, and he 'was not altogether popular',[48] although press reports of the warm appreciation he received at hunt committee meetings and public appearances in the county suggest the reverse.

Queensberry still maintained an interest in naval affairs. In 1870 the unstable and top-heavy vessel *Captain* capsized, with the loss of 472 lives. When this provoked a letter from Admiral Rous blaming the tragedy on 'ignorance of the first rudiments of seamanship', Queensberry responded with a letter to the *Hampshire Telegraph* criticising the design of the ship in terms that showed he had not forgotten his training.[49]

Queensberry's third son was born at Ham Hill on 22 October 1870 and was named Alfred after his grandfather, and Bruce after his godfather Lord Robert Bruce who had been in the navy with Queensberry. The golden-haired child was eventually to supplant Francis as his mother's favourite. She called him 'Boysie', an affectionate variant on 'boy', which soon became 'Bosie', a name which stuck with him for the rest of his life and was used by all his family and friends except for Alfred Montgomery.

With all her affections focused on her children, Sybil's lack of interest in her husband became more apparent, and she actively encouraged him to stay away. When he was at home, the children could see that their mother was unhappy and that there was conflict between their parents. This was hard for everyone concerned and Queensberry, made miserable by the situation, spent more and more time apart from his family. Inevitably, since the children saw their gracious, gentle and indulgent mother far more than their gruff father, they supported her in any dispute. Despite Bosie's later assertions that he had once hero-worshipped his father, this was only for his sporting prowess. The eleventh Marquess believed that none of Queensberry's children actually liked him. The stresses of the crumbling marriage began to tell, exposing in public for the first time the high-handedness and hair-trigger temper for which Queensberry later became notorious. In June 1871 he was sued by Mr Whiting, an innkeeper for putting his carriage on a pitch at a racecourse that Whiting had already hired for a refreshment tent. According to Whiting, Queensberry refused to move his carriage until the races were over. Whiting was awarded £2 for loss of profit.

The Dowager Marchioness Caroline remained vigorous in her efforts to stir up opposition to the Home Rule movement. Thus far Queensberry, a supporter of Home Rule, had made no public comment on his mother's beliefs, but an incident in 1871 made his position plain. In Dublin on the night of 11 July Head Constable Talbot was accosted in the street and shot, the ball lodging in the back of his neck. The assailant, Robert Kelly, was captured after shooting Constable Mullen in the thigh. Talbot died from his wounds five days later. When Kelly was tried for murder Caroline wrote a letter of comfort to his wife, addressing her as 'My poor dear friend' and closing with 'Tell your husband I think of him and pray for him.'[50] To the surprise of most observers, Kelly was acquitted.

On 21 November a representative of Queensberry sent a letter to the *Dublin Mail*, which demonstrated his firm rejection of his mother's principles and also shows that Sybil might have been experiencing some embarrassment.

Sir – I have been directed by the Marquis of Queensberry to remit to you a cheque for £50 (which I accordingly do), for the next of kin of the late Head-constable Talbot, as a mark of his lordship's sympathy for the family of a man who was assassinated in a most cruel and cowardly manner, simply because he discharged his duty faithfully; and who, by his fearless conduct, contributed to no small degree to save this county from the horrors of rebellion and civil war. Lord Queensberry has also requested me to state that the letters which have appeared in some newspapers in reference to the recent trial of Kelly are the productions of the Dowager Marchioness of Queensberry, and not of the Marchioness of Queensberry.[51]

What effect this may have had on the relationship between the dowager and her son and daughter-in-law is unknown. Caroline, despite her devotion to the land of her birth, never visited that country after leaving at the age of two; nevertheless, over the years she continued to write passionate letters to the newspapers demanding justice for Ireland. Queensberry, by contrast, was a regular visitor to Dublin where he and his family stayed at the Bilton Hotel and he rode in the Punchestown Races. In February 1872 when Kelly was tried for the shooting of Constable Mullen and sentenced to fifteen years, Caroline wrote to Kelly's wife with her condolences, offering to pay for the education and maintenance of one of her children and enclosing money for the support of the others.

Queensberry's personal standing was unaffected by his mother's actions, and his fellow Scottish peers were happy to have the promising young nobleman as one of their number. When a Scottish representative peer died in January 1872 it was soon determined to propose Queensberry for the vacant place. The *Bristol Mercury* denounced the whole process as a 'hollow sham', declaring that the Duke of Buccleuch was 'the only peer-maker north of the Tweed, and his nominees are, as a matter of course, ultra-Tories like their master'.[52] If the noble peers of Scotland were expecting twenty-seven-year-old Queensberry to toe the line they were in for a shock. 'I should think that if I was to speak out my opinions I should be set down by the world as the most dangerous out and out radical' he wrote in 1879, although he admitted that 'I am a Conservative in so far as I wish to retain my things'.[53]

At Holyrood House Edinburgh on 7 March the Marquess of Queensberry was unanimously elected a representative peer for Scotland, entitled to sit in the House of Lords. Only two days previously he had been thrown from his horse at the Windsor Military Steeplechase, and was not thought to be badly hurt. He returned to London to see his medical attendant Mr Alfred Cooper, who found that Queensberry had fractured two ribs. All hopes of riding in the Grand National had to be abandoned for that year, although he was soon back in the saddle for flat racing, and had an active season at cricket.

A fourth son, Sholto George was born on 28 July 1872 at 8 Chesterfield Street. There were no obvious external signs of the slow breakdown of the Queensberry marriage, and the couple still attended social events together. Sybil accepted the situation with calm regret, but Queensberry was undoubtedly under stress. On the morning of 4 December he entered the Charing Cross Hotel to ask after a friend. The friend could not be located, and to his growing irritation he found himself being referred from one porter to another. After a fruitless search, the delay causing him to miss a train, his temper boiled over and he called the porters 'a lot of humbugs' among other choice words.[54] Tom Toby, the hotel's detective, believing that Queensberry was about to strike one of the porters, decided to intervene. The evidence as later given at the Bow Street Police Court, where Queensberry was charged with assault, was confused and contradictory. Queensberry claimed that Toby came up and put a hand on his shoulder and told him to go, and that this had caused him to strike the detective. Toby, who admitted that he had not asked what the matter was, said he had not laid a hand on Queensberry first but had asked him to leave and been struck on the mouth with a stick. A constable was called, and there was a certain amount of struggling and kicking before the angry nobleman was apprehended. A porter claimed that he had been assaulted, but showed no sign of injury; however, Toby's lip was swollen. Queensberry was fined 20 shillings.

The incident seems not to have injured Queensberry's reputation, although the radical *Reynolds's Newspaper* – complaining that the magistrate had 'allowed him to occupy another place than that allotted to plebeian rowdies and roysterers' – described the penalty as 'trumpery'.[55] For the next few years Queensberry remained, in the public eye at least, a popular sporting nobleman.

CHAPTER 6

The Game and Sporting Lord

THE sport with which Queensberry is now most closely associated is boxing, but while his actual contribution to the revival of a sport that had by the 1860s virtually been declared dead was not, at the time, regarded as ground-breaking, what he did was to set in motion a series of events that were to have far-reaching consequences.

The legislation that had doomed the prize ring was the Metropolitan Police Act of 1839 which made it lawful for any constable to take into custody, without a warrant, anyone he found disturbing the public peace, or whom he suspected of having committed or being about to commit a breach of the peace. The prize ring attracted big money for purses, ticket sales and gambling, and inevitably it also attracted rogues, rowdies and thieves. As the reputation of the sport dwindled, respectable backers abandoned it. 'The Ring was doomed,' said the editor of *Pugilistica*,

> not less by the misconduct of its professors than by the discord and dishonest doings of its so-called patrons and their ruffianly followers, unchecked by the saving salt of sparring gentlemen and men of honour, courage and standing in society. Down, deeper down, and ever downward it went, till in its last days it became merely a ticket selling swindle in the hands of keepers of Haymarket night-houses and slowly perished in infamy and indigence.[1]

By 1866 the days when the 'noble art' of professional boxing was openly patronised by royalty and the aristocracy were over. Competitors in any proposed fight were arrested and fined, as were their backers, the spectators, and the officials of any railway company transporting supporters to see a fight. Many professional pugilists went to America, where the sport was also being driven underground, while others fought in fairground boxing booths, or became publicans, staging illegal fights in back rooms. Professional boxing was then governed by the London Prize Ring Rules of 1853. There was no limit on the number of rounds or their length. A round ended when a man was down, and the fighters then had thirty seconds' rest and eight seconds to come back unaided to the mark in the centre of the ring known as the 'scratch'. A man who failed to 'come to scratch' was declared the loser. The wearing of shoes with spikes no more than three-eighths of an inch long and no less than one-eighth broad at the point was permitted.

Those who still supported the prize ring from a genuine love of the sport were anxious to bring it into better repute. In January 1867 revised rules were published by the committee of the Pugilistic Benevolent Association, which limited the number of spikes to three per boot, but did nothing to curb the duration of contests, which were still deemed to end when one of the men could no longer continue. The new rules made no difference to police action. The *Sporting Life*, reporting that the police had prevented a planned championship fight in October 1867, predicted that pugilists would soon 'find their occupation gone'[2] and in the following month when yet another fight was called off it commented, 'The fortunes of the Prize Ring have of late fallen so low that any announcement of another failure will not cause much surprise. ... How much longer will backers continue to find money for similar farces?'[3] In January 1868 it declared that 'The police's blood is fairly up at last and the prize ring is dead as a doornail,'[4] and, by the end of the year, that the prize ring had 'perished out of the land'.[5]

There was, however, a very clear distinction in the eyes of press, public and police between the disgraced and illegal prize ring, and amateur contests which were considered to be a branch of athletics, and a manly sport suitable for gentlemen. This enabled some former pugilists to open gymnasiums and give private lessons in sparring. Many young men on leaving university wanted to continue the sports they had enjoyed there, and this demand led to the creation of amateur sporting clubs. Queensberry's Cambridge friend John Graham Chambers formed the Amateur Athletic Club, which first met in March 1866. Competitions took place in the grounds of Beaufort House Walham Green, and featured track and field athletics.

On 16 July 1867 the second meeting of the club introduced a 'new feature ... in the shape of boxing'.[6] The competition was open only to gentlemen amateurs, i.e. 'Any gentleman who has never competed in any open competition, or for public money, or for admission money, or with professionals for a prize, public money or admission money; and who has never taught, pursued or assisted in the pursuit of athletic exercises as a means of livelihood; nor is a mechanic, artisan or labourer.'[7] Entry cost 10 shillings. Chambers, 'though not very handy with the gloves himself ... thoroughly understood boxing'.[8] Nevertheless Queensberry was the enthusiast and it seems probable that the introduction of the competition was his idea.

Queensberry donated three challenge cups valued at £25 and was there to present them as well as the club medals for contests at light (under 9st 4lb) middle (under 11st 4lb) and heavyweight. Attendance was poor, but because of 'the fine character of the boxing and the fine racing for the 440 yards handicap'[9] it was felt that the meetings would be better attended in future. Boxing for the Queensberry Cups was thereafter an annual event, with steadily increasing attendance, and in the early years the marquess was on hand to judge winners and present prizes. The rules employed in 1867 were not mentioned in the sporting press, but they may not yet have been fully developed. Spikes were still permitted and in that first contest one of the boxers accidentally spiked his opponent. At the end of the year *Land and Water* commented: 'boxing is well recognised at the Universities and elsewhere .... in short, its importance as a healthy English recreation has been appreciated in London by the institution of valuable challenge cups for gentlemen under the management of the Amateur Athletic Club'.[10]

As eventually formulated, the rules that governed the competition for the Queensberry Cups made a number of important stipulations. The contest was to last for just three rounds, each of three minutes' duration (in later versions the final round lasted four minutes) with a minute's rest between rounds. A man who was down had ten seconds to get up and if he failed to do so the contest was awarded to his opponent. Gloves were to be worn but spiked boots were forbidden. There was no provision for the award of points. Queensberry never made any secret of the fact that it was Chambers who drew up the main body of the rules, which he then approved with some small amendments concerning weights. In 1885 Queensberry told the press, 'The rules were named after me because some twenty years ago I put up some cups to be boxed for, and that was the first time that boxing was conducted by those rules'.[11] The 'organisation, after framing them, named them after [me] in compliment'.[12] It was of course no mean publicity for the club to attach the name of a well-known sporting nobleman to an event. Despite many subsequent claims to the contrary, the Queensberry Rules were not universally adopted at once for professional boxing, which remained in the doldrums for some years, with fights having to be arranged in secret, being interrupted by the police and often failing to take place at all.

For amateur boxers things were far more promising. In November 1871 the *Birmingham Daily Post* stated:

Since the Marquis of Queensberry presented three silver challenge cups to the amateur athletic club for annual boxing competition, this branch of athletics has made rapid strides in public favour amongst university, rowing, cricket, football, and athletic men. On Monday night, the London Gymnasium was the scene of a boxing carnival, in which gentlemen of nearly all the walks of life took part, and a finer display of muscular development has seldom been seen, and the greatest good humour was observed in all the bouts.[13]

Two years later the *Daily Graphic* was drawing a firm distinction between 'glove fights . . . at which even ladies do not disdain to appear, where amateurs contend for a limited time before judges, who award the prize for dexterity rather than for savage violence' and 'glove fights of another sort, where the only limit of time is the utter exhaustion of one of the combatants'.[14]

While Queensberry's name helped to popularise the Rules, the converse was also true, and the marquess became inextricably associated with the emerging acceptability of the sport of boxing. In 1873 when the Shah of Persia made a state visit to London, and demanded to see a boxing match, Queensberry was the man asked by Lord Knollys, the Prince of Wales's private secretary to organise the entertainment. It was intended to be a discreet event, in a quiet spot near the royal stables, but some bishops who happened to be assembled nearby became alarmed, and made a protest. Lord Sydney the Lord Chamberlain wrote to Queensberry asking him how he dared turn Buckingham Palace into a boxing saloon. Queensberry's reply was to enclose the letter he had received from Knollys, asking, 'Might I ask my lord to what department of Her Majesty's Government I am to apply to be refunded the £25 which I paid the pugilists?'[15] He did not receive a reply.

The Queensberry competition was sufficiently well known that when a prizefight was held at Grafton Hall, Soho on 21 April 1873 it was reported incorrectly that the contest was for the 'Marquis' of Queensberry's prize. The fight between two professional pugilists lasted an hour and a half, until the supporters of one of the contestants, seeing their stake money disappearing, invaded the ring and the fight ended amid scenes of uproar. Queensberry, who was staying at the Turf Club, wrote angrily to the *Telegraph*:

> It appears to me that I am to be made the scapegoat of the so-called prize-fight in London. Allow me to make the following statement:– I have given no cup or prize whatever; with the exception of the challenge cups to the Amateur Athletic Club. I was neither present at nor did I know anything at all about the sparring match on Tuesday [*sic*] night at the Grafton Hall. Had I known of it, it is quite probable that I should have been present, as, thank-God, I have no objection to see a good fight with gloves, or without them for the matter of that. I have nothing to say for the blackguardism which appears to have predominated on Tuesday night. Unfortunately, this has always been one of the evils that has attended the encouragement of the still 'noble art of self-defence.' It appears to me to be doomed by public opinion; let it be so. Yet England may regret some day that her sons should substitute for the use of their fists the first deadly weapon that comes to their hands.[16]

After 1873, however, Queensberry's personal and emotional problems meant that he spent an increasing amount of time abroad. He continued to attend and referee boxing matches, remaining a popular figurehead for the manly sport and a draw for crowds, but it was left to others to continue his initiative. In 1880 two former Queensberry Cup champions, R. Frost-Smith and John H. Douglas formed the Amateur Boxing Association. Chambers was present at the first meeting but, unhappy with the proposals, took no further part in the organisation although he continued to support the Queensberry championships. The possibility of approaching Queensberry to become the first president of the ABA was discussed, but this was not followed up.

Queensberry, always the all-rounder, continued to enjoy the occasional game of cricket, at which he was an indifferent batsman and a moderately successful bowler. On 27 June 1870 he was out for a duck playing for Worcestershire against a North of England eleven. The top scorer for the Worcestershire side was W. G. Grace. Queensberry's connection with boxing also tended to overshadow his reputation as a horseman. Although he never kept a stud he both owned and raced horses, and rode many winners during his career as a gentleman jockey, having registered the crimson and black cap as his colours. He was, like his father, a bold rider across country, and hunted to hounds for five seasons, never missing a day despite frequent injuries, which he regarded as a temporary inconvenience. Once, he strained a muscle in his thigh so badly that it was impossible for him to ride astride, but 'nothing daunted, he rode in a side-saddle!'[17] Given his fearless – even reckless – feats in the saddle, it is surprising he was not injured more often although there were some narrow escapes. On one occasion he was leading a field of thirty-six at Punchestown races, when he fell. As the rest of the field thundered towards him he wisely resisted the temptation to rise and remount, and relied on the fact that horses do not like treading on people. 'He lay flat, while the other horses passed over, or close to him.'[18]

Queensberry's greatest ambition was to win the Grand National and it was rumoured that he had taken a £25 bet at a hundred to one that he would one day ride the winner. This great classic steeplechase, first run in 1836, matched the new breeds of vigorous hunters over a course with thirty challenging fences and would have appealed to Queensberry as racing's ultimate test of strength and courage. He rode True Blue in the Grand National in 1873 but was last going over the water jump and withdrew from the race. Despite this failure he opposed all campaigns to do away with jumps in steeplechases. 'Lord Queensberry proved conclusively some years ago that the agitation against the open ditch was a most unreasonable one, instancing the number of times it was negotiated in the Grand National without any casualty.'[19]

One of the few critics of his horsemanship was Amy Menzies, who said 'he was not a first-rate man on a horse, and, as far as racing was concerned, never did anything wonderful . . . his ambition as a rider was greater than his ability'.[20] She did not, however, meet him until 1876, when the best of his racing days were over. There are numerous records of Queensberry's wins and places at race meetings, although he never owned a great champion horse or won the great prizes. A favourite mount was Morris Dancer, which he bought for £700, but the horse was over-handicapped and did badly. At one race meeting he was so irritated that he offered the horse for sale at the end of the last race to anyone who made him an offer. No one took him seriously except for an Edinburgh butcher who offered £5, which Queensberry accepted. Not long afterwards he found to his surprise not only that the horse had been entered for two races but at a handicap two stone lighter than before. Feeling sure the horse would now have a good chance of winning, he offered to ride in both races and the new owner agreed. Queensberry backed the horse, rode and won. He offered to buy the horse back and did so, reputedly for either £100 or £200. Unfortunately the horse was over-weighted thereafter and never won another race.

Queensberry was often asked to steward races, when the organisational skills he had learned as a midshipman must have been called into play. His experience of racing, knowledge of the rules, decisiveness, air of authority, powers of observation, and impartiality were invaluable in his frequent appearances in this role. Despite the scandals that were to dog his later years, he was, throughout his life, a highly regarded and trusted judge in more than one sport.

He was not sentimental about animals; nevertheless, he liked and respected them, especially horses, and treated them well, 'but they had to do some work'.[21] He could not tolerate wanton cruelty. In June 1873 he was riding in Lowndes Street when he saw a wash-cart driver leading a horse so weak it was hardly able to walk. Queensberry at once offered to buy the horse for two sovereigns so it could be humanely destroyed. The owner, James Lister, refused, as he felt he could still get some work out of the animal. Queensberry called a constable, and Lister was taken to Westminster Police Court where he was fined 10 shillings with the alternative of seven days in gaol for deliberate cruelty. Queensberry then bought the beast and had it taken to be put down. 'The young Marquis of Queensberry is a true descendant of old Q', enthused the *Era*, in the days when the press considered that to be a good thing. 'The youthful nobleman's veins are full of the true blood of an old racing family. He is passionately fond of horses, not only because they are useful and beautiful and are a means of gambling, but because they are companions and man's best friend.'[22] The *Illustrated London News* also praised Queensberry as 'a kind-hearted nobleman'.[23]

Whatever he attempted was marked by a single-minded determination and disregard for danger that his friends could only admire. 'Perhaps the pluckiest man I ever met,' said Amy Menzies. 'A wonderful sportsman, nothing came amiss to him, he did not know the meaning of the word fear and would tackle people stones heavier than himself.'[24]

Another great admirer of the marquess's pluck was Sir Claude Champion de Crespigny, a baronet who after a military career had devoted himself almost entirely to sport, including the steeplechase and ballooning. Like Queensberry he relished a physical challenge, and was quick to settle conflicts with his fists. Queensberry, he said, 'was the bravest man of my acquaintance; he laughed at odds'.[25] The men became lifelong friends and shared a great many activities. They had 'a good deal in common, being both aristocratic Bohemians, with a taste for doing outrageous things and shocking the [British public]'.[26] Crespigny, much as he admired the sporting lord, was not blind to his flaws. Queensberry, he said, never aspired to be a 'perfect man' and 'it is a weak trait in an otherwise noble character to write his mind a little too plainly when face to face with some foul injustice. He would scorn to do a petty meanness, and likes to come to the point without any beating about the bush. . . . More than once, at the risk of giving offence, I have got him, to use his own expression, "to throw it off his chest" with the plain Saxon a bit toned down.'[27] The one thing they did not have in common was that Crespigny enjoyed a long and happy marriage.

There were many occasions when Queensberry's skill with his fists was seen outside the roped ring, and he either got into fights or threatened them. He was not, however, a bully. Had he been the kind of man who used violence on those smaller than himself this would undoubtedly have been remarked upon in less happy times, but all the evidence points the other way. Queensberry's constant *need* to prove himself could be gratified only by matching himself against men who would test him. One looks in vain for evidence that he ever struck an animal, child, woman, or a smaller man, apart from one occasion when, he confessed, he had administered a fatherly spanking to Percy. The diminutive Queensberry's success in fights was due in part to his fitness: 'he was always in hard training'.[28] There was no ill will after these contests; on the contrary, 'it was noticeable the way those he conquered became great friends and admirers'.[29] Admiral Grenfell, who had been 'the strongest man and hardest hitter in the navy of his days' and was two stones heavier than Queensberry, had boxed with the smaller man. 'Could you beat him?' he was asked. 'Beat him! I should have to kill him first,' he exclaimed.[30]

Amy Menzies recounted how Queensberry was 'utterly infatuated with a beautiful actress who was married to a huge bully'.[31] The husband, angered by Queensberry's 'attentions and admiration . . . hired a professional pugilist to hammer him'. The pugilist accosted Queensberry in a cul-de-sac, saying '"My Lord, I've got to give you a hiding." "Right," said Lord Queensberry'. The contest, a victory for Queensberry, was over in less than three rounds. Afterwards, whenever the pugilist encountered Queensberry in Piccadilly he would make an 'exaggerated salute saying "Good-day, my Lord!"'[32]

Queensberry was not a man who could be slandered with impunity. Once, after finishing second in a steeplechase, he was carrying his saddle to the weigh-in when a large bookmaker standing in the ring called out 'Well pulled, My Lord.' This was an insult not to be tolerated. 'Down went the saddle and bang went the fists between the bookie's eyes. He was removed by the police, yet Lord Queensberry had made a friend for life.' The man 'was about the best pugilist in England, and in training to fight the following week. His admiration for a man of Lord Queensberry's weight and inches tackling him knew no bounds.'[33] At the following day's races Queensberry took a bad fall, and his new friend 'left his stand and ran across to where Lord Queensberry was lying, picked him up, put him into a fly and packed him off to town'. The next day the bookmaker sent 'a present of some famous bone oil, in hopes of accelerating the recovery of the game and sporting lord'.[34]

In the autumn of 1873 Sybil was pregnant with her fifth child when the couple made a brief tour of Scotland. At the general election in the following February the sixteen sitting Scottish peers came up for re-election and Queensberry was again returned to the Lords. It was still common for landowners to expect their tenants to vote as they did, but Queensberry had firm ideas about this. 'I wrote a letter to all my tenants in which I said that I wished them to vote independent of me as their conscience directed them to vote. I think they all perfectly understood me so that they will certainly not be influenced by me either one way or another.'[35]

Benjamin Disraeli, after more than five years in opposition, was back in power. Although Queensberry was a Liberal, he felt a greater personal affinity with Disraeli than Gladstone. He had once sat next to Disraeli at a public dinner and there had been little conversation until halfway through the meal, when he had startled Disraeli by asking him whether it might ever be possible to 'consider breeding our own race'. Disraeli had replied that he thought so and an interesting discussion ensued which later led Queensberry to assert that Disraeli was at heart 'a true Freethinker', while Disraeli for the rest of the meal called Queensberry his 'young philosopher'.[36] It was probably shortly after Disraeli's return to power that Queensberry approached him and asked if he might be employed in some official capacity in the colonies. When Disraeli asked 'in what way did [he] think [he] could get employed',[37] the young marquess could only make a vague reply. 'I would have gone to any part of the world and even taken a subordinate position supposing that it would eventually lead to my obtaining the Governorship of some minor Colony,'[38] he wrote later. Queensberry's suggestion came less from the desire to live abroad than from the feeling that if he and his family could settle in a warm climate it might enable them to live together harmoniously. The approach came to nothing.

In March he and Sybil arrived at Chesterfield Street for the season, and on the 31st a daughter, Edith Gertrude, was born. Sybil was not yet twenty-nine, yet this was her last child. The physical side of the marriage was over. By the time Edith was born Queensberry had been giving a great deal of thought not only to his own situation but also to the legal and moral constraints on marriage in general. It was most probably just after the birth of Edith that Queensberry made an extended trip to the United States. This long absence abroad without Sybil is another strong indication that the marriage had by then broken down. Later descriptions of the trip give conflicting accounts of when it happened, why he went, and who accompanied him.

The eleventh Marquess suggested that Queensberry went to the United States shortly after his twenty-first birthday on a fact-finding journey to look into ways of promoting the prize ring, and that he took as his companion a boxer called Arthur Chambers. Both of these claims seem unlikely. Would Queensberry have gone on an extended holiday abroad so soon after his brother's death, when he had inherited his estates and was courting Sybil? Arthur Chambers is a most improbable companion. An iron-moulder by trade, the young bruiser's career began in October 1864 when he was nearly eighteen and he became noted as an unscientific slugger who engaged in long, brutal bouts. He has almost certainly been confused with John Graham

Chambers. Arthur Chambers and his wife emigrated to the USA in 1871, which has also led to the assumption that Queensberry's trip was in that year. There is no evidence, however, that Queensberry went to America with either Arthur or John Graham Chambers or that he ever went on a fact-finding mission about the prize ring. The Queensberry Rules were intended for amateur contests only, and he hardly needed to go abroad to learn about boxing, although he took the opportunity on his many trips to watch and sometimes referee bouts.

The absence of any mention of his activities in the English and Scottish newspapers for nearly a year after Edith's birth suggests that the American trip took place during this period. Queensberry was not by preference a solitary traveller; he always looked for a companion on his journeys, and on this occasion he was accompanied by twenty-one-year-old Viscount Mandeville, son of the seventh Duke of Manchester. During this trip, Queensberry, according to Mandeville's son many years later, had an adventure in a saloon bar. (In Brian Roberts's *The Mad Bad Line* it is suggested that the visit was made around 1866, but it seems very unlikely that Queensberry took a thirteen-year-old boy into a saloon bar.) Queensberry and Mandeville were staying at a ranch in California and rode into the nearest town to have a look around.

> Queensberry must have been an incongruous-looking figure among the cow-punchers, for he was dressed in the height of Mayfair fashion, as if he were setting out to an important social function. He wore a pair of brightly polished leather boots, and the two men had hardly been inside the bar more than a few moments when a gigantic cowboy appeared in the doorway and cast a menacing look around the assembled company that finally came to rest on that shining footgear. The sight of them proved the final straw. Lolling his six foot of flesh and muscle across the bar counter, he muttered a profane request to the Divinity to consign all Britishers to a hot climate, and spat vigorously on the cause of the offence.[39]

Queensberry said nothing to the offender, but reached out, pulled a red silk handkerchief from the cowboy's breast pocket, bent down and, while continuing his conversation with Mandeville, used the handkerchief to wipe his boots. He then straightened up and tucked the handkerchief back in the owner's pocket. The cowboy, 'letting out a roar like a wounded grisly [sic]', hurled himself at Queensberry with bunched fists.

'At this period Queensberry was the finest amateur boxer in existence, and so he remained quite unperturbed.' A scuffle ensued during which dust rose from the floor in clouds sufficient to obscure the two fighters, and when it finally settled Queensberry was seen 'leaning nonchalantly against the bar-counter, immaculate as on his first entrance, minus even a scratch' while lying on the floor, 'occupied in taking astronomical observations, and making dazed enquiries as to his whereabouts, was about two hundred and twenty pounds in weight of "bad man"'. As a final insult, Queensberry 'treated the incident as too trivial to trouble about'.[40]

Queensberry must have been using his time away from Sybil to consider what do to about his failed marriage. There were a number of options open to a gentleman in such a situation. He could simply have tolerated the position; but Queensberry was not a tolerant man. He might have maintained the outward appearance of a happy marriage and taken a mistress; but Queensberry did not believe that a married man living with his wife should do so. Then there was divorce, but he had no grounds for divorcing Sybil. A separation could be effected legally, and would have left Queensberry free according to his principles to have liaisons with other women, but this would not give Sybil grounds for divorcing him even if she had wished to. Adultery alone was then insufficient grounds for a wife to obtain a divorce in England – cruelty had to be additionally cited.

It was in this frame of mind that Queensberry arrived in Salt Lake City, home of the Church of Jesus Christ of Latter-Day Saints, which at the time permitted polygamy, and picked up a leaflet on the subject. Although when roused by circumstances he was quick to dash off furious letters, other things that moved him developed slowly in his mind, sometimes for many years, and so it was with this. Queensberry undoubtedly discussed his new ideas on religion and marriage with family and close friends, but for the moment these thoughts remained essentially private. When he finally revealed his views to the world it would establish him for ever in the public mind as an eccentric, and possibly a madman.

On his return, he probably, if he had not already, broached the subject of divorce but Sybil remained resistant to the idea for many years. For Queensberry the only solution to his failed marriage that tallied with his conscience was to live apart from his wife. For most of the rest of his life he was on the move, living in hotels and apartments, staying with friends and sporadically returning to Scotland. If he was in search of anything it was a place he could call home, but he never found it. There were occasional visits to see his children, and newsy letters enclosing money, but for the most part they rarely saw their father. There are hints in some of Queensberry's later comments and letters that one reason for his frequent absences abroad was medical, and like many gentlemen of his time he sometimes stayed in spa towns such as Aix-les-Bains. In 1880 he was to claim that he could obtain doctors' certificates regarding his ill health, but he did not mention the cause. He may have been advised to take a holiday to relieve stress or depression.

In 1874 however the only eccentric Douglas, in the opinion of the public and press, was Caroline, a Douglas by marriage only. After briefly examining the case being made for Home Rule for Ireland, she had firmly rejected it as 'a most destructive, yes, a suicidal doctrine' and wrote long letters to the newspapers to make her point. 'The basis of the real hopes of Ireland is Irish union around a just cause. That cause is Restoration. There is your flag. Look to it!' she thundered.[41]

Early in 1875 Queensberry was back in England for the wedding of his sister Florence to twenty-three-year-old Sir Alexander Beaumont Dixie, Bt, of Bosworth Hall, Leicestershire. Florence, then nineteen, was about five feet tall and weighed less than eight stone, while 'Beau' as he was called, whom she ruled 'with a rod of iron',[42] stood 6 feet 2 inches. The wedding took place on 3 April, at St Peter's Church Eaton Square, and Queensberry gave away the bride. It was a happy union, yet Florence did not mean to retreat into a contented domesticity; like her mother and brother she had wandering feet, an independent mind and a strong need for a mission in life.

Queensberry was not long in finding a new cause to stir him, and one that came with an opportunity for more travel. In May 1875 a deputation including the Duke of Manchester, then president of the Royal Colonial Institute, had approached the Colonial Office suggesting the annexation of New Guinea to the British Crown. Queensberry, attracted by the challenges the scheme offered, may well have accompanied his friend. The visit was inspired by the recent discoveries of Captain Moresby which had culminated in a paper read to the Royal Geographical Society the previous February about New Guinea; its lush cultivation, good harbours, friendly natives and the promise of abundant gold. New Guinea and its untapped prospects suddenly became a hot topic. The deputation received a cool but friendly reception from Colonial Secretary Lord Carnarvon, who informed its members that the primary interest in New Guinea was not British but Australian. Undeterred, the would-be adventurers formed a private association with the object of sending out 200 men to colonise New Guinea with the intention of ultimate annexation. Queensberry subscribed 'some thousands of pounds and propose[d] to join the expedition'.[43]

On 30 October, however, Lord Carnarvon advised that he could not approve the scheme. Alarmed at the prospect of the formation of 'a military or quasi-military force' he pointed out that 'it was not open to any independent association of Englishmen to take possession of the land as proposed'. The disappointed members asked the government to advise a legal course 'for private persons to pursue in order at once to acquire possession of land in that portion of New Guinea unclaimed by the Dutch Government'.[44] Carnarvon while not absolutely forbidding the expedition said that 'if its members acquired land wrongfully their title to it would not be recognised by the English Crown, and that they were, in his opinion, embarking upon a most unusual and a most dangerous course'.[45]

It appears that the proposed expedition never sailed.

Queensberry's restlessness was a sign of growing unhappiness, and of dissatisfaction with the current status of both marriage and religion. In the early summer of 1876 he took a trip that must have had something of the character of a pilgrimage to a place where he had once found enlightenment and perhaps hoped he might do so again – Zermatt, and the slopes of the Matterhorn.

CHAPTER 7

Original Notions

———— •━•━ ————

Q UEENSBERRY'S long spiritual journey which had begun in 1865 with grief and confusion would pass through a process of enquiry followed by enlightenment leading to bombastic certainty, missionary zeal and finally rage, but its progress was almost certainly slowed by the responsibilities of marriage, family and estates and the consolations of sport. Outwardly he would not have struck an observer as concerned with anything beyond the living of life in the present. His sporting acquaintances, though not his close friends, would have been amazed at the notion of Queensberry as a thinker. C. M. Croker Pennell, an admiral's son from Dumfriesshire described Queensberry in 1882 as 'a youth, who, when I saw him some years ago, did not appear to possess a thought above the level of a 16-hand horse, or if his meditations ever soared beyond that height, they might have centred on its rider'.[1]

Queensberry's first return to Zermatt after his brother's death was in 1870 when, hearing that Florence, then fifteen, was making the trip, he impulsively decided to follow her. Florence, who was accompanied by four adults, kept a journal. After spending the night at an inn high in the mountains, her party made an early start, 'climbing across tottering bridges, narrow passes and rugged crags beneath which mountain torrents fell with crash and roar'.[2] They rested at a pavilion where Florence found Francis's name in a visitors' book. He had signed himself 'a lover of the Alps'.[3]

After crossing the glacier, Florence was leaning on her alpenstock gazing down into the Zermatt valley when she was startled to hear herself being greeted by Queensberry, and saw him fifty yards below, ascending the mountain pass. Brother and sister hugged, and Queensberry revealed his plan to follow and meet up with her. He pleaded with her not to return with her companions, but to stay with him and enjoy the glorious view. Together they sat on a grassy slope covered in alpine flowers and he pointed out to her the part of the Matterhorn where Francis had died and also where he had managed to climb in search of his brother's body. The conversation naturally turned to death and the concept of an afterlife. Florence said that, although she had no proof, she felt sure that death was not the end of everything and that she had lived before and would live again. Queensberry suggested that she only felt it to be true because she wished it to be true, but she told him that she often had flashes of memory of places she had never been which she thought came from a past life. Queensberry told her that he, too, thought deeply on the same subjects but could only respond from a scientific point of view. Science suggested that death ended human life and could not prove the existence of a soul. 'I am still searching for the Truth and trying to sift mysteries,' he said. 'Science helps us to think, but as you say, it has many problems yet to solve about which it knows nothing.'

It was soon time for Florence and her companions to move on, but Queensberry decided to stay for another week or so. 'It has done me a lot of good, this visit here has,' he told her, 'and I am so glad you have been with me. God bless you. Good-bye.'

Florence put her arms around his neck and kissed him, asking him to write to her, and confessed that she would feel 'dreadfully lonely' without him. Her companions were very kind but 'It is different when you and I are together.'

He kissed her. 'I am going to write out a lot of my ideas too, and I will send them to you.'[4]

As he returned to the life of a sporting country gentleman and celebrated the birth of his third son, Queensberry was still carefully shaping his thoughts, but the big changes in him always seem to have been due not to single catastrophes but to the collision of more than one. Had his marriage been satisfying his controversial religious beliefs might never have surfaced in public, but contemplating the nature of the soul against the backdrop of the collapse of his relations with Sybil threw his misery and uncertainty into sharp relief.

The failure of the marriage was not yet public property, but once Queensberry had acknowledged it to himself, it is probable that he was never a happy man again. He was about to spend many restless years searching for a truth that would make sense of his existence, and a cause that would give his life meaning. All of Archibald and Caroline's children were on a mission to find some great principle they could believe in, and the happiest may have been those who found peace and certainty in the Catholic Church. Queensberry and Florence were to turn their back on established religion, which for Florence could never have the same consequences as it would for a man in public life. Her twin, James, never found anything that would give him comfort or contentment.

Queensberry's enquiries brought him to the work of polymath and agnostic Herbert Spencer, an advocate of the theory of evolution, best remembered today for his phrase 'survival of the fittest'. Queensberry was especially attracted to Spencer's *Social Statics: or, The Conditions Essential to Human Happiness Specified, and the First of Them Developed* and the chapter entitled 'The Evanescence of Evil'. Spencer, who believed in both social and biological development, declared that 'All evil results from the non-adaptation of constitution to conditions'.[5] The human race, although currently imperfect, was, said Spencer, undergoing a process of adaptation leading to 'complete fitness for the social state . . . so surely must man become perfect'.[6] So forcibly did this theory strike Queensberry that he learned the chapter off by heart, a feat that took him two months to achieve, and it formed the foundation of his beliefs thereafter.

On 1 June 1876 Queensberry returned to Zermatt in the company of Florence and her husband. They were the first visitors of the year, and travelled on little one-horse traps, traversing four tunnels through the snow. The last tunnel was 120 yards long, and the tourists were obliged to descend from the traps and continue on foot, conducted by guides with lanterns. As Queensberry wandered the snowy foothills he recited Spencer's work to himself and from this emerged the idea for a poem, which took him three days to write, *The Spirit of the Matterhorn* which he dated 10 June 1876. It was not made public immediately, but was circulated to friends and probably family (almost certainly Florence) for comment. His new system of belief, which had begun as a means of dealing with the tragic and senseless loss of his brother, had blossomed into an attempt to save not only Francis but mankind, and thereby, ultimately, himself. The poem, emerging from the depths of the author's unhappiness and sense of isolation, reveals some of the reasons for his later unsatisfactory relationships with his children. It opens with the writer sitting beneath the towering slopes of the Matterhorn, which has come to symbolise

... the everlasting laws
Of endless life proceeding from decay.[7]

As a new day dawns, he calls for the 'Spirit of eternal truth divine'[8] to shed its light on his soul, but it is clear that he is seeking far more than personal understanding. A true son of his campaigning mother, Queensberry was unable to perceive a great and important truth without wanting to announce it to the world, and created in his poem a spirit that would give him divine authority to do so.

The spirit duly appears, to guide his thoughts 'to help the future of thy race',[9] teach him that his identity is 'part of the eternal all'[10] and purify it for its mission on earth, 'perfecting man's body for his soul'.[11] The writer expresses the hope that his brother has found eternal rest, but the spirit advises him

Death sinks all individuality
In the great essence of an eternal power
Only later do they
... breathe again, through other forms of life,
A new born individuality.[12]

Man's future, it is revealed, is to build 'perfection of the body and the mind',[13] and this progress is 'no chance but the results of an eternal law'.[14] Even when the fabric of the earth has melted away in some distant future, mankind would be

... part of an eternal endless force
Merged in the ocean of the mighty all.

Faith, says the spirit, will 'ring the knell of war, disease, and crime!'[15] The spirit then commands the author to proclaim these thoughts. 'And this shall bring thee peace, soothing thy mind.'[16]

The ideal of mankind was 'vigorous frames with healthy minds endowed',[17] and while in the perfect future all might claim an equal right to reproduce, that was not yet so, for there are some who 'Possess no right to be progenitors'.[18]

The ultimate aim of perfection, said the spirit, was to experience what Queensberry deep in his innermost desires most wanted: 'perfect love' when 'perfect souls harmoniously combine'.[19] The spirit sympathises with the bitterness the author has felt in being unable to find true love, which in the present imperfect state of things is impossible, but reveals that the author's soul has lived on earth before, many times:

> . . . maybe thy happiest time was when
> Blessed with a giant frame, and savage strength,
> Free as the untamed beast, thou roam'st the earth
>
> . . .
> Thy progeny, a glory to thine eye,
> Were all thou could'st desire in lustiness.[20]

Parents will naturally see some aspects of themselves in their children, but for Queensberry his children were the continuance of his soul on earth.

One of the friends to whom Queensberry sent a copy of the poem was the Earl of Rosslyn, to whom he wrote in October 1876. Queensberry was staying at Glen Stuart, and worrying about the future of his estates. He was not the only landowner with these concerns. An agricultural depression in the British Isles from about 1873 had seen income from rents fall, while the cost of living remained the same; and the value of land went into an increasingly steep decline. Uneconomic estates subject to an entail could not be sold or mortgaged, forcing the owners to look for other sources of income, reduce outgoings and sell moveable assets such as paintings. The next few years would see a continuing erosion of land values and rising taxation on property, but as early as 1876 Queensberry could already discern the threat to his status, finances and peace of mind. Owners of prime agricultural land and handsome houses close to London stood a better chance of riding out the depression, but Queensberry became ever more despairing about the burden of his cold grey remote castle.

Dear Rosslyn

Thanks for your letter: you must not think that I mind your refusing what I asked. I know it is disagreeable to refuse this sort of request. I am afraid there is little chance of my ever pulling off a big stake on the turf I don't think I shall even try. I am very hopeful of finding coal here which will be as good.

But all the money in the world would never make up to me for other things, and I am turning into a very bitter unhappy man. Nothing will ever persuade me that I have had a fair chance. I have been handicapped out of it from the very first. I am thinking of going out to S America next month. Should like to come and see you before I go –

I send you my Spirit of Zermatt I wrote it wandering about in Switzerland this summer & have tried to express my thought on the subject I know you wont [sic] agree – but it is my faith & the only thing I do believe in, the ultimate perfectibility of mankind.

Ever yours

Queensberry

In a note written across the top of the letter he added: 'I want you to second my brother for Boodles he is a very good boy I will propose him.'[21] Boodles was a gentlemen's club and the brother in question was James, who did become a member.

This 'bitter unhappy man' was just thirty-two.

Queensberry's financial worries are often cited as evidence that he was insane, mainly by Bosie who was never able to see past the concept that the Scottish estate was part of the family birthright and should be retained at all costs. In 1879, it was estimated the Dumfriesshire estates had an annual value of £13,384,[22] but it is far from certain that this was what Queensberry actually received. Queensberry had regular consultations with his estate manager and solicitor, and his decisions, guided by their advice, were the same as those made by many another nobleman caught in the same position.

Queensberry was gradually becoming known as a man with unusual ideas. So far he had amused rather than outraged society. 'He used to be laughed at a good deal, and very many were the weird stories in circulation about him.'[23] His appearance in 1877 is epitomised by a cartoon that appeared in *Vanity Fair*: traditional, but with his own little touches of colour and style. Slim, trim and active looking, he wears a plain black suit, black boots with spats, white shirt, gloves and cravat, but the handkerchief in his left breast pocket is edged and spotted with red, and his top hat is perched at a jaunty angle. In one hand is an umbrella and in the other a piece of paper – racing form, perhaps. Mrs Menzies described him as

> clean-shaven, except for the little fuzzy side-whiskers then considered chic. When wearing a tall hat his black wiry hair stood out under it like a frill, especially as his hats were invariably a size or so too small for his head, and [he] indulged in very curly brims. He was a small man, smart in his own way, but with curious theories on dress, women and a variety of other things. I wondered at anybody with such a pronounced nose daring to box.[24]

Vanity Fair commented: 'He has original notions on most subjects, and views all men women and things by the light of novel and startling theories. He is a good light-weight boxer, a fair husband, a capital jockey, generous, amiable, surprising, and a favourite with all his friends.'[25]

Sybil was undoubtedly unhappy. Amy Menzies, who saw her often, said 'she used to come and sit with me and talk about her sorrows and many disappointments'. Mrs Menzies, however, recognised both sides of the situation and described Queensberry as 'a good friend and kindly to all'.[26] Summing him up she said, 'he had become his own master too soon. A little more discipline in early years was all that was wanting.'[27]

Florence, a popular figure whose 'geniality, courtesy, and humour, have made her a great many friends, who esteem her for her kindly disposition',[28] was yet to be accounted eccentric in her own right. She was then best known for her skilled handling of horses and for coming from 'a fear-despising race. She is sister of the Marquis of Queensberry who went to Spain to help the Carlists in the late war, and daughter of the same Marchioness of Queensberry who was made such a heroine of by the Fenian rebels of ten years ago.'[29] Whether or not Queensberry did indeed go to Spain is unknown, but it was the kind of project that might well have attracted his interest. The Dowager Marchioness was not silent for long, but by now everyone had heard what she had to say many times, and hers was an increasingly marginalised voice. Queensberry's quietly devout brother, Archibald Jnr, was able to avoid controversy. After further study at St Thomas' Seminary, Hammersmith, he was ordained by Cardinal Manning in June 1876. In the following year the young priest made a pilgrimage to Rome and was received by the Pope.

Queensberry was still racing, although less frequently than before, and was a member of the Grand National Hunt Committee. In December 1877 he was riding his own mount, Image, at Sandown Park when the horse, which was running well, blundered against a fence and was impaled. It was able to run on a little before it fell, and had to be destroyed. Queensberry escaped without injury. In 1878 he joined the executive council of the British Empire Horse Supply Association, established to 'remedy the existing scarcity of good sound horses in the United Kingdom by drawing on the unlimited supplies which exist in America and Canada'.[30] He may have seen this as a further opportunity for travel, but the company held only one sale, in August 1878, before it was wound up.

In December 1878 he again rode in a steeplechase, but he was also busy preparing for another trip abroad. Florence, 'Palled for the moment with civilisation and its surroundings',[31] had decided to escape to the most 'outlandish' and 'far away'[32] place she could think of, and lighted on the vast open spaces and unexplored wilds of Patagonia (now a region of Argentina and Chile). Florence assembled a party, which consisted of her husband, Queensberry, her twin James, traveller and writer Julius Beerbohm and a servant.

On a cold, rainy December day they joined the steamer *Britannia* at Pauillac, and were welcomed on board by Captain Brough and shown over the ship, admiring its 'sumptuous and comfortable fittings-up'.[33] After dinner the party retired to the captain's deckhouse for whist, while outside the weather had worsened and a gale was blowing. The ship suddenly heeled over so violently that Florence thought they had struck a rock, and they ran out to see what was happening, but it was only a massive wave. Queensberry who had experienced far worse was probably less alarmed than the rest. Three days later they reached Lisbon where the ship stayed for the day taking on coal and provisions, then headed out across the Atlantic, passing the island of Palma two days later. Christmas Day was spent in tropical heat and celebrated with a traditional banquet 'at which much merriment reigned and many speeches were spoken'.[34] On 28 December they called briefly at Pernambuco and did not go ashore, but bought white pineapples from a boat that came alongside. The following day the ship dropped anchor at Bahia, which, 'half hidden among huge banana trees and cocoanut palms', looked picturesque from a distance, but on going ashore Florence thought it dirty, ugly and pervaded by 'disagreeable odours'.[35] They took a hydraulic lift to the upper town, then a mule-tramway took them quickly from the town along a pleasant high road to the ridge on which Bahia was built. On the way they had to change vehicles more than once, as there were descents so steep that they could be traversed only by carriages worked by hydraulic machinery. Arriving at the seashore they enjoyed a magnificent view of the bay dotted with catamarans, but the heat soon drove them into a café, where they had lunch. They were not sorry to return to Bahia and the 'cool clean ship',[36] which weighed anchor and set off for Rio de Janeiro. On the way they celebrated New Year's Day 1879 with 'much festivity'.[37]

Four days later they were steaming into Rio. Florence the intrepid traveller was less than enamoured of the heat, dirt and ugly buildings, and they hired a carriage drawn by four mules to go to Tijuca, high up in the hills. As they descended a steep incline, one of the mules became reluctant to move, and the driver started to whip it. The travellers all got out, and in the confusion the other three mules bolted, causing the fourth one to fall. Carriage and mules all disappeared down the slope in a cloud of dust and the travellers hurried after them, to find their vehicle overturned. It was damaged but surprisingly neither the driver nor the mules were injured. The party decided to walk down to the Hotel Whyte, which they found clean and cool. A little stream fed into a basin hewn out of rock forming a swimming pool, and the gentlemen refreshed themselves with a plunge. Florence later also took a swim, and the day ended with dinner and 'a cheery musical evening'.[38]

The next morning they were up early, as they had to be on board the steamer by midday. The captain, Florence, her husband and James sat in a carriage drawn by two mules with Queensberry and Beerbohm following in a victoria. Florence, realising that her driver was the same man who had driven so recklessly the previous day, cautioned him to be careful but he took no notice and headed off at a gallop, the terrified occupants hanging on and waiting for the inevitable accident. Catching the corner of a stone bridge the carriage heeled over, hurling the driver into the brook below and burying the passengers under its wheels, freeing the mules, which galloped away. The driver emerged dripping from the brook to be showered with the wrath of the fortunately unhurt party. With time of the essence and only one remaining vehicle, there was some debate as to what to do, but at that moment a diligence arrived with vacant seats. Florence joined Queensberry and Beerbohm in the victoria, whose driver assured her that his mules were perfectly steady. Unfortunately as soon as they reached a steep descent the coachman urged his animals into a gallop, they promptly bolted, and one of the reins broke. The road was winding down the side of a steep hill by the side of a 300-foot precipice and the occupants, terrified of being thrown over the edge, jumped out of the carriage as soon as it was safe to do so. All were cut and bruised but no bones were broken. Luckily for the driver one of the mules fell, and this held back the coach, enabling him to check the others. The travellers, vowing that they had had 'enough of Brazilian coachmanship to last us all our lives',[39] completed the journey on foot arriving two hours late, hot and dusty with cuts, bruises and torn clothes. Luckily the *Britannia* had waited for them and they steamed away from Rio.

It was probably on this trip that Queensberry had another boisterous adventure. A large American had boarded the steamer and was making a nuisance of himself: 'He was always more or less in liquor and gratuitously insulted everybody.'[40] Harry Grenfell, a future admiral, was a passenger and when he checked on some ostriches he was shipping, the American dealt him a heavy smack, saying 'You – liar! They're not ostriches, they're emus.'[41] Queensberry weighed in and 'the fun began'. Soon the bully was lying unconscious in the scupper. 'Lord Queensberry, always alert, immediately had him carried sideways over the gangway and took him ashore in a boat with his head hanging over the gunwale, thinking a little rest on shore again would be good for him!'[42]

Four days later they arrived at Montevideo, but since there was yellow fever at Rio the ship was placed in quarantine. They were unable to go ashore on the mainland and went on to an island where Queensberry decided to leave the party, saying he wanted to stay in Montevideo for a fortnight and would follow on by the next vessel. 'The quarantine island, which was a bare, rocky little place, did not look at all inviting, and I certainly did not envy my brother his three-days' stay on it,' commented Florence.[43] 'He told me afterwards that he had never passed such a miserable time in all his life, the internal domestic arrangements being most primitive.'[44]

Queensberry did not rejoin the party and Florence's account of the trip never mentions him again. He stayed for a time in Buenos Aires, where he was openly testing and talking about his new theories of the soul, but he had other adventures in mind. On 7 April he was passing through the Straits of

Magellan on the mail steamer *Potosi*, when he wrote to Prime Minister Benjamin Disraeli, now the Earl of Beaconsfield, asking once again if he could obtain a colonial posting. 'I have come down here with the idea of making enquiries as to forming an expedition across Terra del Fuego next summer as the Chileans are anxious to have it explored and it has not yet been crossed. Am thinking of volunteering an expedition if they will assist me.'[45] He was at Montevideo on 10 April when he wrote more fully, suggesting that he might apply for a potential appointment there, and appreciating that he required more qualifications than a desperate desire to leave the UK. 'I speak French, Spanish slightly, & would very soon perfect myself in that last language. I am pretty well known here, I trust respected. I know Latorre the President well I am confident I could get on with the people here.'[46] More revealingly he added:

> I am aware that you will say that I have done nothing all these years nor brought myself forward that you should place any confidence in me, but my Lord, I tell you privately that I have passed through a great domestic unhappiness the last 5 or 6 years it has perfectly unfitted me for anything & I have only just kept my head above water as it is – I know that I have been much maligned or fancied so, and sensitive as I am I have shrunk from any publicity.[47]

He cited his naval service where he 'held a good character'[48] and suggested that Admiral Hornby, under whom he had served on the *Edgar* and was 'known to be one of the strictest men in the service',[49] would speak well of him.

On a very personal and unhappy note the letter shows that Queensberry had not given up on a reconciliation with Sybil, and had been desperately missing his children:

> I trust that you will see your way to giving me a chance. I am perfectly well & in health and will go anywhere & try anything even if you send me as a consul to Mozambique which is about the most God forsaken place I have ever been in . . . . the Climate here is beautiful and there is no reason why Lady Queensberry and my children should not come.
>
> I don't know how much you know of my private affairs but I assure you that I feel confident it would give me a better chance of our being brought

together again as it is we have lived almost separated for 5 years & the loss
of my children is misery to me – there is no possibility of my settling down
at home with all the difficulties I have to face; I was quote broken in heart
and health when I last left England: but am as well as ever again & feel that
I have all the energy to undertake what I offer to do.[50]

Sybil, whose idea of foreign travel was a holiday in Cannes, was hardly likely
to agree to such a suggestion, and the idea came to nothing.

By the end of 1879 Queensberry was ready to tell the world about his
new beliefs. In doing so he brought upon himself a storm of disapproval and
ridicule. In his search for happiness he was to find only public rejection and
bitter disappointment. The catalyst for his action was the death on 5 October
1879 of Lady Truro. Her husband carried out a possibly illegal, and certainly
highly novel method of burial. Her body was placed in a plain wooden box,
lightly constructed so as to hinder the process of natural decay as little as
possible, and at midnight Lord Truro and his gardener buried her in a spot
previously selected by the lady – the lawn in front of her home at Falconhurst,
Shooter's Hill.

Vanity Fair, a popular weekly magazine of current affairs, commented on
this 'eccentric conduct',[51] and expressed concern for the health of the public.

Queensberry wrote a letter to the editor Thomas Gibson Bowles, urging its
publication. Bowles at once recognised the damaging effect this was likely to
have on the author and asked Queensberry to reconsider. Queensberry stood
by his principles, and the letter was published 'not without hesitation, at Lord
Queensberry's earnest solicitation and request . . . . When a man of his position, with nothing to gain and so much to lose by it, displays so settled a
determination thus to avow himself, things must seem to have come to a pass
which requires very serious attention and a very serious remedy.'[52] The editor,
with a typical Victorian euphemism, was politely suggesting that Queensberry's
insistence on publication was evidence of mental instability.

Queensberry, while agreeing that public health should be considered as
well as individual freedom, revealed that he had left instructions in his will
that he was not to be buried in consecrated ground or in a leaden coffin, but
in either a wooden or wicker coffin 'on the earth-to-earth principle' which he
considered a 'blessing' as the body would become 'clean dry mould' in a few
months.

'I am not a Christian,' he went on, 'and I will not allow at my death that my burial should give the lie to what I have declared during my life. . . . I have given the matter anxious consideration, and have long made up my mind publicly to declare myself, as I have already done in America, and will do here whenever I have the opportunity . . . . it is time that those who think as I do should boldly step forward and declare themselves, as I do now. One word to the many to whom I shall give offence, because they will not understand me. The man Christ I love and respect, as I do all great humanitarians.'

He asked his critics to try and understand the spirit in which he made his statement by reading the chapter entitled 'Are We Still Christians?' In *The Old Faith and the New* by theologian David Friedrich Strauss, in which Strauss concluded that although people were no longer Christians they had not renounced religion. 'My avowal will do no harm,' Queensberry ended, 'and wild horses won't hold me from declaring myself now.'[53]

Of course it did do harm, and the person principally harmed was Queensberry. The *Belfast Newsletter* described Queensberry as 'an eccentric Scotchman' and mentioned his mother's benevolence towards 'political prisoners'.[54] The *Aberdeen Weekly Journal* was far crueller:

> Like . . . the bray of a donkey . . . the Marquis has burst upon the public with a suddenness and vehemence that are perfectly appalling. Nobody was thinking of him, dreaming of him, apprehensive of him – or wanting him. . . . Lord Queensberry . . . takes occasion to inform the world that he is an infidel . . . and to show how destitute he is of the least rag of common-sense or of common decency.[55]

The *Journal* was not far from the truth in declaring Queensberry's letter to be 'an act of outrageous folly'.[56]

Some letters to *Vanity Fair* commended the marquess's courage while others deplored his views. Queensberry replied in a mild vein, saying that he had not been understood and the views he expressed were not his alone. 'I am only acting as the mouthpiece of thousands – perhaps millions with whom I have a faith in common . . . perhaps most of your readers are unaware that churches of this religion already exist. . . . If people only knew what a passionate love for poor struggling humanity is entertained by all the leaders of the faith, they would examine into it,'[57] he added hopefully.

The *Aberdeen Weekly Journal* was merciless. 'That misguided man . . . has again returned to his craze . . . . with the conceit of a small mind, he seems to think that what creates a sensation in his own little circle must necessarily interest the world.'[58] Archibald also wrote to *Vanity Fair*, citing Scripture, including St Peter's second epistle, which warns against false prophets. The deluge of correspondence was so great that *Vanity Fair* had to declare the subject closed.

On 23 November the Reverend Charles Voysey founder of the Theistic Church, gave a lecture at Langham Hall on 'The Marquess of Queensberry's Religion' repudiating any suggestion that there was an agreement between Queensberry's opinions and that of his congregation.

In the wake of the controversy Queensberry felt he needed to explain his actions to Lord Rosebery who was then busy organising William Gladstone's election campaign. 'I should like very much some day to get to know you better,' he wrote. 'I really think that I have thought more than most men of my age particularly on religious and social questions. I am perfectly determined that if no one else will do it that I will endeavour to head a movement myself to get the faith I hold in common with thousands of others recognised and established. Why should we not be recognised and respected the same as all other religious bodies are?'[59] He intended to write individually to all his fellow peers explaining his actions, though whether he actually did this is unknown.

There was, in any case, a powerful public platform for his views which he fully intended to use – the House of Lords.

CHAPTER 8

Judged by his Peers

Q UEENSBERRY expected, somewhat naïvely, that at the next general election he would be automatically re-elected as a Scottish representative peer. The smart money was on an autumn 1880 contest, and if Queensberry had been able to bide his time – although it must be admitted that the chances of his remaining silent were slim – there was almost a year for the furore about his *Vanity Fair* letters to die down and his position to be better understood. In the event Prime Minister Lord Beaconsfield astonished practically everyone by dissolving parliament in March 1880. Queensberry had yet to publish a statement of his beliefs and many of his critics had assumed that because he had denied Christianity he was an atheist, something he never claimed to be. It is a misconception that persists to this day.

Newspapers were soon rife with rumours that Queensberry would not be re-elected to the Lords, which must have taken him by surprise. A movement was afoot to oust him, and Scottish peers met in London to discuss the issue, a gathering to which Queensberry was not invited. A vacancy had arisen on the retirement of Lord Sinclair, but it was decided that voting was to proceed on the basis that there were two available seats. The election took place in the picture gallery of Holyrood House on Friday 16 April 1880, before a large public assembly. Once the names of the peers present had been read out, Queensberry addressed the company, pointing out that there was only one vacancy and not two, as there was a mistaken impression that he had withdrawn. 'I beg to take this opportunity of declaring that I have never done so; and therefore, if I leave my seat today it must be considered that I am pushed out.' He could not, he said, be ignorant of the reasons, and referred to the way his declaration 'actuated by my feeling of sacred duty to the welfare and advancement of mankind' had been received by the press, especially the

Scottish press. 'Is this to be done at their dictation?' he asked, unwisely. 'My Lord, I never gave myself a thought, nor regarded how this declaration might affect my future prospects, neither do I do so now.' He did not see, however, how his religious opinions made him unfit to hold a seat in the House of Lords. He admitted that he had not attended regularly: 'my having been abroad so much the last few years was necessitated by my health, for which I have certificates from the best doctors in London, and I hope it will not happen again'.

The Earl of Glasgow, who as Lord Clerk Register was presiding, responded coldly, pointing out that it was 'scarcely competent or desirable' to discuss the motives of the voters, adding 'it would perhaps be better to be satisfied with what has fallen from you'.

Queensberry, aware that it was 'perhaps the last chance I shall have of making the statement before my Peers', pressed on, arguing 'That any human creature, be he Peer or peasant, man or woman, pauper or millionaire, should be visited with pains and penalties because of his or her speculative opinion on a subject whereon but few even amongst professed Christians are agreed, is a bitter satire on your vaunted liberty.' He condemned the spirit that dictated his rejection as 'the spirit that lighted the martyr fires of Smithfield'. With only a few more words to say (cries of 'No, no,' from the floor) he added that were he re-elected he would take his seat on the cross-benches as 'I am in no way a party politician but am one of those who can see good on both sides'.

The Marquess of Lothian, riled by the suggestion that the noble assembly might have been influenced by what they read in the press, told his fellow peers 'you will probably, as I hope you will, come to the conclusion that he is not a fit representative . . . the noble Marquis,' he declared, 'has denied that he is a Christian – denies as far as I understand him, the existence of God.'

'I did not,' said Queensberry, making the point that there were Jews in the House of Commons. Lothian was unmoved, and denounced Queensberry to the assembled peers as 'an absolute negation not only of what you and myself esteem, but of what all the people of this country hold most sacred and most dear'.[1] He was met with applause. The voting began, and the sixteen peers elected received between forty-four and fifty-seven votes each. Queensberry received only three, from the Duke of Roxburgh, the Earl of Caithness and the Earl of Kintore, who were all Liberals. Lord Balfour of Burleigh later claimed that he had voted against Queensberry 'only because that noble Lord did not seem to pay much attention to his parliamentary duties', but Lord Galloway voted against him 'solely because of that noble Lord's religious opinion, or rather because of his want of any'.[2]

The *Glasgow Herald* observed what many must have been thinking, that while it was 'greatly to be regretted that a man's private theological opinions should be dragged into the arena of public discussion', Queensberry had taken the initiative 'in drawing attention to his own peculiar views'.[3] The *Aberdeen Weekly Journal* commented 'it is cheering to find the Peers of Scotland ... purging themselves of the taint of being represented by an avowed infidel'.[4]

Queensberry often stated that he cared nothing for public opinion, yet he could not help but feel crushed by this rejection. In May he wrote to Rosebery from 9 Bolton Street, lodgings just off Piccadilly, admitting dispiritedly, 'I hardly ever go racing now'. He asked for a meeting to discuss the loss of his seat. 'I have no one to ask advice of, but don't intend to let the matter remain as it is without making as much row as I can, not on account of myself but because of the cause I consider myself associated with intentionally now.' He asked Rosebery if there was any chance of his being made an English peer by the Liberals, and whether there was any point in asking for it:

> If I am to be kicked out ... I shall write a pamphlet clearly stating the whole case and get it published and sent to every peer in the House. .... I always have been much more of a liberal than a conservative, but was placed rather in an awkward position by being elected without even being consulted. I think they have treated me very badly. I have been in great trouble the last few years and it has been quite impossible for me to remain in England. I am much stronger and better again now, and I feel losing my seat very much.[5]

Queensberry also wrote to Gladstone, who had supplanted Beaconsfield as Prime Minister after a Liberal election victory, and received a sympathetic but unhelpful reply. 'I had not failed to notice ... the sacrifice which you had been called upon to make to your opinions. .... But I ... had not considered that the change of constitution on which you had (of course in my view most unhappily) been called to act constituted a ground for your being now named by the Queen for a British Peerage.'[6]

When Queensberry published *The Spirit of the Matterhorn* in January 1881 he dedicated it to 'the Peers of Scotland' in the hope that it would 'show with what little actual foundation those charges were alleged against me'. In a preface he stated 'I have never at any time denied the existence of God, or ventured to express a decided opinion on the matter'. Declining to give a name to 'a Power which, to me, appears undefinable by man', he preferred to speak of 'The Inscrutable'.

The crucial question he addressed was the nature of the soul. The prevailing religious theory was that humankind did not create the souls of future generations; this was a function of the supreme power. Queensberry, however, argued that the soul was 'not an essence distinct and separate from the body, but . . . *the actual result of the body itself* . . . as much dependent upon it for its tone and quality, as the sound of a musical instrument depends upon the excellence and actual construction of that instrument'. If the soul was inseparable from the body, then man 'becomes responsible, directly responsible, for the souls of his posterity'. When we reproduce, Queensberry argued, 'we certainly reproduce *their* [i.e. our children's] *Souls as well*, and thus become directly responsible for what those Souls may be, and are'. Queensberry on paper would have us believe that what ultimately moved him was the good of future generations, but underneath this one can sense something more personal: the desire for that elusive thing he had only ever tasted briefly – happiness. Religion, he advised, should encourage living for posterity, 'endeavouring to attain a more perfect existence', and to do this 'one should lead the most temperate and virtuous life, which of itself would result in happiness. Live purely, and be healthy both in mind and body.'[7]

'It seems that he is not an atheist,' observed the *Liverpool Mercury*, hitting it on the button at last. 'We must not live for the inscrutable, not so much for man generally, as for our children and those who succeed them, then mankind will be perfected.'[8]

Queensberry sent a copy of the pamphlet to Herbert Spencer, saying it 'ought to have been dedicated to you really', with a letter expressing his admiration for Spencer's work acknowledging that it was the 'parent' of the poem. He revealed that after he had memorised The Evanescence of Evil 'For years after I used to say it off to myself every day once at least. . . . I should much like to know you,' he added.[9] He also sent his pamphlet to the Archbishop of Canterbury, writing across it: 'From one who hopes some day to be found foremost in the van fighting to the death against all ignorance and superstition'.[10] He received no reply. The furore did, however, bring Queensberry new acquaintances amongst like thinkers, in whose company he felt comfortable, but some of the consequences, then unforeseen, would rattle on through the years and come to influence his greatest conflicts and tragedies.

His ejection from the Lords had thrown a strong spotlight on to another man: Charles Bradlaugh, atheist, and newly elected member of parliament. Queensberry's rejection, it was felt, 'will . . . offer a strong precedent against the admission of Mr Bradlaugh to the House of Commons'.[11] Charles Bradlaugh was born in 1833, the son of a solicitor's clerk. After a basic education he was sent to work at the age of twelve. His political awareness was formed during the agitation of the Chartist movement, and although originally a public advocate of Christianity, his religious studies had led to doubt. By 1849 he had declared himself to be a freethinker. Threatened with the loss of his clerking job because of his beliefs, he struggled to make a living while attending meetings of secularists and freethinkers where it was soon acknowledged that despite his youth he was a talented speaker. Under his influence the secular and freethinking movements expanded and became more formally organised. Secularism was then defined as 'the study of promoting human welfare by material means',[12] its principles 'intended for the guidance of those who find theology indefinite, or inadequate, or deem it unreliable'.[13] Secularists did not deny the existence of God or the truth of Christianity but did not profess to believe in either. Freethinkers were more consciously antireligious, and believed in forming their opinions on the basis of science and logic, rather than faith. Queensberry must have been familiar with these principles, since his grandfather Sir William Clayton had been interested in the opinions of prominent secularist George Jacob Holyoake. Florence later recalled Clayton singing the praises of Holyoake to Disraeli at a dinner party she attended at the age of six.

Bradlaugh's lectures and participation in public debates soon brought him to national prominence. For three years he edited a secular newspaper, the *National Reformer*, and became the first president of the National Secular Society in 1866. In 1877 Bradlaugh and associate freethinker Annie Besant were prosecuted for publishing an obscene book, *The Fruits of Philosophy*, a frank treatise on sex and contraception. In 1880 Bradlaugh was elected Liberal member for Northampton, a two-seat constituency, his co-member being Henry Labouchère, agnostic and founder and editor of the outspoken journal *Truth*. Bradlaugh's election excited dismay amongst the ultra-religious, and in the wake of Queensberry's fate comparisons were made in the press between the actions of the Scottish peers and the electors of Northampton. Bradlaugh, who had championed the right to affirm in a court of law rather than take a religious oath, claimed the right to affirm when taking his oath of allegiance before parliament, and was publicly supported by Labouchère. Bradlaugh's claim was denied, but when he relented and asked to take the oath on 23 June he was told to withdraw from the House, which he refused to do, and was eventually removed in the custody of the serjeant-at-arms.

Bradlaugh fought on for the right to take his seat, launching a campaign of meetings and lectures. Queensberry naturally saw some parallels in their positions and in May sent Bradlaugh £50 towards his expenses, 'to show my sympathy for the great battle you are fighting'.[14] Some sceptics saw Queensberry's interest as little more than jumping on Bradlaugh's bandwagon to get publicity for his own grievances, and there may well be some truth in this, since when speaking at public meetings he was unable to resist referring to his ejection from the Lords. The secularists, however, were happy to admit a peer to their cause, and when Queensberry joined the National Secular Society, a conference held at the Memorial Hall, Farringdon on 9 June 1881 proposed him as president of the British Secular Union. This small breakaway group had been formed in 1877 by Holyoake and writer and publisher Charles Watts following a disagreement over Bradlaugh and Besant's policy on contraception. Queensberry's precise views on this are unknown although he believed that some members of society were unfit to reproduce and was giving some thought to the question of limitation of births. There is no evidence that he ever fathered an illegitimate child.

Queensberry received letters from Christians, and one which asked for supplication to 'the Great first Cause who holds the Golden Chain of cause and effect in His Hand' he forwarded to the *National Reformer* with the comment, 'It amazes me that you orthodox people should have the conceit to define such a "Cause" and to call it "Him." Why should it not be "Her?"'[15]

On 16 June 1881 a meeting of Bradlaugh's supporters was held at St James's Hall, and on the platform, amongst others, were three men who each in his own way was to play a part in the Oscar Wilde scandal many years later: Queensberry, Henry Labouchère, and the benevolent and open-minded Revd

Stewart Headlam, who while not agreeing with Bradlaugh's anti-Christian stance, admired his work in the east of London for the moral elevation of people whom the clergy could not reach. In his vote of thanks for the chairman, Mr Councillor Adams of Northampton, Queensberry took the opportunity to compare his position with Bradlaugh's, declaring that the religion of humanity was an outgrowth of Christianity and would in future take its place. He was received with cheers.*

The press was scathing as ever: 'The member for Northampton will hardly thank Lord Queensberry for his indiscreet advocacy ... the less of such mischievous and wholly irrelevant talk the better'.[16] Not only was Queensberry being openly declared an eccentric, but it suddenly appeared that he had always been known to be eccentric, as had his Douglas ancestors. The *Western Mail*, denouncing him as 'this eccentric descendant of a "degenerate Douglas"', dug up stories of the exploits of Old Q again and mentioned Caroline's Fenian sympathies, adding that she had married an Irish manservant, a rumour for which there was no foundation. The letter to *Vanity Fair* was blasted as 'a ridiculous production, showing great ignorance, an utter incapacity to reason, and very bad English', and compared unfavourably with the 'vein of simple piety in Lord Archibald's letter'. The Queensberry Rules were, however, 'like the laws of the Medes and the Persians, unalterable'.[17]

On 31 July, Queensberry was at Secular Hall, Leicester with many of the luminaries of the movement for the annual conference of the BSU. Holyoake, presiding, commented on the 'singular coincidence' that two men of such diverse opinion as Queensberry and Bradlaugh should both be excluded, one from the Lords and one from the Commons, because of their beliefs. Queensberry, praised for his 'bold and liberal stand', was unanimously elected president to 'vociferous cheering' and made a long speech.[18] The BSU, he said, was 'not an Atheistic society, but one wherein all persons are left at perfect liberty to entertain their own views with regard to the Deity and a future life'.[19] He hoped that it would one day be recognised as a religious body. Bradlaugh's writing on delicate issues, he said, was 'a subject of grave importance to society ... which ... must be discussed and studied if we would really advance the material and moral welfare of our posterity'.[20] Queensberry, now dubbed 'the Bradlaugh of the House of Lords', later

---

* Bradlaugh's struggles were to continue until the passing of the Oaths Act of 1888 which made it legal for the Oath of Allegiance to be affirmed.

published his address as a sixpenny pamphlet called *The Religion of Secularism and the Perfectibility of Man* in which he claimed to be 'covered with the impregnable armour of truth' and said he intended 'to throw a bombshell into the enemy's camp'.[21] It may have been no coincidence that the *Leeds Mercury* in December chose to publish the story of the third marquess's foray into cannibalism.[22]

In February 1882 Queensberry was invited to address the Plymouth Liberal Association, at a meeting held to protest against the exclusion of Bradlaugh from parliament. He wrote, declining on the grounds that he avoided public speaking, not perhaps the quality one would desire in the president of the BSU:

> I am not prepared at present to enter into a crusade against all existing institutions. I do not see the use of banging my head up against a brick wall. At the proper time it will come down of its own accord when it has been properly undermined. Some of it is rotten enough already. I have declared myself, and consider that that is all I am called upon to do at present, as an honest man. I dislike offending people's prejudices, and it is so hard to make yourself understood. We cannot revolutionize things. As man becomes more adapted to his circumstances, and becomes more equal, and therefore more perfect, he will gradually alter his own institutions. But if you give a perfect law to imperfect men, I think we should all be just as badly off as before. I fear that I am not much more than a tinker. Sometimes I have burst out when I could contain myself no longer against some glaring falsehood about which no reasonable man could have doubt. I know no fear of consequences, as witness my declaration which had the effect of losing me my seat in the House of Lords. You have my warmest sympathy as regards the abolition of the oath. I look upon it as already gone. There will be a row, no doubt, but it is sure to go, and that Mr Bradlaugh will take his seat is a foregone conclusion.[23]

On 6 August he chaired the annual conference of the BSU at the Cooperative Hall, Greyfriars Gate, Nottingham, and was re-elected president. He revealed that he had written to both Gladstone and Foreign Secretary Lord Granville about his exclusion from the Lords. Their replies suggested that 'nothing would be done until he went down to the House at the heads [*sic*] of processions, with yards of petitions, to get his coat torn off his back like Mr. Bradlaugh'.[24] Amused by this image, the meeting resolved to send a request to Mr Gladstone for Queensberry to receive an English peerage. Speaking at the opening of a branch of the Secular Union at Stockport in November, Queensberry declared that 'They were mistaken who thought that secularists cherished a blind animosity to Christianity and its doings'.[25] As time passed, however, and his life was overtaken by new tragedies, his attitude changed and an increasingly depressed and embittered Queensberry was to attribute his personal grievances to the actions of those he saw as his Christian opponents.

An opportunity soon arose for an extraordinary public demonstration of his views. On 11 November a new rustic prose drama by poet laureate Alfred Tennyson, *The Promise of May* opened at the Globe Theatre. The play received a stormy and unsympathetic reception, its serious passages greeted by roars of laughter. The central character was Philip Edgar, a freethinker who did not believe in an afterlife and who had therefore determined to live for pleasure, caring nothing if by so doing he caused pain to others. Edgar had been courting a virtuous young woman but intended to abandon her as he hated the idea of marriage. The derision with which the play was greeted and the inevitability that it would soon close should have suggested that no action was required by the president of the BSU but Queensberry saw the chance of a public platform for his beliefs, and one not confined to fellow secularists. On 14 November he attended the play with a friend, journalist and poet Edward St John Brenon and they took seats in the stalls. Queensberry 'instantly became deeply interested' in the character of Edgar, and on listening to Edgar's avowed beliefs grew 'so horrified and indignant' that at the end of the first scene he stood up and said, 'These are the sentiments that a professing Christian has put into the mouth of his imaginary Freethinker, and it is not the truth.' Then he sat down. There was naturally some alarm in the theatre but as Queensberry declined to say any more the performance continued. When the curtain fell at the end of the first act, 'there were several good-natured cries and calls upon myself from different parts of the theatre to explain myself'. Queensberry rose and attempted to do so, 'naturally most anxious that the motives of my interruption should not be misconstrued'. He was well aware that it was not just the theatre patrons who required an explanation, and was trying to explain himself when he was, in his own words, 'forcibly but kindly removed'.[26] The manager, Charles Joseph Abud, approached and asked him to leave, but when Brenon explained who the offender was it was decided that they should all go to Abud's private room. Here they were joined by author and critic Joseph William Comyns Carr, and Queensberry was persuaded that his best mode of expression was the press. Queensberry and Brenon left and Brenon suggested that they go to his club, the Savage, to write the letter but Queensberry said he would be able to 'write it more composedly' at the nearby Turf Club.[27] This done, he took it to Brenon at the Savage to read, and both went to deliver it to the offices of the *Daily Telegraph*. The result was that the weak play became a curiosity and limped on rather longer than it might have done. 'My object,' Queensberry explained, 'was not only to make a public protest against the supposed sentiments of a Freethinker (on marriage), but to attract public attention to that protest.'[28] Unfortunately the chief effect was on the protester's reputation.

The newspapers had a field day with Queensberry's outburst, which labelled him thereafter in public opinion as a borderline madman from whom anything might be expected. *Fun* suggested satirically that it was 'a truly grand idea ... for infusing new blood into the contemporary British drama' and published an extract from *Macbeth* in which the action was repeatedly interrupted by members of the audience.[29] Predictably the *Aberdeen Weekly Journal* denounced Queensberry as 'an unmitigated ass' from 'a curious family, from which we can only expect eccentricities' and accused him of 'militant atheism', suggesting that he 'ought to be looked after by his relations',[30] a polite way of saying that he required confinement for insanity. Observing that Britain was built on Christian principles it added indignantly: 'If the people of Britain were to be guided by the Marquis of Queensberry, they would simply decree that any man and wife who were evilly disposed to each other could obtain a divorce' and accused him of simply being 'anxious to acquire a factious notoriety'.[31]

Queensberry had a few supporters. Edward Aveling the biologist, socialist and atheist, had been at the performance, which was 'rendered notorious – and perhaps historic – by the protest',[32] and wrote to the theatrical newspaper *Era* in support of Queensberry's outburst. *The Graphic*, too, was sympathetic. 'We do not wonder at his indignation,'[33] said the editor, although the theatre critic thought 'he seems to have rather odd notions of the proper time and place for objecting'.[34]

The *Daily News*, missing the entire point suggested that Queensberry was indignant at seeing 'his own ideas' in the mouth of a 'cowardly cur'.[35] Queensberry replied: 'everything is fair in war: and this is war'. What frustrated him was that 'Our great difficulty at present is even to get a hearing from our orthodox opponents'. His own opinion of marriage was that it 'ought to be and is, a human institution; and not a Divine one'; marriage law should be kept as it was, but not 'bolstered up with the unnecessary falsehood that any Supreme being has bound two unfortunate people together for life, however unsuitable they may turn out to be to one another'.[36] It was divorce law that needed reform.

Many observers objected to a place of entertainment being used to debate serious issues, and some simply deplored Queensberry's behaviour, which 'could not be excused in a New Cut rough. We expect ordinarily decent behaviour from a nobleman.'[37] Even *The Freethinker* described him as 'more zealous than wise'.[38] The incident may have been trivial but it stuck in the public mind.

Queensberry decided to retire from the chairmanship of the BSU and did not go to the 1883 conference in Birmingham, sending a message saying he was prevented from attending as he had anticipated, as he was about to leave for the Continent. He wished a hearty success to the organisation. The delegates applauded his sentiments and Charles Watts was elected in his place. The British Secular Union, though it promised much, 'was never able, however, to get on its feet, and its leaders presently abandoned it'.[39] It finally disbanded in 1884.

The controversial marquess, still hoping for a return to parliament, was actively courting the approval of Gladstone. In April 1883 Queensberry wrote to the newspapers and Gladstone in support of a bill which would have enabled members to affirm. Pointing out that he was unable to sit in either legislative House or exercise the vote, he asked 'why should the few Scotch peers who are left out in the cold be ineligible to sit in the House of Commons?'[40] The bill was defeated. In November 1885 he wrote to *The Standard* about the issue of disestablishment of the Church, and wrote to Gladstone asking him to read the letter, reiterating his grievance at being excluded from the Lords on the statement of Lord Lothian. 'I wish,' he added, 'you would allow me some day to have the pleasure of making your personal acquaintance.'[41] Politically he remained a Liberal. 'I generally find my sympathies pulling with the Party of Progress. We are going up hill, not down. I prefer to leave it to the Conservative Party to put on the skid.'[42]

By 1889 Queensberry had still not got his wish, and tried a different approach, aware that he might have bored a few people with his personal problems. On 7 April he again wrote to Gladstone, drawing his attention to a letter he had written to the newspapers on the subject of divorce, adding 'We are close neighbours & I have always wished to meet you so much, if you could ever give me a spare half hour it would be a great pleasure to myself & I would not trouble you with any grievances of my own'.[43]

Queensberry wrote further earnest and respectful letters to Gladstone in February 1891 asking that agnostics should be recognised as religious, and enclosing a copy of his pamphlet on secularism. His appeals were unsuccessful and he was never accepted back into politics. When the House of Lords ejected Queensberry it lost a colourful personality who would have excited controversy and relished debate. Queensberry lost a formal outlet for his views and acquired a deep sense of injustice that would eat away at him like a corrosive for the rest of his life.

CHAPTER 9

An Undercurrent of Eccentricity

THE public vilification of Queensberry after he declared himself an
agnostic destroyed his chances of ever being well thought of in respectable society, but in the more bohemian world of gentlemen's entertainment,
it was another matter.

A slow, quiet revolution had been taking place in the sport of boxing, and
the resurgence of pugilism gave Queensberry another arena, a place where
he could meet people who were good company and didn't care about his
religion or what he thought about marriage. The rules devised for the
Queensberry Cups had become established in the public mind as the
Queensberry Rules, and the assurance that a contest was held under those
rules was regarded as a stamp of quality, discretion and respectability.
Occasionally, promoters caught arranging illegal prizefights claimed in their
defence that the contest had been arranged under the Queensberry Rules, but
the differences were readily apparent. *The Graphic*, which deplored unscientific 'endurance contests', stated that 'Boxing pure and simple is a manly
exercise, which is deserving of all possible commendation and encouragement'.[1] In 1881 Ned Donnelly, who described himself as a professor of
boxing, advertised lessons in 'the noble art . . . the fact of having taught seventeen winners of the Marquis of Queensberry's Cups . . . testifies to his
capability'.[2] The name had become a brand.

Queensberry and Chambers had ensured that a sport that might well have
died out was able to continue in an orderly and regulated fashion, albeit still
with amateur status. In 1880 the increasingly popular contest for the
Queensberry Cups was for the first time held under the shared auspices of the
Amateur Athletic Club and the new Amateur Boxing Association (ABA),

'which has received the support of all the best known amateurs in the metropolis',[3] and enjoyed its largest attendance since it began.

Some revision had been made to the rules, although the essentials remained. The roped ring was on a platform three feet above floor level. The first two rounds were of three minutes' duration and the last of four. The chief differences were in the judging. There were two judges and a referee, the referee to have the casting vote, but if he was undecided he could order another round of two minutes. A further improvement was that 'all byes had to be regularly sparred off with a professional, which prevented any competitor gaining an unfair advantage by the having the good luck to obtain a rest'.[4]

In 1882, according to the *Birmingham Daily Post*, 'since the Queensberry boxing cup contests were established about fifteen years ago, amateur boxing has become one of our most popular recreations'.[5] Queensberry's sporting fame had spread to the United States. Allowing for some hyperbole from the *New York Times* correspondent, this article shows the battling marquess's standing in the boxing fraternity, if not in polite drawing rooms:

> The Marquis of Queensberry, who is now accepted as an authority upon all glove fights, was a grand pugilist in his heyday. The stories that are told by old 'sports' about his prowess are innumerable. He went about seeking adventures as zealously as the so-called 'good Haroun al Raschid' and the tougher the adventure the more gusto he had in encountering it. He was a kind of Guy of Warwick with his fists. The story about his driving a four-in-hand drag full of ladies and gentlemen is well-known. A brewer's dray blocked the way. The brewer, a powerful surly fellow, refused to move out of the way to allow the drag to pass. The Marquis handed over the ribbons and whip to a companion, took off his coat, leaped down from the box-seat, 'sailed in' at the dray-man, thrashed him in two or three rounds, compelled the man to move away his dray, then jumped back onto the drag, put on his coat, apologized to the ladies for the trifling interruption, and drove away, while the drayman, wiping his ensanguined nose, looked after the party and muttered, 'Blowed, but that must be either the Markiss or the devil.'[6]

On 4 March 1883, Queensberry lost an old friend and positive influence, and sport a respected ambassador, when John Graham Chambers died at the age of forty.

There was another sector of society in which Queensberry felt comfortable – the theatre – and his tastes ran more to the musical and comic than the serious stage. He established new friendships in the theatrical profession, was known to be an admirer of pretty actresses, and in 1883 wrote the lyrics to a ballad, 'My Only Love'.[7] 'My father had quite a pleasant baritone voice,' said Bosie, 'and he was for ever "practising" songs and hammering out the tune with one finger on the piano. He tried all his life to play the piano, but never succeeded in getting beyond the stage which is painfully reached by the average unmusical child of ten.'[8] The musical marquess's lack of ability did not stop him criticising others, and this led to a typical quarrel with Beaumont Dixie. Queensberry and Bosie had been staying with the Dixies and Beau's lack of prowess on the piano had led to some sarcastic comments by Queensberry and a row. All Florence's efforts to pacify the stubborn pair failed. Eventually Queensberry, pale with rage, rose and said, 'Very well, I shall leave this house, and you had better send the boy back to his mother.'[9] He then rushed out, slamming the door hard enough to make the china ornaments in the drawing room rattle. Bosie, then a child himself, found it all rather childish. Beau took the view that Queensberry would soon come back, which he did half an hour later, and after some initial awkwardness was persuaded to play a game of tennis, all disagreement forgotten. Bosie, having seen how best to handle his volatile father, learned a valuable lesson, which he later chose to ignore.

Although Queensberry remained a staunch freethinker, his public profile in that movement was to decline after 1883. In September that year, however, a book of weak but earnest poems, *Songs by the Wayside of an Agnostic's Life*, was dedicated to Queensberry in his capacity as president of the BSU.

Douglas scandals were to become a regular staple of the press, but the next one came from a very unexpected source. Given the radical difference in tastes and beliefs between Queensberry and his brother Archibald, they were never destined to be close, but neither did they quarrel. On some issues they were in agreement; for example, Archibald devoted his life to charitable work, a principle that Queensberry supported irrespective of whether the motives were religious or not. In March 1878 Archibald had paid £7,000 for a large house in Woodfield Terrace, part of Harrow Road at what is now numbers 333 to 339, and established St Vincent's Home for Destitute Boys, providing accommodation, meals, education and training in practical skills. The building had a garden, schoolroom, playground, workshops and a bakery, and a cart bearing 'St Vincent's bread' made its daily round to Catholic homes. Gertrude joined her brother as housekeeper, and when funds were short she was content to undertake some of the menial work.

In June 1882 Archibald left for Canada with forty boys who were to be resettled as farmers. In his absence the home was left in the charge of his sister. While in Canada, Archibald received a letter from Gertrude which must have astonished him. She was about to be married to Thomas Henry Stock, one of the senior boys at the school, who was in charge of the bakery. Stock's origins are obscure, but he stated in the 1881 census that he was born in Market Harborough, and if this is true the only likely Thomas Stock was born on 8 December 1864, the son of James Henry Stock, a tin worker. In 1871 six-year-old Thomas was one of a number of 'homeless children' living in Birmingham. If this was indeed he, then at the 1881 census when Stock was living at St Vincent's Home, he would have been sixteen, but he was claiming to be two years older. Archibald telegraphed and wrote from Canada asking Gertrude at least to delay the wedding, but it took place on 3 October 1882 at the Roman Catholic Church of the Most Holy Trinity, Hammersmith. Forty-year-old Gertrude gave her age as thirty-eight and her new husband, described in the newspapers as 'good-looking and well-behaved',[10] was said to be twenty. Thomas gave his father's name as Thomas Henry Stock of unknown profession, but if he had been essentially homeless from an early age these details may have been unknown to him.* The couple settled in Hammersmith where, the astonished and amused press was eager to inform the public, they opened a bakery.

Florence Dixie was also becoming a public figure, and Queensberry supported her during controversies that would have tested many a brother's loyalty. Although Beau Dixie enjoyed an income of £10,000 a year he was a keen gambler at the racetrack and slowly ran through his fortune. Beau was also a heavy drinker, and Florence, who had as a child written a poem deploring drink, must have joined him, since according to an acquaintance they were known as 'Sir Always and Lady Sometimes Tipsy'.[11] The Bosworth estate was sold and the Dixies moved to a smaller residence called the Fishery about three miles from Windsor, on the banks of the Thames, where

---

* Stock was vague about his age. In the 1891 census taken eight and a half years after the wedding he claimed to be thirty.

Queensberry was a regular visitor. Florence, as spirited as her mother and with the physical courage of her father, was reputed to have attacked a Thames angler who had fished in the waters opposite her house. There were large numbers of pets – Bosie claimed she never had fewer than fifteen dogs – which included a jaguar brought back from Patagonia, kept on the front lawn on a long chain. Anxious neighbours would watch Florence from a respectful distance, playing with her unconventional pet. Some alarm was caused in September 1879 when it escaped and roamed at large in Windsor forest, killing several deer. Florence was obliged to send it to the zoo.

In 1880 Florence published her first travel book, *Across Patagonia*. It was well received and widely read and Florence looked for more fields to conquer. The first shots of a war with the Boers in Africa had been fired in December of that year and Florence, concerned about her husband's continued heavy gambling and investment losses, saw an opportunity to make some income. She wrote to Thomas Gibson Bowles of *Vanity Fair* – the same man who had tried to dissuade Queensberry from making his damaging public rejection of Christianity – asking him to use his influence to secure her an appointment as a war correspondent, promising that she would 'never shirk danger, fatigue or trouble'.[12] Strings were pulled and Florence was engaged by the *Morning Post*. On 1 February 1881 Queensberry and the Dixies attended a lecture given by Edward Whymper, and on the 17th Florence and her husband sailed for the Transvaal.

By the time the ship docked at Cape Town on 11 March, the war was over and Florence, clearly frustrated, wrote to Bowles complaining that 'there has been little doing . . . on account of this wretched peace'.[13] She was, however, able to meet and interview the Zulu king Cetewayo who was being held in detention. The Dixies returned in the following October, and Florence's next travel book *In the Land of Misfortune* was published in 1882.

Florence had now become that formidable thing, a Douglas with a cause – or, to be more accurate, an offspring of Caroline Clayton with a cause – and her cause was Cetewayo and his restoration to the throne of Zululand. She commenced a vigorous campaign, writing impassioned letters worthy of her mother, but before long she was caught up in a furore that was to cast serious doubts on her veracity. In January 1882 the *Morning Post* published a letter which Florence said had been sent to her by Cetewayo in which he was supposed to have stated that he could not trust Henriquez Shepstone, the man appointed to be his interpreter on a proposed visit to England. Shepstone resigned, letters were written to the press defending him, and Cetewayo responded that he had never written the offending lines. An official inquiry confirmed that there was no such passage in the original letter. Florence was obliged to admit this but said she had inserted the words from another letter of Cetewayo's which she was unable to produce as she had destroyed it. Cetewayo said he had only ever written to her once, and further inquiries showed that the missing letter could not have been sent by the mail Florence mentioned. Florence, it appeared, had tried to influence events by inventing the passage about Henriquez Shepstone.

In 1883 Florence was to strengthen the public perception of the Douglases as a family of eccentrics. When anonymous letters were addressed to the press suggesting that there were irregularities in the funds of the Irish Land League, Florence believed the accusations and demanded an inquiry. The treasurer of the Land League denied irregularities, pointed out that the accounts had been audited by an eminent firm of accountants, and suggested that the letters were malicious. An acrimonious correspondence ensued, but when Florence had become opposed to something she was, like her mother and brother Queensberry, immovable and implacable, and the furore raged on. Members of the Irish National Invincibles – an organisation that had supported the Land League – had assassinated two prominent government officials in Phoenix Park in May 1882. In the following March the murder trial was dominating the news, when it was revealed that on 17 March an attempt had been made to assassinate Lady Florence Dixie. Florence claimed that she had been walking in a shrubbery near the Windsor road, which ran beside her property, when she was assaulted by two men disguised as women: they had thrown her to the ground, crammed her mouth with mud to stop her crying out, and tried to stab her with a dagger. She had been saved from death only by the steel of her stays and the intervention of her faithful St Bernard dog, Hubert. The sound of a passing vehicle had put the assailants to flight.

Messages of sympathy poured in, from nobility, gentry and the Queen herself, while the press, concluding that the attack had been a punishment for Florence's outspoken criticism of the Land League, demanded that its president, Charles Stewart Parnell make an immediate statement. Florence confirmed that she had received threatening letters and thought that the attack was a warning to hold her tongue. Sympathetic visitors arrived, and

Queen Victoria sent her trusted servant John Brown to investigate. It was not long before doubts were expressed. The police scoured the area for clues, but found nothing. The proprietor of nearby Surley Hall Hotel had been close to the Windsor road at the time of the alleged attack, and the Dixies' gardener had been potting geraniums just thirty yards away. Neither had seen or heard anything. When John Yorke, MP made a serious request in the House of Commons for more information on the incident he was greeted with laughter.

As early as 20 March the press chose to disbelieve the story. The charitable explanation was that Florence had fainted, and awoken imagining that she had been assaulted. 'Lady Florence . . . is a woman of romantic and eccentric temperament. She has a vivid imagination.'[14] 'There is,' said the *Birmingham Daily Post*, 'an undercurrent of eccentricity running through the family, which gives evidence of vast amounts of imagination in every one of its members. The Marquis of Queensberry himself has been amply provided with this family gift.' The paper cited the *Promise of May* outburst, which 'astonished us all', mentioned Archibald, who had 'no other eccentricity than an excess of zeal', and Gertrude's marriage.[15] The *Freeman's Journal* said that Florence 'has a public reputation of her own and by her mother . . . . For letter-writing to the newspapers she inherits a taste.'[16] 'The Queensberry family enjoy an almost unique reputation for eccentricity,' commented *The Echo*. 'Every member of it is distinguished by some startling singularity.'[17] This statement was followed by a list of Douglas forebears, in which the unfortunate third marquess and Old Q were prominent.

Florence, said Mr Gallagher, president of the Land League in New York, 'is regarded by the League as a sort of "crank." She keeps repeating lots of false-hoods.'[18] Inevitably the Cetewayo incident was revisited, and parliament was asked 'whether Lady Florence Dixie has on a former occasion hoaxed the public by the fabrication of a letter'.[19] It was perhaps too controversial for any paper to state outright that the entire incident was a publicity stunt cooked up by Florence to add verisimilitude to her campaign against the Land League, but the *Dundee Courier* came close, referring to her story as 'catalogued with those of Baron Munchausen [*sic*]'.[20] When John Brown fell ill on 24 March a rumour arose that he had caught a cold as a result of his visit to the Fishery, and that when he died three days later the Queen blamed this on Florence; however, this was repudiated in a court circular which confirmed that he had died of erysipelas.[21]

Ten days after the alleged attack, a gentleman from Eton, whose name was never published but who was said to occupy a high social position, came forward and made a deposition. He stated that he had been in the neighbourhood at the time of the supposed incident, and that Lady Dixie had been in his sight the whole time. She had been taking a stroll and had not been attacked by anyone. Queensberry chose to believe Florence, and wrote to the press angrily refuting the implications in the Eton gentleman's statement, maintaining that the timings given in the deposition were not incompatible with Florence's account, and accusing the newspapers of publishing false and libellous statements. Archibald wrote a gentler letter of brotherly support to the Catholic *Weekly Register*, but the public, the police and the government had come to the conclusion that there was nothing worthy of inquiry. As with Queensberry, Florence's efforts to promote a cause backfired and damaged her own reputation. She was never again an official correspondent, and her future pronouncements were not treated with the respect she had once enjoyed. She had become another unstable and unreliable Douglas. This incident and the Cetewayo letter together must cast grave doubts on the accuracy of Florence's memoirs. Her high-flown dreamy romantic style and her idealism work well for fiction, but there was a tendency to apply the same gloss to her journalism.

In the wake of these events a satirical piece was published in the magazine *Moonshine*, listing persons to whom the governor-generalship of Canada might have been offered and their reasons for refusing it. A few names inevitably stand out. Mr Bradlaugh: 'His peculiar views on population would be all of no use in Canada'; Queensberry: 'he is too busy just now getting up a book to be entitled "Hallucinations and Affirmations" to be published in the summer'; and Oscar Wilde: 'His time was taken up to a too great extent in curling his hair.'[22]

Queensberry's brother James, Florence's twin was rarely in the news. In 1880 he was declared bankrupt because of a promissory note of £2,000. As the youngest son of the family he might have been expected to enter a profession but there is no indication that he ever attempted to do so. He did, however, write some readable novels. *Royal Angus*, published in 1882, recounts the adventures of a young nobleman in the throes of a hopeless love, who plunges into sporting activities of every kind. *Estcourt: a Novel of Sport and Love* was published in 1883 to faint praise. 'Lord James Douglas has a happy style,' observed the *County Gentleman*. 'His men are gentlemen and his women are charming.'[23] *Vanity Fair* thought 'Lord James Douglas has a very remarkable and very rare talent of describing modern life and the talk of people in modern society as they are'.[24] *The Graphic*, however, while allowing the 'spirit and dash' of the piece to pardon its 'multitudinous' literary shortcomings, felt that its 'prodigious platitudes' and 'milk-and-water reflections' required the firm stroke of an editor's pen.[25] *Queen Mab*, which again mingled sport and love, followed in 1884.

In 1882 the Settled Land Act offered some relief to landowners who had seen a steep decline both in income and in the value of their land, making it possible for them to sell smaller outlying properties though not the core estates. Noblemen started to dispose of uneconomic holdings, which enabled them to clear their debts and invest the remaining proceeds to provide an income. Properties that were expensive to maintain but could neither be sold nor let were simply closed down. In April 1883 Queensberry's estates of Tinwald and Torthorwald, comprising 7,000 acres, were placed on the market. They were finally sold in June 1884 for £220,000.

Kinmount was retained, but it was no longer a family home, and had probably not been regularly occupied as such for some time. Whatever charm the castle and its lands had had for Queensberry in his financially carefree childhood had gone, and it remained a burden for several years to come. Sybil and the children moved to London, first to 67 Cromwell Road, Kensington, where Sybil, Francis, Sholto and Edith were living at the time of the 1881 census (thirteen-year-old Percy and ten-year-old Bosie were then at school in Berkshire), and later 18 Cadogan Place, Belgravia. In the summer they stayed at a country house called the Hut, overlooking the Thames, opposite Monkey Island, in Bray, a few miles from Bracknell in Berkshire. It was 'a picturesque, rambling ranch of a house, larger than its name might imply',[26] capable of accommodating up to twenty-five people. Queensberry occupied a series of lodgings in London before he settled on 24 St James Street, between Pall Mall and Piccadilly. His accommodation consisted of three rooms: a sitting room, a bedroom and a dressing room. He lived alone.

In December 1883 Queensberry was home from his trip to the Continent that had prevented him attending the BSU conference, and back in the saddle, but after dealing with estate business he was keen to be on the move again. A crisis in Bechuanaland, with Boer claims on the territory and a call for military volunteers, seemed the ideal opportunity and it was reported that he had volunteered and that his services were accepted. On 27 November 1884 the mail steamer *Pembroke Castle* carrying 1,000 tons of war stores as well as 300 volunteers including eighty army signallers and balloonists left East India Dock with the early tide. Queensberry was said to be amongst them. The expedition, under the command of Sir Charles Warren, arrived at Cape Town on 19 December and the men signed up for service of six to twelve months. It must be doubted, however, that Queensberry ever arrived at the Cape. He may never have sailed or, if he did he may have become disillusioned, bored or distracted by another impulse, and left the ship at an earlier port. In February 1885 the Scottish peers met to elect new representatives to take the places of two deceased peers. The fact that Queensberry did not attend the voting suggests that he was abroad at that time and may not have known about the election.

Soon he embarked on another, more pleasurable trip, accompanied by his friend, the writer and adventurer Moreton Frewen. On 18 May they arrived in New York where they stayed at Brevoort House Hotel. Queensberry was among the fashionable crowd attending the Jerome Park races, where as the 'brother of Lady Florence Dixey [*sic*], who wrote a delightful book on Patagonia, [he] attracted a great deal of attention'.[27] Referring to his previous trip 'some twelve years ago' and saying he had gone 'as far west as Colorado'* he said that on this occasion, after staying in New York for six or seven days, he intended to 'cross the Continent'. After spending some time with Frewen at his ranch in Wyoming, he would go on to visit Percy, who was then in the Royal Navy stationed at Vancouver Island with his ship, the *Triumph*. Queensberry also intended to visit Sir John Lister-Kaye, an English baronet, in Knights Landing, California. The whole trip would take about six months.

Later, dressed jauntily in light striped trousers and a short jacket, he told a reporter that he had gone to California to buy land, but had given up on the purchase as the distance was too great. 'I had an idea that my sons, in time, might locate in this country. I do not like my own country . . . I am disfranchised, an alien in my own land, and politically dead.' He believed, however, that times in England and Scotland were changing. 'The

---

* He was probably referring to the 1874 trip during which he went to Salt Lake City.

people generally are becoming more liberal in their religious opinions. Prejudice is dying, superstition is being choked by science and progress is on the march. It is only a question of time when bigotry must perish and the true era of reform and progress begin.'[28] The trade depression and falling value of land had often, he said, made him consider coming to America to live permanently. It was probably during this trip that he acquired a property in Vancouver.

He returned to England to find that he was as unpopular as before, and wrote to Rosebery on 21 September: 'I see I am not yet elected to the Reform Club. I was passed over in fact, does that mean being blackballed ... I presume it has something to do with my known religious opinions ... that of course would be extremely bitter to me, I should feel it keenly.'[29] Queensberry's return must have been prompted by the forthcoming general election in November, to be followed by the selection of Scottish representative peers, and he was as anxious as ever to regain his seat in the Lords. On 23 November he sent another letter to Rosebery: it has a serious, official look, as it is not in his own untidy scrawl but the neat writing of another, presumably a clerk, although with Queensberry's signature. He stated that his rejection in the last election 'was based entirely on erroneous and mistaken views as to certain agnostic opinions I hold in common with such men as Mr Herbert Spencer and Professor Huxley' and asked for his eligibility to be reconsidered.[30] Rosebery's response is not known, but subsequent correspondence shows that for the time being the men remained on cordial terms.

The peers met on 10 December 1885 and Queensberry was there to say his piece. He wanted to know how candidates for the sixteen seats were nominated, pointing out that since the great majority of peers were Conservatives, virtually only Conservatives were returned. 'When he was first selected ... no question was asked him as to his political opinions, – indeed he was quite unaware that he was to be selected – and no test was ever applied to him as to his religious beliefs.' He questioned the justice of his expulsion and asked for the opportunity to answer the charge made against him by Lord Lothian.

The mood of the meeting was clear: the peers did not want to hear what Queensberry had to say and shouted for the chair to restore order. When the Earl of Glasgow, who was chairing the meeting, unwisely declared that they could take no notice of anything said in private, Queensberry was obliged to remind him that Lord Lothian's accusation had been made in that room before the peers and the public, and he wanted to reply to it. Glasgow responded that it was not customary to have speeches on such occasions, but Queensberry said it was 'a peculiar case. From the accusations that had been made he had suffered intensely, and he might almost say that through them he had almost become an outcast. He claimed the right to be heard, and if he was refused he would deliver speeches in England and all over the world.' This was greeted with derisive laughter.

Glasgow said they couldn't hear him, and Lord Forbes supported the chair, saying he 'thought the noble Marquis had been sufficiently heard already'. Queensberry repeated his threat to give worldwide speeches 'and lifting his papers, hat, and overcoat, and protesting against the way the noble Lords had treated him, left the room'.[31] The voting proceeded and Queensberry received only one vote, from the Earl of Buchan.

The issue remained a burning one in his mind and he took every opportunity to mention it, inevitably becoming something of a bore on the subject. His outspoken agnosticism offended many, and as the cause held him more strongly in its grip with the passage of time he found it hard to keep it out of his conversation. As a result he was occasionally the butt of false rumours, especially in the satirical and popular press, but he read a wide range of newspapers and was quick to respond to articles that concerned him. 'He addressed Steel, the bookmaker, one day in a railway carriage on the subject of Purgatory,'[32] claimed a theatrical paper, *The Bat*; a story that Queensberry denounced as 'pure fabrication'[33] but, taking the view that any mention in the press was publicity for his cause, he wrote thanking them 'for further advertisement'.[34] He referred *The Bat* to comments in *The Scotsman*, one of the few papers to support him over the election:

> They reject a man's name on the hearsay evidence that he is an atheist; they allow him to begin a statement in which he proposes to prove that the accusation is unfounded, and that, apart from the fact that he is the most deeply religious person present . . . they abruptly cut short his defence . . . his speech on Thursday, if it proved anything, showed that he is possessed of a single-hearted passion for the truth, and a strength of devotional feeling which we do not invariably find amongst professed Christians, or even among representative Peers.[35]

Queensberry also wrote to Herbert Spencer, leaving a copy of the *Secular Review* for him at the Athenaeum. Spencer replied cordially on 22 December thanking him and promising to send Queensberry a copy of his *Ecclesiastical Institutions*:

> I was interested in reading the incidents of your conflict with the Scottish peers as reported in the daily papers, and am glad to have the report of your suppressed speech. Though you are now suffering from the candour and courage with which you have expressed your opinions; you will no doubt hereafter receive a compensatory admiration from many who will see how much you have sacrificed on behalf of truth.[36]

The Queen opened parliament on 21 January 1886. Two days later a report appeared in the *Pall Mall Gazette* claiming that Queensberry had presented himself at the ceremony and passed the police by giving his name, but was stopped by an official at the entrance of the House of Lords and told that he had no right of admission. According to the story, Queensberry had insisted on his right, and the official, appearing to relent, conducted him to the robing room and, once he was inside, closed and locked the door. There the marquess was said to have remained until discovered by the peers returning from the ceremony. On the 28th the *Pall Mall Gazette* was obliged to admit that it had been misinformed.

Queensberry later spoke to Rosebery about the alleged incident, and wrote to him on 30 January to say that the *Gazette* had made him 'a sort of apology & a contradiction of their statement which I had ascertained to be libellous'. He went on: 'However I don't care, it will do me no harm, the insult was to the scotch peers and to the house generally. (Anyone who knows me knows that had such an insult been aimed at me I'd have smashed every window and chair in the place).' It had finally come home to him that his fellow peers were simply not interested in his position and would remain deaf to any appeals: '. . . it mattered not to them whether the statement was true or not,' he said, adding 'I have been unable to ascertain whether I had a right to come into the House or not as a Scotch peer'. He told Rosebery that he had written to two peers, who had not replied, but observed unhappily that no one on the day of the vote had made any protest against the way he was treated.

For all his bluster, Queensberry was undoubtedly hurt by this rejection. It was another pivotal point in his life, turning his personal disavowal of Christianity into outright opposition and hatred, as he now perceived himself as a victim of prejudice and 'a champion against this lying hypocritical superstition of so called Christianity . . . . a monstrous superstition and falsehood which must in time like all these things die'.[37]

Queensberry did not attend any future elections of the Scottish peers. He may have been hoping for what he might realistically have realised was a very remote possibility – an English peerage.

CHAPTER 10

Full of Woes

I N February 1886 Queensberry was officially 'pilled' or blackballed from the Reform Club. He had been proposed by Lord Rosebery and seconded by Lord Kensington, but 'the members of the Reform protest that they do not want in their midst a peer who would destroy all the furniture to prove his belief in nothing at all.' Either Queensberry's comments in his letter of 30 January had been shown to others or the threat of smashing furniture was one he had made before. 'The Marquis is a most unfortunate man,' observed the *Liverpool Mercury*. 'He is not thought fit to be even a representative peer of Scotland. Whenever he enters the theatre he is regarded with suspicion . . . and now he is regarded as too eccentric to be a member of the Reform. The club must draw the line somewhere, and it draws it at the Marquis of Queensberry.'[1]

'. . . in case you did not know,' Queensberry wrote to Rosebery on 15 February, 'they "pilled" me from the Reform the other day which of course has caused me intense delight.' He thanked Rosebery for his support and said there were others who wanted him in: '. . . considering the Christian fanatics I did not do too badly. I suppose it is one more trifle I have to put down to the debit account I owe the Christians.'[2] Whether any 'delight' lasted is questionable. This was another rejection that was bound to fester with time.

In 1886 Queensberry, approaching his forty-second birthday, saw what he must have thought of as his final chance of riding a winner in the Grand National, which was run on 26 March. His second cousin and estate manager Arthur Henry Johnstone Douglas, had bought a hunter, Old Joe, for just £150, but hunted him for only one season, after which he put him in training. Queensberry had ridden Old Joe a number of times, and was anxious to ride him in the National, especially after the horse proved his worth by winning a race at Sandown. Douglas, however, believing that Queensberry was 'past his best in the pigskin',[3] put up a professional jockey instead, and Old Joe won at forty to one. Queensberry was understandably 'rather sore about having been "done out of his chance"'.[4] He retained his interest in the turf – in November he was proposing an institute which would provide benefits for decayed jockeys – but he never raced seriously again. Bosie claimed that a great change came over his father when he gave up riding. 'As long as he went on riding he was comparatively all right in his mind, but when he gave it up . . . his whole character and his brain-power deteriorated. He became very moody.'[5] There were of course numerous other sources of unhappiness, but the thrill of the steeplechase may have been a release from stress.

The next scandal was already brewing. In January 1887 it was announced that the Queensberrys were to divorce. The news seems to have taken the press by surprise. Queensberry was undoubtedly famous as a sportsman and eccentric, but due to his frequent and extended absences abroad and Sybil's quiet and gracious acceptance of her position, very little was publicly known about his personal life. Queensberry had no grounds to divorce Sybil so it was necessary for her to divorce him, but it is almost certain that he was the instigator of the action, volunteering to admit adultery, and she unwillingly acquiesced. The hearing, which would normally have taken place in London, was removed to the Scottish Court of Session, Edinburgh, since the sole grounds were adultery and in Scotland it was not necessary for a wife to cite cruelty in addition.

According to Sybil's adoring Bosie, Queensberry won his wife's agreement to the divorce by wearing her down with 'brutally abusive letters' (unfortunately he did not provide examples),[6] and insulting and exasperating behaviour. 'My father was a madman, and his mania was to persecute my mother,' said Bosie, adding – and one needs the entire quote for balance – 'My mother was and is an angel and a saint, who has never done a wrong thing or thought a wrong thought in her life.'[7] Bosie recounted how on one occasion Queensberry arrived at Sybil's house near Ascot, and turned her and the children out at a day's notice because he wanted to come there for the races with a party of his friends, 'including a certain lady whom it was impossible for my mother to meet'.[8] Sybil had already invited some friends for race week and had to telegraph them to put them all off. Queensberry never made any secret of his affairs; according to Bosie, the final straw was when his father wanted to bring a mistress to the house and proposed that they all lived together under one roof.

There may well be some truth underlying these stories but, given Bosie's tendency to exaggerate, how much is hard to judge. Based on Queensberry's later statements on marriage reform it is possible that what he wanted and may have suggested to Sybil was to live with his mistress as his wife, and with Sybil, for whom he still retained affection, in a harmonious but platonic relationship. Few women would have countenanced such a radical proposal and Sybil was not one of them. Queensberry must have written to his father-in-law about his marital problems, perhaps asking Alfred to persuade Sybil either to divorce him or to agree to his unorthodox suggestion, and Montgomery passed the letter to his great friend, the Prince of Wales. 'I never read such a production in my life!' replied the Prince. 'He, I presume considers himself still a gentleman! The sooner he is put into a Lunatic Asylum the better. He is certainly unfit to go about at large. If I were you I would neither answer or take any notice of the letter . . . . indeed yr poor daughter is greatly to be pitied.'[9] The Prince continued to take an interest in Sybil's happiness and later wrote to Montgomery: 'I rejoice to hear that you found your daughter better and have been able to shield her against her insane husband! It is I think nearly time that he was shut up.'[10]

The divorce petition was heard on Saturday 22 January 1887 before Lord Trayner, and the small court was crowded, with many people unable to obtain admission. Sybil had made her one court appearance the day before, taking the Oath of Calumny, which required her to declare that there had been no arrangement between herself and her husband in bringing the action. The court learned – and this must have been something of a disappointment to the press and public – that the evidence of the principal female witness had already been taken in London as she was unable to be present due to ill health.

There were three witnesses. Sybil's cousin, Major Hugh Montgomery testified that he had been present at the wedding. Thomas Gill a valet said that he had entered Queensberry's service in October 1885 having previously been valet to his brother James for some years. On 22 November Queensberry had instructed him that a lady was to be admitted to his rooms, and that dinner for two with champagne and ice was to be prepared. He was not to admit anyone else. The lady called in the afternoon and she and his employer had dinner. During the course of the afternoon Gill had had occasion to go up to the sitting room and saw the couple dining. Later he cleared away the dinner things and found the room unoccupied. At half past seven he brought up some hot water that had been ordered and trying the bedroom door, found it locked. Queensberry answered from within, asking what he wanted and when Gill said he had brought the hot water his employer told him to set it down outside. Gill returned to the sitting room at eight o' clock, and this time he saw the young lady standing at the bedroom door, the marquess still being inside. Gill let her out of the house at eleven o'clock. The lady called again on the following day and the same events occurred, with the exception that on this occasion he had walked into the bedroom with the hot water and found both the marquess and the lady there.

Gill had seen the lady again at the beginning of April 1886 when His Lordship returned from a fishing trip in the north. The lady's hat was in the sitting room but the lady and the marquess were in the bedroom. She had dined again with the marquess on 15 October and they had been in the bedroom together.

William Huckings had been valet to Queensberry until 8 May 1885. He had admitted the same lady to his master's rooms on several occasions and had seen her and the marquess together in the bedroom. Both Huckings and Gill had been present when the witness made her statement in London, and both identified her as the lady they had admitted to the marquess's rooms. Queensberry offered no defence. The divorce was granted and he was ordered to pay the costs.

But who was Queensberry's mistress? The divorce papers name her as Mabel Gilroy, residing at 217 Hampstead Road, London, and also refer to 'other women one or more whose names and places of residence were unknown to the Pursuer'.[11] Mabel Gilroy, almost certainly not her real name, was probably an actress in Queensberry's favourite genre, musical theatre.* Number 217 Hampstead Road in 1891 was a family home with two households, comprising seventeen residents in all, and may have been Mabel's temporary lodging in 1887.

When the critic John Ruskin remarked that he would like to see Scotland ruled by a king, proposing, in the words of a popular song of the period, 'a

---

* A Mabel Gilroy was appearing at the Coventry Opera House in 1903.

Douglas tender and true', a wag calling himself 'Ixion' enquired as to whether the newly divorced Queensberry was the 'tender and true' Douglas to whom Ruskin referred. Queensberry replied in the pages of the *Pall Mall Budget*:

'Ixion' seems to imply that because a person has been divorced he can be neither tender nor true any longer. I am quite aware that prejudice must still for long affect divorced people, and indeed cast a slur upon them that they are no longer quite respectable. Does it, or may it not now, strike 'Ixion' when I suggest to him that fearful and timid natures may be forced to prefer the lie to the truth – to prefer infidelity in marriage to an honourable and open dissolution of it, and to avoid the odium attached to divorce by still seeking the protection of a guilty wedlock which exists in name only? May not a divorced person be an exceptionally truth-loving nature, who hated any compromise with his or her conscience, and therefore welcomed a divorce, however painful it might be, as under our existing laws in this country the only escape from an unbearable and cruel position? I consider infidelity to one's husband or one's wife, when they are living together as such, a disgusting crime; then why force people to commit it when it has become no longer possible for them to live together as man and wife? Don't be a hypocrite, dear 'Ixion,' and throw stones and mud. We are all living in glass houses: you might smash some of your own windows, you know. I have no ambition to be King of Scotland.[12]

Bosie was later to claim that society turned its back on his father, and there were undoubtedly many worthy religious and respectable persons who would not have wished to associate with him. The feeling must have been mutual. A gregarious man, Queensberry may have decided that he would no longer hammer on the doors of clubs that would not have him, but enjoy the company in those where he was welcome. In the boxing fraternity he was, after all, still 'game and plucky Lord Queensberry'.[13] At a tournament held in Islington in April 1888, 'The announcement that the Marquis of Queensberry would be referee was alone an attraction.'[14] He was also a welcome guest at celebrations held by theatrical companies. Outwardly, he may have seemed to be living an unfettered and carefree existence, but his deep underlying unhappiness was apparent to his close friends.

Shortly after the divorce Queensberry was in Monte Carlo. Moreton Frewen was there and wrote 'Q. is here, too, full of woes.'[15] In March

Queensberry went on to Paris where he took lessons in a French martial art, *savate*, a form of kick-boxing. It was probably on his return later that month that he wrote an affectionate and rather wistful letter dated 'Thursday 24th':

> My Dear Bosie
> I daresay a tip will be acceptable, so I send you a cheque for £20 as I have some spare cash. Have not heard of or from you for ever so long.

After encouraging Bosie to improve his handwriting he mentions the trip to Monte Carlo and Paris and that he is thinking of going back to Paris for a fortnight for more lessons in *savate*. He was also planning 'another globe trot',[16] starting on 15 April, travelling to America in the company of some friends, and taking a look at his property in Vancouver before going on to Japan and coming home via India where he would call in on Percy.

Percy changed his mind about India and sailed for America instead. If Queensberry did make his 'globe trot', his departure was delayed. On 28 April he attended the 200th performance of *Dorothy*, an opera in which the lead role was sung by the graceful and charming Marion Hood, followed by a supper and ball held by the comic actor Fred Leslie's company. Queensberry was back in England for the Brighton season in October, and the next months were mainly spent in sporting circles.

He was not entirely free of obligations, as the Scottish courts had fixed an annual sum he was to pay for support of Sybil and education of the children. The allowance was due twice a year, but the payments were frequently late; always, according to Bosie, who said that Sybil had to initiate legal proceedings to obtain the money, which he described as deliberate 'torture'.[17] Despite Bosie's claims, there were no obvious signs of Sybil being short of funds. While still based in fashionable Cadogan Place, she was spending her summers at the Hatch, a seventeenth-century manor house near Melksham in Wiltshire, surrounded by elegant gardens and affording views of Salisbury Plain.

Queensberry's brother James had given up writing books about the pain of lost love, a subject that reflected his own unfocused life. In 1885 his engagement to Maud Mackenzie, youngest daughter of the late Edward Mackenzie Esq. of Fawley Court, Henley-on-Thames, was broken off, for reasons that can only be guessed at, but based on subsequent events it is probable that by then James had become a heavy drinker. James next turned his amorous attentions to Mabel Edith Scott, daughter of the late Sir Claude Edward Scott, Bt. James's repeated proposals of marriage were refused, and became so oppressive that Mabel's anxious mother sought a court order for the protection of her daughter. In April 1887 an injunction was granted restraining James, who was nearly thirty-two, from having any communication with eighteen-year-old Mabel. James repeatedly breached the injunction and there were further court hearings. Undeterred, he sent Mabel a Christmas card, the nature of which was considered to be 'at the least in bad taste'.[18]

In May 1888 James was arrested and brought before Mr Justice Chitty, charged with contempt of court. His counsel stated that James wished to 'express his profound sorrow for the acts complained of' and promised that it wouldn't happen again. Chitty, describing the Christmas card as 'an insult to any lady or any woman in any position of life',[19] committed James to prison. He was released in June. This prompted the *Aberdeen Journal* to publish an article headed 'The Eccentricities of the Douglases'. The *Promise of May* incident was dredged up again, with the comment that Queensberry's career 'as a secularist lecturer and pamphleteer, exhibits the literary taste which seems to run in the family'.[20] Other newspapers too, ignoring Queensberry's popular, worthy and conventional immediate forebears and any characteristics that might have descended though the female line, attributed all family peculiarities to the Douglases: 'there seems to be something untameable in the Douglas blood which makes this special branch of the family almost as incapable of discipline as was the original Black Douglas himself'.[21]

On 4 September 1888 at the Catholic Church in Hawick, James married Martha Lucy Hennessey, a thirty-four-year-old widow with four children. His family must have hoped that marriage would give him the happiness and stability he needed.

Queensberry did not attend his brother's wedding; he was again abroad. In 1888 the Gaiety theatre company headed by Fred Leslie was preparing to set out on a world tour and Queensberry decided to go with them. A grand ball and supper, which Queensberry attended, was held at the Metropole to bid God-speed to the popular leading actress Nellie Farren and the company. On 28 April they sailed from Plymouth on the Orient Line steamer *Liguria* bound for Australia and calling at Gibraltar, Naples, Suez, Albany, Adelaide and Melbourne, arriving in Sydney on 12 June. The company had a pleasant voyage in good weather, with a great deal of feasting, entertainment and sporting activities on board. On 5 June they gave a concert in which Queensberry performed a song.

Early one morning, while the *Liguria* was anchored at Adelaide, an enterprising reporter from the *South Australian Advertiser* boarded the ship, and finding Fred Leslie asleep in bed woke him up and obtained an interview. He then rapped on Queensberry's cabin door and woke him too. On being told that a reporter was outside hoping to interview him, Queensberry is said to have retorted, 'Oh does he? Well kindly tell him to wait till I get my 3oz gloves on.'[22] The journalist didn't wait.

The 'Marquis of sporting and pugnacious celebrity'[23] was a popular figure in Australia and a biography with a flattering portrait sketch was published in several newspapers. Not everyone was so welcoming. Queensberry was staying at the Imperial Hotel Wynyard Square, Sydney when *The Bulletin* published a satirical article, referring to Florence's encounter with 'some non-existent Fenians' and stating that 'The noble Marquis is chiefly at home in private boxes – pugilistic and theatrical. He dotes on the leg-drama and reveres prize-fighting.'[24] Queensberry replied:

> I have noted your inhospitable impertinent remarks anent myself in your last issue. I see you define me as 'a boisterous Freethinker.' I may, I am sure, return the compliment, and define you as a lying Christian; lies and Christianity go well together. I . . . have never seen but one fight in my life, and would not go across the street to see another, and would much rather fight myself than see others do so, though fond of the art and science of boxing as a manly exercise. . . . I am rather proud of my position as an exiled peer for no other sin but that I am, and hope to remain, an honest man.[25]

At Melbourne Queensberry found himself the idol of the boxing fraternity, although the *Northern Star*, perhaps expecting someone more physically impressive, described him as 'a diminutive dark man with black side levers and very little chest'.[26] When it became known that Queensberry was to referee a fight at the Hibernian Hall on 9 July, the crush of spectators was so enormous that he was unable to enter the hall by the usual entrance: 'he was hoisted on the shoulders of half a dozen men, and having successfully clutched at a window ledge three feet higher up and drawn himself through the aperture, this British peer tumbled on to the platform where the contest between Burke and Slavin was being fought for £200, and forthwith proceeded to act as referee.'[27]

Queensberry also attended the University Ball at Melbourne and scandalised respectable society as 'the leading spirit on the occasion'[28] when he arrived at 11 p.m. with members of the Gaiety Burlesque Company and paid 'marked attention to one of the ladies of the chorus'.[29] Melbourne gentlemen who had been attending carefully chaperoned young ladies were unwise enough to desert their partners and flock to the theatrical party. The young ladies naturally felt slighted, and put on their cloaks to leave. The gentlemen quickly realised their error and returned, but in the eyes of the virtuous chaperones at least, it was too late to rectify matters and the crestfallen gentlemen were obliged to escort the ladies home. The lady to whom Queensberry had been paying his attentions may have been singer Marion Hood, to whom it was reported he was 'wildly devoted'.[30] Miss Hood (born Sarah Ann Isaac) was then thirty-four, and had the physical appearance that Queensberry so admired, tall and slender with abundant fair hair. She was married to a stock-broker, Frederick Beaumont Hesseltine, by whom she had two children, although the fact that she had returned to the stage and undertook overseas tours suggests that the couple had separated. She did not reciprocate Queensberry's ardour.

On 27 October the Gaiety company arrived at San Francisco, and was later to go on to New York. Queensberry probably travelled with them, and was lauded as a sporting figure in New York, where he attended a number of events including a six-day walking match where he gave the starting signal. The *Pall Mall Gazette* suggested that it was a role in which he did not shine, since when the clock struck he hesitated so long over the starting word that someone else had to shout out 'Go'.[31]

In the United States he again found himself reputed to be an atheist and wrote to the newspapers to explain that he was an agnostic, describing himself as 'A most earnest, though humble disciple of Mr Herbert Spencer and Charles Darwin . . . there lives no man upon this earth who ponders and wonders more earnestly than myself in the presence of the eternal evidences of the Eternal Power.' His comments were reported in the English papers, and *The Globe,* probably thinking of his theatrical outburst, commented, 'this is at least in much better taste and tone than some former public utterances of the Marquess'.[32] He also wrote a long letter to the *New York Herald*, describing himself as a 'marked and ostracized' man in England who had, 'both politically and socially, suffered intensely' for daring to express his opinions. Feeling that he would have a better hearing in America he wrote movingly on the subject of marriage and divorce. He believed there should be 'such a thing as an honourable and friendly divorce' in which the couple might remain thereafter on amicable terms if they so wished. It might be thought of as a kind of plural marriage if either party married again. He denied being a Mormon, as he did not believe in polygamy, although he found 'many good things in their system of marriage'. Nevertheless, he stated, Mormon laws were 'not just to women, for they make slaves of them' – although to a lesser extent 'our women are still slaves'.[33] He deplored the Roman Catholic Church's opposition to divorce, which he believed led to hypocrisy, deceit and immorality.

He returned to England before the Gaiety company, sailing on the White Star steamship *Celtic* in May 1889. Discontent seemed to follow him wherever he went. At his lodgings in St James's Street he wrote a miserable letter to Moreton Frewen, whose wife was the sister of Jennie, Lord Randolph Churchill's wife:

Dear Moreton
Pray excuse me & I am rather mixed just now as I am worried to death & I have quite given up going out in what is called English society they don't understand me & I don't care much about them but I would have dined with you I came by and called but was not certain about the days. I will come & call again on your Missus as she was always kind and civil to me. Pray excuse me & did not mean to be rude.[34]

Back in England he plunged into the sporting world. In October, a young muscleman, Eugen Sandow, had caused a sensation at an exhibition of strength by emerging from the audience to challenge and defeat a rising British star known as 'Cyclops'. Cyclops's mentor 'Samson' responded by issuing a challenge to Sandow, and a trial of strength was held at the Royal Aquarium. The judges of this crucial contest needed to be knowledgeable, trustworthy and fair. The men selected were Queensberry and his friend Lord de Clifford. Sandow made an impressive showing and was judged the winner, to enormous popular acclaim. Even the *Aberdeen Journal*, which had deplored Queensberry's religious beliefs, respected his sporting knowledge and published an extended interview with him on the subject of 'Men and Muscle'. The feat of bending a poker, said Queensberry, was not so much about muscle as 'knack'. He thought Sandow 'the superior man. Samson has developed only certain sets of muscles, while Sandow is splendidly developed all over. He stripped the other night at the Pelican Club, and all his muscles were like whip cord.' Queensberry did not think that a man of average strength could train himself to Sandow and Samson's level of accomplishment. 'You must have a sound and powerful man to start with.' Asked if such men would make good boxers, he said: 'for boxing you do not need muscles so much as quickness, dexterity and alertness . . . but Sandow is so alert, so well developed in every way, so loose in the shoulders, that if he ever learned to box I should say he would box very well indeed.'[35] Samson's brother, who performed as Hercules, issued his own challenge to Sandow, and the trial took place eight days later at the Royal Music Hall, Holborn. Queensberry was one of three judges and acted as spokesman. It was a close contest, but the judges, who felt that Hercules had completed his tests more cleanly and easily, awarded him the honours, an unpopular decision. Hercules and Samson took out advertisements commenting that the verdict had been awarded 'by Three Judges whose integrity is beyond dispute'.[36]

In January 1887 a sporting gentlemen's club known as the Star Club had opened in Denman Street near London's Piccadilly Circus. It later moved to larger and more elegant premises in nearby Gerrard Street and was rechristened the Pelican Club after a large stuffed pelican in a glass case on the mantelpiece. The easygoing club accepted members from all walks of life: the aristocracy, tradesmen, actors, journalists, artists and moneylenders, the main qualification being an enthusiasm for sport. The club boasted a large smoking room, and cocktail bar. Its boxing hall was the largest in London, and here gentlemen in top hats and formal evening wear could watch contests held under the Queensberry Rules through a haze of cigar smoke, and there were gymnasiums, changing rooms, a billiards room, dining facilities and bedroom suites. An atmosphere of bohemian and high-spirited good-fellowship reigned. It was the perfect environment for Queensberry, who was an active member. He once brought over a French *savate* master for a demonstration before the Pelicans, and fighter Jim Donahue was matched against the Frenchman. Donahue won, and the experiment was not tried again. Sir Robert Peel (son of the former Prime Minister) liked to invite his sporting friends to an evening of boxing, then entertain everyone, including the contestants, to a champagne party followed by a concert. Queensberry took part on at least one occasion, costumed and made up to look like music hall star Albert Chevalier and singing 'Knocked 'em in the Old Kent Road', 'with,' said sports journalist Robert Watson, 'wonderful and realistic effect. . . . In voice, make up and gesture it was a really marvellous imitation of Albert Chevalier. We all laughed until we nearly cried, the rendering of the song being so irresistibly comic.'[37] Another less complimentary description suggests that Queensberry sang 'with unconsciously comic effect, endowing the coster with all the heavy "hee-haw" manner of a society swell'.[38]

Despite the rowdy and juvenile antics of the Pelicans, who often liked to round off the evening with a food fight, one of the aims of the club was to bring boxing into better repute. It was decreed that contests and betting should be fair, and that fights should not be an excuse for thieving and violence outside the ring.

The writer and editor Frank Harris, a close friend of Oscar Wilde, was a member of the Pelican Club. When in London, Queensberry was there almost every night, and Harris, aware of the *Promise of May* incident, was eager to be introduced to the man 'who could be so contemptuous of convention. Had he acted out of aristocratic insolence, or was he by any possibility high-minded? To one who knew the man the mere question must seem ridiculous.'[39] Although Harris claimed to know Queensberry well, he overestimated his height at five feet nine or ten. The pencil annotations in Bosie's copy of Harris's book on Wilde corrects the description to 'five feet seven in height, broad and strong'.[40] Harris described Queensberry's

plain, heavy rather sullen face, and quick, hot eyes. He was a mass of self-conceit, all bristling with suspicion, and in regard to money, prudent to meanness. . . . He cared nothing for books, but liked outdoor sports and under a rather abrupt, but not discourteous manner, hid an irritable and violent temper. He was combative and courageous as very nervous people sometimes are, when they happen to be strong-willed – the sort of man who, just because he was afraid of a bull and had pictured the dreadful wound it could give, would therefore seize it by the horns.[41]

Queensberry's temper sometimes got him into rows at the Pelican. Harris recounted an incident where Queensberry, determined to pick a fight with a stockbroker called 'Haseltine', repeatedly insulted his quarry, a large man, who refused to be drawn. As the story stands, this was unprovoked senseless antipathy, but could 'Haseltine' have been Frederick Beaumont Hesseltine, the husband of the lovely and unattainable Marion Hood?

Eventually, the frustrated marquess made a run at his prey, who hit out at him, catching him full in the face and 'literally knocking him heels over head'.[42] Queensberry got to his feet, a 'sad mess' his nose swollen and bleeding, his eye blackened.[43] A hasty effort to wipe blood from his shirt front only smeared it around and made matters worse. Harris commented that any other man would either have continued the fight or left the club at once. Queensberry did neither. He 'took a seat at a table, and sat there for hours silent . . . the butt of derisive glances and whispered talk of everyone who came into the club in the next two or three hours'.[44] Harris's only explanation was that Queensberry, suffering an acute impulse to fly from the scene of his disgrace, had decided to resist it. Queensberry, of course, had never run away from a fight, but there was no one who knew better when it was over and he was beaten. What can have been going through his mind in those hours? Harris didn't date the incident which, if true, would have occurred not long after Queensberry abandoned racing. Was it dawning on him that his powers of combat were also on the decline?

In December 1889 a bare-knuckle fight was arranged under the rules of the London prize ring between the English champion Jem Smith and American Frank Slavin that was to bring the Pelican Club to its knees, but would enhance Queensberry's reputation as a fair-dealing sportsman. The location was Bruges, and the audience was to be limited, but the news got out and supporters, some of whom were Pelicans, arrived in Bruges to find the area swarming with English ruffians. Queensberry was not present at the event, which was accompanied by outbreaks of violence. One of the more unstable Pelicans, the dissolute George Alexander Baird, drew a revolver. On 8 January 1890 Queensberry, then a member of the committee, was at a special meeting of the Pelican Club where a report attempted to exonerate the Pelicans of blame. Queensberry, however, proposed that there should be a further inquiry and after some discussion the meeting voted to refer Baird's behaviour to the committee for a report. The committee, with the exception of Queensberry, saw this as a vote of no confidence, and resigned as a body. *Freeman's Journal* later commented that Queensberry, 'whatever his other eccentricities, seems to be honestly desirous of preserving to the prize ring the only characteristic which in the least degree separates its exhibitions from undiluted savagery'.[45] The *Birmingham Daily Post*, stating that Queensberry 'has a special title to speak upon matters of fisticuffs,'[46] gave Queensberry the credit for frustrating the committee's attempt to whitewash everyone concerned in the Bruges fight. Queensberry later claimed he had no idea his amendment would conflict with the committee's original report and withdrew it. The old committee was reinstated and Baird was expelled but took out an injunction against the club. This was heard on 28 February at a meeting to which Queensberry gave evidence. Asked to swear on the Bible he said, 'I do not wish to make a scene, but my principles are well known.'[47]

He was allowed to affirm, and handed in his original notes on the affair, which stated that Baird's behaviour was 'a disgrace to the Pelican Club and the sense of justice and fair play of the whole of England'.[48] Baird lost his case, but the reputation of the Pelicans had suffered a fatal blow. The Pelican's neighbours took out an injunction claiming that the activities of the club and its patrons created a noise nuisance. They were successful and the conditions imposed spelled the end of the club, which was obliged to close. From the ashes of the Pelican, however, there arose the National Sporting Club, established by a former member of the Pelican committee, the fifth Earl of Lonsdale; this club completed the process of gaining acceptance for boxing as a sport which Queensberry had commenced. Queensberry along with many other Pelicans did not join the more respectable National Sporting Club, but formed their own offshoot, the Barn Club.

Ever since his visit to Salt Lake City Queensberry had been thinking about the reform of marriage and divorce laws. He may well have bored his friends with the subject but made few public statements until his 1889 letter to the *New York Herald*, which was not reported in England. Later that year he wrote to the *Pall Mall Gazette* concerning the case of Florence Maybrick, who had been found guilty of poisoning her husband. While Florence's supporters were ardently claiming she was innocent, Queensberry was less interested in the verdict than in the position of the woman in an unhappy marriage. With a strong-minded mother and sister, he was more willing than most men of his generation to sympathise with a woman's point of view.

Appealing for mercy he wrote,

I myself have the deepest sympathy and pity for this unhappy woman. If indeed she has committed this murder a terrible crime has been committed no doubt, but behind it exists another crime as horrible and as unnatural ... unhappy marriages that could not be dissolved are the frequent causes of atrocious murders and ... no woman should be coerced to go on living with a man as his wife when such a terrible calamity had come upon him that he was loathsome and hateful to her.[49]

Writer and theosophist Mabel Collins wrote to the *Pall Mall Gazette* to thank Queensberry for pointing out the 'social and legal crime' that had resulted in the Maybrick tragedy. 'It seems strange that it is a man who points this out, when so many women know it; but it comes at the outset with a better grace from a man, and therefore I feel that we women who agree with the Marquis of Queensberry should thank him publicly.'[50]

In 1890 General William Booth of the Salvation Army published *In Darkest England* to raise public awareness of poverty, unemployment and homelessness. In it he suggested the formation of self-helping and self-sustaining communities, to supply the necessities of life and give employment. There was an immediate public response, and subscriptions poured in. To the great surprise of many, one of the subscribers was Queensberry, who wrote to Booth from Glenlee, New Galloway, Dumfriesshire on 21 November, enclosing a cheque for £100 and offering, if the scheme was carried out, a yearly subscription. Queensberry said he had read Booth's book 'with the greatest interest, also with thrills of horror that things should be as bad as they are.... You say you want recruits. When I come to town I should very much like to see you to talk this matter over, for I see no cause in which a man could more put his heart and soul into than this one of endeavouring to alleviate this fearful misery of our fellow creatures.' Queensberry made no bones about the fact that he was

no Christian and am bitterly opposed to it. A tree, I believe, is to be judged by its fruits. Christianity has been with us many hundreds of years. What can we think of it when its results are as they are at present with the poor, whom Christ, I believe you say, informed us we should always have with us? ... It appears to me our common and plainest duty to help and try to change the lot of our suffering fellow creatures.[51]

Addressing a meeting at Exeter Hall on 24 November, Booth stated that he had been reproached for accepting money from a professed opponent of Christianity, but said that he would take money from anyone to help him in his work, for not only would it help him benefit humanity but it would enable him to get at the heart of the marquess himself.

In January 1891 Charles Bradlaugh died at the age of fifty-seven, and Queensberry attended the funeral on 3 February. Henry Labouchère was there, as was journalist John Boon with whom Queensberry had a conversation; a trivial incident, but one which Boon later recalled. He was to play his own minor but crucial role in the Wilde scandal.

At the 1891 census Queensberry was a visitor at the home of retired Colonel John Edward Varty Rogers, his wife and two daughters. Another visitor was thirty-seven-year-old Edith Courtenay and she may well have been Queensberry's mistress. Edith Courtenay had enjoyed a successful acting career since the 1870s, appearing as the lead in both drama and light comedy, and touring major cities in England and Ireland. She was acclaimed for her intelligent and realistic interpretation of roles, the power and earnestness of her depiction, a graceful and refined delivery and a sweet voice. In March 1891 she had just completed an extensive tour. Little more is known about Edith, whose career faded over the next few years, but she seems to have been an accomplished woman. Happiness for Queensberry was, however, a fleeting thing and his private thoughts were hard to bear. He lost another admired friend when Fred Leslie died of typhoid fever in London on 7 December 1892 aged thirty-seven. Queensberry was at the funeral, 'deeply moved in spite of outward calm'.[52]

Queensberry once asked Annie Besant, formerly a close friend of Bradlaugh, the reason for all his sorrows in life. Mrs Besant, who had moved away from secularism after embracing theosophy, told him it was 'the result of karma'.[53] Queensberry, it seemed, was destined to be unhappy.

CHAPTER 11

Four Sons and a Daughter

As a father, Queensberry must have been a source of ambiguity and confusion to his offspring, the children who by his own lights carried on the existence of his soul. Although absent for most of their upbringing he remained a distant presence whose activities were constantly reported in the newspapers. A source of notoriety and money, he would visit them infrequently, correspond occasionally and hover over the family like some rumbling unpredictable cloud that might either storm or reveal sunshine. 'As a boy I adored my father,' wrote Bosie in 1929, 'and looked up to him as a wonderful man of almost legendary prowess as a sportsman and a fighter. My intense admiration of my father was doubtless not at all impaired, but on the contrary greatly increased, by the fact that I hardly ever saw him.'[1]

Bosie's complaint was not ill-treatment, but neglect. 'He did nothing for us boys,' he commented. 'When he saw us he was generally good-natured and kindly, but he never lifted a finger to teach, admonish or influence us in any direction.'[2] In later years Bosie recognised the effect that the lack of fatherly guidance had had on his life. 'My mother's spoiling would not have harmed me if my father had been a real father, and had ever taken half as much interest in his children as he did in his dogs and his horses,' he observed.[3] Queensberry, despite knowing what it was to lose a father early, could not bring himself to spend more time with his family, and Bosie never understood the deep-seated wretchedness that kept him away. 'All through my childhood and youth the shadow of my father lay over me,' said Bosie, who was unable to reconcile his love and admiration for Queensberry with what he saw as 'his infamous treatment'[4] of Sybil.

Nevertheless, the boys enjoyed a happy childhood on the Scottish estate, educated by a succession of governesses, riding their ponies and playing with wooden swords, shields and spears. Sybil had been brought up as a Protestant, but although the Douglases were regular churchgoers, she passed on no religious teaching to her children.

One of Queensberry's constant concerns was that his sons should be able to support themselves financially, since a son with no source of income would be obliged to rely on his father. The only one of his four sons who never gave him any anxiety on that score was his eldest.

Francis Viscount Drumlanrig, or 'Francie', as he was affectionately known,[5] was a son to be proud of. Short and with the prominent Clayton nose like his father, in personality he was more like his namesake uncle, good-natured, considerate and well-mannered, with an engaging sense of humour. At the age of ten, he was sent to a private school, Lambrook, in Berkshire, which, said Bosie, was '"classy" . . . chiefly populated by sprigs of the nobility'. Francis went from Lambrook to Harrow (against the wishes of his father who wanted him to go to a Scottish school) and thence to the Royal Military College, Sandhurst. The eleventh marquess described Francis as 'a highly nervous boy with considerable charm but no great intelligence'.[6] This may be doing him a disservice, since if Francis was no soaring intellect he made up for this by application to his studies and did well enough in his education to establish a reputation as a young man of merit.

In June 1887, aged twenty, Francis was appointed second lieutenant in the Coldstream Guards, serving with the second battalion stationed at Windsor. His ultimate ambition, however, was for a career not in the military, but in public service. Like his grandfather, he wanted to go into politics. Queensberry must have been delighted when Lord Rosebery took an interest in the boy. Rosebery, who had served as foreign secretary in Gladstone's 1886 administration, was already looked upon as a future Prime Minister. In 1878 he had married Hannah, daughter and sole heiress of the Jewish banker Baron Meyer Amschel de Rothschild and the couple had four children. Although the friendly correspondence between Rosebery and Queensberry appears to have lapsed following the divorce from Sybil, Rosebery did not let any antipathy he felt for the father affect his mentoring of the son. In 1890 when Francis was engaged in musketry training at Pirbright Camp he spent his spare moments studying papers on the Home Rule question which Rosebery had lent to him. Francis, who had thoughtfully had a brown paper cover put on the papers, later wrote to Rosebery to say that he had 'found material in them to last me some time', adding that the documents 'furnished me with material for most animated discussions'[7] with the captain of his company, who was an Irish landlord.

In September 1890 Francis was promoted to lieutenant, but that month he left Windsor, and moved to London where he took rooms in Sloane Street. Later he went to live with his grandfather Alfred Montgomery, who was devoted to him. Francis's name began to appear regularly in lists of those gracing royal levees and society dinners, where his natural charm ensured popularity. Probably not destined for greatness, his quiet diligence, good disposition and the family connection with Rosebery were more than enough to ensure his progress. In November 1892 Rosebery, then Secretary of State for Foreign Affairs in Gladstone's fourth administration, appointed Francis to be one of his assistant private secretaries, and it was rumoured that he was being considered as a future candidate for parliament. Rosebery, it was said, liked to gather 'smart young men' about him,[8] and Francis was one of those smart young men. His career was a model of which any father could be proud.

The same, unfortunately, could not be said of the younger sons. Percy had a cheery affectionate nature and a sunny optimism that were eventually to lead him seriously astray. According to Bosie, who called him by the pet name 'Turts', he was 'the kindest-hearted and sweetest-tempered man I ever met',[9] although Percy, like his father, could also snap under pressure. Percy had always been especially fond of Bosie, and until separated by schooling they paired up in almost every recreation. The two brothers remained emotionally close for the rest of their lives.

Destined for the navy, Percy was sent to school in Portsmouth, and joined HMS *Britannia* as a cadet on 15 January 1882, studying mathematics, navigation, French and drawing. He was a good but not exceptional student. In an examination in December 1883 he came sixteenth out of thirty-two and was awarded a second-class certificate. His ability was stated to be 'fair' and conduct 'v good'.[10] Percy also earned a second-class certificate in seamanship coming eighteenth in his class. He was appointed to HMS *Alexandra* on the Mediterranean station and on 15 June 1884 was promoted to midshipman. A report dated December 1884 describes his general conduct as good, ability and professional knowledge as fair, and habits temperate. Despite this, Captain Rawson remarked, 'Weakly, & I should not think of strong intellect.'[11]

In December 1884, Percy was appointed to the armour-clad HMS *Triumph*, flagship of the Pacific squadron. The ship sailed from Plymouth in February 1885 and on 25 August after calling at Madeira, St Vincent, Montevideo and San Francisco, moored at Constance Cove, Esquimalt, British Columbia. Queensberry understandably took an interest in Percy's naval career, and some years later revealed in a letter that 'I twice went right across the world to see him'. The first of these occasions would have been the American trip in the spring of 1885. Unfortunately, seventeen-year-old Percy was deep in the throes of teenage rebellion, and Queensberry was obliged to step in:

> I on one occasion waited 3 months for him at San Francisco, and then spent 2 months on his ship, and was in perfect misery the whole time at his disgusting position. One admiral said he was not fit to mix with gentlemen, the other that he was damned glad to get rid of him, and when on shore if he was not in hospital I believe bawdy houses were his principal attraction where he used to soak.[12]

It should be noted that this unhappy diatribe was written on 18 May 1895 when Queensberry was enraged with Percy for his support of Bosie over the Oscar Wilde affair; however, Percy was undoubtedly in disgrace, since the *Triumph*'s log records on 2 December 1885 'Placed Midshipman Lord Percy S. Douglas under arrest.'[13] The reason is not given, and there was no trial. Alcohol and gambling may have been involved. On 10 December Percy was 'allowed to withdraw from Service at request of Father. Father paying cost of telegram and passage home. Discharged to shore at Esquimalt.'[14]

Well-meaning, constantly optimistic Percy was never able to settle and apply himself to anything. He undoubtedly shared the family love of travel, and his next project was to learn ranching in north-west Canada. He soon gave up this idea, bought a horse and made his way to the borders of Alberta and Montana. Here he managed a roadside house, his customers according to his own account being 'whisky smugglers, miners and cowboys'.[15] He was his own master but that meant having to do all the work, including the cooking and cleaning. This was hardly going to last, and he returned to England.

His despairing father next decided that Percy should enter the army. This was very much against Percy's inclinations, but he accepted it. Percy's naval education was unsuitable for an army appointment so Queensberry arranged for intensive coaching and Percy was sent to Cornwall with a tutor. Why he chose Cornwall is unknown but he may have felt that it was far away from the temptations that had put an early end to his son's naval career. While in Cornwall, Percy became acquainted with the vicar of Boyton, Reverend Thomas Walters, whose daughter Anna Maria, known as 'Minnie', was three years Percy's senior. In February 1889 Percy was appointed second lieutenant of the 3rd Battalion King's Own Scottish Borderers, but his heart was not in it, and he made no real attempt to succeed in his second military career. According to Queensberry, Percy 'failed for the Army, then refused to go on trying'.[16]

Already Percy was drifting towards the alcoholism that was to affect the rest of his life. In 1890 he was living at Ogbeare Hall near Holsworthy in Devon, going through a course of army training, when on 23 February he and three other students lunched at the Stanhope Hotel. That afternoon a constable saw him returning to his quarters on horseback, riding at a furious pace. The constable tried to stop the horse but Percy prevented this by urging on his mount with a stick. Realising that the horseman was drunk, the constable followed him out of town to the foot of a hill where horse and rider both fell. Percy scrambled up and remounted, but had not gone far before he tumbled off the horse. The constable caught up with him and said that the offence would be reported. Percy promptly threw off his hat and coat and challenged the constable to a fight. The constable cautioned him and Percy struck him on the shoulder. By now a crowd of spectators had gathered, one of whom intervened, calmed Percy down and had him taken home in a carriage. After failing to respond to the initial summons on charges of 'drunkenness whilst in change of a horse' and assaulting a policeman,[17] a subdued Percy finally appeared at Holsworthy Petty Sessions on 17 April 1890, where he said he was very sorry and that he 'had taken too much champagne and lost control of himself'.[18] He was fined £5 with £2 costs.

Percy and Minnie had become romantically attached and were eager to marry, but dared not tell Queensberry. Even Percy realised that a series of failed careers was not a sound basis for marriage, and must have known that his father would never approve until he could support himself. Once again he looked abroad to make his fortune. In 1892 Percy went to Ceylon (now Sri Lanka), seeking opportunities in the flourishing tea industry. Here he met twenty-one-year-old David Wynford Carnegie, youngest son of the ninth Earl of Southesk, who was working on a plantation. Carnegie gave up the idea after a few months – and Queensberry alleged that Percy was 'chucked out again neck and crop'[19] – and the pair of adventurers decided to try their hand in the goldfields of Western Australia. With a joint capital of 30 shillings they sailed on SS *Ophir*, which arrived at Sydney on 5 October and Albany on the 29th.* In Albany the friends learned that prospector Arthur Bayley had recently found gold at Coolgardie. The little mining town was then hardly more than an encampment, hot and dusty, with both food and water in short supply. While Carnegie was roughing it Percy went to the rather more civilised environment of Southern Cross, 'trying to carry through some business by which our coffers might be replenished'.[20] To his credit, when Percy heard that Carnegie was virtually starving he hurried back to Coolgardie with supplies of tinned food. They pegged out a claim together, work began, 'and here', wrote Carnegie, 'we spent several months busy on our reef, during which time Lord Douglas went home to England, with financial schemes in his head',[21] leaving Carnegie and a new associate to work the land as best they could.

Percy sailed from Albany on the RMS *Austral* on 11 February 1893 and arrived in England full of optimistic plans for his mining ventures, but this was far from being a settled career or an assured income. He was starting a long involvement in finance for most of which time he would be in debt.

Alfred, Sybil's blue-eyed, golden-haired, pink and white complexioned favourite 'Boysie', was unfortunate enough to inherit both the delicate beauty and cultural tastes of his mother and the uncontrollable temper and obstinacy of his father. The personalities that had been so ill matched in marriage were even more violently conflicted and ultimately destructive when rooted in one individual. 'That flower-like sort of beauty must have been a horrible handicap to you,' George Bernard Shaw once wrote to Bosie: 'it was probably Nature's reaction against the ultra-hickory type of your father.'[22] Oscar Wilde was to write to Bosie of 'that dreadful mania you inherit from your father, the mania for writing revolting and loathsome letters; your entire lack of any

---

* Carnegie's memoirs suggest a September arrival but these dates are as per the shipping registers accessed via Ancestry.com

1 Queensberry's great uncle Charles, the popular sixth marquess, builder of Kinmount Castle, is pictured at a ball at Almack's Assembly rooms in 1815. He is the jolly looking man seen on the far left, enjoying the scene.

2 Kinmount Castle, Scottish home of the Marquesses of Queensberry was built in 1812 at a cost of £40,000. This 1823 illustration shows the castle without the decorative urns and balustrades, which were not added until 1899.

3 Glen Stuart, the cottage nestling in the woodlands of the Kinmount estate, traditionally the Scottish residence of the marquess's heir and his family.

4 The parish church of Cummertrees where the Douglas family worshipped, and where Queensberry and his siblings were christened in 1855.

5 The Queensberry enclosure at Cummertrees parish church, burial place of the marquesses and their family until 1891.

6 Queensberry's mother, the Dowager Marchioness Caroline, pictured in 1874 aged 54. Queensberry inherited her short stature, dark hair, prominent nose and passionate campaigning nature.

7 John Graham Chambers, an all-round sportsman, was Queensberry's friend at Cambridge University. Chambers founded the Amateur Athletic Club in 1866, which introduced a boxing tournament in 1867 under the Queensberry Rules which were mainly drafted by Chambers.

8a and b Sketches by the mountaineer Edward Whymper of Queensberry's younger brother, Lord Francis Douglas (*above*), and of the Matterhorn (*left*), made in 1865 shortly before the tragic events on the mountain.

9 Alfred Montgomery, father of Sybil Marchioness of Queensberry, as a handsome young society dandy in 1839.

10 Queensberry and Sybil Montgomery, a double portrait taken on the occasion of their engagement in 1865.

11 Queensberry in 1868 aged 24 when he was still the popular young sporting lord.

12 A young, slender Queensberry in riding habit.

13 Queensberry's sister, Lady Florence Dixie was an author, traveller, and outspoken campaigner for women's suffrage and Home Rule for Ireland. When portrayed in the *Whitehall Review* in January 1877 21 year old Florence was best known as a fearless horsewoman.

14 Cartoon of Queensberry aged 33, by 'Spy', captioned 'A Good Light Weight' published by *Vanity Fair* in 1877.

15 Francis Archibald Douglas, Viscount Drumlanrig, Queensberry's eldest son and heir born in 1867 is pictured in 1890 in the uniform of the Coldstream Guards before he decided on a political career.

16 Cartoonist Phil May made a series of sketches of sporting subjects at the Pelican Club. This affectionately satirical portrait of Queensberry shows him with boxing 'On the Brain'. Note the Pelican symbol.

17 *Moonshine*, a humorous weekly periodical published a series of illustrations entitled 'Days with Celebrities'. This dates from 1893.

18 Lord Percy Sholto Douglas, Queensberry's second son and later tenth marquess.

19 Lord Alfred Douglas (Bosie), February 1894, a portrait dedicated to Oscar Wilde.

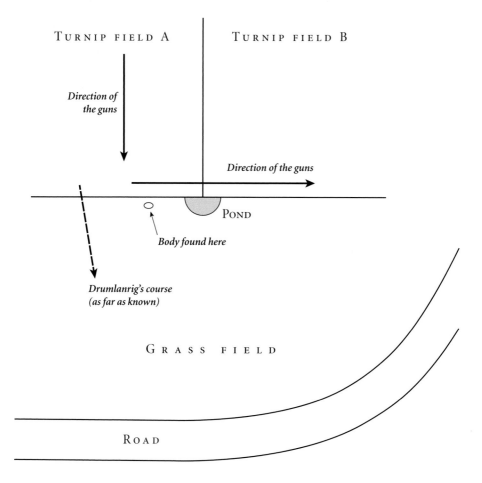

20 The location of the death of Francis Viscount Drumlanrig on 18 October 1894, from a contemporary sketch. It shows where he was last seen entering the grass field which was separated from the turnip fields by a bramble hedge, and the position of the body.

POST OFFICE TELEGRAPHS.

No. of Telegram............

Office Stamp.

If the accuracy of an Inland Telegram be doubted, the telegram will be repeated on payment of half the amount originally paid for its transmission, any fraction of 1d. less than ½d. being reckoned as ½d.; and if it be found that there was any inaccuracy, the amount paid for repetition will be refunded. Special conditions are applicable to the repetition of Foreign Telegrams.

Charges
to pay

£ s. d.

Handed in at the *Piccadilly* Office at 10 27 M. Received here at 10 45 M.

TO { Lord Douglas 31 St Philips Rd
Surbiton

Letters refused must telegraph until wicked accusation of causing scandal withdrawn shall stop Extra allowance also. now feel justified in publishing to friends and relations hideous story of a at

N.B.—This Form must accompany any inquiry made respecting this Telegram.

POST OFFICE TELEGRAPHS.

No. of Telegram............

Office Stamp.

If the accuracy of an Inland Telegram be doubted, the telegram will be repeated on payment of half the amount originally paid for its transmission, any fraction of 1d. less than ½d. being reckoned as ½d.; and if it be found that there was any inaccuracy, the amount paid for repetition will be refunded. Special conditions are applicable to the repetition of Foreign Telegrams.

Charges
to pay

£ s. d.

Handed in at the Office at M. Received here at M.

TO { (2)

Oxford which up until now have suffered and not told a soul not drew you unless you instantly retract. Queensberry

N.B.—This Form must accompany any inquiry made respecting this Telegram.

21 Telegram from Queensberry to Percy on 16 February 1895 threatening to tell family and friends about Bosie's Oxford scandal.

22 The card that brought matters to a head. Queensberry's card 'For Oscar Wilde posing somdomite [*sic*]' left at the Albemarle Club on 18 February 1895.

23 Two newspaper sketches of Queensberry in the dock of the Old Bailey during his trial for libel in April 1893. These are rare pictures of him middle-aged and hatless.

24 A cartoon by 'Quiz' of Mr Justice Henn Collins, who presided over Queensberry's trial for libel in 1895.

25 Queensberry's youngest son, Sholto George born in 1872, shocked society and was widely featured in American newspapers, when he married a singer, Loretta Addis, in California in 1895.

26 In 1895 Queensberry and his son Percy were at loggerheads over Percy's support for Oscar Wilde. On 21 May a chance encounter on Piccadilly led to a fist fight. This artist's impression is from the *Illustrated Police News*.

27 The private burial ground on the Kinmount estate, first established in 1891. The final resting place of James Douglas, Lady Florence Dixie, John Sholto and their mother Caroline.

control over your emotions, as displayed in your long resentful moods of sullen silence, no less than your sudden fits of almost epileptic rage'.[23]

It was a similarity that Bosie was never fully to recognise. In his 1929 *Autobiography*, which often degenerates into a self-justifying whine – the most 'constant cross'[24] he had to bear in his life was, apparently, being born a lord without money – he characterised his father as 'entirely self-centred ... utterly selfish', having been 'from his early youth used to having his own way about everything',[25] whereas he described himself as a generous, selfless and giving person, traits he said he inherited from his mother. His nephew the eleventh marquess saw him very differently, as 'arrogant and full of self-pity ... with an unintelligent egoism which caused him to be totally unaware of the rights of anyone save himself'.[26]

Bosie's first school was Lambrook in Berkshire, where he stayed for a year; after its closure he was moved to Wixenford School, Wokingham, together with Sholto. Bosie was nearly fourteen when he went to Winchester. He and his mother both wanted him to go to Eton but, according to Bosie, Queensberry 'stopped it at the last moment, and said he would not have any of his sons turned into "Belgravian loafers"'.[27] Bosie claimed that his father knew nothing about Eton or any public school, but it should be recalled that Queensberry's father was educated at Eton, and chose not to send his heir there. Bosie added, and there is considerable truth in this, that his father's 'prejudices once formed were as utterly insurmountable as they were often unreasonable'.[28] Nevertheless, Bosie took great pride in his father's sporting achievements. While at Winchester 'one of my favourite occupations was looking up the old numbers of *The Field* newspaper ... for records of races ridden by my father in the sixties and seventies'.[29]

Often angered by his father's sudden changes of mind, Bosie was a volatile and contradictory creature himself. In *Without Apology* (1938) he repudiated *Oscar Wilde and Myself*, which he had written in 1914. Telling the truth about his relationship with Wilde in 1914 would have been a more sensitive matter than it was in 1938 but it might also be argued that if he was unable to tell the truth it would have been better not to have written the book at all. The fact that he was willing to go into print with what he later admitted was lies makes it hard to assess anything he wrote subsequently. In *Without Apology* he expressed surprise that readers of his autobiography published nine years earlier in which he described Winchester school as 'like that of *Tom Brown's*

Schooldays ... an awful place ... a sink of iniquity' with its very own Flashman figure,[30] had gained the impression that he had been unhappy there. In 1938 he wrote 'my whole life at Winchester was one long joyous "rag"' and his 'most enchanting dream . . . is that I am still there'.[31] At the age of sixteen he experienced his first 'violent mutual attraction'[32] to another boy. Although many of his friendships at Winchester and Oxford were not of a sentimental nature and some were sentimental but 'perfectly pure and innocent',[33] there were, he said, others that were neither.

Both Winchester and Oxford encouraged physical recreation to build the healthy physique and moral character of the youthful elite. Bosie was not, on his own admission, much of a cricketer or footballer, but at the age of sixteen he won a cross-country steeplechase. As he breasted the tape and fell on the grass, he saw his brother Sholto bending over him saying 'Bravo Bosie.'[34] Sholto was at a private school in Winchester and had come over for the day to watch the race. When Queensberry heard of Bosie's win he sent him £5.

How often Queensberry wrote to his schoolboy sons is unknown; however, this chatty letter, undated, but written during Bosie's Winchester days survives.

My dearest Bosie

This week is Epsom the Derby & Oaks & I shall be down both days although I rarely go racing now except to see these big races but I will try and run down and see you after that either after or before Ascot.

It is hardly weather for cricket but I have not touched a bat yet & indeed I do not know that I have the spirits or the possibility to begin playing again but if I begin practising & find I am in any form I will come down & play at Winchester that is to say if I do play in any matches at all. But I fear I am getting too ancient for cricket now and as I should be particularly anxious to make runs should be sure not to get any that was always my way if I was particularly keen generally got out first ball.

If I came down for a couple of days should I be able to get any practice with you ? . . .

Give my best love to Sholto, I enclose a fiver give him two sovs.

Your affectionate father Queensberry[35]

Although Bosie often said that he hardly ever saw his father, he did recount many anecdotes of time spent with him in his childhood and youth. Having been brought up by French nurses he always, even as an adult, called his father 'Papa' pronounced in the French way.

> I used to stay with him occasionally in some lodgings which he occupied from time to time at Brighton in Oriental Place. He was an embarrassing person to be with because he had a disconcerting way of not listening to and completely ignoring what one said. After dinner he invariably went and sat in the hall . . . of the Hotel Metropole, which had then only just been built.* He sat there in silence and smoked a cigar, conversation not being encouraged and one's remarks being received with stony silence.[36]

Queensberry would address the teenage Bosie as if he was the same age as himself, his favourite topic being his brother James's drinking habits. The conversation would start with a gloomy: 'I wish your uncle James did not drink so much, he now drinks at least three bottles of brandy a day.' 'Does he really?' Bosie would say, trying with some difficulty to maintain an appearance of polite interest, but having heard it so many times before, the statement made very little impression on him. 'Yes, four sometimes, and that's not counting what he drinks at meals, claret and port and champagne.'[37] It would then suddenly occur to Queensberry that his son might want to amuse himself by going on the pier or to the aquarium, and he would hand over a sum of money far greater than required.

Queensberry, said Bosie, had no idea of the right amount of money to give to a schoolboy and was 'always very lavish in the way of tips'.[38] As a result Bosie had far more money to spend than any other boy in his house. Whenever he was on his way back to school after the holidays he would go to see his father if he was available, and was always given some money. These handouts were accompanied by an apology: 'Of course, I know, my dear boy, this is not much, but you must learn to do the best you can with very little. I am a very poor man, and you had better realise once and for all that you will never have any money. If I were a rich man I would give you more, but as things are, I'm afraid you'll have to make this do.'[39] Queensberry would then give Bosie four sovereigns, twice as much as his friend brought back whose father had £30,000 a year. On one occasion, halfway through term, he

---

* The Metropole was built in 1890.

wrote his father a 'fishing-letter'[40] and was sent two or three more pounds. Bosie often heard his father speak compassionately about someone who 'hardly had a shirt to his back'[41] only to find that this unfortunate had £10,000 a year whereas Queensberry – or so Bosie believed – had £40,000. Bosie later claimed that it was his father's attitude and the disregard of expenses in his mother's house that led to his having no sense of monetary values, and no concept that he would ever be without funds.

Bosie adored and admired Alfred Montgomery, his handsome, cultured and dignified grandfather, who was generous to the boy with his sovereigns and £5 notes and sometimes came to see Bosie at Winchester and later Oxford, entertaining him and his friends to lunch. Alfred's fondness for his grandson was to survive later scandals and vicissitudes and last to the end of his life.

Bosie left Winchester at Christmas 1888 and early the following year he was sent abroad with a tutor. Queensberry was on his world tour at the time, so the trip may have been Sybil's decision. Here, Bosie experienced his first affair with a woman, a divorcee twelve years older than himself, and was sent back to England in disgrace. In the following October he went to Magdalen College, Oxford. There were three recognisable kinds of undergraduate – the studious, the sportsman and the aesthete. Bosie neglected his studies, although his looks and emerging talent as a poet assured his place in the aesthetic set. He was sent down for a term and spent time at a 'crammer', together with Sholto, who also needed extra coaching. He continued to be a successful athlete but in 1892, disappointed at his failure to win a three-mile race, he gave it up (one is reminded of Queensberry's abandonment of racing after the 1886 Grand National) and concentrated on literary pursuits. 'I might just as well have done both things,' he observed, 'but then, of course, Oscar Wilde had come into my life, and his influence was certainly not in an athletic direction.'[42]

In his holidays, Bosie mixed with the cream of society. With his mother and grandfather he spent two seasons at Bad Homburg, a favourite German watering spot, where they dined with the Prince of Wales. His mother's country house was only four miles from Ascot and there was a party for the races every year, Drumlanrig providing his family with tickets for refreshments in the Coldstream Guards' tent.

One of Bosie's closest friends at Oxford was poet Lionel Johnson, who was engaged in his own private struggle with homosexuality. Johnson had met

Oscar Wilde during his visit to Oxford in 1890. Wilde was already noted in society for his witty conversation, and as a poet, essayist, lecturer on the aesthetic movement and writer of short stories. In 1884 he had married Constance Lloyd, and the couple had two sons, Cyril and Vyvyan. His only novel, *The Picture of Dorian Gray* was first published in *Lippincott's Magazine* in June 1890 and was denounced in the press as offensive, notably by the *Daily Chronicle* which described it as 'a poisonous book, the atmosphere of which is heavy with the mephitic odours of moral and spiritual putrefaction – a gloating study of mental and physical corruption of a fresh fair and golden youth, which might be horrible and fascinating but for its effeminate frivolity'.[43] It appeared in a bound and much revised edition in April 1891.

That summer Bosie was staying at 18 Cadogan Place, when Lionel Johnson called and took him to meet Wilde at his family home at 34 Tite Street. The three men had tea, and Bosie was introduced to Constance. The meeting was, said Bosie, 'the ordinary interchange of courtesies. Wilde was very agreeable and talked a great deal, I was very much impressed.'[44] Bosie at twenty was at the height of his attractiveness, and looked very much younger than his years. Wilde, charming, successful, witty, and a thirty-six-year-old man of the world, was both sexually and artistically inspired by beautiful youths. Neither man was a stranger to homosexual love. Before Bosie left, Wilde asked his new acquaintance to have lunch or dinner with him at his club, and he accepted. Wilde was undoubtedly smitten and invitations to lunch and dinner, flattery and gifts followed, although at first the two did not meet frequently and the relationship was not romantic or sexual. It was to be some months before they were caught up in a passionate and ultimately destructive obsession.

Queensberry's son Sholto George was in the meantime doing his bit to maintain the reputation of the Douglases as an eccentric family. Blond and blue-eyed like his mother, he had inherited the boldness and energy of his father but none of his missionary zeal or sense of duty. In March 1892, aged nineteen he had been appointed to the 3rd Battalion of the Northamptonshire Regiment of infantry. Like Percy, he did not try to make a success of the military life, although he did pass a further examination in October 1892. Perhaps it was during his less than creditable military career that Sholto went missing for ten days. A private detective called Cook was employed to find him. The youthfully high-spirited and sociable Sholto was a keen devotee of the popular theatre and having a noisy good time. In November 1893 at the Alhambra Music Hall his rowdy behaviour – imitating hunting cries, throwing coins and whisky into the pit, refusing to desist when asked and resorting to 'very strong language'[45] – brought him before the county magistrates at Hythe on a charge of creating a disturbance. One of his friends had attempted to terrorise the music hall attendants by telling them that Sholto was the champion amateur boxer in England. Sholto was fined £2 10s. with costs.

Sybil must have been anxious about her undisciplined and erratic youngest son. In 1894 he was sent to Bakersfield, California, where the sunny climate is ideal for citrus crops. There he was to take charge of a forty-acre fruit farm bought for him by his hopeful mother.

The quietest of Queensberry's children and the one about whom least is known was his daughter Edith. She was occasionally a bridesmaid at fashionable weddings, and attended society events, often in the company of her mother. Edith's public life was more limited and less controversial than that of her brothers, but when she married in 1898 it was to St George William Lane Fox-Pitt, a remarkable man with unconventional religious views who was eighteen years her senior. She and her husband were to be a sympathetic support to Queensberry in his declining years.

CHAPTER 12

The Antipathy of Similars

IN 1891 seventy-year-old dowager marchioness Caroline had lost none of her fire, and remained an ardent Fenian, although her letters to the newspapers were less frequent than in her heyday. Florence had effectively taken over her mother's campaigning role, supporting the women's suffrage movement and Home Rule for Ireland, although her reputation had been permanently damaged by her long discredited story of the attempt on her life at Windsor. The Dixies' finances continued to slide, and they were obliged to give up the Fishery and settle in Glen Stuart where they lived in 'somewhat reduced circumstances'.[1] Florence returned to her outdoor life, but another cause was waiting for her. A sudden revelation led her to become an opponent of blood sports.

Archibald had relinquished his charge of the St Vincent's home in 1887 and retired to a quieter life of mission work in Scotland, where he was appointed a canon in Galloway, and travelled about in a mobile 'gypsy van chapel'.[2]

For some years James Douglas's mental condition had been giving cause for concern. In 1891 he was summonsed for submitting a false census return in which his wife was described as a 'crossing sweep' and 'lunatic' and her son as a 'shoeblack' born 'in darkest Africa'.[3] At the West London Police Court he 'expressed regret and shame for the childish and foolish return'.[4] He claimed that he had been ill and had given the return to his wife and stepson to complete, who had made the entries for a joke. He had then added his own name in pencil. The court accepted this unlikely but contrite explanation, and the summons was withdrawn.

Queensberry saw James in late April. His brother was suffering a severe attack of 'rheumatic gout' (arthritis) and it was decided that he should holiday in Ireland for his health. He was away for ten days, returning on Monday 4 May. While travelling on the overnight steamer to Anglesey, James was acting so erratically that the staff became concerned, and when he boarded the train at Holyhead railway officials ordered a man to accompany him. On arrival in London James took a room at the Station Hotel, Euston where his behaviour was considered to be rather strange. He may have been experiencing hallucinations, since a waiter observed that James imagined that someone had spoken to him in the hall. The same evening, Queensberry received a telegram advising him of his brother's arrival and mental condition. He consulted Florence and they contacted James's physician, Dr Bloxham, asking him to visit their brother. They also discussed arranging a trip to Scotland for him.

No one believed that James required urgent attention and it was not until after 10 a.m. the following morning that Bloxham arrived at the hotel and asked chambermaid Charlotte Hudd to take his card up to James's room. She knocked twice, but there was no reply, and she entered. James was lying on the floor between the dressing table and the bed. There was a large pool of drying blood on the carpet and a blood-smeared razor lay beside the body. Charlotte ran to get a waiter, who alerted the manager, and Dr Bloxham came up but James was beyond all assistance. A deep incised wound in his neck was undoubtedly self-inflicted. He had been dead for at least ten hours. He was thirty-five. A telegram was sent to Queensberry, who arrived at the hotel that afternoon to be told of his brother's death. He did not see the body then, but later made a formal identification.

The inquest opened at the St Pancras Coroner's Court on 6 May. Bloxham said that he had been James's doctor for the last three years, and due to his patient's very excitable nature he had thought it very likely that he might one day commit a rash act. He believed James's relatives were of the same opinion. Queensberry explained that he was an agnostic and was permitted to affirm. He said that in the last two or three years he had noticed James suffering from 'great depression of spirits'[5] although he had never seen him attempt self-injury. However, he had feared that his brother might commit suicide. The inquest jury returned the verdict that James had committed suicide while of unsound mind.

Early on the morning of 9 May the body of Lord James Douglas, enclosed in a leaden case inside an oak coffin, arrived at Annan, and proceeded by hearse to Cummertrees followed by two mourning coaches. Lord Archibald read the burial service, and the other relatives present were Queensberry, Percy, Sir Beaumont and Lady Dixie, Gertrude and her husband, and cousin Arthur Johnstone Douglas. Although it was intended that the funeral should be a quiet family affair, many of the public attended, including a number of workpeople from the estate who came to pay their respects. James was the first of his family to be interred in a new private burial plot on 'a green knoll amid some scattered beeches'[6] by the side of a lake on the Kinmount lands. A St Andrew's cross dedicated to his memory was later placed on the site. Florence may not have wanted to admit to herself that her beloved and wayward twin had taken his own life. In 1901 she referred to James as 'killed in 1891'.[7]

If Queensberry was a reader of Henry Labouchère's *Truth* he would already have heard the rumours about Oscar Wilde, since in 1883 during Wilde's lecture tour the paper, predicting the poet's descent into oblivion, had described him as 'the epicene youth' and 'an effeminate phrase-maker' indifferent to 'the sneers of his own sex'.[8] He might also have formed his own opinion when he chanced to meet Wilde for the first time, at the home of a mutual acquaintance around 1880 or 1881. Cultured men with artistic, feminine tastes, the antithesis of the manly ideal, were not then necessarily assumed to be homosexual, but unspoken – and in polite circles unsayable – suspicions may have been aroused. Wilde's marriage had quelled the gossip, but his paper of 1889 claiming that Shakespeare was passionately devoted to a beautiful boy actor would have raised a few eyebrows.

The publication of *The Picture of Dorian Gray* precipitated fresh rumours about Wilde, and 'very unpleasant stories which led to his arrest and downfall began to be freely circulated in the West End of London'.[9] Queensberry's acquaintance John Boon had – and he felt this was his duty – personally warned two young men, the sons of friends, who had become part of Wilde's circle of admirers, 'of their dangerous situation'.[10] He also spoke to the father of one of them, and ordered Wilde to stop attending his club. When the gossip reached Queensberry he saw Bosie and advised him that Wilde was not a fit man to associate with. 'I must do my father the justice to say that at this stage he was not unkind or offensive, as he became afterwards,' said Bosie. 'He light-heartedly told me that I must give up knowing Wilde, and seemed to think that this was quite enough.'[11] After some thought Bosie wrote a 'perfectly respectful and affectionate letter' to his father refusing to give up his friend, and 'begged him not to interfere'.[12] Queensberry replied, telling Bosie he was 'a fool and a "baby"' who 'did not understand what [he] was doing'.[13]

In May 1892 Bosie was being blackmailed over an indiscreet letter, and wrote to Wilde for help. Wilde obligingly came to Oxford and stayed with Bosie in his rooms; later he dated the origin of their close friendship to that event. What Bosie called 'familiarities' were to continue occasionally, but ceased about six months before the court appearances: 'of the sin which takes its name from one of the Cities of the Plain there never was the slightest question,' he added.[14]

Wilde asked an old friend, prominent society solicitor George Lewis, to make the threat go away and, after a payment of £100, it did. But the incident had not only damaged Wilde's friendship with Lewis; Queensberry came to hear of it. The details of Bosie's indiscretion are unknown, although his nephew commented 'he had more than once got into trouble through his passion for little boys'.[15] Later events suggest a preference for boys in their mid teens. Bosie himself admitted that his sexual tastes, before he repudiated homosexuality as sinful, were 'all for youth and beauty and softness';[16] however, Wilde declared that the trouble came from Bosie's fascination with 'The gutter and the things that live in it'.[17] On another occasion the two had been staying in Salisbury and Bosie, alarmed by a threatening letter from a former companion, had begged Wilde to see the writer which Wilde did, taking the blame for what Bosie had done.

Queensberry cannot have been unaware that in a closed all-male environment some sexual experimentation will occur between otherwise heterosexual young men. He may have hoped that Bosie's indiscretions were a passing phase that would not recur once his son entered society and met young women, but there must have been fears at the back of his mind that his son was by preference homosexual. The youth's appearance and tastes were too similar to those of his mother and his cultured, lisping grandfather for Queensberry to ignore. The anxious father kept his knowledge a secret and did not mention the 'horrible story'[18] until the Wilde scandal broke and he revealed that Bosie's 'infamous conduct . . . ranked him before with this lot and showed me what he was long ago'.[19]

To call Queensberry homophobic or bigoted, as is so often done, is meaningless in the context of his time. Society in general was homophobic; as Bosie later said, homosexuality was then regarded as 'far worse than murder' or as a form of insanity.[20] In 1895 *The Echo* referred to what the press in general was unable to name as 'one of the most heinous crimes that can be alleged against a man – a crime too horrible and too revolting to be spoken of even by men'.[21] Bosie's poem 'Two Loves', published in December 1894, which ends with the line 'I am the Love that dare not speak its name',[22] is today intensely sad and moving. At the time it was regarded in most sectors of British society as a piece of filth. The homosexual, who was assumed also to be a sodomite, was believed to be a threat to manliness and the traditional family, but fortunately he could be instantly identified because his inverted sexual tastes were apparent in his appearance: pale, languid, weak and unhealthy.

In Queensberry's time, no heterosexual man would have dreamed of openly condoning homosexuality at the risk of becoming suspect himself, though many turned a blind eye when the individuals concerned were discreet. For the man who was openly homosexual, prison, exile, destitution, and possible suicide, all beckoned. Queensberry, although he shared the prevailing public opinion, never took any action against or campaigned against homosexuals in general; his ire was aroused only when his sons were involved. One might wonder why men such as Queensberry and Henry Labouchère who fought so hard for freedom of worship and more relaxed divorce laws could not be more charitable about sexual freedoms, but society's deeply entrenched horror was centuries old and not easily overturned.

Wilde and Bosie spent a great deal of the summer of 1892 in each other's company, and Bosie invited Wilde to Bad Homburg, where he was introduced to Alfred Montgomery and the Prince of Wales. Montgomery, according to Bosie, 'took a violent and invincible dislike to [Wilde] and declined to meet him again'.[23] Queensberry wrote several more letters to Bosie forbidding him to see Wilde, but Sybil could see nothing wrong in a friendship with such a cultured man whose career at Oxford University had been one of considerable distinction. In October 1892 Wilde was staying at the Hut, Sybil's home near Bracknell, when the anxious mother spoke to him dispairingly about her idle, vain and spendthrift son. In the coming year she was to turn to Wilde more than once for advice about Bosie's future.

Not long afterwards Bosie was lunching with Oscar at the Café Royal when Queensberry came in without noticing that they were there, and sat at another table. This fashionable Regent Street restaurant with its long mirrors, and painted and gilded ceilings, was world famous for its exquisite French food and a wine cellar said to be second to none. Its relaxed café-style atmosphere appealed to artists and writers, and it was also patronised by sporting and political celebrities who enjoyed its informality. It was the perfect place for Oscar Wilde to hold court, charming and entertaining his youthful friends. Bosie, seeing an unmissable opportunity to introduce the two men, went at once to his father's table and asked him to join him and Wilde for lunch. Queensberry at first refused, but on being pressed said '"Very well" and came rather sulkily over to our table'.[24] After the introductions Queensberry observed that this was not their first meeting, something Wilde had forgotten. Wilde, who had a legendary ability to win over with his charm and wit those who had previously been dubious about him, 'exerted himself to be agreeable. He was in good form, and in about ten minutes he had my father laughing and listening eagerly to his conversation.'[25] By the time they got on to the inevitable subject of Christianity, the lunch, which had begun at 1.30, had ended and they were at the cigar, liqueur and coffee stage, talking so animatedly that Bosie, left out of the conversation, felt bored. Knowing what to expect once his father began to expound on his favourite bugbear, he left them still talking at ten to three. When Wilde told Queensberry that he and his family were going to stay in Torquay, Queensberry said that he too was going there, to give a lecture, and asked Wilde to come and hear it.

That evening Oscar told Bosie with some pride that the lunch had gone on for another hour, that he had 'completely "got round" [Queensberry], that they were now great friends and had arranged to meet again'. Somehow Oscar had 'succeeded in doing what no one else had been able to do for many years at that time', said Bosie: 'charming my father into pleasant and happy conversation, and leading him right out of the quagmire of boredom and argument in which he invariably landed himself when he began to talk about religion'. Wilde told Bosie that he had greatly enjoyed the meeting and felt great sympathy for Queensberry, who 'had a lot in him which appealed to him'.[26] In the event Queensberry changed his plans, and sent a note to Wilde saying that he was not going to Torquay after all.

Queensberry often appeared to suddenly and unaccountably change his mind, adding fuel to claims that he was insane, but he is rarely given credit for making enquiries about situations and people that concerned him and gathering additional information and opinions. One of the people he consulted about Wilde was an old friend, Lord de Grey, who assured him that Wilde was a friend of his and Lady de Grey and a frequent guest at their house, and that he was '"perfectly all right" in every way, besides being a man of genius and a most delightful and amusing talker'. Two days after meeting Wilde Queensberry wrote to Bosie saying he 'wished to take back all he had said about Oscar Wilde, that he considered him a charming fellow and very clever, and that he did not wonder [Bosie] was so fond of him'.[27] This state of affairs lasted, said Bosie, about two months, and a third amicable meeting with Wilde never took place. 'It is tragic to think,' said Bosie, optimistically, 'that if only the acquaintance between the two had gone on and been refreshed by other meetings, Oscar would probably have succeeded in curing my father's "melancholy madness."'[28]

Queensberry was not the only person worried about the unusual friendship. Frank Harris, who described Bosie as 'self-willed, reckless, obstinate and imperious', thought he was a bad influence, introducing Wilde to 'youths of the lowest class', demanding extravagant expenditure, and encouraging 'an insolent arrogance' and 'aristocratic disdain' in the older man.[29] Harris had observed that Wilde's accommodating nature led him to adopt some of the characteristics of his admirers. The recklessness Bosie had inherited from his father influenced Wilde: his boldness gave Oscar boldness, and the change astonished and distressed Harris. Unsurprisingly, Bosie later denounced Harris's memoir of Wilde as a 'clumsy farrago of lies and misrepresentations'[30] but another friend of Wilde, the writer André Gide, noticed the same change. 'He seemed determined to break through his reserve, and I think Lord Alfred Douglas's presence encouraged him to do so.'[31]

Harris, witnessing Bosie's venomous rage, 'was suddenly struck by a sort of likeness, a similarity of expression and of temper between Lord Alfred Douglas and his unhappy father. I could not get it out of my head – that little face blanched with rage and the wild, hating eyes; the shrill voice, too, was Queensberry's.'[32] 'He is the son of his father,' Oscar eventually admitted, 'violent and irritable with a tongue like a lash.'[33] Later, more perceptively, he told Bosie: 'whenever there is hatred between two people there is a bond or brotherhood of some kind. I suppose that, by some strange law of the antipathy of similars, you loathed each other, not because in so many points you were so different, but because in some you were so like.'[34] Wilde met Queensberry just a few times, and was only partly right. Queensberry did not loathe Bosie, but he was undoubtedly appalled, distressed and infuriated by him. There was, in an antagonistic and destructive way, a bond of affection between father and son, but it was rarely to be seen, and when it appeared, it was more often than not quickly crushed away out of sight.

In January 1893 Bosie sent a poem to Wilde, who responded with a letter that was to have serious repercussions. It began:

My Own Boy,

Your sonnet is quite lovely, and it is a marvel that those red rose-leaf lips of yours should be made no less for music of song than for madness of kisses.

Your slim gilt soul walks between passion and poetry. I know Hyacinthus, whom Apollo loved so madly, was you in Greek days.

It ended 'Always, with undying love, Yours, Oscar'.[35]

Bosie later stayed with Wilde at Torquay, where he was coached by a tutor for his final examinations. On the night before Bosie left his temper got the better of him and there was a terrible scene, which determined Wilde to end the relationship. The tutor later told Wilde that he thought Bosie 'at times quite irresponsible for what [he] said and did, and that most if not all of the men at Magdalen were of the same opinion'.[36] Despite this, they were reconciled. These scenes and reconciliations were to be repeated throughout the relationship.

Back at Oxford, Bosie took over the editorship of an undergraduate journal, the *Spirit Lamp* and published some of his poetry. 'I suspected that I was a great poet when I was twenty-three, and as the years went by my suspicion became a conviction.'[37] He also published poems by Wilde and one by his father. Queensberry was rarely moved to poetry, and only when inspired by some tragic event. On this occasion it was the early death of his friend, the actor Fred Leslie. A sentimental piece, on the theme of the mingling of the souls of the dead, it opens:

When I am dead, cremate me;
    Please let my ashes lie
In mother earth's dear bosom;
    I have no fear to die.[38]

Bosie described this as 'not very good, I fear', although he thought *Spirit of the Matterhorn* 'had a lot of good lines in it'.[39]

Both Bosie and Wilde had by then begun the fatally dangerous practice of casual sexual encounters with young men. Carelessly, Bosie left Wilde's exquisite January letter and others of a similar unambiguous nature in the pockets of a suit he gave to a seventeen-year-old youth, Alfred Wood, who used his find to demand money from Wilde. The money was paid, Wood went abroad, and the problem was apparently over. Bosie, devoting his last months at Oxford to poetry and pleasure fended off his father's anxiety about his future by promising that he was intending to enter a respectable profession. Time, however, was running out.

After years of introspection Queensberry at last felt able to formally promote his unorthodox marriage theories in England. On 18 January 1893 he gave an address at Prince's Hall, a concert and lecture hall at 190 Piccadilly, entitled 'Marriage and the Relation of the Sexes, an address to women'. Inevitably this attracted satirical attention from the press. There was a small audience: 150 ladies in the gallery and about another 150 people in the body of the hall of whom about fifteen were men, members of sporting clubs, hoping perhaps for some near-the-knuckle entertainment. Queensberry shared the platform with the venerable George Jacob Holyoake and publisher Charles Watts, who advised the audience that the pamphlet could be purchased at the door for sixpence.

The *Pall Mall Gazette* described the forty-eight-year-old marquess thus:

Height about 5ft 7in in his boots.
Weight about 10st 3lb 2oz.
Hair black and sparse: more sparse than black.
Dress: swallow-tail coat, coat, black; trousers, black; patent-leather boots,
    No. 8, black, waistcoat, white; shirt and tie like new-laid snow.
Hands reddish white.

Eyebrows black.

Whiskers black, about a quarter of an inch wide at the summit, and one and a quarter inches at the base, running in a straight line from the ear to the lower jaw, abatt [sic] the cheekbones.

Cheek-bones not prominent.

Forehead so-so.

Speech intermittent, full of hills and valleys, short cuts and unexpected corners.

Memory fitful, not noticeably bad so long as he kept his eyes glued to the manuscript, but otherwise not to be depended upon except at odds of not less than 40 to 1.

Enunciation cloudy.

Pose straight up and down, but uneasy on his feet.

Manner serious; impossible to imagine a joke thriving in his vicinity.

Stutter picturesque for fifteen minutes; for an hour apt to generate a thirst for gore.[40]

Watts made the introductions, stating that he thought the marquess was 'a bold man to come forward in favour of such a radical reform'.[41] Queensberry rose to speak and began by stating that he wished to correct the allegation that he advocated polygamy. He was suggesting instead 'a kind of plurality of marriage' and he appealed specifically to women because he 'was quite confident that he would get no assistance from men in the furtherance of his project. Besides,' he added, 'women would soon get the franchise'. Queensberry was not a natural public speaker. His audience listened patiently as he read from his manuscript, which took an hour. Every so often he would raise his eyes from the paper, lose his place and find it again only after a struggle. Sometimes he did not find it and skipped a page or so, eliciting a sigh of relief from those in the audience who had the pamphlet with them. His pronunciation of some words was 'singularly original' and he spoke as if in a hurry, sometimes cutting off syllables, not, the *Pall Mall Gazette* felt, because he actually was in a hurry but from force of habit. Many of the women applauded his sentiments and a few of the men 'then looked rather ashamed of themselves'. He concluded with a reading from *Spirit of the Matterhorn*. 'The Marquis,' observed the *Pall Mall Gazette*, 'has a way of grinding out poetry. It is difficult to discover whether he is beginning or ending a verse.'[42]

The address, when published as a twenty-eight-page pamphlet, was wordy, rambling and repetitive. If this was Queensberry's considered writing style then it is no wonder that some found his verbal arguments dull and tiresome. His message was that the current marriage laws were not in harmony with basic human needs. The evils resulting from prostitution – the cruel degradation of women, and the spread of disease – were the direct consequence of strictly enforced monogamous marriage. Where a marriage had broken down, and sexual relations had ceased, the couple should be able to avoid the misery of separation and divorce and live together as brother and sister. The idea that a man should have marital relations with just one woman for the whole of his life was a law that scarcely one man in ten thousand could obey. His answer, which avoided the taking of unlawful wives in secrecy and dishonour, was legal concubinage, which would enable men to acknowledge mistresses and children currently branded as illegitimate.

This did not, he emphasised, mean enslavement for women – a recent case which had established that a woman could not be compelled to live with her husband against her will was, he stated, 'one of the most glorious victories that woman has yet gained in the progressive emancipation of her sex towards freedom'.[43] Queensberry did not suggest plurality of marriage for women, because there was one way in which men and women could not be equal: the biological – a woman knew that her child was her own. For that reason he advocated easier divorce for women and reducing the necessity of divorce for men. The one essential was that husband and wife should act by mutual consent.

Queensberry's Mars/Venus theory was that a man could never fully know the tenderness of a mother's love while a woman could never fully know the purity of man's conjugal love. He did not claim that his ideas were original, and acknowledged his debt to an anonymous pamphlet called *The Future of Marriage*, from which he quoted extensively. In Queensberry's ideal world, wives who admitted other women into a union with their husband would solve many problems, reducing the numbers of single women and competition for marriage, sharing the burdens of wifehood and motherhood, and avoiding the stresses that maintained prostitution. He anticipated that wives might object to this idea but did not see it as an insurmountable problem; it was just a matter of education and custom. What he advocated was, he said, in any case what men were already doing, but deceitfully. In Salt Lake City some twenty years earlier he had spoken to a Mormon woman who had told him that the hatred and jealousy that existed in monogamous marriages did not exist there. Monogamy was the ideal of the perfect man, but man was not yet perfect.

When the address was over, Holyoake rose and gave a vote of thanks 'in a voice that sounded painfully like an asthmatic penny whistle'.[44] Another publisher, Stuart Rose, seconded the vote of thanks, and it was hinted that *Spirit of the Matterhorn* was also for sale. Queensberry, before departing to entertain Holyoake to dinner at Albemarle Street, thanked the audience with the parting observation that he might be a hundred years ahead of the times.

CHAPTER 13

A Serious Slight

B Y 1893 Queensberry was no longer the trim figure of his youthful days. Thickset and muscular he had given up riding and, looking for new ways of burning energy and keeping himself fit, he became a keen cyclist. "'Q" as his intimate friends called him, once spun up from the Star and Garter, Richmond, to his place in town in forty minutes. A punch-ball used to be one of his favourite methods of taking exercise, and that, again, if one has a suitable room for it, is a rare good way of keeping oneself fit in town.'[1]

In his late forties, however, he began to experience a severe and embar-rassing problem: he became impotent. Later evidence suggests that he may have developed what is now known as Peyronie's disease, which had first been described in 1819. Peyronie's usually starts in the forties or fifties, when the formation of lesions results in distortion of the erect penis. The condition can be painful, making erection impossible. There are many possible causes, including injury during energetic coition, as the tissues of a man in his forties are less flexible than in his younger days, resulting in abnormal and excessive scarring. In the 1890s it was untreatable. For this intensely active masculine man, who believed that body and soul were indivisibly linked, and to whom physical strength and endurance were central to his perception of self, the onset of impotence must have been a catastrophe of no small order. Its psychological effects are well known – lack of self-esteem and confidence, feelings of frustration, anxiety, irritability and depression. The effects of this pressure on a volatile man like Queensberry who was going through one of the most traumatic periods of his life can scarcely be underestimated, for between 1893 and 1895, while he was privately combating this distressing and humiliating condition, he was to suffer a series of fateful hammer blows which turned him into the raging termagant that history remembers.

Queensberry's life, which had been a series of shocks and rebuffs, some due to his own uncompromising nature and, for his time, unorthodox views, was entering a phase of almost permanent open conflict. Had each crisis arrived individually he might have been able to deal with them with some dignity and restraint, but as scandals and tragedies piled on top of and sometimes interacted with each other it took very little to make him distracted with rage and misery. The next two years were to establish Queensberry in the public eye as a monster and a lunatic who ruined his family, but there is another point of view. 'I maintain,' said the eleventh marquess, 'that seldom in family history has such provocation been given to a father, provocation from wife and children alike.'[2]

Bosie who on his own admission 'wasted time in a shocking way at Oxford'[3] was due to leave in the summer of 1893, and that March was making a final effort to catch up on his neglected studies. In May Oscar Wilde enjoyed an extended stay at Oxford, and there was a round of delightful dinners but probably not a great deal of study. Bosie and Wilde's relationship was now a public matter and fresh rumours reached Queensberry, who wrote to Bosie 'repeating his old accusations',[4] ordering him to drop his acquaintanceship with Wilde and give his word of honour that he would have no more to do with him, or his allowance would cease. Bosie responded angrily, refusing to drop Wilde, reminding Queensberry of his years of neglect which he said gave him no right to interfere in his son's life, and saying that 'if he was mean enough to stop my allowance he must do so'.[5] 'I am the last person in the world who can be bullied or threatened into doing anything,' wrote Bosie. 'In that respect I very much resemble my father. Neither of us would give way. My father wrote to me in insulting terms, I replied in the same vein.'[6]

'What happened to make him change his mind in so strange and fatal a manner?' Bosie later wondered. 'Obviously someone made mischief and deliberately inflamed my father against Wilde. But who it was, or why he did it, must ever remain a mystery.'[7] It is unlikely, however, that there was only one informant. Even if Henry Labouchère and John Boon had not had a word in Queensberry's ear there were many other London clubmen of like mind. Two of Queensberry's closest friends and advisers were men whose opinions and veracity he trusted far more than those of his own family: property dealer Edward James Pape of Portland Place, and his old sporting comrade Sir Claude de Crespigny. Both men were to guide Queensberry's actions in his efforts to keep Bosie away from Oscar Wilde.

While Bosie was largely marking time at Oxford, Francis was taking the first steps in a political career, visiting Scotland in March 1893 as the prospective Gladstonian Liberal candidate for the Northern Burghs. His fortunes, however, were about to make a further, dizzying advance in a way that no one, least of all his father, could have anticipated. That spring, Gladstone's private secretary Algernon West informed Lord Rosebery that he had not been able to complete the number of appointments required for lords-in-waiting, and suggested a solution. With the Liberals anxious to increase their numbers in the Upper House, both these problems could be addressed by offering young Drumlanrig the post. This would necessitate his being awarded a British peerage. It was an extraordinary and unprecedented idea to elevate a man of twenty-six who had manifestly done nothing to deserve a peerage, and to do so during the lifetime of his father, who had not received a similar accolade.

The unusual proposal understandably took Rosebery by surprise, but he felt honour bound not to conceal it from Francis, and mentioned it to him 'not thinking for a moment that he would entertain it';[8] when he found that his protégé did not reject the idea at once, he strongly urged him not to accept. Not only was it 'a dreary fate at his age to be buried in the House of Lords', but the issue was a highly sensitive one, since Rosebery knew very well the long-standing Queensberry hopes for a British peerage. He reminded Drumlanrig that Queensberry's consent would be necessary, and 'it was impossible to predict what line his father might take'.[9] Francis agreed, and went away to think about it, but two days later returned and told Rosebery that he was 'strongly minded to accept' because he 'wished greatly to enter on a political life & considered this an easy and economical method of doing so'.[10] Francis may have been thinking about his grandfather, who had had the political career he had always wanted taken away from him when he succeeded to the marquessate. A British peerage would ensure that Drumlanrig could never be excluded from parliament, and for all he knew this might be his only chance. Rosebery still disagreed, but 'found, as I discovered afterwards when opposing Lord Drumlanrig's leaving the Guards, that I had not the slightest influence on his resolutions'.[11]

Francis went to see his father who was staying in Brighton. Queensberry, according to Bosie, was 'all smiles' and happily 'wrote to Gladstone thanking him and expressing his great satisfaction at the honour done by Her Majesty to his son'.[12] If he did, the letter has not come to light, and this claim may be one of Bosie's exaggerations, but Queensberry did write to Rosebery stating that although the event 'revived the memory of the insults that had been heaped upon him by the Scottish Peers . . . he would not allow his feelings to stand in his son's way'.[13] Queensberry maintained that by the time Francis told him about the peerage the matter had effectively been arranged, and it is possible that Francis may have given him that impression to avoid opposition. He advised Francis that he would not stand in his way – 'could I have done so if I wished?' he later commented – but 'reserved to myself the right of making some protest'.[14] Queensberry decided to keep quiet and wait on developments. Perhaps he hoped that if his son was elevated he would receive a corresponding honour, a not unreasonable expectation under the circumstances. Francis reported back to Rosebery but was told that this grudging approval was not an adequate form of consent and was obliged to go and see Queensberry again; this time he returned to say that he had 'received a full and free consent'.[15]

On 3 June 1893 the name of Viscount Drumlanrig appeared on the Queen's birthday honours list. Queensberry's did not. Since Francis had been very little in the public eye and had done nothing exceptional, many newspapers expressed frank puzzlement. *The Graphic* theorised that the reason for the 'very unusual promotion' was that Rosebery would have the convenience of a secretary in the House of Lords, or more probably so that Drumlanrig could be appointed lord-in-waiting.[16] The *New York Times* approved, describing Francis as 'the only sane adult of either set [*sic*] which that family has contained for a long time'.[17]

That same morning Queensberry, having decided to write to the Queen, called on Holyoake and asked his advice about the planned letter. When Queensberry made his protest, however, he was met on every side with a series of rebuffs that fuelled his suspicion that there was a conspiracy to slight him. Both Gladstone and Rosebery had underestimated the violence of Queensberry's reaction, and neither was prepared to mollify his hurt feelings. As his frustration and anger grew, his language became more extreme in order to provoke a response, and it was increasingly easy for anyone who wished to dismiss his views to declare them to be the ravings of a madman. Queensberry's first appeal was to Gladstone, and on 5 June Algernon West had a meeting with Sybil. Saying that the marquess was 'for the moment furious . . . and had written a very offensive letter', he promised that he would send 'a soothing answer'.[18]

Queensberry's letter to the Queen was written on 5 June from the Bedford Hotel, Brighton. 'I trust your Majesty will pardon my troubling you with this letter on a personal affair,' he began. After thanking her for the honour conferred on his family he went on: 'I would respectfully call to your Majesty's consideration, that under the circumstances of my own rejection . . . what has now happened is a most gratuitous slight to myself & keenly accentuates the injustice of my position.' After commenting on his exclusion from the Lords he pointed out that Gladstone 'bringing my son in over my head and into my shoes during my lifetime, as an English peer [is] a thing unprecedented but which in justice he could therefore have done for me long ago. I can only look upon this on his part as an intentional slight . . . it is to say the least most unfair to strike at me again through my own son and may be to set us in antagonism to one another over this . . . I should regret very much to give you any annoyance or to place myself in opposition to your wishes. But after this further rebuff I can hardly keep silent.'[19]

On 12 June Rosebery wrote to the Queen: 'He understands that Lord Queensberry has recently written to Your Majesty with regard to Lord Drumlanrig's peerage. It is doubtless unnecessary to warn Your Majesty that that nobleman does not appear to be in complete possession of his senses on all occasions.'[20] On 13 June Sir Henry Ponsonby, the Queen's private secretary replied to Queensberry. 'I am commanded by The Queen to acknowledge the receipt of Your Lordship's letter. As the name of Lord Drumlanrig was recommended to her for a British Peerage by Mr Gladstone, Her Majesty has sent your letter to him to consider.'[21]

Two days later, Queensberry responded:

Dear Sir

I am obliged for your acknowledgement of my letter to Her Majesty though I cannot help feeling that it is possible Her Majesty has not received it at all and that it has just been sent on to Mr Gladstone. If this is not the case, I would beg you to inform Her Majesty that I had already written to Mr Gladstone & that his only reply to myself was through his secretary that he considers my sons elevation to a peerage would be unobjectionable &

agreeable to myself though he never consulted me, indeed it is only a few weeks ago when he was down here that he very rudely declined to allow me to call upon him I at the time knowing nothing of this intended step. My son was the first to inform me of it when I wrote to Ld Rosebery I used these words. While thanking you for your kindness to my son and in no way wishing to stand in his way I must tell you that I cannot consent to waive my own claims of being relieved from a very intolerable and unjust position & that if my son is brought in over my head and I left out in the cold I could consider it nothing else but a studied insult to myself.[22]

On 20 June Gladstone received a 'long and abusive letter from Lord Queensberry about the peerage, which Rosebery recommended not answering'.[23] Queensberry was later assured that all his letters had been seen, but since there were no further developments, he concluded correctly that he was being deliberately ignored.

Francis's maiden speech to the House of Lords on 25 June on the work of the Society for Prevention of Cruelty to Children, confirmed his gentle, thoughtful nature. On 1 July the Queen appointed Francis, now Baron Kelhead – although he continued to use the Drumlanrig title – to be one of her Lords-in-Waiting in Ordinary and on 4 July he took his oath in the House of Lords, where he was now entitled to vote, and did so, supporting Lord Rosebery. Over the next year he made his mark in parliament. 'His constant attendance, his fair hair and pleasant, boyish face drew the attention of casual visitors. . . . The world was all before him with every promise of a brilliant future.'[24] Socially he was also a success: 'his manner was the acme of politeness and suavity . . . and his grace and gaiety of deportment made him a special favourite in the company of ladies'.[25]

On 17 July Queensberry was staying at the Hôtel des Bains at Spa in Belgium when he again wrote to the Queen:

Madam

I regret to have to trouble your Majesty again on the subject of my son's peerage but I feel compelled to inform Your Majesty that I can receive no satisfaction from either Mr Gladstone or Ld Rosebery in answer to my protest, which was forwarded to the former by Your Majesty's command for his consideration as they both refuse to communicate with me in any way.

He wanted to know

> how Mr. Gladstone could represent to your majesty that the circumstances
> of my son's elevation to the peerage while I was passed over & slighted could
> be anything other than painful & objectionable to myself, particularly after
> my strong protest addressed to Ld Rosebery. It is clear that one of two
> things must have occurred either Mr Gladstone knowingly deceived your
> majesty or that Ld Rosebery deliberately and for purposes of his own with-
> held my letter and the contents of it from Mr Gladstone and gave him
> assurances contrary of the truth.
>
> As the former supposition, is I hope inadmissible, the latter is assuredly
> what has occurred, Ld Rosebery who is a connection of my wife's family by
> marriage, has evidently made himself the instrument of family spite against
> myself & strikes by the most unjustifiable means to bring about a state of
> things which not only constitutes a serious slight to myself, but will continue
> I fear through life to be a subject of discord and disturbance between me and
> my son. . . . your majesty must see that a most grievous wrong has been done
> to me and that I have good reason to complain of the reticence and decep-
> tion that has been practised on your majesty in this matter, to say nothing
> of the conspiracy of silence with which my protest which was forwarded to
> Mr. Gladstone by your majesty's command is now being treated.[26]

This letter appears to have been passed to Rosebery to deal with, as the
original is amongst his and not the royal papers. Queensberry's missives to
Rosebery were now adopting 'a more violent and insulting tone'.[27] Rosebery's
only response to this flood of correspondence was to inform Queensberry
that the idea of the peerage was not his, but another's. On Saturday 5 August
Rosebery left London for a holiday in the spa town of Bad Homburg. Shortly
before his departure he had received another letter from Queensberry 'to say
that he intended to take the first opportunity of publicly assaulting me'.[28]
Queensberry was in Nice when he wrote a further letter on 6 August, which
Rosebery did not receive for another five days.*

Rosebery had understandably not named Algernon West as the originator
of the peerage idea but this secrecy set Queensberry's mind working and he

---

* At f. 258 Rosebery writes 'May 11' but it is clear he is referring to the letter he received on 11 August.

jumped to a wrong but not unreasonable conclusion. Francis was a favourite of his grandfather Alfred Montgomery, and Montgomery was a close friend of the Prince of Wales. Queensberry convinced himself that Montgomery was the unnamed man, and perceived Rosebery as the 'channel of an insult to him carefully plotted by' his ex-wife and her family.[29] Rosebery saw, far too late, 'that this idea, brooded over & dwelling, has produced the monomania which makes him act and write as he has'.[30] Unfortunately, Queensberry had gone so far down the route of blaming his family that he was almost certainly open to no other interpretation.

There was another concern, and one that was to have critical importance over the next two years. Rosebery's preference for 'smart young men' and reticence over his private life had led to widespread but discreetly guarded gossip that he was homosexual. Whether he was or not cannot be proven and is still a matter of debate; Leo McKinstry in *Rosebery: Statesman in Turmoil* argues strongly that the allegations were untrue and unfounded, while Neil McKenna in *The Secret Life of Oscar Wilde* believes that Rosebery and Drumlanrig were lovers. The most detailed descriptions of the supposed affair are in the colourful and highly dubious memoirs of Sir Edmund Trelawny Backhouse who claimed to have had affairs with, amongst others, Rosebery, Drumlanrig, Bosie and Oscar Wilde. Irrespective of the truth of any rumours, if Queensberry had heard a whisper that his son had been given a peerage because he was the object of Rosebery's sexual inclinations, he would have been appalled. There is no conclusive evidence that Francis was homosexual or that Queensberry even suspected he was, but the mere fact that his son was the subject of such gossip would have been painful enough.

While Queensberry's relations with Rosebery had once been cordial, Labouchère had long been an opponent of the earl. If anyone was going to pour insinuations about Rosebery into Queensberry's ear that man was Henry Labouchère, who may have delighted in stirring up the rage of the volatile marquess against his enemy. Queensberry, said Frank Harris, 'was just the sort of person a wise man would avoid and a clever one would use – a dangerous, sharp, ill-handled tool'.[31]

Queensberry's letter of 6 August was not, however, an uncontrolled rant; it was a deliberate attempt to goad Rosebery into some sort of physical confrontation with every insult he could reasonably commit to paper. 'Cher fat Boy,' it began, 'this shall be my concluding letter to you'. Complaining that he had

had no response to his letters to the Queen he went on: 'I presume the savoury odour of your Jew money bags has too delicious a fragrance to allow me to expect any justice in high quarters. Which would brand yourself as what I have always heard you described the greatest liar in Europe.' He adds, in an odd moment of calm explanation, 'I wish to insult you & that is why I address you in this fashion . . . I would prefer having 15 minutes with your fat self in a 16 foot ring & hand gloves to being created an English Duke or even a Bishop . . . therefore oh fat Boy keep yourself fit, use a skipping rope mighty man of valour, you will find it good for your fat carcass.' He tells Rosebery that he has a 'pounding ball', which he is having inscribed in black letters 'The Jew pimp' and will 'daily punch it to keep my hand in, until we meet once more'. Of Francis he says:

I make allowances for him. The title he should have taken is Dufferhead. Obstinacy and foolishness were the principal qualities that allowed him to lend himself to such a gross slight to his father. I do not think he really saw it when I told him of it, he will certainly eventually have to choose between his father and your fat self, but no doubt as he grows older he will find you out. He is very green & childish yet even for his age.

Queensberry added that the individual who suggested 'this dirty scurvy business' (McKinstry transcribes this as 'dirty Jewry business') is 'Alfred Montgomery a pimp of the first water and quite fitted by nature to run in double harness with yourself . . . it would be the hell of a race & you might win by a foreskin'.

Rosebery read the first page of the letter, then set it aside. Queensberry was in Monte Carlo when he learned that Lord Rosebery was at Bad Homburg and determined to tackle him personally. On 14 August, however, he sent a taunting telegram: 'Intended coming today. Too hot. Will keep. Strongly recommend skipping rope.'[32] Rosebery decided to take no notice of either letter or telegram but mentioned them to his secretary, Munro Ferguson. On the evening of the 19th Rosebery was out taking a walk when Ferguson hurried up and told him he had just seen Queensberry in the gardens. They decided to consult solicitor Sir George Lewis (knighted in the same honours list that had elevated Francis) who was also at the resort. Lewis begged Rosebery to go back to his lodgings 'to avoid any collision with a lunatic'[33] while he went to fetch the chief of police. Rosebery returned and read through the whole of Queensberry's letter, only then realising that it contained a challenge to fisticuffs. The chief of police arrived and it was decided that on the following morning Rosebery should not go to take the waters, while the police chief would visit Queensberry and tell him he would not be allowed to cause trouble.

Early next morning, according to Rosebery's account – the information presumably communicated to him by others – 'Lord Queensberry paraded the promenade tramping about with great ferocity informing everyone – even the ladies – of the direful things he was going to do to "that b-y pimp" or that "b-y b-r Rosebery"'.[34]* At 9 a.m. the chief of police spoke to Queensberry and received his 'word of honour to commit no assault & offer no insult while in Homburg'. Queensberry changed his lodgings twice before noon, perhaps to evade the police, but he must have been observed and his movements reported to Rosebery. That afternoon Queensberry made a number of visits 'informing people that he was playing an infallible system at Monte Carlo through three men whom he was superintending'. He had advised Rosebery, 'I also some day may have the Queensberry money bags, but dear Jew Christian friend they will not be acquired in the same way as yours were.'[35]

The Prince of Wales was also staying at Bad Homburg and that evening Queensberry called on him, saying that he intended to leave the next morning. 'The best thing you can do,' said the Prince. 'We are quiet people in Homburg & don't like disturbance.'[36] Before Queensberry left he sent a note to the Prince calling Rosebery a liar. He left on the 7 a.m. train bound for Metz and Paris.

Rosebery's secretary wrote to the Queen from Bad Homburg on 29 August:

> Lord Queensberry has been here with the object of carrying out his avowed intention of publicly insulting Lord Rosebery, having previously written him a letter which alone would prove the writer insane. It is however a material and unpleasant addition to the labours of Your Majesty's service

---

* Hyphens as per the original manuscript. McKinstry has transcribed this as 'boy pimp and boy lover' but Rosebery's dashes are more likely to be taking the place of swear words. 'Bloody pimp' and 'bloody bugger' are possible.

to be pursued by a pugilist of unsound mind. On this occasion however Lord Queensberry, on an admonition from the police, left Homburg for Monte Carlo . . .[37]

It is often claimed that Queensberry threatened Rosebery with a whipping and walked up and down outside Rosebery's hotel with a dog-whip in his hand. The sole source of this allegation is Bosie's *Autobiography*. Bosie, who was not a witness to the events in Bad Homburg, was himself a mean hand with a whip when roused. No one actually present mentioned a whip; indeed, the correspondence and memoranda suggest that Queensberry was after a man-to-man glove fight.

As expected, Francis's peerage caused a rift between father and son. This was probably mostly Queensberry's doing as he nursed his hurt feelings, but Francis may have found it easy to stay away from his difficult father. The new peer took his duties seriously. That September he visited some Wyndham relatives and impressed Walpurga, Lady Paget as 'an excellent, amiable little man',[38] although his conscientious nature made him the bane of the house-maids as he was always up by 8 a.m. writing his letters in the drawing room.

On 22 August Queensberry arrived in Monte Carlo still smarting from his slights and defeats. Here he discovered letters and telegrams left for him by Percy, expressing his confidence in financial success in the Australian goldfields on the basis of which he asked his father's consent to his marriage with Minnie.

'You really cannot expect me to take in all this at once,' Queensberry replied:

it sounds much like fairy tale but of course I shall be glad if you have dropped into anything good. Don't you think it is rather premature to talk about marriage on the strength of what may turn out of all this. My dear fellow it is no use to ask my consent to such a marriage. I know nothing of the girl & you have given me no opportunity of even knowing anything at all about her. It seems to me you have always done pretty well without my consent. When you are in a position to marry you can marry whom you please. At present after all that has happened and with you with no assured prospects of even keeping yourself I cannot and will not encourage such a thing as this. In saying I give my consent suppose nothing comes of all this.

Are you going to handicap yourself further with a penniless wife. What are you going to do carry her about on a camel after you in that rough country out there. If there is anything in all this & you have really dropped on your feet it is time enough for me to say give my consent. . . . having a lot of penniless children I really do not wish the burden increased by a lot of similar grandchildren.[39]

Queensberry wrote to Sybil, a letter which he later told Percy 'was perfectly kind, speaking about your girl . . . and saying that of course I could not object to your going and seeing her sometimes but that I could not have you living down there altogether and doing nothing for yourself, thereby hinting that you do something for yourself and were in a position to marry should I with-draw my objection'.[40] Queensberry's concern is understandable. At the age of nearly twenty-five, Percy's only reliable means of support was his father, his efforts at establishing a career had so far proved to be unrealistic and chaotic, and Queensberry could see the prospect of Percy, his wife and a growing family becoming a permanent financial burden.

Sybil did not reply to Queensberry's letter, and he later discovered to his annoyance and frustration that the marriage had already been decided upon.

On 11 September 1893 Percy Douglas and Minnie Walters were married at Boyton Church, Launceston. Viscount Drumlanrig was best man, and Sybil, Bosie and Sholto all attended. Beau and Florence sent gifts. Queensberry was not at the wedding – he was probably still abroad, and may have been told by telegram. According to the eleventh marquess he was furious, and a 'cascade of vitriolic letters' came pouring in by every post.[41] If true, none of these has survived, but there may be some confusion here with the angry correspondence in 1895 following the Wilde scandal. A letter written by Queensberry to Percy from Carter's Hotel at 14 Albemarle Street on 17 September 1893 shows that he had just returned to England to see his solicitor Mr Jamieson about making a financial settlement on his son. The plans went awry, chiefly it appears because of Percy's indolence, and Queensberry was annoyed. The 'miscarriage of what I wished to do for you & the interference of Mr Jamieson was entirely your own fault,' he wrote. Percy had failed to tell Jamieson what he wanted, written 'most abusive letters' to the solicitor, and set 'that foolish wife of yours upon me to do your own business'. The exasperated father advised his heir '. . . you must be very dense & stupid if you don't see now that what I offered to do for you was entirely in your favour & I should get no advantage from it. . . . The money is perfectly safe you agreeing to re intail'. Here he inserts 'my father was in the same position as is Drumlanrig'.[42]

Percy still felt that his fortunes lay in Australia. In November 1893 he was elected Fellow of the Royal Geographical Society, joined the board of management of West Australian Goldfields Ltd and prepared for an early return. Lord and Lady Percy Douglas sailed for Australia on the Orient Line steamship *Oruba* on 1 December and arrived in Albany on 6 January 1894. Back in Australia, David Carnegie, unsuccessful in his search for gold, had been working as a surface hand on Bayley's mine. After many months of labour he 'took train for Perth, where I eagerly awaited the arrival of my old friend and companion, Percy Douglas. He meanwhile had had his battles to fight in the financial world, and had come out to all appearances on top, having been instrumental in forming an important mining company from which we expected great things.'[43]

Percy did not accompany Carnegie on his subsequent arduous prospecting expeditions. Carnegie never complained about the division of labour in which he seems to have done most of the physical work under tough conditions while Percy dealt with finance. He named two mountains after his friend: Mount Douglas and Mount Hawick, after Percy's title Lord Douglas of Hawick and eventually made enough money to fund his future expeditions. Although Percy was initially unsuccessful in disposing of the claims he had staked, there was a sudden boom in west Australian goldfields and he was reputed to have made about £20,000. Unfortunately, he had got the finance bug and thought he could become a millionaire by playing the stock market. He was, said his adoring brother Bosie, 'recklessly generous, confiding and extravagant'[44] and 'always imagined that he was just on the brink of making an enormous fortune'.[45] Percy started to speculate on a large scale, and the money he made in Australia ran rapidly through his fingers. He later claimed that he had been 'a very rich man one day, poor the next . . . the Stock Exchange knew more than I did'.[46] He spent the rest of his life looking for wealth in financial schemes that never amounted to anything, and getting by on loans and bail-outs.

CHAPTER 14

Wounded Feelings

———•———

THERE was another disappointment awaiting Queensberry on his return from the Continent in 1893. Bosie had left Oxford without a degree, having failed to turn up for his final exams in June. Queensberry was understandably angry, and wrote what Wilde later described as 'a very vulgar, violent and abusive letter. The letter [Bosie] sent him in reply was every way worse.'[1] Bosie claimed that he missed the examination because of illness and might have taken his degree later but that his father was happy for him not to, saying that 'he had never known a degree to be worth twopence to anybody'.[2] Whether or not Queensberry ever said this, his feelings about Bosie's failure to take up a profession are unambiguous. 'All the time you were wasting at Oxford I was put off with an assurance that you were eventually to go into the Civil Service or to the Foreign Office, and then I was put off with an assurance that you were going to the Bar,' Queensberry wrote later. 'It appears to me that you intend to do nothing. I utterly decline, however, to supply you with sufficient funds to enable you to loaf about. You are preparing a wretched future for yourself.'[3]

When Queensberry spoke to Bosie's tutor at Oxford, he received another far greater shock: Bosie had left university in disgrace. Although Queensberry was told the full circumstances he kept the distressing story to himself. The eleventh marquess stated without going into detail that Bosie had left 'at the request of the authorities!'[4] It is not too far a stretch of the imagination to suggest that there may have been a homosexual scandal. In the light of rumours about Francis's peerage this new revelation about Bosie must have been especially stinging.

In the autumn of 1893 Queensberry was holidaying at the Clifton Hotel, Eastbourne when his life took another fateful lurch, in the attractive shape of Ethel Maud Weeden.

Ethel was born in Pendleton, Lancashire, on 23 October 1872, the fourth child of Edward Charles Weeden whose declared occupation was 'gentleman', and his wife Florence, daughter of a Pendleton merchant. Edward's source of income was dividends on railway shares. By 1881 the couple must have separated, for Florence was boarding with a family in Marylebone while Edward lived at Park Villa, College Road, Eastbourne with their five children. On 22 January 1888 Edward Weeden died aged fifty-eight, leaving an estate of just under £2,500. Florence moved into the Eastbourne house, and in 1890 she married Irish barrister and solicitor Thomas De Courcy Atkins.

The family was well known in Eastbourne society, where Atkins was a leading light in the Liberal Party and Ethel's two older sisters were active in church work at St Saviour's. How Queensberry met Ethel is unknown, but the Douglases and the Weedens had some previous acquaintance, since Ethel's brother, Edward St Clair, knew Bosie at Oxford where he was taking his MA prior to entering the Church. On 24 November 1893 Edward wrote a letter to 'My dear Bosie' which ends 'I find that I have one of your books, which must have drifted into my rooms at Oxford. If you will send me an address I will return it.'[5] Edward had been abroad, and returned at the start of November to find to his surprise that Ethel had met Queensberry and they were engaged to be married.

Queensberry could be good company when he wanted to be, gallant and attentive to women, and willing to acknowledge their spirit and intelligence. Ethel was 'an exceedingly graceful woman. She is tall, possesses an admirable carriage, has a charming complexion, and a mass of wavy fair hair.'[6] Like Sybil, Ethel was a publicly acclaimed beauty. 'She is a well-known figure on the Eastbourne parade, and invariably attracts an admiring glance.'[7] It would be cynical though probably not far from the truth to suggest that Ethel saw in her middle-aged swain a title and advancement into the ranks of the landed gentry, while Queensberry saw in Ethel a possible cure for his impotence. Ethel's brother did his best to dissuade her from the marriage, 'to which I was opposed for various reasons, disparity of age and so on', and at last received a promise from Ethel that she would not see Queensberry for six months. Edward assured Bosie that his opposition was 'not due to personal considerations; and indeed I have never seen Lord Queensberry for more than half an hour in my life'. Queensberry, however, was not prepared to wait, and persuaded Ethel that the promise to her brother was not binding because of the promises she had previously made to Queensberry himself. As there was a fifteen-day wait for a special licence, they must have applied on Ethel's twenty-first birthday and there was a quiet wedding at Eastbourne register office on 7 November. The groom was described as '49 years of age, but looks younger, has dark hair and whiskers, his upper lip being shaven'.[8] There were two witnesses, Queensberry's valet Thomas Gill, the man who had supplied the essential evidence at the divorce hearing in 1887, and 'J. Hillman,' probably a clerk. The only others present were John Nicholls the registrar and Albert Hurst, deputy to the superintendent registrar. The couple left Eastbourne and the Weedens were sent a telegram: 'Send Ethel's clothes. Married to the Marquess of Queensberry.'[9] There was no official announcement in the newspapers and news of the event did not filter out for two days.

The marriage was in trouble from the start. The newly-weds spent their honeymoon in three locations, Carter's Hotel and Brown's Hotel, both in London's Albemarle Street, and the Royal Hotel, Ventnor, Isle of Wight, although how long they spent in each and whether they went to London before or after Ventnor is not known. The bride was willing and the groom was keen, but the marriage was not consummated. Were the changes of hotel made in the search for a more conducive environment? One can imagine the increasingly frustrated and despairing marquess suggesting that a change of scene would overcome the problem. The marriage rapidly collapsed. Bosie alleged that his father deserted his new bride – who, he asserted, was only seventeen – on the day after the wedding, both of which statements are untrue, but the cohabitation of the unhappy couple cannot have lasted long and Ethel decided to avoid controversy by going to stay in Marseilles.

In the same month there was more unhappiness for the Douglas family, with the death of Queensberry's sister Gertrude at the age of fifty-one. Gertrude's unorthodox marriage had not brought her the contentment she had craved. The little bakery in Brook Green, Hammersmith, like her writing, had not met with success. In 1887, probably prompted by the relocation of Archibald and her sister to Scotland, Gertrude purchased a small property called Barkerland near Dumfries and renamed it Maryland, where she and her husband lived with the dowager marchioness. She took an interest in animal welfare, joined the anti-vivisection movement and helped to establish the Canine Defence League. Her health, however, was declining as she had tuberculosis. In 1892 her husband Thomas went to South Africa as a volunteer soldier in Matabeleland. In the same year Gertrude published her last book, with the unhappy title *A Wasted Life and Marr'd*, featuring baker's boy Jack Merlin, 'a fair-haired, blue-eyed youth of singularly attractive appearance' with a 'cheery presence and happy smile'.[10] *The Graphic* described it as 'one of those depressing stories in which the characters seem to be created for the sole purpose of being made miserable'.[11] Gertrude and her mother moved to Hendon, but in the autumn of 1893 she was told that her condition was incurable. She entered the convent of the German Nuns of the Sacred Heart of Mary at Hendon, where, with her mother and Archibald at her side, she died on 25 November. She left a personal fortune of £2,000 together with her landed estate at Maryland, all bequeathed to her husband.*

On 8 November, following a spate of arguments with Bosie, Wilde, desperate for a separation, wrote to Sybil saying that her son was 'in a very bad state of health' and 'quite astray in life', and fearing he 'may . . . come to grief of some kind'.[12] He suggested that she make arrangements for him to go abroad, recommending that he stay with Lord and Lady Cromer in Egypt. Sybil wrote to Lady Cromer and Bosie was invited to spend the winter in Cairo. He departed at the start of December, a welcome respite from anxiety for Queensberry. He was probably unaware that Bosie was still writing to Oscar who was refusing to reply to his letters, and also to Sybil, vigorously defending Oscar against her assertion that Wilde had acted towards him as Henry Wotton had to Dorian Gray. Sybil wrote to Wilde deploring Bosie's vanity and behaviour, but saying that she was unable to speak to him about his extravagance and the kind of life he was leading because she was afraid of his temper. Just as Queensberry blamed his children's perceived defects on the Montgomerys, Sybil blamed the Douglases for Bosie's 'terrible legacy'.[13] He was 'the one of my children who has inherited the fatal Douglas tempera-ment',[14] she wrote to Wilde, who agreed with her assessment so far as to reveal to her the trouble Bosie had been in at Oxford although 'forced into reticences and generalities'[15] as to what had led to the friendship, and the fact that he had been 'continually in the same manner troubled'.[16]

---

* In 1896 Thomas Stock was back in England where, on 19 March, giving his profession as 'trooper' and his age as thirty-five, he married hotelier's daughter Annie Louisa Ashley. He returned to South Africa and died at Bulawayo on 8 October 1896.

Wilde also blamed the Douglas heredity for the family woes. 'Through your father,' he wrote to Bosie, 'you come of a race, marriage with whom is horrible, friendship fatal, and that lays violent hands either on its own life, or the lives of others.'[17]

Both parents would have been delighted when Bosie, through the influence of his grandfather and Lord Cromer, then Consul-General of Egypt, was offered the position of honorary attaché to Lord Currie, the ambassador at Constantinople, but he was in no great hurry to take up the post and spent some time in Athens then Paris where, after months of pathetic appeals, Wilde agreed to meet him.

The papers for Queensberry's second divorce had been served on 9 March 1894 and alleged that Queensberry 'was at the time of the said marriage and has ever since been wholly unable to consummate the same by reason of the frigidity and impotence of his parts of generation, and that such frigidity and impotence are incurable by art or skill'.[18] The petition asked the court to declare the marriage null and void and order Queensberry to pay the costs. Queensberry might have gracefully acquiesced, but it was not an allegation he could accept with equanimity, even if rejecting it would require the medical examination of both parties. Perhaps he gambled on his bride not being as innocent as she had appeared. He engaged Sir George Lewis as his solicitor, and on 22 March a counter-petition was filed claiming that the marriage had been consummated and that 'the Respondent was at the time of the said marriage and from thence hitherto hath been and still is apt for coition as will appear on inspection'.[19]

On 30 March the court appointed two medical inspectors, Henry Spencer Smith FRCS and Dr William Sanderson Wyman, to examine the 'parts and organs of generation' of both petitioner and respondent, in Queensberry's case to report on whether he was 'capable of performing the act of generation and if incapable of so doing whether such his Impotency can or cannot be relieved or removed by art or skill'.[20] Wyman was not a specialist, but Smith had been a member of a government commission appointed to inquire into the question of venereal disease in the army and navy and may well have been the court's choice to examine Queensberry. The examination of Ethel was to determine first of all whether or not she was a virgin and, if she was, whether she had any impediment to prevent the consummation of marriage and, if she did, to assess whether this was treatable.

As he awaited this humiliating medical, Queensberry's enquiries had established that Bosie's relationship with Wilde was as strong as ever. He may well have learned of the reunion in Paris. The pair had since returned to London where they had been seen together in numerous public locations and were the subject of scandalous society gossip. It may have been then that he employed Cook, the detective, to discover more about Oscar Wilde, and his worst fears would have been realised. Queensberry, more than ever determined to force Bosie to break with Wilde, sent his son furious letters threatening to thrash him and have him thrown out of restaurants if he ever found him in Wilde's company. He had gone to the restaurants he knew Bosie and Wilde frequented and told the managers and maîtres d'hôtel that he would assault Bosie and Wilde if they were caught together on their premises. Bosie was unworried: 'persons who make threats of the "thrashings" they are going to give, and who "warn" other people about the terrible things they are going to do are very unlikely to be really dangerous. If my father had really meant to assault me or Wilde in a restaurant he would have done it first and talked about it afterwards.'[21] Defiantly, he made a point of going to those very restaurants (he did not say what the management thought) and several times wrote to his father in advance telling him where he would be, giving him the date and time and inviting him to 'come round and "see what happened" to him if he started any of his "ruffianly tricks"'.[22]

The conflict between father and son had come to public notice. Frank Harris later recalled that he was entering his club just as Queensberry was leaving with some friends.[23]

'"I'll do it," I heard him cry, "I'll teach the fellow to leave my son alone. I'll not have their names coupled together."

I caught a glimpse of the thrust-out combative face and the hot grey eyes.' Asking what the matter was, Harris was told that it was, '"Only Queensberry"' swearing to stop Wilde from going about with his son. Harris panicked at the thought of 'that violent combative insane creature pouncing' on his heedless friend, and warned Wilde, suggesting he write Queensberry a conciliatory letter and make a friend of him. Wilde said that if he did so Queensberry would insist he gave up his friendship with Bosie, and that he refused to do.[24]

On 1 April 1894 Queensberry again found Wilde and Bosie lunching at the Café Royal, but this time he had no illusions about the relationship and would not be charmed. He went to their table and shook hands with his son, then accepted Wilde's invitation to join them. There was some friendly conversation about Egypt and Queensberry drank Oscar's wine, but all the time he was watching them carefully, and it may be that some glances of admiration or even affection passed between the couple, which confirmed his fears. Queensberry is usually portrayed in biographies of Wilde as rampaging about out of control, in a permanent froth of rage, but despite all the threats and bluster, Queensberry, when it came to it, did not make a public scene. He was far from being a coward, so his restraint may have stemmed from an unwillingness to create a public disturbance when Bosie was present, or from legal advice, or perhaps from both. His next action, however, demonstrated how he must have been feeling. He returned to Carter's Hotel and wrote an unhappy letter to Bosie.

> Alfred,
>
> It is extremely painful for me to have to write to you in the strain I must; but please understand that I decline to receive any answers from you in writing in return. After your recent hysterical impertinent ones I refuse to be annoyed with such

He suggested that, if Bosie had anything to say, he should 'come here and say it in person'. After taking his son to task for his failure and disgrace at Oxford, and lack of any attempt to enter a profession, he came 'to the more painful part of this letter' and ordered him to stop seeing Wilde. There is some very considered phrasing, a sign perhaps that Queensberry had already consulted a solicitor. 'I make no charge; but to my mind to pose as a thing is as bad as to be it.' Emotion, however, soon took over. Referring presumably to his observation of their behaviour in the restaurant he wrote: 'With my own eyes I saw you both in the most loathsome and disgusting relationship as expressed by your manner and expression. Never in my experience have I ever seen such a sight as that in your horrible features. No wonder people are talking as they are. And now I hear on good authority, but this may be false, that his wife is petitioning to divorce him for sodomy and other crimes. Is this true, or do you not know of it?' he asked, no doubt hoping that the revelation might have some effect. 'If I thought the actual thing was true, and it became public property, I should be quite justified in shooting him at sight.' The letter was signed 'Your disgusted so-called father'.[25]

There is no evidence that Queensberry ever carried a gun except when out hunting, or ever shot at another human being, and this was one of his typical blustering threats, the ramping up from a thrashing to a shooting indicating the intensity of his feelings. The divorce rumour was untrue, but Queensberry was being supplied with many items of ill-founded gossip, some of which may have been malicious lies deliberately intended to stir up trouble. The frantic father hardly knew what to believe.

Wilde, on seeing the letter, realised that he was caught in a war between father – whom he described as 'drunken, déclassé and half-witted'[26] – and son, and wanted to have nothing to do with it, but Bosie was defiant and had already replied with what he later called 'my celebrated telegram: "What a funny little man you are!"'[27]

'I did this deliberately, as being what I considered the most effective way of hitting back at him . . . to show him that I treated his threats with utter contempt. No doubt it filled him with rage, but it had the result of convincing him that I was not disposed to be bluffed.'[28] Wilde realised that the telegram, which he described as 'foolish and vulgar' had 'conditioned the whole of [Bosie's] subsequent relations with [his] father',[29] escalating a private quarrel into a public one.

On 3 April Queensberry, stung by the telegram, replied:

You impertinent young jackanapes. I request that you will not send such messages to me by telegraph. If you send me any more such telegrams, or come with any impertinence, I will give you the thrashing you deserve. Your only excuse is that you must be crazy. I hear from a man at Oxford that you were thought crazy there, and that accounts for a good deal that has happened. If I catch you again with that man I will make a public scandal in a way you little dream of; it is already a suppressed one. I prefer an open one, and at any rate I shall not be blamed for allowing such a state of things to go on.

He then repeated his threat to 'stop all supplies,' adding 'if you are not going to make any attempt to do something' – presumably he meant enter a profession – 'I shall certainly cut you down to a mere pittance'.[30]

The allowance was eventually stopped. From time to time, Queensberry would offer to renew it if Bosie gave up his friendship with Wilde, but without effect. Thereafter Bosie relied on handouts from his mother and grandfather and the generosity of Wilde. Soon afterwards Bosie was told that Lord Currie was furious that he had not yet arrived at Constantinople and declined to have him in the post. It may have been Bosie's indolence that had lost him the position, although he always maintained that he had not been told he was expected to go to Constantinople immediately. It is possible of course that Lord Currie changed his mind after hearing the rumours about Wilde. For once Alfred Montgomery and Queensberry were in agreement: they were both annoyed with Bosie.

While Bosie later said that he believed his father treated him cruelly,

... at the very beginning of the trouble his desire to separate me from Wilde was prompted by a genuine wish to do what he thought right in the circumstances. But his method was doomed to inevitable failure, chiefly because he tried to bully me instead of reasoning with me. He might have guessed that I was quite as obstinate as he was. His threats to stop my allowance (which he actually carried out within a year of the time when he first made it) had simply the effect of exasperating me and making me more determined than ever to stick to Wilde.[31]

There is considerable truth in this. Queensberry, outraged and distressed by his son's behaviour, was unable to perceive that he and Bosie were in many ways very alike. The headstrong youth and the old warrior had charged each other and locked horns and neither was going to back down. Bosie later posed what might have been a solution: 'If instead of ordering me to give up my friendship with Wilde and stopping my money supplies, he had arranged to send me abroad with a decent allowance, he would undoubtedly have succeeded in separating me from Wilde for a long enough period to allow the whole affair to settle down calmly and ultimately fizzle out.'[32]

Unknown to Bosie, this was very nearly the idea that Queensberry had in mind. He was seriously thinking of going abroad and taking Bosie with him, to remove him from Wilde's company and supply some parental supervision. It is interesting to speculate what some quality 'father-and-son' time might have done for their stormy relationship. Unfortunately, Queensberry discussed this scheme with Henry Labouchère, who declared that 'there would be no harm if his lordship gave Wilde a sound horsewhipping; and ... advised his lordship to wash his hands of the son, having done all in his power to reclaim him'.[33] Queensberry dropped the idea.

Bosie, who well knew how little it took to set his father off in a fury that he would later regret, claimed that Queensberry had 'thrown away even the pretence that he was acting in my interest. He was full of vindictive rage against me, and his openly avowed object was to "smash" me.'[34] Somewhere, underlying the whole terrible business was a father's care for his son; indeed, if Queensberry had not cared for Bosie he would not have been so angry, but as the scandal escalated and emotions soared, Bosie was unable to resist goading his father, and Queensberry, frustrated and grieved at being either defied or ignored by every member of his family, made threats he probably did not intend to carry out: 'he was,' said Bosie, 'incapable of understanding any point of view which did not coincide with his own,'[35] an accusation that could have been levelled against more than one member of the family, including Bosie himself.

Much later, in a rare passage of self-awareness, Bosie wondered if part of his father's grievance was based on jealousy:

It never occurred to me at the time, but I believe my father really was fond of me, and I think he sensed somehow that with the horrible heartlessness of youth (the undergraduate who imagines himself to be 'intellectual') I did not appreciate him as he really was, or felt himself to be. I probably showed him (God forgive me) that I thought him rather stupid in comparison with my brilliant friend.[36]

Admitting that he was in those days 'a spoilt and selfish little beast (though of a very attractive appearance)' he wonders 'Did I perhaps unconsciously wound the feelings of poor "Papa"?'[37]

The eleventh marquess speculated on what might have happened had Queensberry understood his obstinate son better, and his suggested solution was what we now call 'reverse psychology'. If Queensberry had ordered his son to stick with his friend through the gathering adversity, Bosie, he believed, would have dropped Wilde at once. Such subtlety was not in Queensberry's nature. What he cannot have known, however, was that the relationship between Wilde and Bosie was fatally unstable.

At the height of these tempestuous exchanges Queensberry's medical examination took place on 10 April and Ethel's ten days later. In view of the sensitive nature of the allegations all court hearings were held in camera. The medical reports are not in the divorce records, but the outcome makes it clear that Ethel was found to be a virgin, and not suffering from any condition that might have prevented intercourse. The marriage was to be annulled 'by reason of the frigidity impotency and malformation of the parts of generation of the said Respondent'.[38] Given that Queensberry was the father of five offspring it can be assumed that any malformation preventing intercourse was not a condition with which he had been born.

Some emotional respite was at hand, for Sybil provided funds to enable Bosie to leave the country once more. This time he was bound for Florence and left on 14 April. Wilde left the country on 27 April.

That summer Queensberry had obtained copies of letters written by Wilde to Bosie. While undoubtedly expressing a passionate affection, these were not in themselves proof that anything illegal had taken place. They would certainly not have proven sodomy, a felony punishable with life imprisonment. Queensberry did nothing at this juncture with either the letters or the evidence he had of Bosie's Oxford scandals. He may have been trying to put the situation out of his troubled mind.

Wilde and Bosie returned to England in June, and Bosie, frustrated that no further confrontations were taking place, goaded his father with, said Wilde, 'telegrams of such a character that at last the wretched man wrote to you and said that he had given orders to his servants that no telegrams were to be brought to him under any pretence whatsoever'.[39]

Sybil heard of this and wrote to Bosie on 20 June: 'As to your father we are told he is in a fairly quiet state now and not inclined to do anything more but your telegrams, which it seems you have sent lately, made him very angry so don't write or telegraph to him at all as he will vent his anger on poor Percy who has already got into trouble enough. I am sure Darling it is best to keep quite quiet now & not notice yr Father at all, people are beginning to understand him better now, & the feeling is getting strong against him.'[40]

The telegrams had their effect, and Queensberry was provoked into trying once again to locate Wilde and Bosie together in public. Bosie, faithful to his mother's instructions, gave up sending telegrams; he wrote to Queensberry on a postcard instead, saying that he was his own master, regarded any threats 'with absolute indifference' and was making a point of appearing with Wilde at restaurants.

If OW was to prosecute you in the criminal courts for libel you would get seven years' penal servitude . . . much as I detest you I am anxious to avoid this for the sake of the family; but if you try to assault me, I shall defend myself with a loaded revolver which I always carry; and if I shoot you or he shoots you, we shall be completely justified, as we shall be acting in self defence against a violent and dangerous rough, and I think if you were dead, not many people would miss you.[41]

The revolver was no empty threat, as Bosie – either by accident, thinking it was unloaded, or intentionally to cause a scene that he knew would be reported to his father – fired it in the Berkeley Hotel.

Queensberry, having been unsuccessful in locating Wilde in a public place, decided to confront him in his own home. The old Queensberry would have been unfazed at tackling a taller, younger man who considerably outweighed him (according to Bosie, Wilde was five inches taller and four stone heavier than Queensberry), indeed he would have relished the challenge, but the new Queensberry, feeling his age and privately suffering the curse of impotence, decided not to go alone. On 30 June, accompanied by another man who was never identified, but was assumed by Wilde to be a prizefighter, he went to Wilde's home in Tite Street. The *Evening News* referred to Queensberry's companion as 'a Mr. "Pip"',[42] presumably a reference to the fist fight in *Great Expectations*. The 'screaming scarlet Marquis',[43] as Wilde used to call him, paraphrasing a line in his poem *The Sphinx*, was shown in by 'Oscar's miniature and trembling footman, a boy of seventeen'.[44]

The only detailed account of the event is Wilde's. The interview took place in the ground floor library and started badly when Wilde walked over to the fireplace and Queensberry ordered him to sit down. Wilde, while no athlete, was no physical coward either, and told Queensberry 'I do not allow anyone to talk like that to me in my house or anywhere else. I suppose you have come to apologize for the statement you made about my wife and myself in letters you wrote to your son. I should have the right any day I choose to prosecute you for writing such a letter.'

'That letter was privileged,' said Queensberry, 'as it was written to my son.'

He was correct, and Wilde, his threat proving ineffective, became angry. 'How dare you say such things about your son and me?'

Queensberry now faced him with the rumours that had been pouring into his ear. 'You were both kicked out of the Savoy Hotel at a moment's notice for your disgusting conduct.'

'That is a lie.'

'You have taken furnished rooms for him in Piccadilly.'

'Somebody has been telling you an absurd set of lies about your son and me. I have done nothing of the kind.'

Queensberry, on the back foot, countered with something he knew to be true. 'I hear you were thoroughly well blackmailed for a disgusting letter you wrote to my son.'

'The letter was a beautiful letter and I never write except for publication,' said Wilde with a hint of his customary flippancy, but then changed his tone to a more considered one. 'Lord Queensberry, do you seriously accuse your son and me of improper conduct?' If he was hoping to entrap Queensberry into making a damaging statement before a witness he failed.

Queensberry chose his words carefully. 'I do not say that you are it,' he said, 'but you look it, and you pose as it, which is just as bad. If I catch you and my son together again in any public restaurant, I will thrash you.'

Wilde, like Bosie, probably knew that a threat and an action were two very different things. 'I do not know what the Queensberry rules are,' he said, 'but the Oscar Wilde rule is to shoot at sight.' He then told Queensberry to leave the house. Queensberry refused and Wilde said if he did not go he would call the police and have him put out.

Queensberry was not yet ready for such a confrontation. 'It is a disgusting scandal,' was his parting shot as he left.

'If it is so,' said Wilde, 'you are the author of the scandal and no one else.'

Queensberry and his companion went into the hallway where Wilde's servant was waiting to show them out.

'This is the Marquess of Queensberry, the most infamous brute in London,' said Wilde. 'You are never to allow him to enter my house again.'[45]

Wilde later wrote to Bosie of the horror he had felt when 'waving his small hands in the air in epileptic fury, your father, with his bully or his friend, between us, had stood uttering every foul word his foul mind could think of, and screaming the loathsome threats he afterwards with such cunning carried out'.[46]

Queensberry wrote to Sybil asking if Bosie had ever stayed at the Savoy Hotel with Wilde, and she wired back saying Bosie denied having been at the hotel in the last year. Queensberry didn't believe them. Sybil must have suggested that Queensberry should go and speak to her father, and initially he agreed, but on 6 July while staying at Skindles Hotel, Maidenhead for the Henley Royal Regatta, he wrote to Alfred Montgomery: 'I have changed my mind, and as I am not at all well, having been very much upset by what has happened the last ten days, I do not see why I should come dancing attendance on you.' Queensberry thought that Sybil, who he knew was funding Bosie, believed that he was making accusations against their son. It may well have been Bosie who gave her that impression. 'It is nothing of the kind,' Queensberry told Montgomery,

> I have made out a case against Oscar Wilde and I have to his face accused him of it. If I was quite certain of the thing, I would shoot the fellow at sight, but I can only accuse him of posing . . . . Your daughter appears now to be encouraging them, although she can hardly intend this. I don't believe Wilde will now dare defy me. He plainly showed the white feather the other day when I tackled him – damned cur and coward of the Rosebery type. As for this so-called son of mine, he is no son of mine, and I will have nothing to do with him. He may starve as far as I am concerned after his behaviour to me.[47]

Queensberry had, however, changed his mind about the origins of Drumlanrig's peerage and now believed that Sybil was behind it. 'I am now fully convinced that the Rosebery–Gladstone–Royal insult that came to me through my other son, that she worked that – I thought it was you. I saw Drumlanrig here on the river, which much upset me.'[48]

Bosie's cousin George Wyndham, MP was anxious to avoid a family scandal, and spoke to Wilde on 4 July to dissuade him from taking action against Queensberry. Nevertheless, Wilde decided to consult a solicitor. His natural choice was Sir George Lewis, but on being told that Queensberry had already engaged his old friend he wrote to check whether this was correct, seeking an opinion about possible proceedings. Lewis replied on 7 July confirming that he was acting for Queensberry and saying that under the circumstances it was impossible for him to provide an opinion. The choice of solicitor was an excellent one for Queensberry and quite probably a fatal one for Wilde. Lewis was highly experienced in settling society scandals out of court, and was the man who had made the blackmail of Bosie disappear. He knew Bosie's reputation better than any other legal man.

Wilde engaged sixty-five-year-old Charles Octavius Humphreys, of Humphreys, Son and Kershaw, a poor choice, since according to Wilde's biographer Richard Ellmann 'homosexuality was quite outside Humphreys' field of knowledge'.[49] Wilde asked if the letter of 1 April was actionable and whether anything could be done to restrain Queensberry's behaviour. Humphreys wrote to Queensberry on 11 July saying that Wilde had 'instructed me to give you the opportunity of retracting your assertions and insinuations, in writing with an apology for having made them' in order to 'prevent litigation'.[50]

There was a not unexpected but dignified response. 'I have received your letter here with considerable astonishment,' Queensberry replied on 13 July. 'I shall certainly not tender to Mr Oscar Wilde any apology for letters I have written to my son. I have made no direct accusation against Mr Oscar Wilde but desired to stop the association as far as my son is concerned.'[51] For a man usually depicted as a rampaging, insane bully Queensberry was steering a very careful course. He also had a powerful counter-threat. On 18 July he went to see Humphreys, and later that day wrote, 'Since seeing you this morning I have heard that the revolver has been given up. I shall therefore not insist on taking the step I threatened to do tomorrow morning of giving information to the police authorities.' He went on, however, to assert that if he continued to be defied 'by further scandals in public places' he would 'give information at Scotland Yard as to what has happened'.[52]

Neither side took legal action, but Queensberry, determined to keep Wilde and his son apart, continued to make the rounds of their usual haunts. 'Your father is on the rampage again,' Wilde wrote to Bosie '– been to the Café Royal to inquire for us, with threats etc. I think now it would have been better for me to have him bound over to keep the peace, but what a scandal! Still, it is intolerable to be dogged by a maniac.'[53]

Matters seemed to have come to a head, but instead things suddenly simmered down. Wilde had received an advance on a new play, and that summer he departed with his family for Worthing where he wrote *The Importance of Being Earnest*.

CHAPTER 15

Catastrophe

PERHAPS Queensberry had taken Labouchère's advice and was trying to wash his hands of Bosie. Made miserable by events in London he felt a need to get away, and headed off to Scotland, staying at Glen Stuart. 'I am so much better in the country and have taken such a horror of London life that I feel I shall never go back there and live the terrible life,' he wrote. 'I was so utterly depressed and wretched when I left London.'[1]

He had become reconciled to Percy's marriage and sent him an affectionate letter with a 'small cheque' a 'pony' (£25). 'I am going to stay here a week or ten days and shall get some shooting as I believe the partridges are pretty good this year.'[2] On learning that he was about to become a grandfather for the first time, he sent Percy £100. Dorothy Madeline Douglas was born in Perth, Australia, on 5 July 1894. Queensberry received the good news with an invitation to visit the family in Australia and replied to Percy:

I am glad . . . that Minnie got through alright what appears to have been a trying time but whether children are a matter of congratulation I hardly know. I am afraid they are not when they come to very young married people. I really don't know if I shall get out to Australia but there is a chance I may this winter . . . I am in so much better spirits since I came up here what with the splendid life stalking and out all day on these glorious hills and being with people I like that I feel quite different and up to making a start from here. If I get back to London where I get all by myself – there is nothing so terrible to me as living alone in a crowd. I get utterly unhinged and fit for nothing in a week. Well, if I wish to avoid London and don't hunt, I must travel, and if I go anywhere will come out to you as I shall be able to look forward to meeting you both and shall not feel so terribly, so

fearfully desolate as I always do now when I go alone on these travels. . . .
Give my best love to Minnie and thank her for her letter. This will answer
you both as I am not good at writing. I have heard of the great gold find at
Coolgardie, it was in all the papers here, and I wished only that you had
been one of the lucky ones who found it, but saw that you were not. . . . I
hope that you may have some luck yet.[3]

Bosie continued to see Wilde. On 19 August, while staying at Worthing,
he wrote to 'dearest Turts' complaining that ever since his return from Egypt
'that brute' had been giving him a 'fearful time', going

all over London spreading vile scandals . . . he has been to nearly every
restaurant [saying] that he was going to hit O W across the face with a
cane the next he saw us together . . . I need hardly say that the whole
family (with the exception of course of darling Mamma) simply backed
out of it; & Francy absolutely refused to even stick up for me to the
small extent of dining in public with me & O W to show that he did
not believe what my father said, though I implored him to do it. He
declined to have anything to do with it at all, & actually went out of
town to escape from any chance of being 'drawn into it' as he said! I never
had much opinion of Francy but I never before thought he was such a
cur as he proved himself to be. . . . Of course I am now absolutely
penniless. . . . If the beast would only die, it would be all right but I fear he
will live for ever![4]

Bosie continued to send postcards to his father, but Queensberry replied
from his Scottish retreat on 21 August that his son's writing was 'utterly
unreadable. . . . My object of receiving no written communication from you
is therefore kept intact. All future cards will go into the fire unread.' After
sarcastically congratulating Bosie on his autography suggesting that it might
get him a living as a crossing-sweeper, he added, 'I shall keep it as a specimen,
and also as a protection in case I ever feel tempted to give you the thrashing
you deserve. You reptile. You are no son of mine, and I never thought you
were.'[5] Queensberry, whose own handwriting is difficult to read, no more
thought Bosie was not his offspring than he intended to thrash him, but he
was unable to see any trace of himself in his wayward son.

Bosie replied in a telegram sent to Carter's Hotel, which was forwarded to Scotland by post. On 28 August Queensberry replied in a sorrowful but fatalistic mood, stating that he had torn it up and told the hotel not to forward any more:

> I have learned, thank goodness, to turn the keenest pangs to peacefulness. What could be keener pain than to have such a son as yourself fathered upon one? . . . it is the only confirming proof to me, if I needed any, how right I was to face every horror and misery I have done rather than run the risk of bringing more creatures into the world like yourself, and that was the entire and only reason of my breaking with your mother as a wife, so intensely was I dissatisfied with her as the mother of you children, and particularly yourself, whom, when quite a baby, I cried over you the bitterest tears a man ever shed that I had brought such a creature into the world, and unwittingly had committed such a crime.

After expressing the usual doubts that Bosie was his son he went on: 'No wonder you have fallen prey to this horrible brute. I am only sorry for you as a human creature. You must gang your ain gait. Well, it would be rather a satisfaction to me, because the crime then is not to me. As you see, I am philosophical and take comfort from anything; but really, I am sorry for you. You must be demented; there is madness on your mother's side.'[6] He told Bosie not to write to him again.

That September, having enjoyed some partridge shooting and salmon fishing, Queensberry was deer stalking in Ross-shire when he received a heart-warming piece of news. Francis, whose ascendant career had received another boost the previous March when Lord Rosebery was appointed Prime Minister, was preparing to announce his engagement. The prospective bride was twenty-three-year-old Alexandra Mina Ellis, third daughter of General (later Sir) Arthur Edward Augustus Ellis whose distinguished military career had been followed by the post of equerry-in-waiting to the Prince of Wales. Queensberry was still not on speaking terms with his eldest son, but Francis decided to travel north to ask his father's blessing. On 18 September Drumlanrig was staying with General Ellis and his family at Mothecombe near Ivybridge in Devon when he wrote to Lord Rosebery.

My dear Lord Rosebery

You have always shown me so much kindness and affection that I feel I cannot delay a moment writing to tell you that I am engaged to marry Alexandra Ellis who is Arthur Ellis's third daughter. I am leaving this [*sic*] today for Hatch House to see my mother and then go north to Dumfriesshire to see my father. What the result of the interview will be I don't know, and I feel it is not exactly an auspicious moment! However that cannot be helped and of course I know in any case that I shall have to look forward to considerable difficulties and that we shall probably have to wait some time, and I don't really know as far as my father is concerned that one moment is better or worse than another.

I am going north tomorrow and shall stay with Arthur Douglas at Comlongon Castle, Ruthwell, Dumfriesshire, and shall then go on to Edinburgh most probably to see a lawyer. You were kind enough to say that I might come to Dalmeny, so if you are there the end of this week and would like to have me for a night or two I should like very much to come. I hope you will not consider that marriage is likely to impair the efficiency of a private secretary, or that it is a crime to be visited with as heavy a penalty as lack of moustache on a Military Attaché!

I am yours sincerely and affectionately,

Drumlanrig[7]

There is no hint of homosexual feelings in this letter, but it reveals the warmth of Francis's regard for his mentor. Rosebery was twenty years his senior, and Francis may have seen him as a father figure and preferred his support to that of the frequently absent and unpredictable Queensberry. The marquess might well have been jealous that another man – and a man moreover who he believed had deliberately slighted him – was enjoying the respect and confidence to which he felt he as a father should be entitled. At Hatch House, her Wiltshire home, Sybil's initial reaction to the engagement was not good and she wrote to Bosie. 'We have all been thrown into confusion . . . it is all so sudden that it has been quite a shock to me and made me quite ill. . . . He is in town expecting to be sent for by yr Father who seems quite amiable about it . . . I am too frightened to do anything but cry I cannot be sure she is good enough for him.'[8]

On 20 September Francis was back in London where, in strict confidence, he revealed his marriage plans to his colleagues. He was clearly very excited, saying that his intended "'simply fizzes like – like champagne dear old chap, don't you know!'"[9]

There was one person who might have been very unhappy at the prospect of one of Rosebery's favourites marrying into the Ellis family: Henry Labouchère, first cousin to Alexandra's mother Mina. Queensberry and Labouchère were unalike in many respects. Labouchère was a man of words, while Queensberry preferred physical action. Labouchère acted after considered thought; Queensberry was more likely to fly off the handle. Queensberry was openly sympathetic towards women's position in society and supported female suffrage, whereas Labouchère believed that women were 'mentally flighty' and unfit to exercise the vote.[10] Although anti-Semitism was a commonplace of Victorian society and homosexuality was regarded with abhorrence, Queensberry's antipathies were on a personal level, aimed at individuals he disliked or whose behaviour affected him; Labouchère, by contrast, was openly opposed to Jews in public life, and anti-homosexual in principle. Despite these differences they were united as freethinkers. Labouchère must have known that if he wanted a man dealt with, without consequence to himself, the best way to go about it was to wind up Queensberry like a clockwork toy and set him going.

In 1885 Labouchère was in parliament late one night debating the Criminal Law Amendment Act, which was designed to protect young girls from sexual exploitation. He proposed the introduction of a new section and in the early hours of the morning it became law. This notorious piece of legislation (inspired perhaps by the 1884 Dublin Castle scandal, whose proceedings were held to be too revolting to publish), made undefined acts of 'gross indecency' between males a misdemeanour punishable by up to two years' imprisonment with or without hard labour. Although sodomy and indecent assault had long been against the law, this was the first time that homosexual acts not involving sodomy between consenting adult males in private had been criminalised. The Act, described as 'The Blackmailer's Charter',[11] caused untold misery for eighty-two years and was to be the instrument of Oscar Wilde's downfall. It was first invoked in the 1889 Cleveland Street scandal, which filled the newspapers for over a year from the autumn of 1889 and obliged the Prince of Wales's equerry to flee abroad.

Francis's meeting with his father did not take place, since the peerage slight still rankled, but friendly letters were exchanged and Queensberry approved the match. He stated later that he 'had said I would do what I could to help him the cause of our quarrel was not mentioned, though I had declined all interviews until some expression of regret had been offered for the outrage'.[12]

The summer of 1894 was a time of contentment such as Queensberry would never know again. He had left the conflicts behind, made his peace with Percy and Minnie, become a grandfather and seen the start of a possible reconciliation with Francis. He would have been even happier had he known that the relationship between Oscar and Bosie had reached a final snapping point. That October the pair were staying at the Metropole Hotel Brighton, when Bosie fell ill with influenza and Wilde looked after him. As soon as Bosie had recovered Wilde took to his bed with the same ailment, but was left alone and uncared for by his young lover, who seemed disgusted by his condition and sent him an abusive letter. Wilde had had enough. As soon as he was recovered, he determined to return to London, and ask Sir George Lewis to write to Queensberry to say that he never wanted to see Bosie again and also to send a personal letter to Bosie informing him of his decision. By Thursday 18 October the meeting with Lewis had been arranged, but on the Friday morning Wilde opened his newspaper and saw the news that changed everything – a tragedy that sent him running back to Bosie and destroyed in one shocking and unforeseen moment all of Queensberry's hopes for the future.

In the first week of October 1894 there had been no hint of anything amiss when Francis, Lord Drumlanrig went to stay at the Quantock estate near Bridgwater in Somerset, the country seat of Edward Stanley MP, husband of Mina Ellis's sister Mary. Although rumours of the engagement had been appearing in the press since 4 October, the news was not yet official and Francis intended to make a formal announcement during that visit, probably on 19 October. Notices had already been sent to the local press.

On Thursday 18 October Francis set out with a shooting party. His companions were William Elton of Heathfield Lodge near Taunton, General Ellis's son Gerald, Mr Bevill Fortescue (probably John Bevill Fortescue, a Cornish barrister) and Henry William Mordaunt, manager of an insurance office. They were accompanied by head keeper Richard Webber, his son Frank, under-keeper Alfred Elliott and a beater called Trapnell. Stanley was away from his estate that day, presiding over a dinner of the North Petherton Agricultural Association. The weather was fine, a good number of game birds were shot and a picnic lunch enjoyed. The ladies, meanwhile – Mrs Stanley, her sister, nieces and sister-in-law – had gone out for a drive in a carriage, and on two occasions when stopping at a gate, they encountered and spoke to the shooting party.

The men were shooting partridges and pheasants in a turnip field near Halsey Cross Farm about two miles from Quantock Lodge, starting at the northern end of the field where two birds were shot and picked up. Francis shot a bird halfway down the field, and they spent some time looking for it, then Elton shot a bird, which fell in an adjoining turnip field. They walked halfway across the field and turned to look at a keeper who was still searching for the wounded bird. Elton and Fortescue had a brief conversation at the bramble hedge that separated the two turnip fields from a grass field, and then walked on to a gap in the hedge. 'I think my bird is in the hedge,' Francis told Mordaunt, and climbed through into the grass field, going on for a few yards. When he did not return Mordaunt assumed that Francis had walked on to meet the ladies' carriage. It was four o' clock, and everyone, with the exception of Drumlanrig, had crossed into the second turnip field where the keepers were preparing for 'beating up'. 'Where is his Lordship?' asked Webber, and it was only then that everyone realised that Francis had still not joined them. Webber blew a whistle and called for His Lordship. Moments later they heard a shot, apparently from about a hundred yards away. 'Where can His Lordship be?' asked Webber again.

'I hope he has not shot himself,' said Elton, who later stated that the comment was made 'half in jest'.

'Oh no, we will not think that,' said the keeper. Webber sent his son to look for Francis, but when he replied that he could not see him, everyone went to search. Ellis gave Elton his gun to hold and said he would walk along beside the hedge to see if he could find Francis. He climbed through the gap into a grass field, and had only gone a few yards when he returned and said to the others, 'Come at once, he is shot.'[13]

Ellis's face must have shown that this was no jest. The stunned party followed him, and some seventeen paces further on they found Francis. Any hope that this might be a trivial incident vanished. He lay motionless on his back, his body parallel with the hedge, his head turned slightly to the right and concealed in the brambles. The gun lay across his stomach the muzzle towards the hedge, and his arms were stretched out, his hands some distance from his sides. Elton tried to examine the wound but the brambles made this almost impossible, although he could see a great deal of blood on Francis's face and collar, and thought he had been wounded in the forehead. He raised the left hand and thought he could feel the slight flutter of a pulse, but to all others present it must have been apparent that Francis was beyond help.

The body was left at the spot. Mordaunt took the game-cart and left to summon a doctor. Elton, with the grim duty of remaining beside the body, opened the gun and found that the cartridge in the left-hand chamber had been fired.

The first medical man to arrive, Alfred Egerton Smith, saw at once that Francis was dead. He noticed blood around the mouth and spattered on the leaves and branches of the bushes. He ordered the body to be taken to Quantock Lodge to await the inquest.

Mr Stanley was summoned home by telegraph and left immediately. Telegrams were also sent to General Ellis and Sybil. Someone must have had the terrible task of breaking the news of the tragedy to the cheerful party of ladies. At the post-mortem examination Smith confirmed that the shot had entered Francis's mouth fracturing the lower jaw on the right-hand side and passing through the roof of the mouth on the left. Some of the shot had exited through the face between the nose and eye on the left side. The base of the skull was completely shattered and death had been instantaneous. The lower lip was slightly blued by the powder but the moustache had not been singed.

Publicly, the idea that Francis had committed suicide was never contemplated. Edward Stanley told the press that he believed Francis had been accidentally killed while trying to get through the hedge with a loaded gun. It was confirmed that the young man had been in excellent health and spirits right up to the moment of his death.

It is not known where Queensberry was at the time of his son's death. His contested final divorce hearing was imminent, and he might have been in London or on his way there. How he learned the devastating news and by whom he was told are unknown. There is no mention of his having been sent a telegram, but the family or his agent in Scotland could have done this. The London clubs knew about it late on the evening of 18 October and it was in the newspapers the following morning. Unsupported by his scattered family it was a loss that Queensberry probably had to endure alone. Plunged into a new nightmare, in his desolation, grief turned to rage, and his anger and bitterness focused once more on the Montgomerys, Rosebery, Gladstone, the Queen and Christians in general.

Percy was in Australia and Sholto had only a fortnight before been sent to America. Archibald, who in the last few years had been dividing his time between Scotland and the provinces, was in Walthamstow. George Murray, Gladstone's private secretary heard the news that evening and the following morning went to see Alfred Montgomery, finding him ill in bed, prostrated with grief. Bosie arrived at Quantock Lodge on the Friday evening, to be followed on Saturday afternoon by Sybil, Lady Edith and Arthur Johnstone Douglas all of whom had travelled down from Scotland. They remained at Quantock until midday the following Monday, when they returned north. Queensberry refused to go to Quantock, possibly to avoid a confrontation with Sybil, and Archibald, too, chose not to go.

The inquest was held at Quantock Lodge on the morning of Saturday 20 October. Dr Smith was asked if the deceased's mouth had been open when the shot was fired and he said he thought it was. Gerald Ellis who was the first to see the body did not unfortunately describe the position in which he found it, or how the gun was lying, but said that he had undone Francis's waistcoat to see if his heart was beating and also lifted the body slightly. It seems he did not disturb its position in relation to the hedge. The coroner, Mr T. Foster Barham, summed up the case, remarking that he thought the deceased had tried to return to the others by getting through a gap in the hedge by a tree stump and had accidentally set off his gun. The jury, after a short deliberation, returned a verdict of accidental death. The press accepted the verdict without question – 'Drumlanrig . . . has fallen victim to the fatality which seems to be traditional in his family'[14] – and articles were published on the carelessness of young men while out shooting. The deceased was praised for his 'amiable character'[15] and was said to be 'especially well-mannered . . . generally popular'.[16] The person said by the press to have been hardest hit by the news was Alfred Montgomery who had been devoted to 'his favourite and promising grandson'.[17]

An analysis of the scene of Francis's death must result in a rejection of the coroner's theory. If Francis had been trying to climb through the hedge he would have been found facing it, not lying parallel. The position of the wound, which suggested that Francis had fired upwards into his own mouth, is a strong indication of suicide. Not only was the mouth open when the shot was fired but the lack of singeing on the moustache suggests that the barrel of the gun was inside the mouth. Had Ellis not tried to lift the body then, following such a wound, the arms should have been by the sides, the gun lying vertically and not across the stomach. Murray later spoke to Mordaunt who drew a sketch plan to make the events clearer, marking the point where Francis was last seen alive and where his body was found:

> . . . close up to the hedge and about half way between the gap he originally crossed by and another gap at the pond where the two fences join. It is very difficult to account for his going up to the hedge where he was found – the hedge was barely passable there; but there was nothing that could be called a gap; and it was by no means the natural place to choose if he wanted to rejoin the guns as soon as possible.

Murray, while commenting that being shot through the mouth upwards is 'almost impossible to produce by accident', still found the suicide theory equally improbable 'for want of motive'. Mordaunt, however, told Murray that in his opinion and that of the doctor, Elton and Fortescue it was suicide.[18]

Francis's death was almost certainly suicide, and by the same method his grandfather had chosen, but why? Was the pleasant sunny young man with such happy prospects secretly harbouring some unknown grief, or had he been suddenly overwhelmed by a shattering catastrophe?

There is the tantalising hint from his nephew that Francis was 'highly nervous'. The eleventh marquess had never met Francis, but the obvious source of this information was his father, Percy. The eldest son of warring parents, the much doted on favourite of his mother whose smothering affections had transferred to his younger brother Bosie, might well have been sensitive and eager to win approval. Queensberry's letter to Rosebery suggests that Francis was young for his age, perhaps naïve. The best clue to what might have happened is the timing of the death on the day before the planned formal announcement of the engagement, which suggests that Francis killed himself to avoid either the engagement or the repercussions that might have flowed from it. A popular theory is that Francis was facing the eruption of a homosexual scandal involving himself and Lord Rosebery. Henry Labouchère might well have been horrified at the proposed marriage of Rosebery's favourite into his own family, and may have made his suspicions known. Had

Francis perhaps been told to break off his engagement or ruin would follow? An open homosexual scandal, with or without foundation, would have destroyed both his own career and that of his admired mentor.

Arthur Johnstone Douglas arranged for a hearse to take the body to Bridgwater railway station to be transported to Scotland, and Queensberry made the funeral arrangements, issuing a card announcing that it would take place from Glen Stuart. On 20 October Queensberry was staying at Carter's Hotel, when he wrote a letter to Gladstone sending a copy to Rosebery. He headed it 'copy of letter sent to the Christian whoremonger & hypocrite Gladstone'.[19] The pain of the bereaved father who wrote 'my son and I have parted without reconciliation'[20] is palpable. His undisciplined handwriting sprawls even more violently than usual across the page, with multiple underlinings of the scarcely legible diatribe, mainly against the 'bloated old' Queen, the 'imaginary Christian devil god' and the 'underbred disgusting Jew pimp Rosebery'.[21]

Two days later he wrote to the Queen from Comlongon Castle, the home of his cousin and estate manager Arthur Douglas. Although some newspapers later reported that Queensberry petitioned for a continuation of the Kelhead peerage in his own person, no letters on that subject survive. Why, in any case, should Queensberry have wanted an English peerage then? After Francis's death there was very little that could give him pleasure any more. His letter of 22 October does not claim any honour; he wrote only to express his deep bitterness about the slights that had led to the estrangement from his eldest son for which he blamed 'that liar Ld Rosebery, as proved by the correspondence & that senile old hypocrite Mr Gladstone'. His only consolation was that the tragedy had ended the bad feeling between himself and Francis after the award of the peerage. 'With his death, thank God, all soreness against my boy has disappeared. . . . But my feelings of resentment and anger against those who made bad blood between I & my son are all intensified & until I die I can neither forget not forgive this.'[22]

Arthur Ellis's letter to Rosebery of 22 October was written unreservedly from the heart and made it clear that he at least had no suspicions about the relationship. 'Drummy was devoted to you – as well you know – and so proud to serve you and earn your good opinion. I quite think I shall never see his like again. The most lovable youth I ever met – no wonder my poor child was fond of him. They would indeed have been a bright and happy couple & quite devoted to each other.'[23] Of the grieving father he had this to say: 'The funeral is (in Scotland) on Friday next. His impossible father means to attend, but Q declined to come here – I wish I could believe that he is mad –'.[24]

Francis's body arrived at Annan on 23 October, and was taken to Glen Stuart where the coffin covered by a mass of wreaths was placed in the white-draped drawing room where it was surrounded by a display of flowers. Relatives and close friends crowded into the room to hear the first part of the burial service conducted by the Revd Colin Campbell who was chaplain to the Archbishop of Canterbury and a personal friend of Drumlanrig, assisted by Revd Nichol of Cummertrees. The chief mourners were Queensberry and Archibald. Lady Edith had come from London for the funeral but waited at the graveside. Sybil and Alexandra Ellis sent wreaths, but did not attend. A group of about thirty villagers and tenants arrived, and since there was no room for them in the house, they stood in a wide semicircle in front of the French windows of the room where the coffin lay. Lord Rosebery sent a wreath, and was represented by a private secretary, Neville Waterfield, who later sent his employer a cruel picture of the grieving father. Waterfield arrived at Glen Stuart which he described as 'a small white house buried at the end of a narrow glen and overshadowed by trees. In summer it would be a pretty place, but yesterday it was suggestive of nothing but melancholy and damp.' Queensberry had either neglected or refused to don traditional mourning and was therefore a curious sight:

> Suddenly there emerged from the room a jaunty figure, clad in a darkish grey frock coat and trousers, brown boots & gloves, a large white fox-hunting neck-cloth (no collar) and a top hat somewhat on the side of the head, which after nodding generally to the company & shaking hands with one or two tenants, motioned to the clergymen to begin. . . . you can believe that a clown could not have stepped more incongruously into that dismal circle. However the service began, and shortly the choir headed by the two clergymen filed through the corridor onto the lawn singing a hymn. They were followed by the coffin, which decorated with wreaths, was placed on a wheeled bier and propelled by some half dozen tenants. I am glad to say the wretched man, who had hitherto preserved a more or less self-satisfied air, was forsaken by his bravado, and breaking down shambled tearfully away at the head of the procession which followed the choir & the coffin down the glen.

The procession, swelled by sightseers as it reached the public road, entered the gates of Kinmount, and wound through the park along a boggy avenue until it reached 'a wooded knoll, prettily placed with a view to the distant sea' at the top of which was a rough enclosure where a grave had been dug. Matters were concluded 'without any such display of eccentricity as one might have feared. The whole ceremony was very simple and sincere, and rendered if possible the more sad by the grotesque misery of the chief mourner.'[25] Francis's remains were interred beside those of his uncle James. It was 'a picturesque spot, on a knoll overlooking a little lake and the square grey pile of Kinmount House, and set in lively woodland surroundings'.[26] A memorial was later placed on the site with an inscription stating that Francis had been 'killed by the accidental discharge of his gun'.[27]

The hearing that was to confirm the annulment of Queensberry's marriage to Ethel took place on 24 October. In view of the tragedy the press which might otherwise have made a meal of the end of Queensberry's second marriage declined to do so, although the fact that it was annulled and the hearing was conducted in camera was a powerful clue to the reasons.

The following day Queensberry, still at Comlongon Castle, sent a letter to Revd Nichol thanking him for a kind note conveying the sympathy of the Cummertrees Hall Committee and Bowling Club and tenants and cottagers on the estate: '. . . though words fail on an occasion of this kind to express one's grief, it is some solace to receive the kind messages of sympathy from friendly ones around us'.[28]

Queensberry, convinced that Francis had taken his own life, had been making his own enquiries about what might have driven his son to suicide, something he felt he could have prevented had they not been estranged over the peerage. On 1 November he wrote to Alfred Montgomery. It was a savage letter to send to a man of eighty, but Queensberry, alone with his misery, lashed out like a wounded animal:

Sir,
Now that the first flush of this catastrophe & grief is passed, I write to tell you that I think it is a judgement on the whole lot of you, Montgomerys, the Snob Queers like Rosebery & canting Christian hypocrite Gladstone. . . .
If you & his mother did not set up this business with that Cur & Jew pimp Liar Rosebery as I always thought – at any rate she acquiesced in it, which

is just as bad. . . . I smell a tragedy behind all this & have already got wind of a more ghastly one, if it was what I am led to believe, I of all people could & would have helped him, had he come to me with a confidence, but that was all stopped by you people – we had not met or spoken hardly for more than a year & a half.[29]

Queensberry had received information that he felt accounted for Francis's death, but he never committed those thoughts to paper. His only comment was 'cherchez la femme when these things happen'.[30] Was this a dig at Sybil – or at Labouchère's cousin Mina Ellis?

Back in London, the news of Francis's death stopped Oscar Wilde in his tracks. Knowing that Percy and Sholto were both abroad, and how much must therefore fall upon Bosie's shoulders, Wilde felt unable to desert him and opened his heart to his grieving friend. 'I am perforce the sharer of his pain,'[31] he wrote, and they were reconciled. He may have had other anxieties, since there are occasional threats of suicide in Bosie's correspondence; it was a weapon he was unafraid to use to get his own way.

In November Wilde, who had taken an interest in the recent Queensberry divorce, wrote to Bosie: 'I heard all the details of the Scarlet Marquis the other day: quite astonishing. Arthur Pollen told me all about it: he came to tea one afternoon.'[32] Pollen, a young barrister who had been acting for Ethel, must have been charmed by Oscar into revealing Queensberry's humiliating secret. How much Pollen knew, and how much he told Wilde, is uncertain. It was hardly something Wilde could commit to paper, but having mentioned it, he would have passed on any scandalous titbits to Bosie at their next meeting. There is, however, no evidence that Bosie ever used this information to taunt his father.

If Francis had not died on 18 October, Wilde would have ended his relationship with Bosie, and Queensberry could have gone on to find contentment and harmony with all his children. Even if Bosie and Wilde had become reconciled, Queensberry might, as he had planned, have washed his hands of his wayward third son, made Scotland his main base, and visited Percy in Australia. But the loss of Francis was a shock from which he could never recover, and misery and conflict were to be his constant companions.

CHAPTER 16

A Family Divided

I N the winter of 1894 Queensberry was staying in the forester's cottage at
Comlongon Castle. It was 'dismal and austere, but it was a better life than
I am accustomed to'.[1] Unfortunately he quarrelled with his cousin Arthur
Douglas and his wife 'the holy christian Jane',[2] who decided that she didn't
want him there. He had probably been unable to restrain himself from
diatribes against Christianity, which had become entangled in his mind with
the circumstances of Francis's death. In late December or early January he left
the cottage and went to stay at the County and Station Hotel, Carlisle, 'not
knowing what on earth I am going to do and feeling . . . ill and bad
tempered'.[3] He spent his weekends at Holm Hill, a country house in the
village of Dalston in Cumberland 'as my life is not a particularly cheerful one
at that Station Hotel at Carlisle all alone'.[4]

His irritation spilled over into his relationship with his mother and sister,
and it may have been at this time that he sent Florence some acrimonious and
potentially hurtful letters. Florence knew her brother well; as she anticipated,
he soon simmered down, and their affection for each other never faltered.

On 1 January 1895 Percy and Minnie arrived home from Australia and
went to stay with Sybil at Cadogan Place. Percy, now his father's heir, was able
to raise substantial sums from moneylenders on the expectation of his inheritance, hoping to make a rapid fortune, but he was still drinking heavily, a
tendency that had not been helped by his days on the ranch and in the goldfields. 'When he was under the influence,' said Bosie, 'he was an easy mark
for the unscrupulous.'[5] Queensberry wrote a long letter to 'My dear Minnie'
showing that he was willing to accept Percy's marriage, but was deeply
concerned about his heir's prospects. 'I am quite ready to believe in Percy, but
have waited long, anxiously for him to prove he deserves it from me. . . . I

wrote him a very kind letter. He must not be surprised if I am a little sceptical about this phantom fortune. . . . I was not intending to stand between you two. All I wanted was some assurance he had some prospects to marry on first.' Percy had sent him 'theatrical telegrams' but 'when I propose he should come and see me he makes no reply'. Queensberry had been thinking of inviting the couple to settle with him at 'the Glen' (presumably Glen Stuart):

> I am utterly helpless alone, but of course if he is in business he will want to be in Town. . . . I have no soul to help me as my sister and mother are utterly useless to me. I am perfectly furious. I was driven from Comlongon by a man and woman I have done everything for and picked out of the mud and set on their feet when they were utterly broke . . . .
> Yours affectionately
> Queensberry[6]

On 3 January Oscar Wilde's third comedy *An Ideal Husband* opened at the Theatre Royal, Haymarket. Queensberry was also at the theatre – in Carlisle, where he attended a performance of *A Bunch of Violets* by Sydney Grundy and afterwards invited young dramatist Laurence Irving and director Mr H. Yardley to supper, saying how delighted he had been with the entertainment. The brief charm of a night in the theatre did not affect his fundamental depression, and Queensberry, declaring himself to be 'in a most forlorn state' and wanting to 'let bygones be bygones', invited Percy and Minnie to come stay with him, which they did later that month for a week to ten days. The visit was a success; Queensberry and his son were reconciled, and he got to know and like Minnie.

> I was much comforted and delighted to find that with [Minnie] I was much more able to be friendly with my son and I had thoughts that with them I should be able to make a home again and that we might mutually help one another and that I would have shared their expenses I even proposed that they should come and live in Glen Stuart in fact I would have done anything and everything and of course it would have been an estimable blessing to me once more to have had a home after 22 years of the greatest misery and desolation* I suppose a man has ever been through.[7]

---

* Transcribed in manuscript copy as 'dissolution', but desolation makes more sense.

He later wrote to Minnie about this change of heart – 'before God I wished to be friends with you both & to my joy discovered that you & he together brought me some comfort I had not felt in the last 20 years.'[8]

One inevitable topic of conversation was the relationship between Bosie and Wilde. Queensberry must have hoped that Percy's affection for his brother would give him some sway, which he himself lacked. 'I told him I had been suffering intensely about this affair and hardly dared to return to London in such distress was I in.'[9] To Queensberry's immense relief, Percy promised his father to take all the worry off his hands. No sooner had Percy left Carlisle, however, than Queensberry heard that he had met Arthur Douglas and taken sides with the agent in the quarrel. This was upsetting enough but far worse was to follow. Percy returned to London and spoke to Bosie, who was adamant that the rumours about his relationship with Wilde were 'a pack of lies',[10] adding – and what an unnecessary and vicious twist this was – that it was Queensberry himself who, either from malicious hatred for his son or insane delusions, had invented the allegations. It cannot have been hard, in view of Percy's affection for his brother and a natural unwillingness to accept that a scandal of this nature was affecting the family, for Bosie to convince 'dearest Turts' that he was telling the truth. Sir Claude de Crespigny later observed that Percy's long absence from England had left him ignorant of what was 'a common topic of conversation among the regular habitués of the leading restaurants and theatres'.[11] Sybil naturally believed Bosie, while Minnie and Archibald supported Percy, and Edith sided with her mother. Florence, living in Scotland, afflicted by arthritis and caring for her increasingly frail mother, took no part in the quarrel, but the other Douglases and all the Montgomerys were united and ranged against Queensberry.

On 17 January Bosie accompanied Wilde to Algeria. In Blidah, 'a town much frequented by Englishmen in search of boys',[12] they encountered André Gide, who was shocked at Bosie's outspokenness on sexual matters – 'I have a horror of women. I only like boys'[13] – his 'despotic manners of a spoilt child'[14] and explosions of savage rage. 'Wilde beside him seemed gentle, wavering and weak-willed. Douglas was possessed by the perverse instinct that drives a child to break his finest toy.'[15]

On 18 and 19 January Queensberry was in Edinburgh for a meeting with his solicitor, Mr Jamieson. After a long consultation he found that he was now empowered to sell Kinmount and he wrote to Percy on the following day reassuring him that if he did so he would pass on due compensation. His plan was to invest the proceeds, which would bring him a life interest, and at 4 per cent he estimated that it would provide him with nearly double the income that Kinmount brought in as an estate. The falling value of property remained a serious concern. Ten years earlier Kinmount would have fetched £200,000 or more; currently, it might only realise £150,000 to £160,000. Tinwald and Torthorwald, which had sold for £220,000 would now be worth no more than £150,000.

> . . . this is significant of the way things are going – in another 50 years Kinmount will probably not be worth 100 thousand or even less [*sic*]. I did a pretty good stroke of business selling the other estate it is a clear gain on fifty thousand in my pockets now; about which we are to be congratulated. In my opinion nothing can prevent land going on deteriorating in value. . . . And this must get worse.

While he could understand people who loved to live on their estates and had the money to do so, 'this is not the case with us at least not with me with that great dreary dungeon of a house Kinmount that has been a millstone around our necks the last 4 generations'.[16] He was not, however, going to do anything immediately and promised he would consult Percy first. 'I mean to show Arthur I can be independent of him when he drove me away from my last chance of living in the country. I saw that either you must come & live there and look after things if I could not or that it would be wisest to get out of the place altogether which I have long had thoughts of doing.'[17] Queensberry's other worry was that by returning from Australia, Percy had lost his chance of earning a salary. 'As to your present prospects you don't tell me what they are & it all seems very vague.'[18] He promised that if he could be assured that Percy was making a regular income, he was willing to make it up to £1,000 a year. The only way he could see of funding this was by selling Kinmount.

On 22 January he was staying at Glen Stuart and wrote to Percy again. It is clear that the charms of the location had long since evaporated:

Dear Percy

I am only hanging on here from day to day as I find it very depressing &
have nothing here to occupy me except recently spending a day shooting
over Comlongon. I can only come up here with the notion of trying to stop
here & making it my home, but I fear that there is very little prospect of
my doing so as I find it too dull and lonely & could not stand this stagna-
tion very long then it is for ever raining here & down in this hole it is too
depressing for words I cannot think how people could have been so foolish
as to build a house in such a position.

Family squabbles meant he felt 'more cut off and estranged from you all more
than ever, in fact the only chance I have here is to try to put it all away out
of my mind & not think of it'. He referred to an argument with Percy about
his club after which Percy had written to him asking him to leave him alone.
'I was quite ready to make it up with you that time you came to my rooms
but you made me perfectly rabid by further attacking me again about what
you chose to call my behaviour to you.' The fault, however, was not any
individual's but 'the opinions & laws of these lying hypocritical Christians on
the subject of marriage. . . . For 20 years of my life I was too much of a man
for it to be possible for me to live entirely without a woman's help. Your
mother having utterly failed me before I was 30 because I would not practise
their usual hypocrisies & deceit on the subject.'[19]

On 25 January at the County Hotel Carlisle Queensberry signed a new
will, undoubtedly necessitated by the death of Francis. In another letter to
Percy probably written at the end of January he complained of feeling 'wretched'
at the hotel, which he could not leave until his financial matters were settled,
and was more determined than ever to sell Kinmount. Complaining that Sybil
could not acknowledge a cheque he asked Percy to hand it to her and send him
an acknowledgement. He was planning for the Dixies to move to Glen Stuart:
'Not that Florrie will be much good to me there beyond a housekeeper for
I know I cannot live with them as I have tried often before to do so and failed.'
He was still unhappy with his cousin Arthur. 'Nothing would please me
better or satisfy me, than taking my coat off to him and one of us thrashing
the other.'[20]

When Queensberry, alone in his Carlisle hotel was able to focus his misery
it settled once more on Oscar Wilde. With any rumours about Francis stilled

only by his son's death, this fresh scandal was a waking nightmare; all the more so because in this case he felt sure that the stories were true. He had heard that Wilde had taken Bosie to Algiers, and his informants cannot have spared him the details of why men went there. He may also have learned of the publication of a novel, *The Green Carnation*, a thinly disguised satire on Wilde and Bosie, which even reproduced Bosie's 'funny little man' telegram, of which he was undoubtedly so proud that he had shown it to friends. The book had created some anti-Wilde feeling and had been followed by a satirical cartoon in *Punch* in November, but it seemed that as long as Wilde continued to amuse the public with his plays he was unassailable.

The newspapers were announcing that *The Importance of Being Earnest* was to open on 12 February (it was later postponed by two days) and Queensberry, knowing that Wilde would be back in London for the first night, returned and took a room at Carter's Hotel. Despite his threats he was unwilling to cause a public disturbance when Bosie was present – his target was Wilde, not his son – but this time the pair were not together; Bosie, enamoured of a handsome Arab boy of fifteen had remained in Algeria. The romance did not last. On finding that the youth was seeing a woman, Bosie horsewhipped him until his howls rang around the hotel, then came to dinner with 'livid face and steely eyes'.[21]

Percy was allotted the difficult task of tackling his father over Bosie. A letter from Queensberry to Percy simply dated 'Saturday night' (possibly 9 February) says 'Dear Percy, Come up if you like, I shall be glad to see you, but fear I am in dreadful depressed spirits, Your affect father'.[22]

The meeting ended badly, since Percy revealed that so far from having resolved matters as promised, he now believed his brother's version of events, including Bosie's allegation that Queensberry was the originator of the rumours. Not only had the entire burden of dealing with the potential scandal fallen back on to Queensberry's shoulders, but his hopes of at last finding contentment with his son and daughter-in-law had vanished. An undated letter from Queensberry to Percy written more in dismay than anger may well have been penned shortly after this meeting, since it refers to 'that night when I dined with you' and mentions his discovery that since Percy's return from Carlisle he had spoken disparagingly of his father regarding the quarrel with Arthur Johnstone Douglas. 'There will be a scandal and more disgrace to our family, but none to me. . . . Your mother's conduct is disgraceful, and then you expect me to be friends with you who are hand in glove with them. I regret all this most bitterly as I thought I could, and wished to be, friends to you and Minnie, but you have knocked it all down again, and I wish I had died before I married such a woman who has given me such children.'[23]

Queensberry wanted another confrontation with Wilde, but was unable to discover where his quarry was staying. There was, however, one place and time were he could be sure of seeing Wilde – the St James's Theatre on the opening night of *The Importance of Being Earnest*, when, as was his custom, the author would be present and would take the stage after the performance to enjoy the acclaim of the audience. It was too good a chance to miss.

Queensberry bought a ticket – 'by fraud,'[24] Wilde suggested (presumably orders had been given not to sell him one) – and some vegetables, a wintry mixture including carrots, cauliflowers and turnips.[25] It is unlikely that Queensberry was planning to interrupt the action of the play itself; he had too many friends in the theatrical profession to think of abusing actors because of a dispute with the playwright. Even when enraged by *The Promise of May* he had waited until the end of a scene to make his point. His intention was probably to greet Oscar's appearance with a shower of vegetation and then stand up and make a public announcement. Unfortunately for his plans, he was unable to keep his intentions secret.

Algernon (Algy) Bourke was a cousin of Bosie – his mother Blanche was the sister of Sybil's mother Fanny Montgomery – and somehow he got to hear of it. Bourke wrote to Sybil: 'Q has obtained a seat at the St James Theatre tonight for the 1st night of O W's play. It is his present intention to go there and make a public scandle [*sic*]. Cant [*sic*] you get Bosie to go and see his Father and dissuade him from this. It would be most detrimental to the boy.'[26] Bosie was still abroad but Sybil went one better and informed Wilde, who quickly pencilled a note to the business manager of the theatre, R. V. Shone: 'Dear Mr Shone, Lord Queensberry is at Carter Hotel, Albemarle Street. Write to him from Mr Alexander* that you regret to find that the seat given to him was already sold, and return him his money. This will prevent trouble, I hope.'[27]

On the 14th Wilde sent another brief note, probably to his close friend Robbie Ross. 'Bosie's father is going to make a scene tonight. I am going to stop him.'[28] Wilde had decided that returning the ticket was not enough. He

---

* George Alexander, actor/manager and tenant of the St James's Theatre.

knew that Queensberry might try to bluff his way in, or even adopt a disguise (there was a rumour that Queensberry would try to get in by the stage door disguised as a policeman), so he alerted the police.

Snow was falling thickly, stirred by a bitter wind, when Queensberry arrived at the theatre together with a companion (never identified but assumed to be a prizefighter), only to have his intentions thwarted. There were about twenty police officers guarding the theatre. The same legislation that entitled the police to prevent prizefights also prevented Queensberry hurling vegetables and accusations at Wilde. Having been refused admission at the box office he attempted to enter by the gallery stairs, but the police were guarding that entrance too. According to Wilde, who did not witness the events himself but presumably learned what had happened from theatre staff, Queensberry spent three hours prowling around the theatre trying to find a way of getting in before abandoning his vegetables (Wilde called them 'a grotesque bouquet') and leaving, 'chattering like a monstrous ape'. It was a victory for Wilde, who declared 'This of course makes his conduct idiotic – robs it of dignity.'[29]

Back at his hotel, Queensberry considered his next move. There was no point in repeating the attempt at the theatre the following night since Wilde would not be present, and his attempts to discover where Wilde was staying had been unsuccessful. Learning that the new play was an enormous popular success may have added to his irritation. There was one other place he might encounter Wilde and that was his club, the Albemarle at 13 Albemarle Street next door to Carter's Hotel. Thus far, Queensberry had been protecting Bosie by keeping the Oxford scandal secret, but he now decided on a desperate measure – the only way he could convince Percy of the truth of his accusations was by revealing what he knew. Percy was refusing to receive any letters from his father, so Queensberry wrote to Minnie instead, telling her about the encounter with Percy, and his decision to produce more evidence about Bosie. On 16 February he sent a telegram to Percy at 1 St Philips Rd Surbiton, 'Letters refused must telegraph until wicked accusation of causing scandal withdrawn shall stop extra allowance also. Now feel justified in publishing to friends and relations hideous story of A at Oxford which up until now have suppressed and not told a soul not even you unless you instantly retract.'[30]

He received no reply and suspecting that Percy had intercepted the letter to Minnie, he wrote to her again on 18 February. 'Percy knows nothing of it.

It is a horrible story ... if Percy does not choose to hear this, I shall feel bound to make use of it to clear myself from his wicked accusations. I have been most patient about all this and for two years sat still and did nothing, until everyone was saying "what is his father about, and why does he not interfere?" When I did so I received nothing but insolence and defiance and impertinent telegrams.'[31]

It may have been Queensberry's telegram to Percy that prompted another visit from him on the 18th. The confrontation took place in Queensberry's room, where he spoke frankly about Bosie's brush with blackmail. He 'arrived at my hotel and dared to take me to task and said I was making the scandal and why did I not bring it to a head and in every way taking his brother's and Wilde's part against me. I was then obliged to tell him a lot of things I knew particularly about his own disgusting brother how there had been a scandal at Oxford.'[32] Percy refused to believe his father; he saw the revelation as another delusion and a fresh attack on Bosie, and his usually suppressed aggression surfaced. He 'actually had the impudence to defend [Bosie] in his threats to shoot me'.[33] Queensberry ordered Percy out of his room, and made an angry and momentous gesture: '... it was that very day that driven almost to desperation I left that card on Oscar Wilde and brought matters to a head'.[34]

At 4.30 p.m. Queensberry entered the Albemarle Club, wrote some words on his card and handed it to the hall porter, Sydney Wright. 'Give that to Oscar Wilde,' he said. The words which were later to be misread and disputed were 'For Oscar Wilde posing somdomite [sic]'. Queensberry's handwriting is hard to decipher at the best of times, although his spelling was usually accurate (Bosie's declaration 'I am not sure he is able to read; I am certain that he is unable to spell'[35] is a gibe without foundation), but this was more sprawling than usual, and resulted in the garbling of 'sodomite', a word which he spelled correctly in later correspondence. It is open to question whether Queensberry's message, written in a state of some agitation, was what he intended to write. There was no legal counsel on hand, but he may have been advised on previous occasions not to make an outright accusation of sodomy. To accuse Wilde of posing as a sodomite was one thing, but, as read, the card accused him of being a sodomite. Queensberry had taken matters to another level.

Wright may not have been able to read the handwriting; the suggestion that he had been astonished by the contents came later from solicitor Charles Humphreys and not the porter, who maintained 'I looked at the card but did not understand it.'[36] Wright noted the date and time on the back of the card, and put it in an envelope 'so that the card should not be lost'.[37] Wilde would not see it for another ten days.

When Bosie returned to London Wilde suggested that they tell Percy the truth about their relationship, but Bosie refused. 'So when he came in after dinner we had to play the comedy of your father being an insane man subject to absurd and unaccountable delusions. It was a capital comedy while it lasted, none the less so because Percy took it all quite seriously.'[38]

On 26 February Queensberry again wrote to Minnie:

I am naturally very much annoyed and angry at the way I am being treated, particularly after my saying I was ready to forget the past and to be friends with you both. However this last behaviour of Percy has quite finished me with him. . . . if he is still so obstinate to refuse to recognize what the character of this man is . . . let him speak to Cook the detective . . . he knows more about him (O.W.) than I do, perhaps Percy will be able to impress himself that this is also all imagination.[39]

Queensberry's frustration and bitterness at the new quarrel can only be imagined. Just weeks before he had been heartened by the reconciliation with Percy and Minnie and the prospect at long last of some companionship, even if he was obliged to meet the expenses. Not only was he alone again, but his efforts to save Bosie from disgrace and ruin were being misinterpreted as an attempt to destroy him. In some ways he blamed Bosie least of all; perhaps he felt he was not entirely responsible for his nature, but Percy's betrayal cut deep and was something he would never forgive.

Queensberry had recently promised to increase Percy's allowance, but now declined to do so. 'It would serve him right if I stopped it altogether, but I will continue it as beforehand, £25 a month,'[40] he wrote to Minnie.

I shall be fair, as I cannot object to a settlement on yourself as a future lady Queensberry as a regular burden on the estate, but shall certainly now make this dependent on Percy consenting to re-settle the estate on himself and male heirs. I have nothing to gain by this, as I must be dead before it can come into force, but consider it my duty, to prevent if possible, my successor from having the power of squandering everything.

He declined to make a settlement on Minnie in the event of Percy predeceasing him, and would only increase Percy's income if Kinmount was sold.
As things stood, he thought reconciliation was impossible.

Percy ignored all the evidence Queensberry sent him in support of his
accusations. It is not known if he went to see Cook, but if he did, it made no
difference. He preferred to believe Bosie. Minnie offered to be a peacemaker,
but things had gone too far. Queensberry wrote to her on 27 February.

Dear Minnie

I do not refuse to see you if you insist on doing so but what is the use of
it? & why am I to be put to all this intolerable pain? I cannot discuss this
horrible subject with you nor can I speak to you of what I think of Percy.
I have not quarrelled with you personally but you and he are one as he
chooses to come here and quarrel with me the quarrel must extend to yourself . . . . has ever a man been placed in such a position & then for another
of my good for nothing sons to come and quarrel and attack me and to
dictate to me what I am and what I am not to do in this awful position I
am placed in of having such sons and this one going on with Wilde and if
it was not so intensely painful these quarrels it would be ludicrous . . . .

The quarrel coming so soon after the reconciliation in Carlisle was 'a fresh
terrible blow to me'.[41] The eleventh marquess found the letters 'infinitely
pathetic. Reading between the lines one senses his longing for a little
sympathy, a little affection to soften his rough heart.'[42] It is doubtful that
Minnie went to see her father-in-law, and any intentions she may have had
were soon overtaken by events.

CHAPTER 17

The Peer and the Poet

B OSIE was sufficiently alarmed by his father's bid to shower Wilde with vegetables to buy Wilde a swordstick so that he could defend himself against possible assault. Wilde in the meantime had instructed his solicitor to prosecute Queensberry for threats and insulting conduct. Humphreys responded on 28 February, saying he was unable to comply, 'inasmuch as upon investigating the case we have met with every obstruction from Mr George Alexander, the manager, and his staff at the theatre, who decline to give us any statements or to render any assistance to you'.[1]

> Had Lord Queensberry been permitted to carry out his threats you would have had ample ground for instituting a prosecution against him, but the only consolation we can offer to you now is that such a persistent persecutor as Lord Queensberry will probably give you another opportunity sooner or later of seeking the protection of the Law, in which event we shall be happy to render you every assistance in our power to bring him to justice and thus secure to you future peace at his hands.[2]

Wilde's efforts to prevent a scene had worked against him. He must already have received this frustrating letter when at about 5.30 p.m. on 28 February he entered the Albemarle Club and Sydney Wright handed him Queensberry's card. Wilde at once wrote to Robbie Ross saying he could see no way out except a criminal prosecution. 'My whole life seems ruined by this man. The tower of ivory is assailed by the foul thing.'[3]

The next day Wilde and Bosie went to see Humphreys. They thought that there were three words on the card, 'ponce' (slang for either a pimp or – more probably in this context – an effeminate man), an illegible word and 'somdomite [*sic*].' Wilde gave the solicitor his solemn oath that there was no truth in Queensberry's allegations, and with this assurance Humphreys was happy to take the case. The only issue was cost, since Wilde, due to his extravagance and generosity, had been living above his means for some time and had no money. He was overdrawn at the bank, which was returning his cheques, his creditors, believing that successful plays meant that he had funds, were issuing writs, and his landlord was threatening to distrain for unpaid rent. Wilde had been staying at the Avondale Hotel, but was unable to settle his bill, and the management had impounded his luggage.

Bosie told Humphreys that his family would be delighted to pay the costs. His father 'had been an incubus to them all' and they had 'often discussed the possibility of getting him put into a lunatic asylum so as to keep him out of the way' as he was 'a daily source of annoyance and distress to [Sybil]'.[4] Bosie, eager for a prosecution, was obsessed with the idea of seeing Queensberry in the dock as he mistakenly believed that he would be able to give evidence against his father's character. The issue to be tried, however, was whether Queensberry's allegations against Wilde were true. The accuser's character and his son's opinion of it were irrelevant. Despite Bosie's declaration that his father wanted to 'smash' him, he must have realised that he was in no danger. 'You knew that your father would not attack your life or yourself in any way,'[5] wrote Wilde, and indeed Queensberry took great pains to shield Bosie from any hint of sexual misdemeanour.

For some reason, it was thought that Queensberry, who had been longing for a public platform to air his grievances against Wilde, might ignore a summons to appear in court, and on 1 March Marlborough Police Court issued a warrant for his arrest, 'For that he did unlawfully and maliciously publish a certain defamatory libel of and concerning one Oscar Wilde at Albemarle Street on February 18 1895 at the parish of St George's'.[6]

At 9 a.m. on Saturday 2 March 1895 Detective Inspector Thomas Greet and a detective sergeant ('Shaddock' in the newspapers but possibly Edwin Shattock), both of C Division, arrived at Carter's Hotel. Queensberry's comment on being read the warrant suggests that he was, if anything, relieved and content. Expressing his surprise – 'In these cases I always thought proceedings were taken by summons, but I suppose it is all right' – he asked the date of the libel and on being told 18 February, realised that it related to the card, and added: 'Yes – I have been trying to find Mr. Oscar Wilde for

8 or 10 days. This thing has been going on for over 2 years.'[7] He was taken to Vine Street police station to be formally charged and from there to Marlborough Street Magistrates' Court where he appeared before the 'somewhat irritable' police magistrate Robert Milnes Newton.[8] Humphreys prosecuted on behalf of Wilde and Lewis acted for Queensberry.

Humphreys, describing his client as 'a married man [who] lived on most affectionate terms with his wife and children,' told the court that Wilde 'had been the object of a system of the most cruel persecution at the hands of Lord Queensberry'. He advised that he had first been consulted ten months ago but 'in consequence of the domestic affairs of the Queensberry family' his client had been 'loth and unwilling to take any steps of a criminal nature'; however, matters had 'come to a climax, and he felt bound to take steps in self-protection'.

Queensberry had been standing silently in the dock but when Humphreys described the inscription on the card as 'Three words . . . two being epithets of the foulest nature, while the intermediate word he could not decipher' he interjected 'The word is "posing".'

Humphreys said that he did not intend to rest his case simply upon this libel, but would go into previous cases – by this he undoubtedly meant Queensberry's letter of 1 April 1894. Lewis requested an adjournment to consult with his client, but Humphreys replied that he would call only two witnesses, whose evidence would be very short and the whole matter could be gone into next week. He then called Sydney Wright and Inspector Greet.

Sir George Lewis said, 'Let me say one word, Sir. I venture to say, when the circumstances of this case are more fully known, you will find that Lord Queensberry acted as he did under feelings of great indignation, and—'

'I cannot go into that now,' Newton interrupted.

'I do not wish this case to be adjourned,' Lewis persisted, 'without it being known that there is nothing against the honour of Lord Queensberry.'

'You mean to say you have a perfect answer to the charge,' said Newton.[9]

The 'perfect answer' under provision 6 of the Libel Act of 1843 (Vict. c. 96) was that the statement was true and published for the public benefit. Lewis applied for bail for his client on his own recognisances of £1,000, and Humphreys, who had not yet appreciated that Queensberry was as eager as his son for the case to be heard, asked for a surety.

'Lord Queensberry is not going to run away,' protested Lewis.[10]

Newton adjourned the case for a week, granting bail but requiring that Queensberry find a surety in the sum of £500. There was no difficulty as a friend of Queensberry's came forward. William Haviside Tyser a shipowner of 13 Gloucester Square had connections with Bracknell, and it may have been on one of Queensberry's unhappy visits to Sybil's nearby country home that he and Tyser met.

When news of Queensberry's arrest hit the Monday newspapers, the initial public reaction was to take sides with Wilde. The *London Figaro* referred to Wilde as 'the noble dramatist' and to Queensberry as the author 'of some of the worst poetry that was ever written. The Marquis is an Agnostic, and doesn't let you forget it. He holds peculiar views on matrimony, as many people very often do who have been twice married, even if they do not possess the distinction which the Marquis enjoys of having also been twice divorced.'[11] Sybil, who was in Italy at the time, read about the arrest and wrote a letter:

> My Darling Percy,
> I have seen Monday's paper, how horrible it all is. . . . Do, my Darling, do anything you can for my Darling Bosie you know how passionately I love him. If he is to be dragged in employ anyone you think best I will pay anything. . . . Do beg him from me to keep quiet & not be rude or violent to his Father that would only be worse for him.[12]

The press had revealed that Queensberry was staying at Carter's Hotel and he began to receive anonymous notes and copies of newspapers, which confirmed his belief that not only was he justified in his actions but that the public supported him.

Before the next hearing Lewis, for reasons he never revealed, returned his instructions to Queensberry and declined to act for him. Lewis's long friendship with and regard for Wilde, even after Bosie's Oxford scandal, may have prompted the decision. Queensberry appointed Charles Russell of Russell and Day, the firm that had acted for Ethel in the annulment. Russell at once realised that Queensberry's defence consisted of rumour, which was inadmissible, and Wilde's indiscreet letters to Bosie and published writings, which proved nothing. Russell approached the eminent counsel Edward Carson, QC, but Carson, who had been at Trinity College Dublin with Wilde refused to take the brief. Undeterred, Russell called on him again. This time he was more persuasive and Carson, after consulting the Lord Chancellor for advice, agreed. Carson was initially inclined to advise Queensberry to plead guilty, something his client would never have done, as it would have denied him his public platform.

Queensberry wrote to Minnie again on 4 March, although the letter now began curtly 'Madam' explaining that he did so

> because it was the only way to communicate with this good-for-nothing, white-livered son of mine, if he is so. . . . You must all be mad, and if you choose to make inquiries, you will find the whole town has been reeking with this hideous scandal of Oscar Wilde for the last three years . . . if I were to shoot this hideous monster in the street, I should be perfectly justified, for he has almost ruined my so-called son. That you are all going now and taking sides against me in what must be the most awful trouble that could come upon a father is the most wicked thing that was ever done, and I wish to have nothing to do with such people.[13]

On 6 March Queensberry received a batch of letters, some anonymous and some signed, and passed them on to his daughter-in-law. He was 'overwhelmed with horrible evidence to fortify my own position' and accused Minnie and Percy of 'living in the sphere of ignorance and mist . . . the only thing that can account for Percy's idiotic conduct . . . I am doing the best I can in the most horrible position a man was ever placed in. . . . I have the whole world behind me which is all my consolation.'[14]

On the 9th Queensberry appeared before Newton again wearing a 'long brown Melton coat trimmed with fur'[15] against the chilly weather, and accompanied by several friends and his legal team. Tyser, a 'gentleman of military bearing with a fierce white moustache',[16] and 'looking very much like Henri Rochefort' (a politician with distinctive bushy hair) arrived early. Wilde was represented by Charles Humphreys, and Carson arrived with his junior, Charles Gill. 'The prosecution of a marquis for criminal libel is not a matter of everyday occurrence,' observed the *Evening News* in an article headed 'The Peer and the Poet', and by the time the case was called at 11.30 the little court was packed with spectators, there was hardly any standing room, and 'The score or two of the general public who filled up the nooks and crannies left unoccupied by the Press, were packed worse than sardines in a tin.' Numerous people were disappointed. It was not yet a society event; the *Evening News* noted 'a complete lack of the fashionable West-end element'.[17] Wilde arrived in a carriage and pair accompanied by Bosie and Percy and had some trouble getting seats for them, while Humphreys had to appeal to the magistrate in order to obtain a place for his clerk. When his name was called Queensberry stepped into the dock, but Newton, his hostility of the previous week abated, at once directed that he be given a chair behind his counsel. Several newspapers were to comment suggestively on Bosie's appearance: 'a pale, fair-haired, smooth-faced, rather good-looking youth, observed the *Westminster Gazette*. Newton spotted that Bosie and Percy were in court and ordered them to leave, which they did, Bosie, after touching Wilde's arm in mute appeal, 'looking somewhat surprised and crestfallen'.[18]

The first witness to appear was Wilde, who described his meetings with Queensberry in the Café Royal and how Bosie had afterwards given him the letter Queensberry had written on 1 April 1894. Newton's interruption at this point was the first indication to most of those present that something rather more serious than a calling card with a few insulting words was involved.

'I think you are adopting a course which you had better not pursue,' said Newton. 'I am inquiring about this card.'

'But I have other libels to put in,' protested Humphreys.

'I suggest you should not examine on the letters,' said Newton.

Carson now weighed in saying that he hoped the letters would be put in as his client was acting in the interests of his son. There was a squabble in open court, Carson saying he 'wanted to go into the question of Lord Queensberry giving advice to his son'.

'You do not know that the letter only contains advice to his son,' said Humphreys.

'Don't I?' retorted Carson. 'I have a copy of it.'

Newton interposed, warning Humphreys that he was 'opening the door to let something in which would be very objectionable'.[19]

Humphreys said that he wished only Newton and Carson to read the letters and would not read them in public as in one particular letter 'the names of exalted persons are used', a statement which caused some excitement in court. Eventually Humphreys dropped the issue of the letters but when he had finished questioning Wilde about the card Newton asked

Humphreys and Carson to go with him to his room for a discussion. The men were absent for about ten minutes and the onlookers could only speculate on the reason. That was not the end of the conflict for on their return Carson wanted to cross-examine Wilde. Newton told Carson he had no right to cross-examine in that court and Carson said he had. He intended to ask about the steps taken by his client to end the acquaintanceship of his son with Wilde. Newton said that was quasi-justification and not admissible and there followed another pointed exchange, with Humphreys agreeing with Newton. Carson eventually conceded but not before establishing that his contention was that Queensberry sent the letter of 1 April 1894 because 'he thought it was well for the morality of his son'.[20]

Newton asked Queensberry if he wished to make an answer to the charge. The defendant, who had been following the testimony with head bent forward, now stood, a small figure behind the towering height of his counsel, and replied 'I have simply to say this, that I wrote that card simply with the intention of bringing the matter to a head, having been unable to meet Mr Wilde otherwise, and to save my son, and I abide by what I wrote.'[21]

Newton committed Queensberry to be tried at the central criminal court, with the same bail conditions as before, and Queensberry left the court with his friends. Newton, anticipating a distasteful trial, took the lawyers into his consulting room and strongly urged them to come to a settlement, but without success. 'Queensberry is quite dogged in his resolution to see the matter through,' commented the *New York Times*.[22]

There was some debate in the newspapers as to whether Queensberry would be 'tried by his peers' and it was anticipated by some, not without relish, that a jury of noblemen would be empanelled. The *Pall Mall Gazette* was obliged to point out that this rule applied only to 'heinous' crimes such as treason and felony. On 11 March Queensberry, back at Carter's Hotel, wrote to Minnie again saying she should tell her 'unfortunate husband' of the evidence in his possession. One was 'a most odious work, suppressed on account of its utter filth',[23] which he believed had been written by Wilde. This item was a story called 'The Priest and the Acolyte' in *The Chameleon*, a magazine published in Oxford in December 1894. Wilde had not written it, neither did he nor Bosie edit the collection; however, the story had a horrible resonance for Queensberry since the priest and the boy he loved committed suicide. Queensberry also had copies of 'two so-called poems, if filthy gibberish strung together can be called poetry, by Alfred, and signed with his name'.[24] These were In 'Praise of Shame', and 'Two Loves':

> the last ending with the words 'I am the love that dare not breathe [*sic*] its name' meaning Sodomy. . . . Percy and his brother must have been mad to go into court with this fellow. I hope you noticed they were instantly ordered out of the Court, which was some satisfaction to me. If Percy saw this publication, it might convince him of the utter folly of his and of his brother backing this man up, when I am doing all in my power to keep Alfred out of it.[25]

Percy and Minnie decided not to respond to Queensberry's letters and sent the most recent one to a solicitor, J. D. Stoneham whom they asked to correspond on their behalf. Stoneham wrote to Queensberry on 12 March asking that the correspondence should cease. Queensberry was angry enough to reply with exaggeration worthy of Bosie, objecting to the 'impertinent message from yr client who forced herself upon my family without my consent having inveigled my son into an engagement when he was still a boy at school,' adding, 'What will happen in the next six weeks will amply prove how utterly foolish ungrateful and childish their conduct has been in taking sides with this horrible monster'. He added, however, that since writing his last letter it had come to his knowledge that Wilde had not written the story in *The Chameleon*: 'I am always willing to acknowledge an error everyone gave him the credit of it. . . . We have plenty of filthy evidence without this article.'[26]

Stoneham responded that Lord and Lady Douglas did not wish to be connected with the dispute between Queensberry and Wilde (which, given Percy's actions, was untrue as far as he was concerned) but that Lord Douglas had declared 'his disbelief that Lord Alfred Douglas has been or is capable of being guilty of such an offence as you impute to Mr Wilde'.[27]

There were three weeks to go before the trial. Russell and Day, still without substantial evidence, employed private detectives to make further enquiries, one of whom was retired police inspector Francis Frederick Kerley (misspelled Kearley in trial transcripts).[28] The crucial links were provided, however, by actor and writer Charles Hallam Elton Brookfield. In 1892 Brookfield had produced and performed in a satire on Wilde's *Lady Windermere's Fan* entitled

The Poet and the Puppets, and in January 1895 he played a role in *An Ideal Husband*. According to Sir Max Beerbohm, Wilde, at the peak of his confident celebrity, had once snubbed Brookfield, who never forgave him and hated him thereafter. Brookfield was introduced to Russell by a mutual friend, Queensberry's journalist acquaintance John Boon, and finding that there had been difficulty in tracing some of Wilde's associates, used his contacts to make his own enquiries. Before long, Queensberry's solicitors had the names and addresses of a number of young men.

Another private detective was John George Littlechild, a former detective chief inspector who had retired from the Metropolitan Police in 1893. Whether he was, like Kerley, employed by Russell and Day or directly by Queensberry has never been established. Littlechild had been keeping a watch on Alfred Taylor, an associate of Wilde, who was known to the police, and even got into his rooms by a ruse and searched them but found no evidence to link him to Wilde. It was Kerley, however, who obtained a box of correspondence from the landlady of Taylor's lodgings, which included letters and telegrams from Wilde. Many of the rumours that had been circulating about Wilde centred on events at the Savoy Hotel, and through this connection further witnesses began to emerge. The plea of justification was amended accordingly.

On 23 March Queensberry wrote directly to Bosie, and by now he could see only one remaining way to settle the matter – with his fists. Bosie, whom he regarded as 'miserable, misguided, . . . insignificant, ridiculous and physically wretched' was, he believed, not a suitable match for the fifty-year-old battling lord:

> I would finish such as you in five minutes, but your good-for-nothing, kicked out, run-away, turned it up brother is a different matter. He, too is a wretched creature, but has some pretensions to be a man. What you both require is a damned good hiding. I never could, or would, touch you as children; if ever there was a case of spare the rod and spoil the child, it was you and Percy. What you both required was an unmerciful hiding to knock the conceit and shit out of you before you had arrived at your present state.

He thought 'this squirming skunk Percy . . . has some sort of idea he can fight . . . I will take him on for any sum he likes . . . I will back myself for any ready money . . . and meet him anywhere, fists or single sticks, to fight to the finish and try to give him the licking he deserves. Of course he might lick me, so it's quite fair, but I know what a tame cur and coward he is, so I shall chance it.'[29]

On 25 March a grand jury met at the Central Criminal Court to hear the indictment and consider the evidence supplied by the prosecution, including the letters that had not been read out at Marlborough Street. Queensberry appeared in person and said that he was not guilty and intended to justify his words. On the following day the grand jury found that there was sufficient evidence for the case to proceed to trial. Queensberry wrote an angry letter to Minnie's father about his 'stuck-up, pauper, impertinent daughter' and 'her good-for-nothing, white-livered husband'. Frustrated that neither of them would take any notice of what he said or look at the evidence in his possession, and that they continued to take sides with Bosie against him, he had stopped supplying them with money, and predicted that 'the improvident foolish match' would end in 'nothing but disaster'.[30]

That night Queensberry dined with his friend Mr Pape and spoke of an incident, the date of which is unknown but would have been recent. Queensberry had been staying at Pape's house, and Percy had called to see him. Queensberry was not in, but Percy took the opportunity of telling Pape about his father's quarrel with his agent and the accusations against Bosie. Perhaps Percy hoped to enlist Pape to his side, or thought that Pape could persuade Queensberry to retract his statements. The visit only served to annoy Queensberry further, especially as Percy at first denied having made it. 'He is quite ready to meet you and to meet your denials,' wrote Queensberry to Percy on 27 March. 'You told me first of all you had never even seen him but were obliged to take that back. How is it possible you could forget such an interview. He says you were at Portland St ever so long, and your wife sitting outside in a cab all the time quite an hour and that you were gesticulating and declaiming in a derogatory way about my quarrel with Arthur taking his side. I believe Pape. I don't believe You.'[31] It was probably this event that Queensberry referred to in an unfortunately undated letter to Percy saying that Percy had 'come and forced yourself into not my home I have none but into a friends house where I was resting for a time & try to force an interview upon me'. Bosie, it seemed, tried the same thing soon afterwards. 'Worse because I was in the house & he forced his way in to my presence when I refused to see him'. Queensberry sent him away with 'his tail pretty well between his legs'.[32]

The family was understandably afraid that Queensberry's campaign would end by incriminating Bosie but he pointed out to Percy that he had only told him about the 'scrape at Oxford . . . to show I was trying to screen him all I could which we are doing now, and you two fools rush in and ally yourself with this monster's cause and make our task more difficult'.[33]

Stoneham was unwise enough to write to Queensberry advising him that Lord Douglas did not want to take sides which, since that was exactly what Percy had been doing, further enraged Queensberry and provoked another exasperated rant in his reply of 28 March, in which he wrote bluntly about Bosie going about with a 'notorious sodomite' and the 'hideous publication' with 'a story of sodomy' and 'two disgusting poems, also of sodomy'.[34] Stoneham replied on the following day. 'While making all allowance for your excitement under which you are undoubtedly labouring, I cannot help expressing my surprise you should so far forget yourself and your own dignity and self-respect as to indulge in such invectives as are contained in your last two letters.'[35] Queensberry was calmer when he sent the letter back unopened two days later. 'I regret that I wrote violently to you lately, but in the trouble that I am in, it is beyond human endurance.'[36]

On 28 March Mr Gill appeared before Mr Justice Collins at the Central Criminal Court saying that in ordinary circumstances the case would stand over until the next sessions but 'the defendant was very desirous of having the case speedily tried and he himself was informed that the prosecutor also desired it'. The hearing was scheduled to open on 3 April.

On 30 March Russell filed the amended plea with the additional assertion that the 'alleged libel' was 'true in substance and in fact'. There followed a list of allegations that Wilde had been sexually intimate with ten named young men and a number of others, names unknown. Wilde was also said to have published obscene works, which included *The Picture of Dorian Gray*. The alleged libel was said to have been published 'for the public benefit' in that Wilde was 'a person who exercised considerable influence over young men', his works were 'calculated to subvert morality and encourage unnatural vice', that he had 'corrupted and debauched the morals' of the named young men and that 'his true character and habits' should be known so that Her Majesty's subjects 'being forewarned might avoid the corrupting influence'.[37]

Wilde had been persuaded by Bosie to go with him to Monte Carlo, and they departed on 12 March. It was an absence Wilde later regretted. He should, he acknowledged, have been in London taking legal advice about what Queensberry always referred to as the 'booby-trap'[38] in which he was about to be caught, 'the trap he openly betted in the Orleans club he would lure me into'.[39]

Wilde returned on 20 March. His counsel was the respected and formidable Sir Edward Clarke, who accepted the brief after being personally assured by Wilde that the charges were 'false and groundless'.[40] Wilde and Bosie met Clarke and examined the plea of justification. The list of names, many accompanied by dates and addresses of the alleged intimacies, must have come as a shock. Wilde continued to deny everything. His friends begged him to go abroad but he decided to stay and see it through, and Bosie of course was eager for his day in court.

Queensberry had brought matters to a head, but Queensberry's son made the case an instrument of his anger against his father. Bosie later alleged that Clarke had promised he could give evidence against his father's character, something Clarke always strongly denied. Caught between the clashing Douglases was a loving and foolishly indiscreet literary genius who had never corrupted anybody, and was about to suffer the penalty of a ridiculous law. Inevitably Wilde was later to comment bitterly: 'his father saw in me a method of annoying his son, and the son saw in me the chance of ruining his father, and I was placed between two people greedy for unsavoury notoriety, reckless of everything but their own horrible hatred of each other, each urging me on, the one by public cards and threats, the other by private, or indeed half-public scenes, threats in letters, taunts, sneers'.[41] Of course Queensberry's frantic opposition to the relationship was not 'a method of annoying his son' but an attempt to save him from ruin or worse, but Wilde never seemed to appreciate the horror with which homosexuality was regarded outside his own artistic circles.

Wilde later claimed that three important witnesses were coached by Queensberry and his solicitors to make statements that transferred the actions of another person to himself. The other person would undoubtedly have been Bosie. Each side was to accuse the other of witness tampering, and Queensberry would certainly not have countenanced any witness who imputed criminal activity to Bosie. The young men would have been instructed to say nothing about his son.

On the night before the trial, Queensberry, Crespigny and their old friend Fred Cotton – he of the Bogside steeplechase foot race – dined at Willis's. It was known that Wilde had dined there a few days previously, so Queensberry when booking the table had sent a message to the head waiter 'to warn Wilde, should he turn up, of the fact, so that he could select his choice of remaining or retiring'.[42] As they dined the proprietor came up to them and said that he thought there was little chance of Wilde coming there since at his last visit the other diners had said that if he was permitted to enter again they would dine elsewhere. The dinner continued in peace.

CHAPTER 18

In the Dock

THE trial of Queensberry, commented Sir Travers Humphreys, 'exhibited all the features of a cause célèbre. It is not every day that a Marquess can be seen in the dock of the Old Bailey charged with libel.'[1] Since the plaintiff was a playwright with two plays currently enjoying a successful London run and it was understood that the decency of Wilde's writings would be called into question, there was an immediate clamour by all classes of society for admission to the court. What they expected may have been a demonstration of Wilde's flashing wit, and that, to begin with, they certainly got.

The proceedings opened before Mr Justice Henn Collins. He was due to take his seat at 10.30 a.m., but the court began to fill more than an hour before, and the mood of those present may be gathered from the fact that someone made a joke about 'the importance of being early',[2] which raised a laugh. Unlike the varied throng in the magistrates' court this was a classy crowd of 'well-dressed folk, people who seemed willing and anxious to pay any sum rather than go home disappointed'.[3] The police had been supplied with lists of those who had the sheriff's permit to enter, but 'an eager struggling crowd of lookers-on'[4] some of whom, it was suspected, had bribed their way in, took up the remaining spaces. Soon all the seats were filled, and standing room in the gangways was fully occupied so that 'every space was packed with distinguished, fashionable and well-known people – all men'.[5] The passages leading into the court were so blocked by the crush of people that it was hard for anyone to get in or out. The court usually allowed six places for the press but this time had allocated twelve. Unfortunately, there were twenty-five pressmen.

Queensberry was the first of the principals to arrive. He came in alone, and stood, hat in hand, in front of the dock. Stepping up to the solicitors' table, he had a brief word with his lawyer Charles Russell. He 'looked worried, but wore a marked expression of determination'.[6] He wore 'a long, dark blue velvet-bound somewhat sportishly cut overcoat, and upright collar, with a light blue hunting scarf held with a very fine pearl pin, a black suit, shining new pair of tan gloves', and looked 'pale and not over happy. The light tie and his dark hair, well pomaded, and dark, heavy side whiskers, seemed to vie with each other in making his pallor more conspicuous.'[7] The newspaper sketches of Queensberry in the dock are some of the few pictures of him in middle age in which he is hatless. He is clean-shaven apart from the whiskers, and his dark hair is well combed and sleeked down. One observer later stated 'His lower lip drooped considerably',[8] and this can be observed in his portrait in *The Star*. In *The Sun* his mouth is firm, but he looks strained, tired and unhappy.

Two or three minutes later there was a stir in court as the elegant figure of Wilde appeared. He looked 'intensely grave' and took a seat immediately in front of his counsel, Sir Edward Clarke and barrister Charles Mathews, with whom he at once joined in 'an animated conversation'.[9] The contrast between Wilde and the silent figure of Queensberry a few yards away was closely observed, as were the figures who sat just behind Wilde, 'the fragile-looking Lord Alfred Douglas and the sturdier and more manly looking Lord Douglas of Hawick'.[10] Ex-inspector Littlechild was present, and spoke to Charles Russell. The judge arrived ten minutes late, and once the jury had been sworn in Queensberry surrendered to his bail and took his place in the dock, standing at the front with his arms resting on the ledge. Asked by the warder if he would like to be seated, he shook his head and remained standing. Bosie, according to Wilde, 'feasted [his] eyes with the spectacle of [his] father standing in the dock'.[11]

As Queensberry pleaded not guilty to the indictment on the grounds that the libel was true and published for the public benefit, he 'cast a glance of undisguised contempt' at Wilde.[12] Sir Edward Clarke rose to make the opening statement for the prosecution. As he spoke an intensely attentive quiet fell over the courtroom. Queensberry, perhaps relieved that the trial had begun at last, appeared more at his ease and occasionally smiled and nodded. Clarke was proceeding on the basis that the words on the card were 'posing as a sodomite', that there had been no accusation of 'the gravest of all offences'[13] but that the recipient wished to appear as a person guilty of or inclined to the commission of such an offence; undoubtedly a simpler, and less controversial and distasteful option. Had the publication of the libel been the defendant's only action, said Clarke, the result of some strong but mistaken feeling on his part, this might have extenuated the gravity of the situation but the plea of justification that had followed and the allegations that Wilde had solicited people to commit indecent behaviour made it 'a much graver issue'.[14] Clarke decided to pre-empt any insinuations of the defence and demonstrate that his client had nothing to hide by reading out Wilde's indiscreet 'red rose-leaf' letter to Bosie referring to it as 'the expression of true poetic feeling'.[15] It provoked a brief burst of mirth in court. The prosecution was on rather better ground with the *Promise of May* incident and Queensberry's arrival at the St James's Theatre with 'a large bouquet made of vegetables'.[16] There was more laughter and Clarke added, 'Whether Lord Queensberry was responsible for his actions is a matter on which you, gentlemen of the jury, may have some doubts before this case has ended.'[17] Wilde was shown in a forbearing light when Clarke revealed that he had taken no action over the accusations made in Queensberry's letters as 'he did not wish to – and he will not now further than can be avoided – bring into prominence the relations of Lord Queensberry with the members of his family'.[18]

The literary justification for the libel was easily disposed of, as Wilde had not published anything controversial in *The Chameleon*, and Clarke defied Carson to find anything indecent in *Dorian Gray*.

Sydney Wright was questioned but not cross-examined, and then Wilde took the stand, smartly dressed and confident. From the dock, Queensberry turned slightly to look at him 'with an expression of supreme contempt'.[19] The crowd craned forward, and a hush fell. No one wanted to miss one golden word from the lips of the distinguished playwright.

During Wilde's questioning by Clarke, Queensberry's expression did not change but was 'complemented occasionally . . . by subdued and angry mutterings'.[20] As Wilde described his first meeting with Bosie, Queensberry asked for writing materials and wrote a lengthy note for his counsel. Wilde amused the court with his witty description of the failed attempts to blackmail him about his letter to Bosie and Queensberry's angry visit to Tite Street. He stated that there was no truth in any of the statements impugning his conduct. Thus far the trial was going against the defendant.

Carson, who was suffering from a bad cold and spoke in a subdued voice, opened his cross-examination. He started by catching Wilde out on a point of vanity, since Wilde had claimed to be thirty-nine whereas he was actually forty. Having established that the witness was substantially older than Bosie and that the two had stayed together on many occasions, Carson moved on to the weakest part of his case, the interpretation of literature. The contrast between the stern counsel and the sparkling poet could not have been greater. At the lunch interval which 'came as a pleasant relief for all',[21] Carson applied for and received permission for Queensberry to be allowed his freedom.

After lunch Carson read out large portions of *Dorian Gray*, with Wilde continuing to deny that there was anything indecent in his writing. The examination then moved on to more dangerous ground, Wilde's association with young men. Wilde denied any improper conduct but as the questioning progressed it became apparent to those listening that Wilde had had friendships with a number of much younger men, not of his own social class, whom he had addressed on first-name terms, treated to dinners, taken to hotels and to whom he had given money and other gifts. The faces of the jurymen 'plainly showed signs of surprise . . . and surprise gave way to sheer astonishment'[22] when Carson produced some extravagant gifts which Wilde had given to a boy who sold newspapers on Worthing pier. The examination was interrupted by the end of the day's session and Queensberry was released on bail. It was thought to be significant that Queensberry's bail had been reduced from £2,000 to £500.

The mood of the trial had changed; 'though it was the marquis who was technically in the dock it was quite evident that before the day's proceedings finished it was his accuser . . . who really stood on his defence before the world . . . as the day waned and the centre of gravity, as it were, shifted from the defendant to the prosecutor'.[23] Overnight, a rumour flew around London society that Wilde had left by the night mail to Dover. A journalist checked with Queensberry at 1 a.m. but he had heard nothing.

On the following day the doors opened at half past nine, and once again the court was packed, and buzzing with conversation, mainly about Wilde's testimony. Junior barristers 'monopolised the seating and overflowed into adjacent passages in such numbers as to seriously obstruct the view from many points'.[24] Bosie was described by the press as 'a fair, pale young man, of somewhat delicate mould',[25] while his 'smooth, clean-shaven face, light flaxen hair brushed smoothly off his forehead, and "rose-leaf lips" became the subject of universal attention'.[26] As the crush of onlookers waited for the start of the trial there was the busy rustle of morning papers being eagerly perused.

Queensberry, looking 'cool, hard and determined',[27] was 'again attired in the semi-sporting costume which seems to go far towards making him a distinct personality'[28] although he had exchanged the light blue hunting stock for a cream one. After a brief conversation with his supporters, he took his place in the dock at half past ten. He sat down, but when the judge entered, stood and leaned on the front rail, holding one of his gloves, a pencil and a piece of paper. Carson's questioning of Wilde about his friendships continued, and 'as name after name rolled from Carson's uncompromising lips the witness showed signs of impatience, his own counsel began to feel uncomfortable, and the faces of the middle-class jury got longer and longer'.[29] Queensberry looked on Wilde 'with a gaze of interested curiosity',[30] his eyes flickering back and forth between counsel and witness as the questioning continued. Now and then he smiled as Carson scored more heavily than usual, and made notes. Occasionally he glanced at Bosie, curious to see if the revelations were having any effect.

Thus far Wilde had been calm and firm in his denials, but then he made a fatal slip, which Carson immediately capitalised on. Carson asked Wilde if he had ever kissed sixteen-year-old Walter Grainger, a servant at Oxford. Wilde replied that he had not; adding flippantly that the boy was 'extremely ugly'.[31]

'Was that the reason you did not kiss him?' demanded Carson.[32] There was a sharp exchange of questioning and Wilde became unnerved and, for a time, inarticulate. Had there been just one or two friendships open to misconstruction the gentlemen jurors might have been persuaded to dismiss the rumours, but the catalogue of names and exposure of a hidden side of Wilde's life revealed a pattern which they might well have thought any father of a young son would have viewed with concern.

The cross-examination closed and Clarke started to read out the correspondence, starting with Queensberry's letter of 1 April 1894. When he began to read the letter of 3 April Carson at once interrupted and demanded that Bosie's curt telegram be read, which it was. Clarke then completed his reading of the 3 April letter, following it with the letter to Montgomery of 6 July and the letters of 21 and 28 August to Bosie. The reading of Queensberry's hurt and angry tirades in Sir Edward's calm dispassionate tone caused a sensation in court and there was a considerable stir and gasps of amazement at passages in which the writer appeared to be questioning his son's legitimacy. Queensberry, in a state of great emotion stood grasping the dock for support, his lips quivering. 'Every now and then he turned to the man in the witness-box and ground his teeth together, and shook his head at the witness in the most violent manner. Then when the more pathetic parts of the letters came the poor old nobleman had the greatest difficulty in restraining the tears that welled into his eyes, and forced him to bite his lips to keep them back.'[33] Harsh as Queensberry's letters were, the contrast of his bitter pain with Bosie's petulant insults and Wilde's poetic expressions of love could only arouse in the jurors a fellow feeling for the man in the dock.

Clarke read some extracts from *Dorian Gray* to offset the impression given by the ones read out by Carson, and suggested unconvincingly that Wilde's young male friends were admirers of literature and that Wilde had not suspected that they might be disreputable. When Wilde was late in returning to the witness box after lunch, a rumour flew around the court that he had fled abroad rather than face Carson again. The crowds in the courtroom were now so great that people were almost standing on the judge's bench, and outside a score or more were straining to peer through the glass-topped entrance. At two o'clock when it seemed that not another person could be crammed in, the Lord Mayor appeared. People were sitting two deep on the bench, and one man was actually permitted to perch on the corner of the judge's chair.

Carson requested that Bosie's postcard referring to his possession of a revolver be put into evidence and read. Clarke objected but was overruled. The foreman of the jury questioned Wilde about *The Chameleon* and his opinion of 'The Priest and the Acolyte', and Clarke read the correspondence that had passed between Queensberry and Humphreys, which showed, disappointingly for the scandalmongers, that the references to 'exalted persons' did not relate to the charges made by the prosecutor. The case for the prosecution was closed and Wilde left the courtroom but not the building.

Carson's opening speech for the defence stated at the outset that 'in any act [his client] has done, in any letter he has written, or in the matter of the card which has put him in the present position, he withdraws nothing. He has done all those things with a premeditation and a determination, at all risks and at all hazards to try to save his son. . . . Lord Queensberry's conduct in this respect has been absolutely consistent all through.'[34] Referring to Bosie's poem 'Two Loves' he said, 'Is it not a terrible thing that a young man on the threshold of life who has for several years been dominated by Oscar Wilde . . . should thus show the tendency of his mind upon this frightful subject? What would be the horror of any man whose son wrote such a poem?'[35] He read extracts from *Dorian Gray* to support his contention that it 'advocates the vice imputed to Mr Wilde'.[36]

Carson then played his master card. Referring to Alfred Wood, who had tried to blackmail Wilde over his letters to Bosie and to whom Wilde had given money so he could go to America, he said 'Mr. Wilde . . . I suppose hoped that he would never see him again.' At this point Carson paused dramatically. 'But gentlemen,' he went on, 'as a matter of fact, Wood is here and will be examined before you.'[37] A gasp of amazement and anticipation went round the court.

The evening shadows deepened. The trial had started in an atmosphere of high comedy, but that was long gone. 'Everybody in Court seemed conscious that they were assisting at a great tragedy. . . . the climax . . . seemed to all certain and foredoomed.'[38] After rereading a letter sent by Wilde to Bosie Carson went on:

> I am not here to say anything has ever happened between Lord Alfred Douglas and Mr Oscar Wilde. God forbid! But everything shows that the young man was in a dangerous position in that he acquiesced in the domination of Mr Wilde, a man of great ability and attainments. Against that letter . . . Lord Queensberry protested; and I wish to know, gentlemen, are you, for that protest, going to send Lord Queensberry to gaol? . . . before you condemn Lord Queensberry, I ask you to read Wilde's letter and to say whether the gorge of any father ought not to rise.[39]

Here the session ended for the day.

On 5 April Queensberry arrived in the Old Bailey with a new air of confidence. After leaning nonchalantly against the dock, and looking about him, he climbed into the dock, sat down, took a paper out of his pocket and read it. Onlookers craned their necks to see what he was reading, without success. He folded the paper and put it away. Wilde was in a side room, and did not make an appearance.

Carson told the packed court that he had to approach 'a more painful part of the case . . . to bring before you young men, one after another, who have been in the hands of Mr. Wilde, to tell their unhappy tales'.[40] Wilde had denied in evidence that there had been a scandal at the Savoy Hotel (Queensberry in his letter of 6 July 1894 had referred to the allegations that Wilde and Bosie had stayed there), but a witness would tell the court of 'the shocking acts he was led by Mr. Wilde to perpetrate' at the Savoy.[41] The atmosphere in the court was understandably tense. Carson had not completed his opening statement when Sir Edward Clarke, who had briefly left the court with Mr Mathews in order to consult Wilde, returned, touched Carson's arm and asked for the judge's leave to consult with his learned friend. There were a few moments of whispered conversation, during which the spectators wondered what new drama was about to unfold, and then Carson sat down.

Clarke addressed the court, saying that to avoid 'going through day after day an investigation of matters of the most appalling character'[42] he wished to withdraw from the prosecution. He could not resist a verdict of not guilty, but, anxious to avoid any suggestion that his client had had improper relations with young men, he asked that the finding should be justified only by reference to Wilde's literature and letters. The judge agreed that he would not 'insist on going through prurient details',[43] but could not approve Clarke's suggested limitation. The jury was directed to return a verdict of not guilty and after a few moments of consultation agreed that justification had been proved and that the words on Queensberry's card were published for the public benefit.

'Of course the costs of the defence will follow,'[44] said Carson, and Collins agreed. The decision was greeted with a prolonged outburst of applause and 'round after round of cheering in Court',[45] which the ushers did little to suppress. The cheers were perhaps less for the marquess than an expression of support for the prevalent public view of morality from those who might have liked to strike a blow themselves but did not have Queensberry's personal motives or determination.

Wilde, on the advice of Clarke had already left the building by a side exit, accompanied by Bosie. Even before the formal discharge 'congratulatory handshaking had been going on, the marquis leaning over the dock to reach the palms of his beaming friends'.[46] Once Queensberry was discharged he stepped from the dock amidst renewed applause from the spectators in the public gallery 'which the officials of the court only half-heartedly attempted to stop'[47] and joined his solicitor in the well of the court. Crowds were waiting outside in the street and it was not long before the news reached them. 'The feeling in London against Wilde is very strong,' observed the *Westminster Gazette*, 'and the public indignation finds vent in the freest expressions of opinions.'[48]

When Wilde left the Old Bailey and stepped into his private brougham, two men jumped into a waiting cab and followed him. It is sometimes claimed that these were Queensberry's detectives, but they might also have been pressmen. If Queensberry had engaged detectives to prevent Wilde and Bosie from being together, they failed, and there is no evidence that Queensberry received or acted upon any information that day.

Queensberry was not, as was later confirmed by his solicitor, intending to press for criminal charges to be brought against Wilde; he was content simply to have Wilde parted from Bosie. It was widely reported that immediately after the trial Queensberry's first act was to send a message to Wilde. 'If the country allows you to leave,' he said, 'all the better for the country; but if you take my son with you, I will follow you, wherever you go, and shoot you!'[49] The press was later informed: 'This statement is not correct. The message was sent some days ago, and not after the trial ended. Lord Queensberry did not say he would shoot Mr Wilde. What he said was that if he persuaded his misguided son to go with him, he would feel quite justified in following him, Wilde, and shooting him, did he feel inclined to do so and were he worth the trouble.'[50]

Queensberry's decision to take no part in the prosecution must have been partly financial, since 'the preparation for the defence has involved no little outlay, a considerable part of which has been incurred in the preparation of the details of the sworn testimony, and in bringing witnesses from a distance'.[51] He felt that he had spent quite enough on a case which concerned not only his own but the public interest; he wanted his money back if possible, and he was not going to spend any more.

That afternoon, Wilde, Bosie and Percy occupied rooms at the Holborn Viaduct Hotel from which Wilde issued a statement claiming that he had retired from the case rather than place Bosie in the 'painful position' of giving evidence against his father.[52] Percy told a reporter from *The Sun* that Wilde was unable to bear seeing anyone. He, however, was happy to talk to the press and revealed that both he and Bosie had been under subpoena for the prosecution. 'I and every member of my family, exempting my father, disbelieve entirely the allegations of the defence. It is, in my opinion, simply a part of the persecution which my father has carried on against us ever since I can remember.'[53]

Messages of support for Queensberry began to pour in. On being told by a Sunday newspaper that a further pile of messages was waiting for him he said, 'You know, I have not much to do with distinguished people, but I had a very nice letter from Lord Claud Hamilton, and a kind telegram from Mr Charles Danby, the actor, with "Hearty Congratulations" et cetera. Various clubs have telegraphed also. Here is a message: "Every man in the City is with you. Kill the bugger!"'[54] The *New York Herald*'s London reporter found Queensberry in Carter's Hotel, his 'table littered with congratulatory telegrams which continued to arrive in batches at intervals'.[55] Queensberry declared that he had done his duty, to himself, his family and the community. He confirmed that he had sent a message to Wilde saying that if he left the country he would not lift a finger to stop him, 'but he must distinctly understand that if he takes my son with him I shall follow him and shoot him like a dog. But I think he ought not to be allowed to leave the country. I think he ought to be placed where he can ruin no more young men.'[56] The public, for once, agreed with Queensberry and he was obliged to issue a general note of thanks.

> As the Marquess of Queensberry finds it quite impossible to reply to the number of letters, telegrams and messages he has received in the last few days, he begs to be allowed through the medium of the Press to express his gratitude for the hundreds of kind messages of sympathy he has received, from friends and strangers alike, from every part of the country, and to thank them most cordially for the same, the number of which makes it impossible to send separate replies or acknowledgements.[57]

The verdict of the press was unanimous. 'There is not a man or a woman in the English-speaking world possessed of the treasure of a wholesome mind who is not under a deep debt of gratitude to the Marquess of Queensberry,'[58] commented the *National Observer*. The *St James's Gazette*, which had taken particular pride in its refusal to publish details of 'offences so abominable that they cannot be mentioned' and referred during the trial to 'the remarkable quarrel between Mr. Oscar Wilde and Lord Queensberry, now being fought out to its poisonous end',[59] commented:

> In reality the case was a trial not of the defendant but of the plaintiff. . . . For the Marquess of Queensberry himself there can be nothing but congratulation. . . . Lord Queensberry may not be a very dignified or heroic figure, but we are not surprised at the demonstrations in his favour . . . no one can complain of a father using strong language and action towards a son, when he finds him in association with a man twice his years whose influence is so degrading and corrupting that the miserable youth actually goes within an ace of threatening to murder his own father.[60]

Later Wilde, from the depths of despair wrote to Bosie 'your father became the hero of the hour, more, indeed . . . your family now ranks, strangely enough, with the Immortals, ... your father will always live among the kind pure-minded parents of Sunday School literature'.[61]

Bosie, hoping to see his father condemned and humiliated, was bitter about his triumph, and blamed Clarke for having introduced nothing in the trial to cause Queensberry 'a moment's slight uneasiness. He had assumed the mantle of the heart-broken, loving father, fighting nobly to "save his son".'[62] History, accepting Bosie's furious allegations, and Wilde's later unhappy analysis, has ascribed to Queensberry many unworthy motives for his actions – homophobia, insanity, a vindictive desire to ruin his son and break his ex-wife's heart, or even to boost his own reputation and regain his lost popularity. The simple and obvious answer has been dismissed as improbable, that he really was doing everything he could think of to put an end to a relationship which he believed – and there was abundant justification for that belief – would result in the ruin of his son.

Archibald had rethought his initial support of Bosie in the light of the revelations about Wilde, and wrote to *The Sun*, pointing out that Percy had not been authorised to make a statement on behalf of his mother, his sister or himself. Regarding the allegations of the defence 'we most certainly do believe them, and must repudiate any sympathy with the statement of my nephew'.[63] He later wrote to Percy saying that while his action in siding with Wilde during the libel trial was 'comprehensible . . . you do not act wisely and well in public lamentings over your father's success and you do not do well in quarrelling with your father'. He advised Percy to go to Queensberry and tell him that he was forced to admit that he had had good reason to say what he did. Wilde's acceptance that Queensberry's allegations were justified, said Archibald, 'necessitates my withdrawing my support',[64] but he offered to be the medium of reconciliation between Percy and his father. There is no evidence that Percy accepted this offer. The case had effectively split the family in two, and Percy and Bosie's relations with their aunt and uncle were to be cool for some years.

No one doubted that Wilde was in imminent danger of arrest, or worse. 'There must be another trial at the Old Bailey, or a coroner's inquest – the latter for choice.'[65] Russell and Day informed the press that 'it was not his lordship's intention to take the initiative in any criminal prosecution of Oscar Wilde'[66] but matters were already proceeding very fast without him. Russell had sent the case papers to the Public Prosecutor as soon as the trial had ended, and a warrant was obtained for Wilde's arrest the same afternoon. That evening, Wilde was arrested, taken to Bow Street Police Court, and charged with offences under Labouchère's section 11 of the Criminal Law Amendment Act of 1885. He was refused bail and transferred to Holloway Prison where Bosie visited him every day, something Queensberry seems to have done nothing to prevent. Wilde's plays closed, his sources of income dried up, and the same creditors who had once pursued him turned their attention to Constance. Wilde's distraught wife had abandoned Tite Street some weeks earlier to stay with a friend, and as soon as the libel trial began she took the boys out of school. It was not, as is sometimes believed, Queensberry who forced the sale of Wilde's property, but the landlord of 34 Tite Street who distrained for unpaid rent.

No charges were brought against Bosie. While Hamilton Cuffe, the Director of Public Prosecutions was in no doubt about the nature of Bosie's relationship with Wilde, the official view was that there was no real evidence to corroborate statements made by witnesses who were held to be of bad character. With the spectre of bankruptcy hanging over Wilde's head Bosie could only express his selfish delight that his father would not get his costs.

CHAPTER 19

The Price of Victory

ONLY a brave or foolhardy man would speak out in defence of Wilde but on 16 April a letter calling for more charitable treatment for the fallen poet was published in *The Star*. The writer was author Robert Buchanan, who asked whether those who were casting stones were 'without sin' or 'are themselves notoriously corrupt'.[1] Queensberry thought the question was aimed at him, and responded 'I certainly don't claim to be [without sin] myself, though I am compelled to throw the first stone. Whether or not I am justly* notoriously corrupt I am waiting patiently for the future to decide.'[2]

Bosie also wrote to *The Star* in Wilde's defence, giving his address, which was published. If Queensberry didn't already know where Bosie was staying, he knew then.

Buchanan replied, saying that his words were not aimed at Queensberry but at those who were pronouncing sentence on Wilde before he was even committed for trial:

I am sure that Lord Queensberry, who has himself suffered cruelly from the injustice of public opinion, is quite as sorry as I am for his fallen foe, and is quite as anxious as I am that he should be dealt with fairly, justly and even mercifully. . . . I have too much sympathy with his lordship's creed to think that the man who holds it would approve of such a system. So far from thinking him 'notoriously corrupt,' I think him notoriously brave and honest, anxious that all men should have, under Queensberry and all rules, a fair trial and fair play. . . .[3]

* The original of this letter has not survived. The word 'justly' may be a mistranscription of 'judged'.

After further correspondence Buchanan wrote, 'I heard from the Marquess of Queensberry's own lips that he would gladly, were it possible, set the public eye an example of sympathy and magnanimity.'[4] Queensberry took exception to the word 'sympathy' being placed in his mouth:

I never used it. In my time I have helped to cut up and destroy sharks. I had no sympathy for them, but may have felt sorry, and wished them put out of pain as soon as possible. What I did say was that as Mr Wilde now seemed to be on his beam ends and utterly down I did feel sorry for his awful position, and that supposing he was convicted of those loathsome charges brought against him that were I the authority that had to mete out to him his punishment, I would treat him with all possible consideration as a sexual pervert of an utterly diseased mind, and not as a sane criminal. If this is sympathy, Mr. Wilde has it from me to that extent.[5]

On 22 April Queensberry wrote again to Stoneham offering to settle the matter in the old-fashioned way with

this so called white livered son of mine Douglas of Hawick and Shitters. I want to thrash him or him me. He is 25 I am over 50 but I will meet him anywhere. I never could touch any of my children when they were children though I believe I did spank this boy once but now he is grown up he deserves a real good beating. Of course he might give me one so it is quite fair . . . . his miserable brother I take no notice of he is mad and is too wretched a creature to notice and has some excuse for his outrageous conduct if it had not been for me he would have been arrested before now.[6]

Percy asked Stoneham to apply for a summons against his father, hoping he would be bound over to keep the peace, but the magistrate Mr Hannay refused on the grounds that 'he declined to have any more dirty linen washed in his court'.[7] After a second application was refused Percy considered applying to the Court of Chancery for an injunction against Queensberry to restrain him but was advised that it was doubtful that this would be granted.

On 25 April with Wilde's trial due to open the following day the Douglas family – as if they did not have enough to worry them already – received some very unwelcome news from America. Lord Sholto Douglas who had been packed off to the fruit farm in California had not, as hoped, settled down to a life of dull but virtuous toil. He had quickly acquired a reputation as a lover of sport, and was a regular patron of gambling establishments. At a Bakersfield saloon he had met Loretta Addis, 'an exceedingly pretty young woman',[8] and on 24 April had taken out a licence to marry her. Loretta's real name was Margaret Mooney, and she was a song and dance variety actress of Irish descent. The press claimed that she was seventeen, but she was almost twenty.[9] Loretta had no great desire to be on the stage, but was there at the wishes of her domineering mother whose influence she was eager to escape. One of Sholto's friends had been so alarmed by his marriage plans that he decided to prevent the wedding. The friend, whose name was reported either as M. G. Burwester or Burmester, may have been English-born Maurice George Burmester. Sholto, to his astonishment, was arrested and placed in the county gaol where he learned that his friend had made an affidavit before a magistrate that he was insane and unaccountable for his actions, and that he was obliged to remain a prisoner until he could be medically examined. Sholto was understandably enraged, but once he had calmed down, he instructed counsel, demanded that the examination be carried out as soon as possible and instigated proceedings for the prosecution of Burmester.

The press commented that Sholto had never shown any symptoms of insanity, 'his only weakness being an insatiable desire for sport in any form'.[10] Burmester did not press his charge, and Sholto was released soon afterwards, as determined as ever to marry Loretta. He hoped for his family's blessing but was quite prepared to marry without it. A correspondent of *The World* interviewed Queensberry and observed:

The Marquis has been greatly depressed by the reports of the other affair printed in London, but seemed overwrought in consequence of this latest shock. He said 'I knew nothing of this affair until I heard of it yesterday from America. It came with a painful shock to me.' Asked if he disapproved of the marriage he replied 'I do not disapprove of it on principle . . . if that is what you mean. . . . I believe in permitting a man to marry the woman of his choice regardless of any other consideration. I think it a point on which perfect freedom should exist. . . . As to the particular circumstances of the present case, I know nothing.[11]

Sholto later exchanged letters with both his parents, and Queensberry, on learning that the couple had known each other for less than a month, advised his son to wait before marrying.

Oscar Wilde's trial opened at the Old Bailey on 26 April. Bosie had been entreated by Clarke to leave the country, and on the same day a statement was published in the newspapers. 'The Central News is requested by Lord Alfred Douglas to state that, in response to an urgent telegram from his mother, he started today for Italy to see her, but hopes to return to London in a few days.'[12] How much of this statement was true may only be guessed at. The supposed delicacy of the slender, pale marchioness was an unassailable excuse for any action. Bosie later stated that he left England the day before the trial but went only as far as Calais, where he stayed in the Terminus Hotel until the proceedings were over. On or around the third day of the trial, he sent a telegram offering to give evidence. His offer was refused.

On the 28th Queensberry suffered a cycling accident and did not appear in court on the following day, as he was confined indoors, so he may not have been in attendance when the trial ended on 1 May with the jury unable to reach a verdict. Wilde returned to Holloway but moves were afoot to have him bailed, and Queensberry determined to prevent a reunion with Bosie.

At the beginning of May, possibly on the 2nd or 3rd, Queensberry's friend Pape told him that he had seen Bosie at the theatre and met him at a refreshment room. Was Pape mistaken, or had Bosie returned? On 4 May Queensberry went to Holloway where he spoke to the officials about Bosie, probably to check whether his son had been seen there with Borie.

On the 7th Wilde made an application for bail at Bow Street Police Court. Bail was fixed at £5,000 with Wilde to give his personal security for £2,500, the rest to come from two sureties. One of the sureties was the radical and public-spirited clergyman Revd Stewart Headlam, the man who in 1881 had shared a platform with Queensberry and Henry Labouchère in support of Charles Bradlaugh. Headlam, a keen theatregoer, often entertained theatrical folk at his home. He had met Wilde just twice, and, concerned that publicity had prejudiced his case before it had even begun, had become a surety 'not for his character but for his appearance in court to stand his trial'.[13] The other surety was Percy, who, the press commented, did not resemble Bosie, 'being rather fleshy than thin, dark instead of fair, and dressed after the manner of the philistines, in black frock-coat with silk lapels and the ordinary stand-up collar and black cravat of Piccadilly'.[14] Wilde left the court accompanied by his co-sureties who had arranged for him to stay under another name at the Midland Hotel, St Pancras.

What followed has been described in several different ways, mainly by people who were not there to witness events. Wilde's friend and biographer Robert Sherard, whose memoirs incorrectly have Wilde going directly from Holloway to the hotel, stated that Wilde was followed by some men who had been waiting for him outside the prison gates 'at whose instigation we need not inquire'.[15] Just as he was about to sit down to dinner in his private room, the manager entered and asked if he was Oscar Wilde. Unhesitatingly, he admitted that he was, and was at once ordered to leave. In some accounts Wilde was hunted from hotel to hotel all over London by a gang of hired roughs who threatened to wreck any establishment at which he was allowed to stay, although Sherard states that this happened only at the second hotel and thereafter Wilde was not admitted to others because he was recognised. He eventually found refuge at his mother's house. The London press, however, did not report any public disturbances, which suggests that there were no unpleasant scenes in the street, and stated that Wilde arrived at the Midland Hotel with Percy and Headlam at 3 p.m., spent some time consulting with legal advisers, and left the following day for an unknown destination on the coast.

The only certainties that emerge from this mass of conflicting allegations are that Queensberry was involved in a pursuit of Wilde, that he was accompanied by Sir Claude de Crespigny, there was at least one disturbing scene of unknown location, and that Wilde transferred from the Midland Hotel, St Pancras to the Great Northern at King's Cross, most probably on the evening of 7 May, and then left. Crespigny told Bosie that it was Queensberry himself who went into the hotel and denounced Wilde to the manager. How far the pursuit went thereafter is unknown, but since Wilde did not arrive at his mother's until about midnight, it must have continued for some hours. Queensberry's actions were not, however, as is usually alleged, a vindictive attempt to prevent Wilde from finding a place to stay. He was under the impression that Bosie was in London, and wanted to ensure that the two did not meet.

On 8 May Queensberry sent a telegram to Stoneham: 'Unless I can get some assurance that Alfred is away and does not intend joining this fellow shall keep hunting him and seeking him from every Hotel as I did last night.'[16] Stoneham wired back: 'Assure you Alfred not in England will not return until end of month.'[17] This was followed up with a letter: 'You need be under no apprehension or fear that your son Lord Alfred is with Mr Wilde as a fact I myself saw him off by the continental train some few days ago and I know that yesterday afternoon he was still on the Continent and has no intention of returning to England . . . . every effort will be made by me to induce him to remain abroad for some little time.' Stoneham offered to satisfy Queensberry as to Bosie's whereabouts short of giving him the actual address, 'as I am very desirous of avoiding a repetition of the scene of last evening'.[18]

Queensberry tore up his copy of the letter, but replied to the telegram saying, 'you must either be purposely trying to deceive me or you are yourself mistaken because the wretched abortion of a creature was seen here . . . by my friend Mr Pape . . . I presumed he had intended to meet Wilde and therefore I took the step I did the other night to satisfy myself whether they were together or not. There was no occasion for him to bolt as he did if the wretched boy was not with him.'[19]

The timing of Bosie's train trip mentioned in Stoneham's letter is compatible with Bosie having been in London at the beginning of May, and in a telegram written on 22 May Bosie himself was to say that he had been in France for fifteen days, so it is possible that he did return after the end of the first trial and was sent back.

On the 8th Queensberry wrote to Stoneham with a new tirade, savagely denouncing Percy for his failures in the navy, army, Ceylon and Australia. 'You may inform this so-called skunk of a son of mine (I never believed he was my son) . . . that I will catch him some day and give him the warming he deserves, then we can raise the question whether a father has a right to thrash his son, particularly when he is old enough to protect himself.' He was especially upset at Percy joining in with what he called 'this lot . . . he certainly has all the appearance to recommend him to the fraternity: white-livered smoothed face, sicked-up looking creature, as if he had come up the wrong way. When he was a child swathed in irons to hold him together it used to make me sick to look at him.'[20]

Queensberry, who was then staying with Crespigny at Champion Lodge, Great Totham, Essex, was desperately frustrated as he didn't know where either Bosie or Wilde was and feared that they were together. Wilde was at the Kensington home of his friends, Ada and Ernest Leverson who kept his location secret, and Bosie was in France, his family simply telling Queensberry that his son was 'abroad'. Queensberry suspected that he was being lied to, and that Bosie and Wilde were with Percy. The Douglases were at Chalcott House, Long Ditton a short train ride from Waterloo, and Bosie had been staying with them before his departure for France. On 11 May Queensberry went there to see for himself and confronted Minnie. There followed an emotional scene during which Minnie told her father-in-law that he had no right to come to her house and that she had every right to have Bosie there. He asked for her word of honour that Wilde was not there and she gave it. She then asked him to leave and, not wishing to prolong the unpleasantness, he did, but on the following day he wrote a long letter to Minnie to explain the reasons for his visit. 'I came to your house only because I wished to know if the boy was there, believing and expecting that you were harbouring this villain Oscar Wilde. I have a right . . . to force myself in anywhere to keep this wretched misguided boy apart from such a man. If I had not thought Wilde was there, as I believe he is or was, I should not have come.'[21]

He remained concerned that Percy's support for Wilde would start the rumour that he, too, was homosexual, and was astonished that he and Minnie still refused to see the truth. 'The only possible excuse . . . is that you are all stark staring mad. People all over the world who don't know will for ever say, are they one of the man's lot. . . . As for the other wretched fellow, if it had not been for me he would have stood in the Dock with his friend, as he may do yet.' He ended with a postscript asking Minnie not to refer him to 'any of your sharks of lawyers' and threatening that if she did not acknowledge his letter he would lay the matter before her father so that he would know what was going on. 'I must defend myself as best I can. . . . I ask you a question. What was Wilde doing with these men & boys grooms and loafers.'[22]

On 14 May he wrote again enclosing a letter from Bosie whom he described sarcastically as 'the gilt soul whose rose-leaf lips are made for the madness of kissing . . . so you may see the sort of lot you have got amongst, and are supporting. Look out for your own children, there is such a thing as heredity as is well known, they throw back to the Montgomery grandpere.' He was no longer concerned that Bosie and Wilde were together; perhaps the letter he mentioned was from Bosie in France. 'His letters can be used to shutting [*sic*] him up in an asylum should he return. . . . As for O. W. I can wait for his fresh trial.' Wilde, 'if with you still, will hardly dare show his nose outside your gates. I guessed he was with you, and when I came down, found out he had been seen at your station with the great Lord of Shitters, naturally concluded he had gone on with you. Was I mistaken?'[23] 'Shitters' is an unusual expression for Queensberry to use when writing to a woman, and he must have forgotten himself in the heat of the moment.

The next day, having had no reply from Minnie, Queensberry sent another long letter, this time to Revd Walters with the whole story of the events since Percy and Minnie had returned from Australia. In it he expresses his dashed hopes, disappointments, anger and distress. He found it incomprehensible that after his acquittal on the libel charge and the revelations at Wilde's trial Percy should be standing surety for Wilde and – so he supposed – sheltering him:

> . . . if you think I am ever going to forgive this reptile of a son of mine and your upstart ignorant fool of a daughter you are very much mistaken. . . . I have been through an ordeal few men have passed through but all my pain has been unutterably intensified by the conduct of this son of mine, Hawick and your daughter . . . . even had I been wrong there was no earthly occasion for him to mix himself up in the affair and people will say he is one of the lot by the Lord he looks like it.[24]

Queensberry revealed that he had received a letter from a doctor in New York 'who said to me to be plain this man is a cock sucker' and advised Walters that he had 'better go and save your daughter from further contamination of such a man and Brute'.[25]

Oscar Wilde and his friend Alfred Taylor, who had also been arrested and charged with gross indecency, appeared at the Old Bailey on 20 May where it was decided to try them separately and take Taylor's case first. On the same day a bankruptcy notice was drawn up by Queensberry's solicitors requiring payment of Queensberry's court-awarded legal costs by 29 May. Wilde's unsecured liabilities after the sale of his effects were approximately £3,591 of which only £677 3s. 8d were Queensberry's legal costs. The remaining debts of £2,914 were made up of loans from Constance's family of £2,057, an advance from the St James's Theatre of £414, and numerous small sums, all under £100, for goods and services. None of these creditors intended to petition for Wilde's bankruptcy but Queensberry was hardly likely to hold back from claiming what was legally his. He was well aware that Wilde had no funds but may have believed that his family would support Wilde by coming up with the payment. Wilde, who had been led to believe that the Douglases would pay his legal costs, discovered to his great dismay and lasting bitterness that rather than give money to Queensberry, they preferred that he should be made bankrupt.

On 21 May, Taylor was found guilty of committing acts of gross indecency, though not of procuring for Wilde. Sentence was deferred. Percy and Queensberry were both in court to see this and at 5.04 p.m. Queensberry sent a triumphant telegram to Minnie. 'Must congratulate on verdict cannot on Percy's appearance looks like dug up corpse fear too much madness of kissing Taylor guilty Wilde's turn tomorrow.'[26] Queensberry had been spoiling for a fight with Percy for some time, and at ten past five that evening he got one. He had just come out of the telegraph office in St James's Street and was heading for his hotel in Albemarle Street when he saw Percy walking down Piccadilly with a friend, Mr Wisdom. According to Percy's later account he started 'making grimaces with the apparent idea of attracting my attention'.[27] Queensberry wasn't, however, intending to stop; he had just crossed over Old Bond Street where it joined Piccadilly, and had reached Scott's the hatter at 1 Old Bond Street, when Percy strode up to him. 'Are you going to cease to write those obscene and beastly letters to my wife?'[28] he demanded. Queensberry's response was to 'make a vulgar noise with his lips'.[29] Presumably he blew a raspberry. Percy placed himself in front of his father and repeated the question. What happened next was later hotly disputed. Percy claimed that Queensberry threw a punch, which landed under his left eye. Queensberry said that Percy 'came almost running at me, and pushed me up against a shop window, at the same time speaking at the top of his voice. I struck him in self-defence.'[30]

Percy dropped his umbrella and for some moments there was an exchange of blows. Mr Wisdom parted the pair, but they continued to quarrel and soon began fighting again. Piccadilly was busy with the usual afternoon strollers, and a small crowd quickly assembled which attracted the attention of Constable Morrell (Morrow in some newspaper reports) and Constable Loughlin who had been on duty nearby. Efforts were made to separate the combatants. The police asked the reason for the incident, to which

Queensberry replied 'I am the Marquess of Queensberry, and this is a so-called son of mine'[31] and Percy also gave his name. The constables attempted to reason with them, but Percy declared that it was no use trying to heal the breach in that way and asked to be taken at once to a police court 'so that I might thereby, by acquainting a magistrate of the gross and foul slanders and insults to which I had for some months past been subjected, obtain that protection which every person has a right to demand'.[32]

Queensberry decided to return to his hotel, and walked away, but Percy went after him and they met again outside Stewart's, a baker and confectioner's. 'Will you or will you not cease to write obscene letters to my wife, as I wish to have the matter settled once and for all?' Percy demanded.[33] Another scuffle ensued. Although the police had not seen the start of the first fight they thought that in the second it was Percy who struck the first blow. The fighting Douglases were taken into custody, Morrell arresting Queensberry and Loughlin taking charge of Percy, and escorted to Vine Street station, Percy insisting all the way that he had not been the one to strike first. The crowd followed and waited outside for developments.

At the station both men were charged with disorderly conduct by Inspector Walter Tett of C Division and agreed to appear in court at ten the following morning. Queensberry, who must have anticipated another public stage for his grievances, was content to be charged, and said 'That is quite right, so far as the police are concerned.' He pointed to Percy. 'That is my son who bailed Oscar Wilde. He has followed me about and struck me in Piccadilly before I touched him,'[34] he said, adding that he would willingly fight Percy any time for the sum of £10,000. Percy for his part protested that the incident was caused by his father's offensive letters to his wife. After half an hour both men were released, the visible casualties of the encounter being Percy's left eye and Queensberry's silk hat. Percy hailed a cab for Waterloo, and Queensberry walked through the crowds, who cheered and clapped him; turned into Swallow Street on his way back to Piccadilly, and took a cab.

On 22 May, the day that Wilde's trial was due to open at the Old Bailey, Queensberry and Percy appeared at Marlborough Street Magistrates' Court before Mr Hannay charged with disorderly conduct and fighting in Piccadilly. Mr Stoneham appeared for Percy but Queensberry represented himself. Although the court had opened earlier than its usual hour to hear the case, news of the action had spread, for the court was filled with spectators, and a crowd had collected in the street. When Hannay arrived, Queensberry, wearing a 'big white old-fashioned cravat'[35] and three yellow Maréchal Niel rosebuds in his buttonhole, was already sitting in the counsel's pew, while Percy was at the solicitors' table, sporting a fancy waistcoat and a slightly discoloured eye. Queensberry, 'with the easy air of one to whom legal practice has become familiar',[36] rose and said he wished to make an application.

'Eh? What?' exclaimed Hannay, startled.

'In my case, and I am sorry to say, my son, I appeal to you to take this case first, as I am extremely anxious to get down to hear another case.'[37]

'Certainly,' said Hannay, and Queensberry entered the dock. Percy followed him and father and son 'carefully edged as far away from one another as the limits of their common habitation allowed'.[38] The charge was read and Constable Morrell gave evidence, then Queensberry cross-examined, Morrell confirming that as far as he had observed, Percy had been the aggressor. Loughlin gave much the same account of the incident. Queensberry declined to question him but Stoneham asked about the challenge to fight issued by Queensberry at the police station. Loughlin said that Queensberry had offered to fight Percy at any place but he did not want to make a scene in Piccadilly.

When Queensberry had given his version of events, Stoneham read out the telegram of 21 May and told the court that the marquess had been writing letters 'containing vile charges against Lord Douglas and other members of his family'[39] claiming that Queensberry had been to Percy's house 'with no earthly reason except to cause a disturbance'.[40] Stoneham said that on the previous day all Percy had done was ask his father to stop sending 'obscene and filthy letters to his wife' and Queensberry had 'made grimaces' and struck him in the face with his fist. The whole incident had been caused by Queensberry's letters and 'abusive language'.[41]

Queensberry brought two witnesses, assistants from nearby shops who had seen the start of the second fight. Charles Thomas Sherriff said that he 'saw Lord Douglas rush with great violence' against Queensberry, knocking his father's hat off, 'and then he struck the Marquess with violence' after which there were blows given on both sides. Queensberry asked Sherriff who he thought the aggressor was and the witness replied 'I consider Lord Douglas was the aggressor.'[42] Similar evidence was given by the other witness, Charles Ernest Tyler. Queensberry denied that his letters to Minnie were obscene and asked for the last one to be read, but Hannay said they were not relevant. He had seen the letters when Percy had applied for an injunction and had 'declined to act upon them on the ground that there should be no more family quarrelling'.[43] Percy's friend Frederick Wisdom was the only witness to the start of the conflict. Asked who struck the first blow, he said 'It was a very near thing, but I should say the Marquis was just a shade the quicker,'[44] to which Stoneham replied, 'He naturally would be, seeing that the Marquess is a boxer,'[45] an exchange that provoked laughter amongst the spectators.

Queensberry, denying that his letters were obscene, said that he had gone to Percy's house as he had heard that Wilde was there and wished to see if Bosie was there as well. The letter he had written to Minnie explained the reason for his visit. Hannay took no notice, and ruled that both defendants had behaved in a disorderly manner in a public street, neither had invoked the assistance of a nearby policeman, and both were therefore equally responsible. He bound them over to keep the peace for six months in the sum of £500. Queensberry 'went off gaily in a hansom amid cheers'.[46] Percy was hissed and hooted at by the crowds as he left. Some newspapers reported that it was Bosie whom Queensberry had been fighting, and any crowds who waited outside may have been under that impression. Queensberry wrote to Stoneham on 23 May accusing him of telling falsehoods at the magistrates' court and denying that his letters to Minnie were 'filthy and obscene'. (He may have forgotten the allusion to 'the Lord of Shitters'.) '[I]t was a great satisfaction to me that I so evidently got the best of the scrap . . . I am as fit as a man can be.'[47]

The first witness in Oscar Wilde's second trial was already giving evidence when Queensberry arrived in a rush, evoking a murmur of speculation as to what had occurred at Marlborough Street. He was allowed to take a seat at the end of the judicial bench, where he sat smiling broadly at the weary and haggard defendant, who appeared to be oblivious of his presence.

Queensberry, enlivening his appearance with a white hunting stock and wearing three yellow rosebuds in his buttonhole, was a regular and conspicuous attendee throughout the trial, watching Wilde closely and listening to the evidence with a serious expression.

On 24 May the newspapers published a telegram received from Bosie, who was writing from Rouen, demanding an apology from the press for the falsehoods printed about 'the Queensberry affair' and expressing his regret that it was his brother and not he who had 'corrected' his father.[48] On 25 May, the final day of the trial, Queensberry was seated near the bench. The judge, Alfred Wills, one of the Alpine enthusiasts who had inspired Queensberry's brother Francis, observed in his summing up that 'Lord Alfred's family seems to be a house divided against itself. But even if there were nothing but hatred between father and son, what father would not try to save his own son from the associations suggested by the two letters . . . . Lord Queensberry had drawn from these letters the conclusion that most fathers would draw, although he seems to have taken a course of action in his method of interfering, which I think no gentleman would have taken.'[49] He had not yet completed his summing up when the court adjourned for lunch. According to some newspaper accounts Queensberry did not return when it reconvened, although a privately printed report commenting 'No one, too, will question the indecorousness of the Marquis of Queensberry remaining in court a spectator of one of the most painful scenes the Old Bailey has ever witnessed'[50] suggests that he did. When the jurymen retired to consider their verdict, Queensberry was seen 'pacing the corridor in grotesque impatience'.[51]

Wilde was found guilty on a number of charges of gross indecency, and both he and Taylor were sentenced to the maximum under the law: two years in prison with hard labour. The conviction and sentence, according to writer E. F. Benson, 'probably reflected the bulk of public opinion in England, and a plebiscite would have approved any amount of trials in order to obtain a conviction and the severest sentence possible'.[52] 'Lord Queensberry's conduct in the present appalling case,' said the *Essex County Standard*, 'has received as a whole the approval of people generally. In details no doubt there is room for doubting whether his lordship showed the most perfect discretion, but the result has fully excused, if it has not altogether justified, all the words and actions which the impetuous and justly incensed Marquis considered necessary or inevitable.'[53] 'It is only right to add some word of recognition to Lord Queensberry,' commented the *Westminster Gazette*: 'undoubtedly there has been much in his conduct, as reported in the public Press, which is not calculated to attract sympathy. The judge's censure was, however, decidedly mitigated by a preceding remark that the conduct, though unworthy of a gentleman, was, nevertheless, natural in a father . . . . Lord Queensberry has . . . performed a public service in throwing the search-light of justice upon that hideous circle of extensive corruption.'[54]

Wilde was not without his supporters. A lady wrote to *Reynolds's Newspaper*, disgusted with the prosecution witnesses and declaring that she could not believe in Wilde's guilt. 'I cannot close this letter without saying what I think of the creature who has flaunted about in and out of the Old Bailey with yellow roses in his buttonhole, and his hat stuck airily upon the end of his walking-stick. If I were a man I would meet him face to face and give him his deserts with my own hands. By God, I would! He is the most outrageous little snob it is possible for one to conceive.'[55] Even the absent Sholto's name was dragged into the business. Queensberry received an anonymous card, supplying the name of the secretary of the 'Japan Society' claiming this was 'another of your sons fancy'. The tormented father sent it to Percy on 25 May after writing on the back: 'am also warned Sholto was also taken to these places. I presume by your slim gilt soul brother who[se] friends are sods and suckers what was he doing in Taylor's house now a convicted sod. Why was Wilde friends with all this lot if he was not one of them.'[56]

On 31 May Sholto and Loretta were married in San Jose by a justice of the peace. Sholto notified his family of the wedding by telegram. The new Lady Sholto Douglas demurely displayed a slender gold wedding ring and said that they intended to live in San Francisco where she would continue to dance and sell drinks for a wage of $25 a week.

Percy was a member of the Army and Navy Club and was called before the committee to explain his behaviour in standing by Wilde. Realising it would be unwise to reiterate his former wholehearted support, Percy backtracked, claiming that he had acted as bail 'solely because my brother made that the condition of his leaving the country, which all our family were exceedingly anxious he should do', adding that he had acted under 'very grave provocation'.[57] He also claimed to know little or nothing about Wilde and was 'prepared to accept his and my brother's assurances that the allegations were groundless'.[58] Percy remained a member.

Crespigny later wrote to the Essex newspapers in support of Queensberry's actions, paying tribute to him as a literary man and 'deep thinker', and praising his 'pluck and fighting ability':

A more chivalrous man does not exist. He would be utterly incapable of sending an indecent letter to a lady, and as his letters to Lady Douglas of Hawick were read either by myself or a member of my family I am in a

position to meet Lord Douglas's statement with an unqualified denial . . . .
personally I opposed Lady Douglas being written to at all, as at the visit of
Lord Queensberry and myself to the Great Northern Hotel, when Oscar
Wilde bolted out the back door, and subsequent one to Chalcott, Long
Ditton, full explanation was given of what would happen in a certain
eventuality.

Stoneham retaliated by showing copies of Queensberry's recent letters to
Minnie to a representative of the press; letters which, it was said, 'undoubtedly contain expressions which ought not to have been used in communica-
tions to a lady'.[59]

Queensberry estimated that the total cost of defending himself against
Wilde's accusation of libel was £2,000 and tried to recoup the sum from the
Treasury, but the Chancellor of the Exchequer, Sir William Vernon Harcourt
refused to allow reparation 'on the ground that the payments were . . . bribes
to blackmailers'.[60] Queensberry was offered a small sum, variously reported
as either £35 or £100, which he refused. 'Considering the great public service
he rendered it was surprising that no "whip" was made on behalf of the
marquis,' said the author of *Fifty Years of London Society*. 'Perhaps no other
man in the kingdom would have had the courage to act as Lord Queensberry
acted. He was profusely thanked by the Press and by innumerable private
correspondents of both sexes; but the fact remains that he had to bear the
whole of the heavy expenses . . . .'.[61]

On 28 June Bosie wrote a letter to W. T. Stead, editor of the *Review of
Reviews*, defending Wilde and accusing Queensberry amongst other things
of ruining his mother's health, persecuting her, 'with every fiendish ingenuity
of cruelty and meanness',[62] leaving her with only the money he was forced
to give her, flaunting about with prostitutes, and publishing pamphlets advocating free love. A letter intended for the August edition of the *Mercure de
France* expressing his hatred of his father was not published, but his typescript
survives and later appeared as *Oscar Wilde: A Plea and a Reminiscence*. These
impassioned outpourings are probably the case he intended to make
at Queensberry's libel trial had he been permitted. Claiming that his relationship with Wilde was 'love, it is true, completely pure but extremely
passionate'[63] and that his mother had endured 'years of suffering, of horrible
and nameless misery',[64] he alleged that witnesses against Wilde had been both

threatened and bribed by unscrupulous lawyers. He also stated that cruelty was cited in Sybil's divorce suit and that Ethel had been only seventeen at the time of her marriage and was deserted the day after; but Bosie was never to let facts get in the way of his attacks on his father. The witnesses at Wilde's trial received £5 a week, a not insubstantial sum, but this was from the date of Wilde's arrest, not, as is mistakenly believed, from the start of Wilde's prosecution of Queensberry.[65]

Queensberry, however, had not given up on Bosie. Concerned that he was in the company of exiled homosexuals in France, he wrote to him offering to give him back his allowance if he went away, proposing 'Samoa or any place right away from all these people I believe he is still with,' but the letter was returned apparently unopened with 'all kinds of insulting remarks on the envelope'.[66] Bosie must have read the letter or another one in similar vein, for he later said that his father had offered, on the condition that he gave up Wilde for ever, to supply him with money and an allowance, suggesting rather naïvely that he should go to the South Sea Islands 'where he said "you will find plenty of beautiful girls"'.[67] Bosie, writing in 1929, did not blame his father for trying to separate him from Wilde but did 'blame him bitterly for the way he tried to do it',[68] asserting that it was 'perfectly obvious that he was not thinking of me and of my interests'.[69]

Percy was in some financial embarrassment since, as he might have anticipated, Queensberry had stopped his allowance, but ever the optimist, he remained convinced that he could pull off a financial coup. The funds Percy had made in Australia were gone, he had no source of income, and he was borrowing heavily on the expectation of his inheritance at rates of interest between 80 and 100 per cent. Ultimately, however, he suffered a far greater loss. His support of Bosie cost him his father's love.

CHAPTER 20

'Where Stars shall ever shed their Light'

THE Douglases and Montgomerys were never to admit, at least in writing, that Queensberry's allegations were neither an insane delusion nor a deliberate, malicious invention. Perhaps they preferred to believe that whatever had been true about Wilde and other young men, Bosie had somehow been exempt. Alfred Montgomery, already a broken and declining man after the death of Francis, never recovered from the terrible blow of Bosie's disgrace. He died on 5 April 1896.

Once the public acclaim following Wilde's exposure had evaporated, Queensberry found himself back on the fringes of society, which was probably where he felt most comfortable. Society could tolerate many things as long as they were not made public, and Queensberry had made some very unpalatable things public. The accepted view of him at this time is that he was socially ostracised, miserable, beset by delusions and declining rapidly into insanity. The source of this view is Bosie's memoirs. Bosie claimed that his father was '"cut" by many of his oldest friends, and politely cold-shouldered by others', although he named only one, his godfather Lord Robert Bruce who was in the navy with Queensberry and told Bosie some years later that he had never spoken to Queensberry after what he had done. Queensberry was, according to Bosie, 'metaphorically pursued by Furies ever afterwards'.[1] It is true that after the first heady flush of victory had gone, and the stress of his long and bitter fight was over Queensberry's life lacked purpose. His reported activities following the trial suggest, however, that he was far from being a broken man, could manage his financial affairs, write coherent letters, support charities, make public statements on matters of concern, and was not without friends, interests or recreation.

His main sporting activity was cycling. Interviewed in April 1895 a vigorous-looking Queensberry stated:

No man was ever fonder of riding or of horses than I have been, but the only riding worth having is what you get in racing or in following hounds. Park riding and that sort of thing is not worth talking about. Well, I got tired of riding, and I have given it up, but from my experience of riding and cycling I say that cycling is the better and more useful exercise. I know nothing like it to keep one fit.[2]

He became president of the Bath Road Cycling Club, and often accompanied members on their weekly runs. His favourite mount was the tandem, on which he was paired with a Mr C. A. Smith.* 'The two make a very good tandem pair,' commented the *Penny Illustrated Paper* in July, 'and the speed attained at times has been of the very "scorchiest" description, which the Marquis seems to enjoy thoroughly.'[3]

Percy was refusing to see his father, communicating only through solicitors, which Queensberry found annoying and frustrating. In June Queensberry received a letter from Mr Jamieson proposing a plan which involved not only making a settlement on Minnie in the event of Percy predeceasing his father, but paying £36,000 of Percy's debts. Queensberry wrote to Percy on 11 June, understandably 'very angry', and refused, citing 'your and your wife's outrageous behaviour to me . . . neither will I do anything as long as you refuse all intercourse with me and keep up this bitter enmity'.[4]

Percy capitulated and went to see his father. Soon afterwards Queensberry wrote to Percy asking for his letters to Minnie to be returned: 'Your visit has terribly upset me. Not one word of apology did you offer me, but tried to justify yourself in your outrageous attack on me. . . . I was spoofed into saying I forgave you with my lips, but my heart did not do so, neither can I ever forget what has happened.'[5] Queensberry had not, however, given up on a partial reconciliation and was worried about his heir's financial improvidence. On 29 June 1895, disgruntled at again being asked to settle Percy's substantial racing debts, Queensberry wrote to Minnie, whom he still

---

* This may well be the former Sussex County cricket captain who later became better known as actor C. Aubrey Smith.

addressed formally as 'Madam', saying that he had just heard that Percy had gone away again:

> it could almost be hoped he will not return . . . I suppose you are aware that as you both refuse to communicate with me in any way & to defy me I declined to come forward in any way to assist him. . . . Should I die before him & that he is still going on in this way it must mean utter ruin to his son & all that come after him . . . . Had he come to me with any penitence I suppose I should have been compelled to have seen what could be done though at great sacrifice to myself . . .

He remained concerned that if Percy went on raising huge loans he would reach a point where 'anything I could do for him, even if I chose to do so, would be utterly useless'.[6]

Queensberry returned to Scotland for a period of rest and solitude at Glen Stuart, while the action for Wilde's bankruptcy proceeded through his solicitors, the assistant official receiver acting as his proxy. At the first meeting of Wilde's creditors on 26 August 1895 it was suggested that a trustee be appointed but this was disallowed by Queensberry's vote, as he wanted the matter to remain in the hands of the official receiver, possibly to avoid further delay.

Sholto in the meantime, was looking for business opportunities in the USA, while trying to avoid Loretta's mother. Queensberry had employed an agent, J. R. Wharton an Englishman living in Oakland, to look into the new Lady Douglas's antecedents. Wharton reported that while the Mooneys had never been rich, he was satisfied that 'they were never anything else than respectable, and that Lady Sholto has always conducted herself in a becoming manner'.[7] Queensberry wrote to Sholto saying he hoped to visit as soon as he could find a travelling companion, but the trip was never made. In October Loretta went back on the stage, something probably only her mother, who had swept back into her life to take control, was happy about. In the following December Sholto appeared on stage at the Alcazar Theater, San Francisco in a play called *The Governor*. His role required him to speak eleven words, but his name attracted considerable interest and he was warmly received.

Queensberry continued to support worthy causes, especially where they gave him a platform for his unorthodox views. In October 1895 twenty-three-year-old Miss Edith Lanchester, the daughter of a Battersea architect, announced her intention of living with a Mr Sullivan as his common-law wife. Her disapproving family had her forcibly removed to an asylum. Mr Sullivan received many letters of support, including one from Queensberry offering financial assistance:

> No doubt we hold similar opinions on the marriage question, but were I in your position, I should go through the ceremony of marriage, and the instant it was concluded protest against and repudiate it, saying it was naught to you, and that if mutual love and affection could not bind you together as man and wife nothing else could. If the book 'The Woman Who Did' was meant to teach anything, it was that at present such marriages must not be made.* It is not fair to the woman to place her in such a cruel position, to say nothing of the children of such a marriage. What we want is a protest; change of laws follow, do not precede, change of opinion. . . . What is this idiotic ceremony, except that it gives your wife and future children protection, and by making a public protest you and your wife clear your own consciences, and are free before God and man? . . . I should like to know you and your brave wife and shake her by the hand.[8]

Edith Lanchester was soon released from the asylum. She did not marry Sullivan, but they lived together as husband and wife. Their daughter, actress Elsa was born in 1902.

Oscar Wilde's public examination in bankruptcy took place on 12 November. If the Douglas family had helped Wilde meet his liabilities they would have effectively been paying Queensberry's legal fees, something they had no intention of doing. Percy instead promised Wilde £500 on his release from prison, but he never came up with the money.

On 24 December 1895 Queensberry received an unusual Christmas present from Bosie, a copy of a poem he had written in the previous year. It had been published anonymously with the title 'A Ballad of Hating' in the *Pall Mall Gazette*.[9] Queensberry made a manuscript copy on which he

---

The Woman Who Did (Grant Allen, 1895) is the story of an intelligent freethinking woman who despises marriage, enters into a loving relationship, gives birth to a child, is ruined when her partner dies and commits suicide.

scribbled his own comments and sent it to Percy. Bosie's Yuletide message was: 'I hated you then I hate you a thousand times more now & will be even with you some day wishing you every curse & misery & speedy death with eternal damnation.' It was signed 'Your son [Queensberry here inserted "(Query)"] Alfred Bruce Douglas'.[10] Queensberry's covering note to Percy stated: 'I don't intend to reply to him but he had better be told that if he returns here I will instantly get him put under restraint this last letter will be quite sufficient to get this done as I have already shown it to a doctor anyone will see it is the letter of a lunatic.'[11]

The poem, with Queensberry's annotations, given here in square brackets, starts:

Here's short life to the man I hate!
(Never a shroud or a coffin board)
Wait and watch and watch and wait
He shall pay the half and the whole
Now or then or soon or late
(Steel or lead or hempen cord
And the devil [the Christian one, I suppose] take his soul!)

Queensberry added 'Capital what a pity such genius is exiled'.[12]

There was another unpleasant communication, which Bosie denied sending. Sybil wrote to Bosie 'I am glad to hear you did not telegraph. Your Father had an unsigned telegram from France & a very disagreeable one I believe and concluded that it came from you, Percy says he thinks he knows who sent it & hopes no more will be sent as it only does harm.' [13]

Sholto's finances were a continuing source of concern. In January 1896 the *London Figaro* reported his admission that 'he had property of the value of one cent. and no more "confessing silently," . . . that he "lived on the dollars of people who would pay to see his wife lift her leg a little higher than is usual for ladies."' One American newspaper had referred to him as '"the most contemptible of mankind"'.[14] Queensberry sprang to Sholto's defence: 'I have read your extremely offensive remarks concerning my son, who is in America, and not here to defend himself. I can understand an American paper kicking an Englishman when he is down; but why the English Press should accentuate this I do not comprehend.'[15] The *Figaro* had suggested that Sholto received no allowance from his father, to which Queensberry responded: 'I give him £300 a year as I did to all his younger [*sic*] brothers when they started, but if sons go to distant lands and choose to marry music hall singers without asking with or by your leave [*sic*], why they must take the consequences, and provide for them as best they can.'[16]

He made another attempt at reconciliation with Percy, writing from his friend Crespigny's Essex home, Champion Lodge on 15 January 1896:

Percy

Do you not think it is being foolish keeping up this deadly enmity between us. I was waiting of course after what happened that you should make some approach to me from the quite unreasonable conduct of yourself in this hideous affair in which it was proved beyond all doubt that I was in the right. . . . If it was possible to forgive I never could forget what has happened but still we might have been on amicable saga writing terms about money & business. . . . I don't wish to push you too far but certainly intend to recover some of my two thousand pounds when Kinmount is sold I presume I shall be compelled to pay you a certain sum but had you been reasonable should no doubt before have been willing to meet you half way about money matters I don't consider when you have paid your share of shutting up Oscar Wilde that I have any right to stop your money neither should I wish to do so but really I think some approach on your side was due to me first. Don't mistake me as to our ever being friends again. I think that is impossible for if I could forgive I never could forget & it would be like asking to take to my bosom again a scorpion that had before stung me & would probably do so again on the first opportunity.[17]

The June 1895 meeting was probably the last time Percy and his father conversed amicably. The eleventh marquess stated that his grandfather refused ever to see him or his brother and sister, but whether the estrangement was due to Percy's or Queensberry's intransigence will never be known. He also wrote of Queensberry's 'determination to ruin his eldest son'[18] but the correspondence suggests otherwise. The will signed by Queensberry in January 1895, before Percy sided with Oscar Wilde, was never amended.

On 24 February 1896 Queensberry took part in a ten-mile cycle challenge under the auspices of the Bath Road Club, on a road near Cobham. His opponent was sculptor C. B. Lawes, six months his senior, who had been a noted athlete and rower in his youth. Members of the club including Sir Claude de Crespigny were there to act as pacemakers. Queensberry led from the start and completed the course in 35 minutes 43 seconds, a minute and 47 seconds ahead of Lawes. He was staying at the White Lion Hotel, Cobham and on 28 February was fined 10 shillings at the Thames County Police Court for allowing his dog to wander without a muzzle. He seems to have liked the Cobham area for riding. On 10 April he was fined 15 shillings for riding a bicycle on a footpath at the Drive, Oatlands near Weybridge.

According to Bosie, Queensberry in his later years 'had the strange delusion that he was almost entirely without money',[19] an allegation that has only fuelled the common belief that he was insane. Queensberry, who must have expected to live at least another twenty years, had perfectly reasonable grounds for concern over the dwindling value of his lands, and the failure of his sons to earn a living. In April 1896 Kinmount was put on the market, and there was a sale of paintings at Christie's. The estate finally sold in October for £138,000. So far from being an act of malice designed to prevent Percy from inheriting, as is usually alleged, the sale, made for sound financial reasons, helped preserve the value of his inheritance.

Queensberry cannot have been pleased that June if he read the reviews of Loretta's debut on the New York stage. 'Lady Sholto Douglas is possessed of a voice of which the lower notes are fairly good. Her singing is colourless, and is not greatly enhanced by a disposition to raise her skirts and display her noble nether limbs.'[20] Not long afterwards, Loretta, who was expecting her first child, retired from the stage. Queensberry was anxious for his grandchildren to be born on British territory, and asked Sholto and Loretta to move to Vancouver, where in all probability they occupied his property. Their son, Bruce, was born on 1 April 1897.

Life in 1897 was quieter for Queensberry. He had lost none of his vigour as a cyclist and again fell foul of regulations in February of that year when approaching the White Lion, Weybridge he cycled on a path to avoid muddy roads. His claims that he was a well-known sportsman and president of a cycling club did him no good and he was fined 15 shillings again.

On 19 May 1897 Oscar Wilde was a free man. A week later he was settled in Berneval, a village near Dieppe, using the pseudonym Sebastian Melmoth. Queensberry's two years of respite from bitter anxiety were over, and it was feared that he would set detectives to keep watch on Wilde or even come to France personally and cause a disturbance. On 10 May solicitors Parker Garrett & Holman wrote to Wilde's friend More Adey advising him that 'Lord Queensberry has made arrangements for being informed if his son joins Mr Wilde and has expressed his intention of shooting one or both. A threat of this kind from most people could be more or less disregarded, but there is no doubt that Lord Queensberry, as he has shown before, will carry out any threat that he makes to the best of his ability.'[21]

Wilde and Bosie were soon in touch by letter and telegram, on terms that became increasingly affectionate. Wilde was subsisting on an allowance from Constance, and Bosie on an allowance from Sybil. Both incomes were under threat if the two met. Despite this, a meeting was being actively planned in June. Wilde's solicitor Mr Hansell was warned of the proposed reunion (both Queensberry and his agents and Bosie's anxious friends have been cited as possible informants), resigned, and wrote to Wilde who panicked and wrote to Bosie telling him the meeting was impossible. According to Bosie, Wilde wrote that it would be dangerous for him to come as Queensberry was 'having him watched and would, certainly, intervene and create a fresh scandal'.[22] Wilde's letter makes no mention of his being watched, but he was certainly anxious that Queensberry might turn up: 'if your father – or rather Q, as I only know him and think of him – if Q came over and made a scene and a scandal it would utterly destroy my possible future and alienate all my friends from me'.[23] Bosie later said that he did not believe the report which he described as a '*canard*', a false rumour, and replied 'laughing at the idea of [Queensberry's] supposed plot',[24] suggesting they meet elsewhere. This did not stop him writing to Percy on 5 August, 'The beast has been sending detectives to Dieppe & annoying the poor chap again. It makes my blood boil with rage when I think of it.'[25] How he knew of any detectives is unclear as none of Wilde's extant letters refer to them.

Bosie asked Percy to help Wilde financially, and Percy replied that 'he was "for the moment very pushed for money," but that in a few months he expected to bring off a very big *coup*. . . . "Don't worry, my dearest boy . . . in a short time I shall be a very rich man, and if I am a rich man, you of course will be the same."'[26] A delighted Bosie passed on the good news to Oscar. Percy had given up on Australia and sailed for Canada to try his luck there. Unfortunately some of the mines he purchased turned out not to exist.

Despite all the broken promises Wilde always considered him 'a very good-hearted fellow, kind and considerate'.[27]

Bosie and Wilde were finally reunited on 28 August at Rouen where they walked arm in arm or hand in hand, all day, clearly unworried about snooping detectives or a rampaging father. If Queensberry had sent his spies they were not in evidence.

Despite everything, Bosie and his father had not abandoned each other, and Bosie, in a calmer and more introspective frame of mind was yearning for reconciliation. In September he was staying at Aix-les-Bains with his mother, and Queensberry was also there that month. If they met or saw one another, this may have been the inspiration for Bosie's 'Ballad of St Vitus', which was written there. In this poem a pagan king hears that his son is singing a song of Christian praise. The king's brow grows 'black as a winter night'[28] and he calls his son to him and asks him to sing. Pale with fear the boy goes to take something from under his doublet, alarming the king, who seizes a spear. When the boy reveals that the thing he was about to take out was a crucifix,

> . . . the King grew black with rage and grief,
> And for a full moment he spake no word
> And the spear in his right hand shook like a leaf,
> And the vein on his brow was a tight blue cord.[29]

After this moment of tension the king scornfully orders the 'Christian fool' to be taken away. Vitus is shut up in a dark tower, but before the night was over the king's 'heart's blood yearned for the son he loved',[30] he climbs the tower and finds the room suffused with light and angels playing sweet music to which Vitus danced 'a courtly dance'.[31] The king falls to his knees in wonder and it is assumed that not only are he and his son reconciled but that he has accepted Christianity.

In September Wilde and Bosie took a villa near Naples; however, it was not Queensberry but financial issues and the determination of Constance and Sybil, who held the purse strings, which forced them to give it up. Constance Wilde's death in April 1898 secured an unconditional income for her husband, and he was able to meet Bosie from time to time, but abided by a promise to Sybil that the two would never again live under the same roof.

On 27 March 1898 at Holy Trinity Church, Sloane Street, Lady Edith Douglas married St George William Lane Fox-Pitt, son of Augustus Henry Lane Fox Pitt-Rivers, founder of the Pitt-Rivers Museum. St George was only twelve years younger than Queensberry, a pioneer in the development of the incandescent electric light, a student of psychic phenomena, advocate of moral education and later one of the founders of the Buddhist Society of Great Britain and Ireland. The wedding did nothing to heal old wounds. Queensberry was not there.

In November 1898 Bosie wrote to his cousin Algy Bourke, saying that he wanted to be friends with his father again, and asked Bourke to arrange it. He could not undertake never to see Wilde, but reassured Bourke and his father that their relations were 'entirely harmless' and motivated only by a feeling that he could not abandon Wilde 'now that he is poor and broken after being his friend when he was rich and flourishing'. Pleading the 'sort of dog's life' he had led in the last few years he asked his father to 'meet me half way' and 'not make it impossible for me to bring about the reconciliation I so sincerely desired'. Bourke showed Queensberry the letter and wrote to Bosie within twenty-four hours to say that Queensberry 'would be delighted to see [his son] and had spoken in the most affectionate way about [him]'.

That month a programme of boxing was being held under Queensberry's patronage at the Alhambra Theatre Leicester Square, and he was staying at Bailey's Hotel. The meeting of father and son took place in the hotel's smoking room, and was emotional and very affectionate. Queensberry began by formally forgiving Bosie and then tearfully embraced him again and again. He promised to restore Bosie's allowance and wrote to Arthur Johnstone Douglas (presumably the quarrel had been made up) asking that he start paying an allowance to 'my poor darling boy'. A week later Bosie was at his mother's house, ill in bed with flu when he received a letter from Queensberry. Either Queensberry had forgotten the promises in Bosie's letter or he wanted to make assurance doubly sure, but he told Bosie he could not agree to pay him anything until he knew exactly what his relations were with 'that beast Wilde'.[32] Bosie sent back a stinging reply, saying that 'there was no possibility of lasting peace between us' and hurling his father's promise of an allowance back at him. Bosie later learned that Queensberry had been very much upset by this. Both men had made misjudgements and the reconciliation was at an end, but, said Bosie, 'short as it was, it was sufficient to cure me of the real hatred which I am sorry to say I felt for him for two or three years after the catastrophe'.[33]

Queensberry's health was in decline. The years of stress had taken a hard physical toll and he was looking older than his years. A few months after the failed reconciliation, Bosie was in a cab when he happened to see his father in the street. 'I was struck with compunction at his appearance, for he looked ill and wild and haggard.'[34] He was moved to discuss this with St George Fox-Pitt. Bosie claimed that St George was the only member of the family who was on speaking terms with Queensberry, but this is not true. Caroline, Florence and Archibald remained sympathetic, but all three were living in Scotland and both Florence and her mother were too infirm to travel. St George, however, was available, and he told Bosie that his father was under the impression that he hated him. According to Bosie, Queensberry had told St George that he thought Bosie was responsible for the troubles from which he was suffering, believing that he was being 'persecuted by the Oscar-Wilders' who 'had driven him out of various hotels, and disturbed him at night by shouting abusive epithets at him'.[35] Bosie was upset to learn this and wrote a letter to St George asking if he could show it to his father. In this letter Bosie said his father was 'completely mistaken in imagining that I hated him or had any feelings about him except of kindness and affection' and explained that his last letter had been provoked by his father and was written while in a high fever, that he was 'scarcely responsible for what it contained and in any case did not mean what I said and entirely withdrew it'. He also sent his love.[36]

St George gave the letter to Queensberry and later told Bosie 'I think he was pleased to see it.' Bosie was convinced that it had calmed his father and put a stop to the delusions. Queensberry, who has been described as 'a pathetic victim of persecution mania',[37] may, on later evidence, have been suffering from minor strokes which accentuated his anxieties. Bosie himself wondered if his father's eccentricities 'may have been due to one or other of the terrible falls he got steeplechasing and hunting'[38] and 'ended by having nothing but kind thoughts about him, even though I saw him no more, and I contrived that he should get to know of this'.[39]

Queensberry's health issues did not prevent him from taking an interest in public affairs, and he still wanted to have his say. On 19 July 1899 twenty-two-year-old Mary Ann Ansell was hanged for the murder of her sister whose life she had insured, and there was a public outcry against the execution of a young woman considered by many to be insane. Three days later Queensberry attended a protest meeting where he proposed a motion that 'the time has now arrived, and indeed has long since passed, for the immediate institution of a Court of Appeal in Criminal cases'.[40] The resolution was adopted.

On the morning of 18 December Queensberry, who was staying at the Raleigh Club, was found in bed, unconscious and critically ill. A few days later, having regained consciousness and showing some improvement, he was transferred to apartments at 8 Welbeck Street. It is unlikely that he ever stirred from his bed again.

Percy was in London and sent a telegram to Florence. She replied that she was unable to come to London as she was unfit for travel, capable only of moving about on crutches due to stiffness in her knees, wrists and ankles. 'I would have risked all to go to your poor father only I cannot leave my mother who I fear is dying & I & Archie are constantly by her. . . . She is skin and bone & her face no larger than my hand.' Florence said she had been expecting Queensberry's illness, 'for he has been in a terrible state for so long & quite unmanageable. This brain disease is an awful thing & it makes a man utterly irresponsible for his acts. Remember only that he is your Father & do your best for him and forget all the sad past.'[41]

It was necessary to create power of attorney over Queensberry's assets, which Percy felt unable to do. He must have sent Florence another telegram asking if someone else could take on the task and she replied on 20 December pointing out that he was the heir and successor. She advised him to consult a lawyer and get two doctors' certificates 'to the effect that he is in no fit state to overlook his affairs or take care of himself. This has been clear for a long time but no-one could interfere. Now the time has come.' Florence chose to believe that all of Queensberry's past behaviour was due to mental illness:

As for the past all should be forgotten you must all clearly see that for years past your father's loves and hatred, likes or dislikes, quarrels or misunder-standings have been the workings of his poor brain. It is not his fault but his misfortune & I speak as one who has fully incurred many & many a time his abuse & anger, one day friendly letters, the next day furious ones. I never blamed him for I knew that it was not he but a diseased brain that dictated same.[42]

Percy, still unable to accept his responsibilities, engaged a lawyer, Mr Blythe, to write to Archibald asking him to act for his father. Blythe complied, stating that he did not think it necessary for Queensberry to be placed in an asylum, but he needed to be under the care of a medical man. Archibald replied on 22 December saying he was unable to leave Scotland as he believed his mother to be dying. He disliked private asylums but recommended a Dr Rutherford, who ran a public one.

Sybil visited Queensberry and wrote to Bosie in an undated letter:

I have seen yr poor Father twice but he is too far gone mentally for anything to be of any use to him now. He seemed very pleased to see me & was very affectionate but had nothing to say to me & only rambles on quite incoherently sometimes & at other times telling one long anecdotes of little events just before his illness. It was very distressing to see him but I think he is really happier than he was as he does not seem to realise anything now. I believe he has got worse in the last 4 days & I am sorry now I did not see him sooner.[43]

Archibald eventually visited his dying brother. His only account of this event is a letter written to Bosie in 1911, shortly after Bosie was received into the Roman Catholic Church:

A blight settled on your father's religious life soon after he was 21 and with it his affection for us all snapped and you never got his fatherly & affectionate influence . . . as a boy your father was deeply impressed with religion – then follows that long period during which his hatred of Xtianity seemed to grow always deeper – then suddenly at the end something like a fog bank lifted and he spoke to me like his old self – he saw nothing of the Catholic Church he practically knew nothing of her, but he went to his Eternity with his old child trust for and love for Jesus Christ to whom he told me 'I have prayed with all my heart for the forgiveness of my sins' – I gave him Conditional absolution.[44]

There was no deathbed conversion, as has been alleged, but a return at the end to the religious feelings that had comforted Queensberry before his brother's death on the Matterhorn. Percy went to see his dying father and according to Bosie, Queensberry, unforgiving to the last, spat at him.

Queensberry died on 31 January 1900. The cause of death was certified as 'Cerebral haemorrhage 6 weeks. Syncope'.[45] The informant was Percy, giving his address as 'Smedmore', Corfe Castle, Dorset, who was present at the death, as was Arthur Johnstone Douglas.

Florence replied to Percy's telegram:

Ah! Well, your poor father is at rest & none could wish it other-wise for his mental suffering must have been fearful & so many mistook his actions (I for a long time also did so) for those of a hard hearted & tyrannical being but we now know it was his misfortune, not his fault. You will let me know if he is to be buried near darling Jim and darling Francie. He used to wish it but later on talked of Cremation so I do not know if he left his wishes stated.

The Wilde scandal had clearly created lasting ill feeling between Florence and her nephew for she added 'I know, my dear old Percy, he whom I remember in days gone by is the same now at heart & that is why I grieved to feel a cloud had arisen between us.'[46]

Unusually, a codicil in Queensberry's will regarding the disposition of his remains was later published in the press:

At my death I wish to be cremated & my ashes put into the Earth enclosed in nothing earth to earth, ashes to ashes, in any spot most convenient I have loved. Will mention places to my son Harleyford for choice, I particularly request no Christian mummeries or tomfooleries be performed over my grave but that I be buried as a Secularist & an Agnostic. If it will comfort anyone there are plenty of those of my own faith who would come and say a few words of common sense over the spot where my ashes may lay [sic].

His suggested places were 'The Summit of Criffel, or Queensberry [hill], Dumfriesshire, the end of the Terrace overlooking New Lock, Harleyford, Bucks. No Monument or Stone necessary or required, or procession, as ashes can be carried in one person's hand, failing these places, any place where Stars shall ever shed their light & Sun shall gild each rising morn.'[47]

Some found these romantic ideas in poor taste, observing that Queensberry 'having laughed during life at all conventionalities, met death itself in a mocking spirit. It might almost be said that he was mad. . . . But he preferred to scoff in death, as he had done in life, at proprieties which govern the thoughts and the conduct of the vast majority.'[48]

Queensberry's remains were removed from Welbeck Street in a special cremation shell, covered with a white cloth, and taken to the private mortuary attached to the necropolis station, Westminster Bridge Road. At 11.45 on the morning of 2 February a special train left for Woking crematorium where the remains were cremated. The ashes were placed in a Doulton Ware casket and taken to Scotland by train, which also carried Percy, now the tenth marquess, Minnie, Sholto and Loretta who had recently arrived from America, Bosie and Archibald. Caroline and Florence were unable to attend. Whether the casket was placed in the earth of the family burial ground, 'a quiet enclosure surrounded by its hedge of rusty beech and planted here and there with rhododendrons',[49] or the ashes scattered to become one with nature, is unknown. A memorial to John Sholto was to join those to James and Francis on the western slope of the knoll.

The tone of the obituaries depended a great deal on how well the writer had known the deceased, if at all.

'The Queensberry family,' said the *Belfast Newsletter* taking the accepted line, 'were the most eccentric people for several generations of all those whose names are recorded in the pages of "Debrett's Peerage." It seemed to be an impossibility to any member of the family to conform to the conventionalities of society and walk in the usual lines laid down by tradition for their order.'[50] The writer for the *Birmingham Daily Post* who observed that Queensberry 'neglected to utilise either his talents or his powers', adding that he 'contented himself with living a life of pleasure',[51] had clearly never met him. Inevitably stories were told about Queensberry which may or may not have been true, such as the one in which he was supposed to have arrived at the offices of a society journal threatening to horsewhip the editor over a severe comment, only to be deflated on confronting a bespectacled elderly lady, and there were many tales of him exercising his boxing skill 'on extortionate cabmen and others, who, unaware of his identity, have aroused his anger'.[52]

The *Sporting Times* announced Queensberry's death 'with great regret . . . a not, we fear happy life has come to a close. It is not for us here to inquire into the workings of his peculiar mind. It had a craving for something; it knew not what . . . "Q" as he was called . . . apart from his eccentricities, was a much-liked man, and in sporting there was nothing he could not do. It was a treat to see him and his great friend Sir Claude de Crespigny, backing up each other, and anything that man might do they would do.'[53]

'A man unfettered by conventional observances,' said the *Daily Telegraph*, 'and caring nothing for them, the Marquis lived his own life, went his own way, and expressed his views with unmistakable emphasis and decision . . . the law courts held no terrors for him when he believed himself to be in the right.'[54] 'His lordship,' observed the *Western Mail*,

> seems to have led a somewhat erratic and irregular career, and the conven-
> tionalities of society were not entirely to his liking. . . . he had his good
> qualities, and was very popular among a large section of the community,
> but his eccentricities did not commend themselves to the judgement either
> of the class from which he sprang or of the general public. At the same time,
> the Marquess was an interesting personality, and was open-hearted, straight-
> forward, and generous to a degree.[55]

The Times stated that Queensberry 'was in many ways a man of strong character, but unfortunately also of an ill-balanced mind, and never turned to any
account either his talents or his powers', blaming this failure on his Douglas
inheritance and the 'follies and wildness' of Old Q.[56] This stimulated a
response from Richard Edgcumbe of Crowthorne, Berkshire, who said that
he was a 'life-long friend' (the date and manner of their meeting are
unknown), and that Queensberry was

> almost universally misunderstood. If ever Englishman 'took his pleasures
> sadly' that man was Lord Queensberry. His crowning sorrow and misfor-
> tune through life was an inability to divest himself of a feeling that some-
> thing higher, something nobler than the employment he had in hand was
> expected of him. He suffered, so to speak, of a plethora of conscience.
> Whenever he heard of a wrong he felt that it must be righted, and that he
> himself would be forced to do it, because no one else seemed willing to
> incur the odium. His superlative moral and physical courage (a rare
> conjunction) often placed him in awkward straits, but his conscience always
> supported him through every discouragement. . . . His conduct [in the

Wilde case] was simply heroic, and the pain which it caused him was known only to the few who were in his confidence at that dreadful period . . . . he was undoubtedly a fearless, chivalrous, English gentleman, who never told a lie in his life, who never did a shabby thing, who scorned hypocrisy, and who would willingly have suffered death if thereby he could have made his traducers better or happier.[57]

William Stewart Ross, editor of the *Agnostic Journal* wrote:

I knew the late Marquess intimately for many years; and, like all who really knew him, I regarded him with a feeling akin to affection. He was a man whom those who only partially knew him were apt to quite misunderstand and grossly misrepresent. It may be that his procedure was not uniformly guided by prudence, and that he, on occasions, failed to exercise self-restraint; but a more sincere, single-minded, kind-hearted man did not live.[58]

Queensberry was 'as chivalrously brave a Douglas as had ever borne the name . . . the single-hearted, sincere, and chivalrous Lord Queensberry was of the best mettle of the best men of his illustrious line'.[59]

The official valuation of Queensberry's estate was £307,501 15s. The bulk of this was the proceeds of the sale of his estates on which he received an income during his lifetime, and which had been settled on his heir. Percy also inherited Glen Stuart, which he let to Sir Beaumont and Florence Dixie, and about 2,000 acres of land, which he sold. Queensberry's personal property amounted to £44,880 17s. 5d. (Corrections later increased this to £45,808 4s. 5d.) Of this £21,000 were the proceeds of life assurance policies, £11,624 was cash on current account, £5,000 was a capital reserve against the diminution of the trust estate, £4,722 the value of shares and bonds, and the rest was accrued unpaid income, debts and chattels. This residual estate was divided between Bosie, Edith and Sholto.

Almost half Percy's inheritance was used immediately to pay off moneylenders, but sufficient funds remained to ensure him a comfortable income; Bosie estimated that Percy could have received six or seven thousand pounds a year and made settlements on his children. Unfortunately Percy was still looking for the big coup. Within eighteen months he was declared bankrupt.

Bosie received £8,000 of his legacy at once, and gave about £1,000 to Oscar Wilde. On 22 February Wilde wrote from Paris 'Bosie is over here, with his brother [presumably Percy]. They are in deep mourning and the highest spirits. The English are like that.'[60]

On 5 November 1900 Lady Loretta Douglas gave birth to a son who was named Sholto John Augustus.

Wilde died on 30 November 1900, and in 1902 Bosie married poet Olive Custance. 'Perhaps if [my father] had lived a little longer we might have had another and more lasting reconciliation,' he wrote. 'If he had outlived Wilde, and still more if he had lived long enough to see me married to Olive, I feel pretty certain that we would have come together again.'[61]

The battling dowager marchioness Caroline survived her illness of 1900 but as her strength failed the prayer 'God save Ireland' was frequently on her lips.[62] She died at Glen Stuart with Archibald by her side on 15 February 1904, having borne nine children and outlived all but two of them. She was much mourned as 'a true friend of Ireland and a gentle and blameless lady'.[63]

Florence Dixie, who had become a fruitarian, had for several years been largely confined to her couch in great pain from arthritis and an 'unhealed injury to a limb; but her courage and interest in life never faltered through all this seclusion and suffering'.[64] When able, she had paid visits to the sick, and it may have been on one such visit that she contracted diphtheria. Florence was only fifty when she died at Glen Stuart on 7 November 1905.

Percy, who spent much of the rest of his life chasing after a fortune in mining for precious metals and gems, never made his 'big coup', and was adjudged bankrupt on three more occasions. Minnie died in 1917 and Percy remarried in the following year. He was in South Africa on 1 August 1920 when he died from basal meningitis and an abscess of the brain, aged fifty-one. His body was returned to the UK and buried at Kensal Green cemetery.

On 10 January 1901 twenty-eight-year-old Ethel Maud Weeden, describing herself as a spinster, married thirty-one-year-old Henry Daniel McCarthy, gentleman, at the parish church of Kew. A son, John, was born in 1903 but died at the age of fifteen. Ethel died in Eastbourne in 1948.

Sybil, who retained her pale, fragile beauty well into old age, died in Hove on 31 October 1935 aged ninety.

In 1908 Archibald was appointed pastor at Girvan, Ayrshire, where he remained until 1920. After five years as a chaplain in Cliffe near Dover he withdrew into a quiet retirement. His final days were spent at St Anthony's Hospital, North Cheam, where he died on 13 February 1938 aged eighty-seven. He was buried at Streatham.

Sholto and Loretta were divorced in 1920 because of her drinking and adultery. He married again in 1921 and was adjudged bankrupt in the same year. The marriage was not a happy one and he was divorced again in 1924. He married for the third time in 1926 and died in 1942.

Bosie spent his last years in Hove. While his temperament did not essentially change, time mellowed him and to the end of his life he retained friends who appreciated his good qualities and were understanding of his faults. If Queensberry had lived longer he might also have attained a similar peace. Bosie died on 20 March 1945.

Edith Fox-Pitt outlived her husband by thirty-one years and died on 6 April 1963.

'The thought which has only recently occurred to me is a terrible one,' wrote Bosie in 1939. 'Did my father really love me all the time, as I certainly loved him before he turned against me, and was he only doing what Oscar says in his great ballad all men always do, killing the thing he loved? Didn't we all three, Wilde, my father and I, do it, more or less?'[65]

Epilogue

For too long John Sholto Douglas, ninth Marquess of Queensberry has been represented as an evil, brutal, insane bigot who set out to destroy literary genius Oscar Wilde. In biographies of Wilde and Lord Alfred Douglas (Bosie) the exaggerated and sometimes demonstrably untrue allegations against Queensberry made in Bosie's hysterical and self-justifying letters and memoirs are often repeated as fact without further examination. Events in which Queensberry had no hand, such as the criminal prosecution of Wilde, are attributed to his personal malice. The motives for his actions are frequently misinterpreted, so the prudent financial management of his estates has been portrayed as an attempt to deprive his heir of his inheritance. Anything that shows Queensberry to be an unhappy, ill-used and unjustly maligned man is for the most part ignored. He is a convenient villain, a man you can easily love to hate, a one-dimensional caricature of a wicked, violent type, rampaging about with a horsewhip and frothing at the mouth with hatred.

The downfall of Wilde was undoubtedly a great tragedy, not only for himself and his family but also for literature; but his disgrace was not due to Queensberry, it was a product of the laws and beliefs of the society in which Wilde lived, and of his undisguised passion for Bosie. If there is a villain at all in Wilde's story it is Bosie, whose carelessness, arrogance, vindictive pursuit of his father, and fatal beauty all conspired to bring about Wilde's destruction.

Queensberry's often-quoted angry letters, which were written at the height of emotion, should not be read without a detailed appreciation of the events that led to their being written and the underlying tragedies of his life, which interwove and sometimes collided with each other. They should also be seen together with his more considered, heartfelt and sometimes pathetic letters, which reveal his desperate craving for understanding and affection. Queensberry's exterior – his bombast, his belligerence, his daring – was only the outward appearance of the sensitive and vulnerable man who sometimes emerges from his correspondence.

As we examine his life we encounter numerous pivotal events, all of which caused misery or grief, and desperate attempts to make some sense of his fractured existence. The suicide of his father when he was only fourteen must have been a shattering blow to an adolescent and one about which he never seems to have spoken or written. The loss of a beloved brother on the cusp of the great celebration for Queensberry's twenty-first birthday was a coming of age in another, harder sense, and the night in which he diced with death on the Matterhorn broke his previously devout belief in Christianity and fashioned the course of his religious life thereafter. Queensberry was a deeply spiritual man, who needed to believe passionately in some greater power. Following his brother's death, he felt abandoned by the Christian God, and turned to a more comforting faith – an indefinable natural force, and the justification of science – little realising that his new beliefs would make him a social pariah.

His admiration for beautiful women, preferably tall, slim and blonde, led him into a marriage for which he and his wife were disastrously unsuited, something that he was emotionally and psychologically unable to endure. After the couple separated, Sybil and the children lived in country houses or London elegance, but Queensberry was never able to find a home in which he could settle, living alone in three-room apartments, hotels, or the cold and damp of his Scottish cottages, finding any excuse to escape abroad in his never-ceasing and ultimately futile search, if not for happiness, then at least for some contentment.

His crusading spirit, inherited without doubt from his campaigning mother, led him to try and convert others to his unorthodox views on religion and social reform, and made him an outcast in his own country. He was voted out of the House of Lords, blackballed from his club, and insulted in the newspapers. The final indignity at the hands of the establishment was when his twenty-six-year-old son, who had done nothing to deserve an honour, was given an English peerage while he was overlooked.

His surviving siblings did not give him comfort. His sister Gertrude shocked society by marrying a baker's boy more than twenty years her junior and died aged fifty of tuberculosis. His brother James, a highly unstable alcoholic, committed suicide at the age of thirty-five. His brother Archibald became a Roman Catholic priest, sometimes gently chiding Queensberry for his stand against religion. His true soulmate was his sister Florence, a political activist who destroyed her reputation by forging a letter and creating a publicity stunt to promote her views. When Queensberry was most in need of her support she was disabled with arthritis and unable to go to him.

The clash of opposites in Queensberry's marriage did not bode well for the offspring. He became estranged from his heir, Francis, the only son of whom he could be proud, over the peerage issue. In 1894 Francis unexpectedly committed suicide at the age of twenty-seven. Although his action was never fully explained, there were rumours of a brewing homosexual scandal involving the Prime Minister, Lord Rosebery. It was in the aftermath of this event that Queensberry made his most strenuous efforts to put an end to the relationship between Oscar Wilde and Bosie, which he must have feared could bring about his son's ruin or death.

Bosie, the most conflicted of his children, inherited his mother's beauty and his father's temper, and expected to be supported in idle luxury by his family. Father and son clashed bitterly. When Queensberry alleged there was an improper relationship between Wilde and his son, Bosie said the allegations were either invented or the product of delusions, and his father's efforts to save Bosie from himself were declared to be attempts to destroy him. As a result, all of Queensberry's family who were involved in the dispute became ranged against him. By the time he left the infamous card he was probably ready to explode with frustration. It should also be appreciated that during the Wilde scandal Queensberry was suffering from the humiliation and distress of impotence. He had sought a solution by marrying a much younger woman, but the marriage rapidly collapsed and was annulled.

Queensberry's pursuit of Wilde when free on bail between trials, usually assumed to be a malicious attempt to ensure he had nowhere to stay, was in reality an attempt to prevent Wilde and Bosie from reuniting since he had been told that Bosie was back in London.

After the death of Francis, Queensberry's heir was Percy, an alcoholic who pursued easy wealth in gold mines, lived in debt and was thus a constant source of anxiety. Queensberry's one forlorn hope for contentment was a Scottish retreat and reconciliation with Percy and his wife, but all prospects of a quiet existence in a simple cottage disappeared after a quarrel with his estate manager, and Percy believed Bosie's lies and turned against his father. It was a betrayal Queensberry was never able to truly forgive.

The trials of Oscar Wilde were a tragedy, not only for Wilde, but for Bosie and Queensberry. A great writer was destroyed, and eked out a few more years relying on the generosity of friends, separated from his children, believing himself to be damned for ever and never, as he might well have done, living to see his reputation restored. Bosie, had he not been caught up in a great public scandal, might have matured into a man of letters, but instead he was defined thereafter as Oscar Wilde's petulant boy lover, and spent much of his life feeding off the fame of the greater man, his petty jealousies and rivalries overshadowing his genuine talent as a poet. Of the three, Queensberry suffered least during his lifetime, since his actions accorded with the prejudices of the day and earned him brief public approval, albeit on a subject that society preferred not to talk about. When Wilde's works came to be read and performed once more, the fallen poet made a full transformation into martyred genius and icon, but as Wilde rose, Queensberry fell, and was branded thereafter as a coarse, bigoted bully.

There is only one world in which Queensberry reigns supreme: his name remains a byword in boxing. He provided the sport with a lifeline at a time when it seemed to be heading for oblivion, and throughout his life promoted boxing as an exercise and a skill, rather than the bloody endurance test it had once been. The Queensberry Rules enabled boxing to escape its image of brutality and corruption and become a legally acceptable and properly regulated sport, which nowadays offers opportunities for thousands of young men, and women too, worldwide.

Queensberry was not, as is so often declared, insane; indeed, the true wonder of his story is that he was not, since the terrible events of his life might have caused a lesser man to crumble into irretrievable depression and suicide. He appears to have suffered many bouts of depression, from which he emerged with a firmer resolve or a new scheme with which to escape his demons. We see him at the end of his too short life, still on the fringes of society, where he had been pushed by the rigid mores of his times, but pursuing bodily fitness with bicycle and punchball, outclassing in vigour most men of his age, enjoying the company of like-minded friends, and still promoting his then unorthodox ideas of reform.

Reassessing Queensberry today we might find him difficult, abrasive and opinionated, but fundamentally well-meaning. We might even like him. The bohemian world of sport and theatre in which he moved and felt most comfortable is far closer to our twenty-first-century society than that of the respectable Victorian middle and upper classes that rejected him. Many of his ideas that so appalled the Victorian establishment are now accepted without question. Being a declared agnostic is no longer a reason for someone to be excluded from parliament or shunned by the cream of society, and although Queensberry's idea of legal concubinage has not come about, his hopes for simpler divorce laws have been realised. He would also have approved of the formation of the Court of Appeal and the enfranchisement of women, and also very probably of easier methods and availability of birth control.

Had he lived longer he and his family might have achieved some unity and peace, and he could even, in time, have gained a more acceptable public voice and been admitted back into the House of Lords. Not only would that have blunted his pain and disappointments, but it would have given his life the meaning he craved, and enabled him, with his forceful personality, outspokenness and passion for change, to play a useful part in some of the major reforms of the twentieth century.

Notes

Author's Note

1. Violet Wyndham, *The Sphinx and her Circle*, London: André Deutsch, 1963, p. 55
2. Merlin Holland and Rupert Hart-Davis (eds), *The Complete Letters of Oscar Wilde*, New York: Henry Holt, 2000 p. xviii

Chapter 1: Son and Heir

1. British Library Manuscripts, Add. 81654 p. 4
2. Holland, *Complete Letters*, p. 695
3. See Author's Note, pp. ix–x
4. *Dumfries Standard*, 11 Aug. 1858, p. 4
5. *Leeds Mercury*, 11 Feb. 1860, p. 4
6. *Illustrated London News*, 29 July 1865, p. 99
7. Lord William Pitt Lennox, *Drafts on My Memory*, 2 vols, London: Chapman and Hall, 1866, vol. 2, p. 13
8. *Edinburgh Evening Courant*, 25 Dec. 1856, p. 2
9. *Sporting Times*, 13 June 1885, p. 2
10. Ibid.
11. Lady Gertrude Stock, *Nature's Nursling, a Romance from Real Life*, 3 vols, London: Kegan Paul, Trench, 1885, vol. 1, pp. 14–15
12. Henry Downes Miles, *Pugilistica, the History of British Boxing*, 3 vols, Edinburgh: John Grant, 1906, vol. 3, p. viii
13. Rees Howell Gronow, *Reminiscences and Recollections of Captain Gronow*, 2 vols, London: J. C. Nimmo, 1889, vol. 1, p. 76
14. *Sporting Times*, 13 June 1885, p. 2
15. *Racing Times*, 6 Sept. 1858, p. 282
16. *Sporting Times*, 13 June 1885, p. 2
17. *Satirist*, 19 Aug. 1838, p. 260
18. *Freeman's Journal*, 18 Feb. 1904, p. 5
19. British Library Manuscripts, Add. 40446 f. 17
20. Stock, *Nature's Nursling*, vol. 1, p. 179
21. Ibid., p. 180
22. *Bell's Life in London and Sporting Chronicle*, 2 Nov. 1845, p. 7
23. *Satirist*, 14 Dec. 1845, p. 395
24. *Aberdeen Journal*, 11 Aug. 1847, p. 3
25. *Friend of India (Calcutta)*, 4 Nov. 1847, p. 698
26. *Sporting Times*, 13 June 1885, p. 2
27. Ibid.
28. Ibid.
29. Stock, *Nature's Nursling*, vol. 1, p. 139
30. Ibid., p. 140
31. Ibid.
32. British Library Manuscripts, Add. 44480 f. 242
33. Ibid., Add. 43190 f. 379

Chapter 2: The Queensberry Inheritance

1. University of Southampton, Palmerston Papers, PP/RC/FF/29/1 p. 1
2. Anon., *Fifty Years of London Society*, London: Eveleigh Nash, 1920, p. 210
3. Lady Florence Dixie, *The Story of Ijain*, London: Leadenhall Press, 1903, p. 23
4. *Dumfries and Galloway Standard and Advertiser*, 17 Feb. 1904, p. 4
5. *Dumfries and Galloway Courier*, 6 Jan. 1857, p. 1
6. *Morning Chronicle*, 6 Aug. 1856, p. 4

7. Brian Roberts, *The Mad Bad Line*, London: Hamish Hamilton, 1981, p. 14
8. Royal Archives Windsor, VIC/MAIN/A/25/117
9. Palmerston Papers, RC/F/741/1 pp. 3–4
10. *Caledonian Mercury*, 26 Aug. 1858, p. 2
11. British Library Manuscripts, Add. 79735 f. 143
12. Stock, *Nature's Nursling*, vol. 1, p. 48
13. Admiralty Circular No. 288, 23 Feb. 1857 accessed online at http://freepages.geneology.rootsweb.ancestry.com/~pbtyl/Navy_List_1870/Mid-Exams.html
14. *Sporting Times*, 13 June 1885, p. 2
15. *Era*, 15 Aug. 1858, p. 6
16. *Sporting Times*, 13 June 1885, p. 2
17. *Birmingham Daily Post*, 25 Aug. 1858, p. 1
18. *Evening Herald*, 9 Aug. 1858, p. 2
19. Ibid.
20. *Morning Chronicle*, 14 Aug. 1858, p. 6
21. *Bell's Life in London and Sporting Chronicles*, 15 Aug. 1858, p. 2
22. *Racing Times*, 6 Sept. 1858, p. 282
23. *Caledonian Mercury*, 20 Aug. 1858, p. 2
24. Stock, *Nature's Nursling*, vol. 1, p. 73
25. National Archives of Scotland, SC 15/41/11/323–4
26. National Archives of Scotland, op. cit. f. 325

10. Dixie, *Ijain* p. 14
11. The National Archives London, ADM 53/7751
12. Dixie, Ijain p. 19
13. Ibid., pp. 19–20
14. Ibid., p. 20
15. Ibid., p. 21
16. Ibid., p. 22
17. Ibid.
18. National Archives, ADM 50/329
19. Ibid., ADM 196/37 p. 21
20. *Whitehall Review*, 30 Nov. 1882, p. 7
21. *Caledonian Mercury*, 1 Sept. 1862, p. 2
22. *Pall Mall Gazette*, 31 May 1887, p. 1
23. Dixie, *Ijain*, p. 43
24. *London Figaro*, 16 Jan. 1896, p. 3
25. Ibid.
26. Ibid.
27. Dixie, *Ijain*, p. 43
28. Eardley-Wilmot, *An Admiral's Memories*, pp. 37–8
29. Ibid., p. 38
30. Admiral Sir Robert Hastings Harris, *From Naval Cadet to Admiral*, London: Cassell, 1913, p. 84
31. Ibid., p. 85
32. *Court Journal*, 5 Mar. 1864, p. 231
33. Dixie, *Ijain*, p. 49
34. Marquess of Queensberry, and Percy Colson, *Oscar Wilde and the Black Douglas*, London: Hutchinson, 1950, p. 49

Chapter 3: The Young Gentleman

1. *The Times*, 3 Nov. 1859, p. 6
2. Dixie, *Ijain*, p. 9
3. Ibid.
4. Ibid., p. 11
5. John Stephenson (ed.), *A Royal Correspondence*, London: Macmillian, 1938, p. 10
6. Lieut.-Commander Charles Frederick Walker, R. N. (Retired), *Young Gentlemen. The Story of Midshipmen from the XVIIth century to the present day*, London: Longmans, Green, 1938, p. 155
7. Admiralty Circular
8. *Cape Monthly Magazine*, 1 Sept. 1860, p. 144
9. Rear-Admiral Sir Sydney M. Eardley-Wilmot, *An Admiral's Memories*, London: Samson Low, Marston, 1927, p. 37

Chapter 4: Night on a Mountain

1. *Bailey's Monthly Magazine of Sports and Pastimes*, 1 Nov. 1868, p. 325
2. *Sporting Gazette*, 1 Apr. 1865, p. 233
3. *Sporting Life*, 6 Mar. 1883, p. 3
4. Dixie, *Ijain*, p. 55
5. Edward Whymper, *Scrambles amongst the Alps in the Years 1860–69*, London: John Murray, 1893, p. 13
6. Ibid., p. 96
7. Ibid., p. 368
8. *The Times*, 17 Aug. 1861, p. 11
9. Whymper, *Scrambles* p. 369
10. Ibid., p. 386
11. *The Times*, 2 Aug. 1865, p. 10
12. Dixie, *Ijain*, p. 64
13. Ibid., p. 70
14. Ibid.
15. Ibid.

16. Ibid., p. 71
17. Ibid.
18. Ibid.
19. Ibid., p. 105
20. *Illustrated London News*, 29 July 1865, p. 99
21. Queensberry, *Oscar Wilde Black Douglas*, p. 49
22. Ibid., p. 50
23. Lord Alfred Bruce Douglas, *Without Apology*, London: Martin Secker, 1938, p. 247
24. Lord Alfred Bruce Douglas, *The Autobiography of Lord Alfred Douglas*, London: Martin Secker, 1929, p. 10
25. Ibid., p. 15
26. Queensberry, *Oscar Wilde Black Douglas*, p. 50

Chapter 5: 'He Thought He Loved'

1. *Graphic*, 3 Nov. 1894, p. 518
2. George Washburn Smalley, *Society in London by a Foreign Resident*, 8th edn, London: Chatto & Windus, 1885, p. 61
3. *Graphic*, 13 Apr. 1895, p. 434
4. Sir Henry Drummond Wolff, *Rambling Recollections*, London: Macmillan, 1908, p. 76
5. Sir Algernon West, *Contemporary Portraits*, London: T. Fisher Unwin, 1920, p. 60
6. Ralph Nevill (ed.), *The Reminiscences of Lady Dorothy Nevill*, London: Edward Arnold, 1906, p. 144
7. *The Times*, 13 Jan. 1844, p. 5
8. British Library Manuscripts, Add. 40594 f. 503
9. Sir Algernon West, *Recollections 1832 to 1886*, New York and London: Harper & Brothers, 1900, p. 318
10. Dixie, *Ijain*, p. 79
11. Ibid., pp. 80–1
12. Ibid., p. 78
13. Queensberry, *Oscar Wilde Black Douglas*, p. 50
14. Ibid.
15. Ibid.
16. Stock, *Nature's Nursling*, vol. 1, pp. 152–3
17. Ibid., vol. 2, pp. 242–3
18. Queensberry, *Oscar Wilde Black Douglas*, p. 51
19. Stock, *Nature's Nursling*, vol. 2, p. 243
20. Sir Claude Champion de Crespigny, *Forty Years of a Sportsman's Life*, London: Mills and Boon, 1910, p. 62
21. Amy Charlotte Menzies, *Further Indiscretions*, London: Herbert Jenkins, 1918, p. 205
22. Douglas, *Without Apology*, p. 247
23. *Glasgow Herald*, 25 Nov. 1867, p. 4
24. *Liverpool Mercury*, 26 Nov. 1867, p. 6
25. Ibid.
26. *Preston Guardian*, 23 Nov. 1867, p. 4
27. *Pall Mall Gazette*, 16 Apr. 1870, p. 18
28. *Examiner*, 23 Apr. 1870, p. 11
29. *Freeman's Journal*, 3 Oct. 1873, p. 2
30. *Glasgow Herald*, 10 Apr. 1868, p. 6
31. Menzies, *Further Indiscretions*, p. 206
32. Ibid.
33. Cespigny, *Forty Years*, p. 79
34. Menzies: *Further Indiscretions*, p. 206
35. Ibid., p. 207
36. Ibid.
37. Ibid.
38. Letter said to have been written 31 Aug. 1868 and held by Bodleian Library Oxford, quoted in Roberts, *Mad Bad Line*, pp. 64–5 but original untraceable as at 2012
39. Queensberry, *Oscar Wilde Black Douglas*, p. 51
40. Ibid., p. 69
41. Information supplied by Lord Gawain Douglas
42. *Bailey's Monthly Magazine of Sports and Pastimes*, 1 Nov. 1868, pp. 324–8
43. Dixie, *Ijain*, p. 124
44. Ibid.
45. Ibid.
46. *Pall Mall Gazette*, 12 Apr. 1870, p. 5
47. *Worcestershire Chronicle*, 26 Apr. 1871, p. 2
48. Menzies, *Further Indiscretions*, p. 205
49. *Hampshire Telegraph and Sussex Chronicle* 6 Sept. 1871, p. 2
50. *Freeman's Journal*, 16 Nov. 1871, p. 3
51. Ibid., 23 Nov. 1871, p. 3
52. *Bristol Mercury*, 27 Jan. 1872, p. 5
53. National Library of Scotland, Rosebery Collection (hereafter Rosebery Collection) MS 10075 f. 171
54. *London Daily News*, 4 Dec. 1872, p. 2
55. *Reynolds's Newspaper*, 15 Dec. 1872, p. 4

Chapter 6: The Game and Sporting Lord

1. Miles, *Pugilistica*, vol. 1, p. x
2. *Sporting Life*, 16 Oct. 1867, p. 2
3. Ibid., 27 Nov. 1867, p. 4
4. Ibid., 1 Jan. 1868, p. 2
5. Ibid., 30 Dec. 1868, p. 2
6. *Bell's Life in London and Sporting Chronicle*, 20 July 1867, p. 11
7. *Penny Illustrated Paper*, 2 Mar. 1872, p. 138
8. Crespigny, *Forty Years*, p. 79
9. *Bell's Life in London and Sporting Chronicle*, 20 July 1867, p. 11
10. *Land and Water*, 14 Dec. 1867, p. 327
11. *Daily Alta California*, 20 May 1885, p. 2
12. *Sacramento Daily Union*, 8 June 1885, p. 2
13. *Birmingham Daily Post*, 1 Nov. 1871, p. 6
14. *Daily Graphic*, 26 Apr. 1873, p. 382
15. Menzies, *Further Indiscretions*, p. 188
16. *Daily Telegraph*, 25 Apr. 1873, p. 5
17. Menzies, *Further Indiscretions*, p. 205
18. Crespigny, *Forty Years*, p. 160
19. Ibid., p. 91
20. Menzies, *Further Indiscretions*, p. 205
21. Ibid.
22. *Era*, 8 June 1873 p. 10
23. *Illustrated London News*, 14 June 1873, p. 566
24. Menzies, *Further Indiscretions*, p. 203
25. Ibid. p. 204
26. *Essex County Standard*, 28 Jan. 1893, p. 6
27. Ibid. 8 June 1895, p. 2
28. Menzies, *Further Indiscretions*, p. 204
29. Ibid.
30. Ibid.
31. Ibid., p. 203
32. Ibid., pp. 203–4
33. Ibid., p. 205
34. Ibid.
35. National Library of Scotland, Rosebery Papers, MS 10075 f. 171
36. *Secular Review*, 6 Aug. 1881, p. 86
37. Bodleian Library, Ms. Dep. Hughenden, 125/1 f. 241
38. Ibid., f. 240
39. Duke of Manchester, *My Candid Recollections*, London: Grayson and Grayson, 1932, pp. 34–5
40. Ibid., p. 35
41. *Aberdeen Journal*, 2 Dec. 1894, p. 3
42. Douglas, *Without Apology*, p. 243
43. *Pall Mall Gazette*, 21 Oct. 1875, p. 9
44. *The Times*, 20 Nov. 1875, p. 5
45. Ibid., p. 9

Chapter 7: Original Notions

1. *Hampshire and Sussex Telegraph*, 5 Aug. 1882, p. 7
2. Dixie, *Ijain*, p. 159
3. Ibid., p. 160
4. Ibid., p. 166
5. Herbert Spencer, *Social Statics; or, the Conditions Essential to Human Happiness Specified, and the First of them Developed*, London: John Chapman, 1851, pp. 73–4
6. Ibid., p. 80
7. Queensberry, Marquess of, John Sholto Douglas, *The Spirit of the Matterhorn*, W. Mitchell, London, 1881, p. 19
8. Ibid.
9. Ibid., p. 21
10. Ibid.
11. Ibid.
12. Ibid.
13. Ibid., p. 23
14. Ibid.
15. Ibid., p. 24
16. Ibid.
17. Ibid., p. 25
18. Ibid.
19. Ibid., p. 26
20. Ibid., p. 28
21. National Archives of Scotland, GD164/1942
22. *Belfast Newsletter*, 3 Nov. 1879, p. 5
23. Menzies, *Further Indiscretions*, p. 208
24. Ibid.
25. *Vanity Fair*, 10 Nov. 1877, p. 293
26. Menzies, *Further Indiscretions*, p. 208
27. Ibid., p. 209
28. *Whitehall Review*, 27 Jan. 1877, p. 198
29. *Belfast Newsletter*, 11 Aug. 1876, p. 4
30. *Pall Mall Gazette*, 23 Apr. 1878, p. 9
31. Lady Florence Dixie, *Across Patagonia*, London: Richard Bentley, 1880, p. 2
32. Ibid.
33. Ibid., p. 6
34. Ibid., p. 9
35. Ibid., p. 12
36. Ibid., p. 14
37. Ibid.
38. Ibid., p. 21
39. Ibid., p. 25
40. Menzies, *Further Indiscretions*, p. 207
41. Ibid., p. 208

42. Ibid.
43. Dixie, *Patagonia*, p. 28
44. Ibid., pp. 28–9
45. Bodleian Library, Ms. Dep. Hughenden, 125/1 ff. 239–40
46. Ibid., ff. 241v–242
47. Ibid., f. 242
48. Ibid.
49. Ibid., p. 243
50. Ibid., pp. 243–243v
51. *Vanity Fair*, 25 Oct. 1897, p. 223
52. *Vanity Fair*, 1 Nov. 1879, p. 232
53. Ibid.
54. *Belfast Newsletter*, 3 Nov. 1879, p. 5
55. *Aberdeen Weekly Journal*, 4 Nov. 1879, p. 4
56. Ibid.
57. *Vanity Fair*, 15 Nov. 1879, p. 263
58. *Aberdeen Weekly Journal*, 18 Nov. 1879, p. 4
59. Rosebery Collection MS 10075 f. 171

Chapter 8: Judged by his Peers

1. *Glasgow Herald*, 17 Apr. 1880, p. 5
2. *Glasgow Herald*, 24 Mar. 1882, p. 7
3. *Glasgow Herald*, 19 Apr. 1880, p. 6
4. *Aberdeen Weekly Journal*, 20 Apr. 1880, p. 4
5. Rosebery Collection MS 10076 f. 30
6. British Library unbound manuscripts, Add. 81731
7. Queensberry, *Spirit*, pp. 3, 5, 5–6, 6, 17
8. *Liverpool Mercury*, 15 Jan. 1881, p. 5
9. Senate House Library, University of London, Herbert Spencer Archives, undated letters 791/332
10. *Nottingham Evening Post*, 7 Aug. 1882, p. 3
11. *Hampshire and Sussex Telegraph*, 17 Apr. 1880, p. 8
12. George Jacob Holyoake, *The Principles of Secularism Illustrated*, London: Austin, 1871, p. 11
13. Ibid.
14. *Liverpool Mercury*, 21 May 1881, p. 6
15. *National Reformer*, 29 May 1881, p. 443
16. *Pall Mall Gazette*, 10 June 1881, p. 5
17. *Western Mail*, 9 June 1881, p. 2
18. *Secular Review*, 6 Aug. 1881, p. 85
19. Ibid.
20. *Leicester Chronicle and Leicestershire Mercury*, 6 Aug. 1881, p. 3
21. *Liverpool Mercury*, 7 Sept. 1881, p. 5

22. See Author's Note, pp. ix–x
23. *Leicester Chronicle and Leicestershire Mercury*, 18 Feb. 1882, p. 6
24. *Nottingham Evening Post*, 7 Aug. 1882, p. 3
25. *Moray and Nairn Express*, 25 Nov. 1882, p. 3
26. *Daily Telegraph*, 15 Nov. 1882, p. 5
27. *Era*, 22 Sept. 1900, p. 11
28. *Globe*, 21 Nov. 1882, p. 2
29. *Fun*, 29 Nov. 1882, p. 226
30. *Aberdeen Weekly Journal*, 17 Nov. 1882, p. 4
31. Ibid., 21 Nov. 1882, p. 2
32. *Era*, 18 Nov. 1882, p. 5
33. *Graphic*, 18 Nov. 1882, p. 530
34. Ibid., p. 542
35. *Daily News*, 16 Nov. 1882, p. 4
36. *Daily News*, 17 Nov. 1882, p. 6
37. *Hampshire and Sussex Telegraph*, 25 Nov. 1882, p. 2
38. *Freethinker*, 26 Nov. 1882, p. 1
39. John Edwin McGee, *A History of the British Secular Movement*, 1948, p. 38
40. British Library Manuscripts, Add. 44480 f. 242
41. Ibid.
42. *Standard*, 12 Nov. 1885, p. 3
43. British Library Manuscripts, Add. 44506 f. 154

Chapter 9: An Undercurrent of Eccentricity

1. *Graphic*, 20 May 1882, p. 514
2. *Penny Illustrated Paper*, 17 Dec. 1881, p. 394
3. *Land and Water*, 27 Mar. 1880, p. 274
4. Ibid.
5. *Birmingham Daily Post*, 17 Apr. 1882, p. 5
6. *New York Times*, 23 July 1882, p. 9
7. With music by Isidore de Lara, which was published by Duff and Stewart.
8. Douglas, *Without Apology*, p. 238
9. Ibid., p. 239
10. *Western Mail*, 24 Nov. 1882, p. 2
11. Lady Augusta Fane, *Chit Chat*, London: Thornton Butterworth, 1926, p. 69
12. Leonard E. Naylor, *The Irrepressible Victorian*, London: Macdonald, 1965, p. 89
13. Ibid., p. 90
14. *Leeds Mercury*, 20 Mar. 1883, p. 4

15. *Birmingham Daily Post*, 23 Mar. 1883, p. 5
16. *Freeman's Journal*, 21 Mar. 1883, p. 5
17. *Echo*, 20 Mar. 1883, p. 2
18. *Reynolds's Newspaper*, 25 Mar. 1883, p. 1
19. *Echo*, 24 Mar. 1883, p. 1
20. *Dundee Courier*, 24 Mar. 1883, p. 3
21. *The Times*, Mar. 31, 1883, p. 10
22. *Moonshine*, 9 June 1883, p. 275
23. The Times, 30 July 1883, p. 12
24. Ibid., 18 Aug. 1883, p. 12
25. *Graphic*, 15 Sept. 1883, p. 279
26. Douglas, *Autobiography*, p. 8
27. *New York Times*, 31 May 1885, p. 4
28. *Daily Alta California*, 9 Nov. 1885, p. 6
29. Rosebery Collection, MS 10083 f. 300
30. Rosebery Collection, MS 10084 f. 191
31. *Glasgow Herald*, 11 Dec. 1885, p. 4
32. *Bat*, 15 Dec. 1885, p. 563
33. *Bat*, 22 Dec. 1885, p. 1
34. Ibid.
35. *Scotsman*, 12 Dec. 1885, p. 6
36. British Library unbound manuscripts, Add. 81731
37. Rosebery Collection, MS 10085 f. 36

Chapter 10: Full of Woes

1. *Liverpool Mercury*, 23 Feb. 1886, p. 5
2. Rosebery Collection, MS 10085 f. 69
3. Douglas, *Autobiography*, p. 1
4. Ibid.
5. Douglas, *Without Apology*, p. 247
6. Douglas, *Autobiography*, p. 92
7. Ibid., p. 93
8. Ibid.
9. Royal Archives Windsor, VIC/ADDA5/423
10. Ibid., VIC/ADDA5/438
11. National Archives of Scotland, CS116/43/2/1887
12. *Pall Mall Budget*, 3 Feb. 1887, p. 11
13. *Penny Illustrated Paper*, 15 Oct. 1887, p. 254
14. *Penny Illustrated Paper*, 14 Apr. 1888, p. 234
15. Allen Andrews, *The Splendid Pauper*, London: Harrap, 1968, p. 99
16. Lord Alfred Bruce Douglas, *Oscar Wilde and Myself*, London: John Long, 1914, pp. 91–4
17. Douglas, *Autobiography*, p. 92
18. *The Times*, 30 May 1888, p. 4
19. Ibid.
20. *Aberdeen Journal*, 5 June 1888, p. 7
21. *Liverpool Mercury*, 30 May 1888, p. 5
22. *South Australian Advertiser*, 8 June 1888, p. 5
23. *West Australian*, 13 June 1888, p. 3
24. *Bulletin*, 16 June 1888, p. 12
25. *Bulletin*, 23 June 1888, p. 12
26. *Northern Star (Australia)*, 28 July 1888, p. 3
27. *Western Mail*, 27 Sept. 1888, p. 4
28. *The Mercury (Hobart)*, 23 July 1888, p. 3
29. Ibid.
30. *Sacramento Daily Union*, 24 Dec. 1888, p. 1
31. *Pall Mall Gazette* 19 Jan. 1893, p. 7
32. *Western Mail*, 15 Mar. 1889, p. 2
33. *New York Herald* (US edn), 24 Mar. 1889, p. 24
34. Library of Congress Moreton Frewen Papers, Manuscript Division, Box 43 'Miscellaneous 1889'
35. *Aberdeen Journal*, 14 Nov. 1889, p. 6
36. *Era*, 13 Dec. 1889, p. 25
37. Robert Patrick Watson, *Memoirs of Robert Patrick Watson*, London: Smith, Ainslie, 1899, p. 102
38. *Western Mail*, 20 Oct. 1894, p. 5.
39. Frank Harris, *Oscar Wilde, his Life and Confessions including the hitherto unpublished Full and Final Confession by Lord Alfred Douglas, and My Memories of Oscar Wilde by Bernard Shaw*, 2 vols, Garden City New York, 1930, vol. 1, p. 157
40. British Library unbound manuscripts, Add. 81673
41. Harris, *Oscar Wilde*, vol. 1, pp. 157–8
42. Ibid., p. 158
43. Ibid.
44. Ibid.
45. *Freeman's Journal*, 10 Jan. 1890, p. 5
46. *Birmingham Daily Post*, 10 Jan. 1890, p. 4
47. *Manchester Times*, 1 Mar. 1890, p. 4
48. Ibid.
49. *Pall Mall Gazette*, 10 Aug. 1889, p. 7
50. *Pall Mall Gazette*, 12 Aug. 1889, p. 8
51. *Pall Mall Gazette*, 24 Nov. 1890, p. 6
52. *Daily Telegraph*, 12 Dec. 1892, p. 3
53. Arthur H. Nethercot, *The First Five Lives of Annie Besant*, London: Rupert Hart-Davis, 1961, pp. 388–9

Chapter 11: Four Sons and a Daughter

1. Douglas, *Autobiography*, p. 2
2. Ibid.
3. Ibid., p. 16
4. Ibid.
5. Ibid., p. 14
6. Queensberry, *Oscar Wilde Black Douglas*, p. 51.
7. Rosebery Collection, MS 10089 f. 25
8. *Dumfries and Galloway Courier*, 20 Oct. 1894, p. 5
9. Douglas, *Autobiography*, p. 95
10. National Archives, ADM 6/472
11. Ibid., ADM 196/43
12. Queensberry, *Oscar Wilde Black Douglas*, p. 64
13. National Archives, ADM/53/16349
14. Ibid., ADM 196/43
15. *The Times*, 3 Aug. 1920, p. 15
16. Queensberry, *Oscar Wilde Black Douglas*, p. 63
17. *Royal Cornwall Gazette and Falmouth Packet, Cornish Weekly News & General Advertiser*, 27 Mar. 1890, p. 7
18. *Northern Echo*, 18 Apr. 1890, p. 3
19. Queensberry, *Oscar Wilde Black Douglas*, p. 63
20. David Wynford Carnegie, *Spinifex and Sand*, London: Arthur Pearson, 1898, p. 12
21. Ibid., pp. 14–15
22. Queensberry, *Oscar Wilde Black Douglas*, p. 25
23. Holland, *Complete Letters*, p. 689
24. Douglas, *Autobiography*, p. 4
25. Ibid., pp. 2–3
26. Queensberry, *Oscar Wilde Black Douglas*, p. 25
27. Douglas, *Autobiography*, pp. 16–17
28. Ibid., p. 17
29. Ibid., p. 2
30. Ibid., p. 17
31. Douglas, *Without Apology*, p. 159
32. Ibid., p. 170
33. Douglas, *Autobiography*, p. 26
34. Douglas, *Without Apology*, p. 160
35. British Library unbound manuscripts, Add. 81731
36. Douglas, *Without Apology*, p. 240
37. Ibid., p. 241
38. Ibid.
39. Ibid.
40. Ibid.
41. Ibid., p. 242
42. Ibid., p. 181
43. *Daily Chronicle*, 30 June 1890, p. 6
44. Douglas, *Autobiography*, p. 64
45. *Reynolds's Newspaper*, 26 Nov. 1893, p. 8

Chapter 12: The Antipathy of Similars

1. Douglas, *Without Apology*, p. 246
2. *The Times*, 16 Feb. 1938, p. 14
3. *The Times*, 11 Apr. 1891, p. 15
4. *The Times*, 20 Apr. 1891, p. 13
5. *The Times*, 7 May 1891, p. 7
6. *Agnostic Journal*, 25 Nov. 1905, p. 337
7. Lady Florence Dixie, *The Songs of a Child and Other Poems by 'Darling'*, 2nd edn, London: Leadenhall Press, 1901, p. 66n
8. *Truth*, 19 July 1883, pp. 86–7
9. John Boon, *Victorians, Edwardians and Georgians*, 2 vols, London: Hutchinson, 1928, vol. 1, p. 200
10. Ibid., p. 201
11. Douglas, *Autobiography*, p. 98
12. Ibid.
13. Ibid.
14. Ibid., pp. 75, 76
15. Queensberry, *Oscar Wilde Black Douglas*, p. 29
16. Ibid., p. viii
17. Holland, *Complete Letters*, p. 684
18. British Library unbound manuscripts, Add. 81728
19. Ibid., Add. 81723
20. Lord Alfred Bruce Douglas, *Oscar Wilde, A Summing Up*, London: Icon Books, 1962, p. 22
21. *Echo*, 6 Apr. 1895, p. 2
22. John Francis Bloxam (ed.), *The Chameleon: a Bazaar of Dangerous and Smiling Chances*, Oxford: privately printed, Dec. 1894, p. 28
23. Douglas, *Oscar Wilde and Myself*, pp. 72–3
24. Douglas, *Autobiography*, p. 99
25. Ibid.
26. Douglas, *Without Apology*, p. 252
27. Douglas, *Autobiography*, p. 99
28. Douglas, *Without Apology*, p. 252
29. Harris, *Oscar Wilde*, vol. 1, pp. 149, 150 and 151
30. Douglas, *Summing Up*, p. 14

31. André Gide, *If It Die*, London: Martin Secker and Warburg, 1950, p. 271
32. Harris, *Oscar Wilde*, vol. 1, p. 201
33. Ibid., vol. 2, p. 431
34. Holland, *Complete Letters*, p. 759
35. Ibid., p. 544
36. Ibid., p. 691
37. Douglas, *Without Apology*, p. 11
38. *Spirit Lamp*, vol III no. 1, 3 Feb. 1893, p. 17
39. Douglas, *Without Apology*, p. 14
40. *Pall Mall Gazette*, 19 Jan. 1893, p. 7
41. Ibid.
42. Ibid.
43. Marquess of Queensberry, *Marriage and the Relation of the Sexes, an Address to Women*, London: Watts, 1893, p. 13
44. *Pall Mall Gazette*, 19 Jan. 1893, p. 7

Chapter 13: A Serious Slight

1. Crespigny, *Forty Years*, p. 187
2. Queensberry, *Oscar Wilde Black Douglas*, p. 49
3. Douglas, *Without Apology*, p. 176
4. Douglas, *Autobiography*, p. 99
5. Ibid., p. 82
6. Ibid., p. 100
7. Douglas, *Without Apology*, p. 250
8. Rosebery Collection, MS 10176, f. 257
9. Ibid.
10. Ibid.
11. Ibid.
12. Douglas, *Autobiography*, p. 94
13. Rosebery Collection, MS 10176, f. 255
14. Royal Archives Windsor, VIC/MAIN/L21/83
15. Rosebery Collection, MS 10176, f. 255
16. *Graphic*, 10 June 1893, p. 655
17. *New York Times*, 4 June 1893, p. 2
18. Horace G. Hutchinson (ed.), *Private Diaries of the Rt. Hon. Sir Algernon West, G.C.B.*, New York: E. P. Dutton, 1922, p. 163
19. Royal Archives, VIC/MAIN/L21/83
20. Ibid., VIC/MAIN/D/42/104
21. Ibid., VIC/MAIN/L/21/84
22. Ibid., VIC/MAIN/L/21/86
23. Hutchinson, *Private Diaries*, p. 168
24. *Manchester Guardian*, 19 Oct. 1894, p. 5
25. *Dumfries and Galloway Courier*, 20 Oct. 1894, p. 5

26. Rosebery Collection, MS 10065, f. 39
27. Ibid., MS 10176, f. 255
28. Ibid.
29. Ibid., MS 10176, f. 258
30. Ibid.
31. Harris, *Oscar Wilde*, vol. 1, p. 159
32. Rosebery Collection, MS 10176, f. 260
33. Ibid., f. 255
34. Ibid.
35. Ibid., f. 260
36. Ibid., f. 255
37. Royal Archives, VIC/MAIN/Y/60/234
38. Lady Walpurga Paget, *In My Tower*, 2 vols, London: Hutchinson, 1924, pp. 5–6
39. British Library Manuscripts, Add. 81723
40. Francis Archibald Kelhead Douglas, Marquess of Queensberry, *The Sporting Queensberrys*, London: Hutchinson, 1949, p. 162
41. Ibid., pp. 129–30
42. British Library unbound manuscripts, Add. 81723
43. Carnegie, *Spinifex*, p. 29
44. Douglas, *Autobiography*, p. 186
45. Ibid., p. 84
46. *The Times*, 3 Aug. 1920, p. 15

Chapter 14: Wounded Feelings

1. Holland, *Complete Letters*, p. 759
2. Douglas, *Oscar Wilde and Myself*, p. 34
3. H. Montgomery Hyde, *The Trials of Oscar Wilde*, London: William Hodge, 1949, p. 153
4. Queensberry, *Oscar Wilde Black Douglas*, p. 29
5. British Library unbound manuscripts, Add. 81732
6. *Eastbourne Gazette*, 15 Nov. 1893, p. 3
7. Ibid.
8. *Eastbourne Gazette*, 15 Nov. 1893.
9. *Western Mail*, 10 Nov. 1893, p. 3
10. Lady Gertrude Stock, *A Wasted Life and Marr'd*, London: Hurst and Blackett, 1892, vol. 1, p. 103
11. *Graphic*, 2 July 1892, p. 20
12. Holland, *Complete Letters*, p. 575
13. Ibid., p. 694
14. Ibid.
15. Ibid., p. 769
16. Ibid., p. 694
17. Ibid., p. 701

18. National Archives, J 77/532/16267/1
19. Ibid.
20. Ibid.
21. Douglas, *Autobiography*, p. 101
22. Ibid.
23. According to Harris it was the Pelican Club, but this had closed early in 1892 and if his story is true it is more likely to date from 1894 and to have taken place elsewhere.
24. Harris, *Oscar Wilde*, vol. 1, p. 172
25. Hyde, *Trials*, p. 152
26. Holland, *Complete Letters*, p. 707
27. Douglas, *Autobiography*, p. 100
28. Ibid., pp. 101–2
29. Holland, *Complete Letters*, p. 707
30. Hyde, *Trials*, pp. 153–4
31. Douglas, *Without Apology*, p. 235
32. Ibid., p. 236
33. *Aberdeen Journal*, 30 May 1895, p. 7
34. Douglas, *Without Apology*, p. 237
35. Ibid.
36. Ibid., pp. 252–3
37. Ibid., p. 253
38. National Archives, J/77/532/16267/1
39. Holland, *Complete Letters*, p. 708
40. British Library unbound manuscripts, Add. 81702
41. Hyde, *Trials*, p. 162
42. *Evening News*, 3 Apr. 1895, p. 3
43. Douglas, *Summing Up*, p. 59
44. Ibid.
45. Dialogue from Wilde's evidence at Queensberry's libel trial, Hyde, *Trials*, pp. 118–19
46. Holland, *Complete Letters*, p. 699
47. Hyde, *Trials*, pp. 154–5
48. Ibid., p. 155
49. Richard Ellmann, *Oscar Wilde*, London: Penguin, 1988, p. 395
50. National Archives CRIM 1/41/6
51. Hyde, *Trials*, pp. 162–3
52. Ibid., p. 163
53. Holland, *Complete Letters*, p. 598

Chapter 15: Catastrophe

1. Queensberry, *Sporting Queensberrys*, p. 155
2. Ibid.
3. Ibid., pp. 150–1
4. Douglas family collection
5. Hyde, *Trials*, p. 155
6. Ibid., p. 156
7. Rosebery Collection, MS 10097, ff. 241–3
8. British Library unbound manuscripts, Add. 81702
9. Rosebery Collection, MS 10097 f. 267
10. *Truth*, 11 Apr. 1889, p. 671
11. Hyde, *Trials*, p. 6
12. Royal Archives Windsor, PPTO/PP/QV/MAIN/1894/10728
13. *The Times*, 22 Oct. 1894, p. 12
14. *Illustrated London News*, 27 Oct. 1894, p. 526
15. Ibid.
16. *Graphic*, 27 Oct. 1894, p. 491
17. *Graphic*, 3 Nov. 1894, p. 518
18. Rosebery Collection, MS 10049 ff. 45–7
19. Ibid., MS, 10098 f. 117
20. Ibid.
21. Ibid.
22. Royal Archives PPTO/PP/QV/MAIN/1894/10728
23. Rosebery Collection MS 10098 ff. 140–3
24. Ibid.
25. Ibid., ff. 183–6
26. *Dumfries and Galloway Standard and Advertiser*, 27 Oct. 1895, p. 4
27. *Agnostic Journal*, 25 Nov. 1905, p. 337
28. *Dumfries and Galloway Standard and Advertiser*, 27 Oct. 1895, p. 4
29. Richard Ellmann papers, Coll. No. 1988–012. Department of Special Collections and University Archives, McFarlin Library, University of Tulsa, Tulsa, Oklahoma
30. Ibid.
31. Holland, *Complete Letters*, p. 619
32. Ibid., p. 621

Chapter 16: A Family Divided

1. Queensberry, *Sporting Queensberrys*, p. 155
2. Ibid.
3. Ibid.
4. British Library unbound manuscripts, Add. 81723
5. Douglas, *Autobiography*, p. 186
6. Queensberry, *Sporting Queensberrys*, pp. 151–2
7. British Library unbound manuscripts, Add. 81732

8. Ibid., Add. 81728
9. Ibid., Add. 81732
10. Queensberry, *Oscar Wilde Black Douglas*, p. 54
11. *Essex County Standard*, 8 June 1895, p. 2
12. Ellmann, *Oscar Wilde*, p. 405
13. Gide, *If It Die*, p. 272
14. Ibid.
15. Ibid., p. 275
16. British Library unbound manuscripts, Add. 81723
17. Ibid.
18. Ibid.
19. Ibid.
20. British Library unbound manuscripts, Add. 81733
21. Gide, *If It Die*, p. 289
22. British Library unbound manuscripts, Add. 81723
23. Queensberry, *Sporting Queensberrys*, p. 166
24. Holland, *Complete Letters*, p. 709
25. V. Wyndham, *The Sphinx and her Circle*, London: André Deutsch, 1963, p. 114
26. British Library unbound manuscripts, Add. 81732
27. Holland, *Complete Letters*, pp. 631–2
28. Ibid., p. 632
29. Ibid.
30. Douglas family collection
31. British Library unbound manuscripts, Add. 81728
32. Ibid., Add. 81732
33. Ibid., Add. 81728
34. Ibid., Add. 81732
35. British Library Manuscripts, Add. 81654 p. 3
36. Hyde, *Trials*, p. 115
37. Christopher Sclater Millard (compiler), *Oscar Wilde: Three Times Tried*, Paris: privately printed, 1915, p. 14
38. Holland, *Complete Letters* p. 776
39. Queensberry, *Oscar Wilde Black Douglas*, p. 56
40. Ibid.
41. British Library unbound manuscripts, Add. 81728
42. Queensberry, *Oscar Wilde Black Douglas*, p. 69

Chapter 17: The Peer and the Poet

1. Holland, *Complete Letters*, p. 634
2. Ibid., p. 635

3. Ibid., p. 634
4. Ibid., p. 703
5. Ibid., p. 765
6. Merlin Holland, *Irish Peacock and Scarlet Marquess: the Real Trial of Oscar Wilde*, London: Fourth Estate, 2003, p. 300 n. 43
7. National Archives, CRIM 1/41/6
8. Hyde, *Trials*, p. 31
9. *The Times*, 4 Mar. 1895, p. 14
10. Millard, *Three Times Tried*, p. 15
11. *London Figaro*, 14 Mar. 1895, p. 3
12. British Library unbound manuscripts, Add. 81732
13. Ibid., Add. 81728
14. Ibid.
15. *Evening News*, 9 Mar. 1895, p. 3
16. *Star*, 9 Mar. 1895, p. 3
17. *Evening News*, 9 Mar. 1895, p. 3
18. *Westminster Gazette*, 9 Mar. 1895, p. 5
19. *The Times*, 11 Mar. 1895, p. 4
20. Ibid.
21. National Archives, CRIM 1/41/6
22. *New York Times*, 10 Mar. 1895, p. 1
23. British Library unbound manuscripts, Add. 81728
24. Ibid.
25. Ibid.
26. Ibid., Add. 81723
27. Ibid.
28. Millard, *Three Times Tried*, p. 174
29. British Library unbound manuscripts, Add. 81732
30. Ibid.
31. Ibid., Add. 81723
32. Ibid.
33. Ibid.
34. Ibid.
35. Ibid.
36. Ibid.
37. Hyde, *Trials*, Appendix A, pp. 341, 344 and 345
38. Holland, *Complete Letters*, p. 690
39. Ibid., p. 670
40. Hyde, *Trials*, p. 38
41. Holland, *Complete Letters*, p. 670
42. *Essex County Standard*, 8 June 1895, p. 2

Chapter 18: In the Dock

1. Son of solicitor Charles Humphreys, a junior counsel in 1895, later a noted judge. Hyde, *Trials*, p. 1
2. Ibid., p. 47

3. *Sun*, 3 Apr. 1895, p. 3
4. *Westminster Gazette*, 3 Apr. 1895, p. 5
5. *Sun*, 3 Apr. 1895 p. 3
6. Ibid.
7. Ibid.
8. Millard, *Three Times Tried*, p. 27
9. Ibid.
10. *New York Herald* (European edn), 4 Apr. 1895, p. 1
11. Holland, *Complete Letters* p. 709
12. Hyde, *Trials*, p. 48
13. Ibid., p. 108
14. Ibid., p. 109
15. Ibid., pp. 112–13
16. Ibid., p. 113
17. Ibid., pp. 113–14
18. Ibid., p. 114
19. Millard, *Three Times Tried*, p. 29
20. Ibid.
21. Ibid., p. 30
22. Hyde, *Trials*, p. 51
23. *New York Herald* (European edn), 4 Apr. 1895, p. 1
24. *Glasgow Herald*, 5 Apr. 1895, p. 9
25. *Echo*, 4 Apr. 1895, p. 3
26. *Westminster Gazette*, 4 Apr. 1895, p. 5
27. *Sun*, 4 Apr. 1895, p. 3
28. *Glasgow Herald*, 5 Apr. 1895, p. 9
29. Hyde, *Trials*, p. 52
30. *Sun*, 4 Apr. 1895, p. 3
31. Hyde, *Trials*, p. 150
32. Ibid.
33. *Sun*, 4 Apr. 1895, p. 3
34. Hyde, *Trials* p. 164
35. Ibid., p. 167
36. Ibid.
37. Ibid., p. 168
38. Edward Marjoribanks, *The Life of Lord Carson*, 3 vols, London: Victor Gollancz, 1932, vol. 1, p. 222
39. Hyde, *Trials*, p. 169
40. Ibid., p. 170
41. Ibid., pp. 171–2
42. Ibid., p. 174
43. Ibid.
44. Ibid., p. 176
45. Ibid., p. 11
46. *Pall Mall Gazette*, 5 Apr. 1895, p. 9
47. Ibid.
48. *Westminster Gazette*, 5 Apr. 1895, p. 5
49. Hyde, *Trials*, p. 57
50. *Sun*, 6 Apr. 1895, p. 3
51. *Westminster Gazette*, 5 Apr. 1895, p. 5
52. Holland, *Complete Letters*, p. 637
53. *Sun*, 5 Apr. p. 3
54. H. Montgomery Hyde, *Oscar Wilde*, London: Magnum, 1977, p. 292
55. *New York Herald* (European edn), 6 Apr. 1895, p. 1
56. Ibid.
57. *The Times*, 9 Apr. 1895, p. 4
58. *National Observer*, 6 Apr. 1895, p. 547
59. *St James's Gazette*, 4 Apr. 1895, p. 3
60. *St. James's Gazette*, 5 Apr. 1895, p. 4
61. Holland, *Complete Letters*, p. 691
62. Douglas, *Autobiography*, p. 106
63. *Sun*, 6 Apr. 1895, p. 3
64. British Library unbound manuscripts, Add. 81732
65. *National Observer*, 6 Apr. 1895, p. 547
66. *Aberdeen Journal*, 6 Apr. 1895, p. 5

Chapter 19: The Price of Victory

1. *Star*, 16 Apr. 1895, p. 4
2. *Star*, 19 Apr. 1895, p. 3
3. *Star*, 20 Apr. 1895, p. 3
4. *Star*, 24 Apr. 1895, p. 2
5. *Star*, 25 Apr. 1895, p. 2
6. British Library unbound manuscripts, Add. 81723
7. Millard, *Three Times Tried*, p. 347n
8. *Glasgow Herald*, 25 Apr. 1895, p. 8
9. She was born on 2 June 1875. Information provided by Loretta's cousin Linda Hahn
10. *Glasgow Herald*, 25 Apr. 1895, p. 8
11. *San Francisco Call*, 26 Apr. 1895, p. 1
12. *Sun*, 26 Apr. 1895 p. 3
13. *Reynolds's Newspaper*, 2 June 1895, p. 5
14. *Star*, 7 May 1895, p. 3
15. Robert H. Sherard, *The Life of Oscar Wilde*, New York: Mitchell Kennerley, 1906, p. 358
16. British Library unbound manuscripts, Add. 81723
17. Ibid.
18. Ibid.
19. Ibid.
20. Ibid.
21. Ibid., Add. 81728
22. Ibid.
23. Ibid.
24. Ibid., Add. 81732
25. Ibid.
26. Ibid., Add. 81728

27. Queensberry, *Oscar Wilde Black Douglas*, p. 67
28. Ibid.
29. *Lloyd's Weekly*, 26 May 1895, p. 20
30. *Western Mail*, 23 May 1895, p. 6
31. Queensberry, *Oscar Wilde Black Douglas*, p. 67
32. Ibid.
33. Ibid.
34. *Western Mail*, 23 May 1895, p. 6
35. *Pall Mall Gazette*, 22 May 1895, p. 8
36. Ibid.
37. Ibid.
38. Ibid.
39. *York Herald*, 22 May 1895, p. 5
40. Ibid.
41. *Western Mail*, 23 May 1895, p. 6
42. Ibid.
43. Ibid.
44. *Pall Mall Gazette*, 22 May 1895, p. 8
45. *Star*, 22 May 1895, p. 5
46. *Pall Mall Gazette*, 22 May 1895, p. 8
47. British Library unbound manuscripts, Add. 81723
48. *Pall Mall Gazette*, 24 May 1895, p. 8
49. Hyde, *Trials*, p. 331
50. Millard, *Three Times Tried*, p. 428
51. *Star*, 27 May 1895, p. 2
52. E. F. Benson, *As We Were*, London, New York, Toronto: Longmans, Green, 1930, p. 227
53. *Essex County Standard*, 8 June 1895, p. 2
54. *Westminster Gazette*, 27 May 1895, p. 7
55. *Reynolds's Newspaper*, 2 June 1895, p. 5
56. British Library unbound manuscripts, Add. 81723
57. Ibid. Add. 81732
58. Ibid.
59. *Essex County Standard*, 1 June 1895, p. 2
60. Patrick Jackson (ed.) *Loulou. Selected Extracts from the Journals of Lewis Harcourt (1880–1895)*, Teaneck: Fairleigh Dickinson University Press, NJ, 2004, p. 261
61. Anon., *Fifty Years of London Society*, p. 153
62. British Library unbound manuscripts, Add. 81732
63. British Library Manuscripts, Add. 81654 p. 3
64. Ibid., p. 4
65. Horst Schroeder, *Additions and Corrections to Richard Ellmann's Oscar*

Wilde, 2nd edn, Braunschweig: privately printed, 2002, p. 174
66. British Library unbound manuscripts, Add. 81723
67. Douglas, *Autobiography*, p. 121
68. Ibid., p. 122
69. Ibid.

Chapter 20: 'Where Stars shall ever shed their Light'

1. Douglas, *Autobiography*, p. 122
2. *Westminster Gazette*, 17 Apr. 1895, p. 8
3. *Penny Illustrated Paper* cycling supplement, 6 July 1895, p. 2
4. Queensberry, *Sporting Queensberrys*, p. 161
5. Ibid. pp. 165–6
6. British Library unbound manuscripts, Add. 81728
7. *San Francisco Chronicle*, 22 Aug. 1895, p. 11
8. *Pall Mall Gazette*, 30 Oct. 1895, p. 8
9. *Pall Mall Gazette*, 5 Sept. 1894, p. 2
10. British Library unbound manuscripts, Add. 81723
11. Ibid.
12. Ibid.
13. Ibid., Add. 81702
14. *London Figaro*, 9 Jan. 1896 p. 3
15. *London Figaro*, 16 Jan. 1896, pp. 2–3
16. Ibid.
17. British Library unbound manuscripts, Add. 81723
18. Queensberry, *Sporting Queensberrys*, p. 160
19. Douglas, *Without Apology*, p. 214
20. *Reynolds's Newspaper*, 21 June 1896, p. 3
21. British Library unbound manuscripts, Add. 81701
22. Douglas, *Autobiography*, p. 151
23. Holland, *Complete Letters*, p. 901
24. Douglas, *Autobiography*, p. 151
25. Douglas family collection
26. Douglas, *Autobiography*, p. 84
27. Holland, *Complete Letters*, p. 680
28. Lord Alfred Bruce Douglas, *The Collected Poems of Lord Alfred Douglas*, London: Martin Secker, 1919, verse 13
29. Ibid., verse 17
30. Ibid., verses 18, 22
31. Ibid., verse 22

32. Douglas, *Autobiography*, pp. 123 and 124
33. Douglas, *Without Apology*, p. 248
34. Douglas, *Autobiography*, p. 124
35. Ibid.
36. Ibid., p. 125
37. Hyde, *Trials*, p. 10
38. Douglas, *Without Apology*, p. 247
39. Ibid., p. 249
40. *Western Mail*, 25 July 1899, p. 5
41. British Library unbound manuscripts, Add. 81733
42. Ibid.
43. Ibid., Add. 81702
44. Ibid., Add. 81726
45. Death certificate
46. British Library unbound manuscripts, Add. 81733
47. National Archives of Scotland, SC 15/41/26/1086
48. *Northampton Mercury*, 23 Feb. 1900, p. 5
49. *Agnostic Journal*, 25 Nov. 1905, p. 337
50. *Belfast Newsletter*, 5 Feb. 1900, p. 3
51. *Birmingham Daily Post*, 2 Feb. 1900, p. 4
52. *Northampton Mercury*, 2 Feb. 1900, p. 2
53. *Sporting Times*, 3 Feb. 1900, p. 5
54. *Daily Telegraph*, 2 Feb. 1900, p. 3
55. *Western Mail*, 2 Feb. 1900, p. 4
56. *The Times*, 1 Feb. 1900, p. 6
57. *The Times*, 7 Feb. 1900, p. 13
58. *Agnostic Journal*, 10 Feb. 1900, p. 84
59. *Agnostic Journal*, 18 Nov. 1906, p. 330
60. Holland, *Complete Letters*, p. 1173
61. Douglas, *Without Apology*, p. 249
62. *Cork Examiner*, 27 Feb. 1904, p. 5
63. *Freeman's Journal*, 18 Feb. 1904, p. 5
64. *Illustrated London News*, 18 Nov. 1905, p. 740
65. Douglas, *Without Apology*, p. 253

Bibliography

Archive sources

Bishopsgate Institute

Holyoake 2/42 1893 Diary of G. J. Holyoake 1893

Bodleian Library Oxford

Ms. Dep. Hughenden 125/1 ff. 230–240 Letter from Queensberry to Lord Beaconsfield, 7 Apr. 1879
Ms. Dep. Hughenden 125/1 ff. 241–244r Letter from Queensberry to Lord Beaconsfield, 10 Apr. 1879

British Library Manuscripts

26 Aug. 1841, Add. 40446 f. 17, Letter from Archibald Viscount Drumlanrig to Sir J. R. G. Graham
30 June 1846, Add. 40594 f. 503, Letter from Fanny Montgomery to Sir Robert Peel
18 Feb. 1848, Add. 44367 f. 81, Letter from Archibald Viscount Drumlanrig to W. E. Gladstone
c. 1852, Add. 43190 f. 379, Letter from Archibald Viscount Drumlanrig to Sir J. R. G. Graham
3 Jan. 1857, Add. 79735 f. 143, Letter from Sir J. R. G. Graham to Archibald, 8th Marquess Queensberry
18 Apr. 1881 unbound manuscripts, Add. 81731, Letter from W. E. Gladstone to Queensberry
24 Apr. 1883, Add. 44480 f. 242, Letter from Queensberry to W. E. Gladstone
Undated probably between 1884 and 1888, unbound manuscripts, Add. 81731, Letter from Queensberry to Lord Alfred Douglas
16 Nov. 1885, Add. 44493 f. 84, Letter from Queensberry to W. E. Gladstone
22 Dec. 1885, unbound manuscripts, Add. 81731, Letter from Herbert Spencer to Queensberry
7 Apr. 1889, Add. 44506 f. 154, Letter from Queensberry to W. E. Gladstone
11 Feb. 1891, Add. 44512 f. 92, Letter from Queensberry to W. E. Gladstone
14 Feb. 1891, Add. 44512 f. 103, Letter from Queensberry to W. E. Gladstone
22 Aug. 1893, unbound manuscripts, Add. 81723, Letter from Queensberry to Lord Percy Douglas
17 Sept. [1893?] unbound manuscripts, Add. 81723, Letter from Queensberry to Lord Percy Douglas
24 Nov. 1893, unbound manuscripts, Add. 81723, Letter from Edward St Clair Weeden to Lord Alfred Douglas

20 June [1894?], unbound manuscripts, Add. 81702, Letter from Sybil, Marchioness of Queensberry to Lord Alfred Douglas

Undated but probably Sept. 1894, unbound manuscripts, Add. 81702, Letter from Sybil, Marchioness of Queensberry to Lord Alfred Douglas

20 Jan. 1895, unbound manuscripts, Add. 81723, Letter from Queensberry to Lord Percy Douglas

14 Feb. 1895, unbound manuscripts, Add. 81723, Letter from Algy Bourke to Sybil Marchioness of Queensberry

18 Feb. 1895, unbound manuscripts Add. 81728, Letter from Queensberry to Lady A. M. Douglas

26 Feb. 1895, unbound manuscripts Add. 81728, Letter from Queensberry to Lady A. M. Douglas

27 Feb. 1895, unbound manuscripts Add. 81728, Letter from Queensberry to Lady A. M. Douglas

4 Mar. 1895, unbound manuscripts Add. 81728, Letter from Queensberry to Lady A. M. Douglas

6 Mar. 1895, unbound manuscripts Add. 81728, Letter from Queensberry to Lady A. M. Douglas

11 Mar. 1895, unbound manuscripts Add. 81728, Letter from Queensberry to Lady A. M. Douglas

12 Mar. 1895, unbound manuscripts Add. 81728, Letter from Queensberry to Lady A. M. Douglas

21 Mar. 1895, unbound manuscripts Add. 81728, Telegram from Queensberry to Lady A. M. Douglas

23 Mar. 1895, unbound manuscripts, Add. 81732, Letter from Queensberry to Lord Alfred Douglas

27 Mar. 1895, unbound manuscripts, Add. 81723, Letter from Queensberry to Lord Percy Douglas

10 or 16 Apr. 1895, unbound manuscripts, Add. 81732, Letter from Revd Lord Archibald Douglas to Lord Percy Douglas

Mar.–May 1895 unbound manuscripts, Add. 81723, Letters and telegrams between Queensberry and Stoneham

12 May 1895, unbound manuscripts, Add. 81728, Letter from Queensberry to Lady A. M. Douglas

14 May 1895, unbound manuscripts, Add. 81728, Letter from Queensberry to Lady A. M. Douglas

15 May 1895, unbound manuscripts, Add. 81732, Letter from Queensberry to Revd. Walters

28 June 1895, unbound manuscripts, Add. 81732, Letter from Lord Alfred Douglas to W. T. Stead

29 June 1895, unbound manuscripts, Add. 81728, Letter from Queensberry to Lady A. M. Douglas

Undated letters [c1895?], unbound manuscripts, Add. 81723, Queensberry to Lord Percy Douglas

c. July or Aug. 1895, Add. 81654, Oscar Wilde by Lord Alfred Douglas, typescript of unpublished article

Undated, but probably 1895, unbound manuscripts, Add. 81732, Letter from Lord Percy Douglas to the committee of the Army and Navy Club

Undated but probably 1895, unbound manuscripts, Add. 81702, Letter from Sybil, Marchioness of Queensberry to Lord Alfred Douglas

25 Dec. 1895, unbound manuscripts, Add. 81723, Letter from Queensberry to Lord Percy Douglas

15 Jan. 1896, unbound manuscripts, Add. 81723, Letter from Queensberry to Lord Percy Douglas

19 Dec. 1899, unbound manuscripts, Add. 81733, Letter from Lady Florence Dixie to Lord Percy Douglas

20 Dec. 1899, unbound manuscripts, Add. 81733, Letter from Lady Florence Dixie to Lord Percy Douglas

Undated but either Dec. 1899 or January 1900, unbound manuscripts, Add. 81702, Letter from Sybil, Marchioness of Queensberry to Lord Alfred Douglas

2 July 1911, unbound manuscripts, Add. 81736, Letter from Revd Lord Archibald Douglas to Lord Alfred Douglas

Copy of *Oscar Wilde His Life and Confessions, with memories of Oscar Wilde by Bernard Shaw*, by Frank Harris, with undated pencil annotations by Lord Alfred Douglas, Add. 81673

Douglas family collection

Letter from Lord Alfred Douglas to Lord Percy Douglas, 19 Aug. 1894
Telegram from Queensberry to Lord Percy Douglas, 16 Feb. 1895
Letter from Lord Alfred Douglas to Lord Percy Douglas, 5 Aug. 1897

Library of Congress, Washington, DC

Moreton Frewen Papers, Manuscript Division, Box 43 'Miscellaneous 1889'

National Archives, London

ADM 6/472 Records of Royal Naval College
ADM 38/3797 Ship's muster, HMS *Illustrious*, 1 Jan. 1858–30 June 1858
ADM 38/3798 Ship's muster, HMS *Illustrious*, 1 July 1858–31 Dec. 1858
ADM 38/5487 Ship's muster, HMS *Aboukir* Jan.–Sept. 1860
ADM 38/5737 Ship's muster, HMS *Britannia* Jan.–Dec. 1859
ADM 38/6090 Ship's muster, HMS *Edgar* 11 July 1862–Mar. 1863
ADM 38/6091 Ship's muster, HMS *Edgar* Apr.–Dec. 1863
ADM 38/6092 Ship's muster, HMS *Edgar* Jan.–June 1864
ADM 38/6093 Ship's muster, HMS *Edgar* July–Dec. 1864
ADM 38/6730 Ship's muster, HMS *Nile* July–Dec. 1862
ADM 38/7334 Ship's muster, HMS *Victory* Apr.–June 1862
ADM 38/7337 Ship's muster, HMS *Victory* to 31 Mar. 1863
ADM 38/7338 Ship's muster, HMS *Victory* 1 Apr. 1863–30 June 1863
ADM 38/7434 Ship's muster, HMS *Aboukir*, 25 May 1859–15 Oct. 1862
ADM 38/7719 Ship's muster, HMS *Cadmus* 14 May 1859–6 May 1863
ADM 38/8031 Ship's muster, HMS *Emerald* 12 May 1859–7 Nov. 1863
ADM 38/8149 Ship's muster HMS *Forte* 14 Jan. 1860–8 Sept. 1864
ADM 38/8876 Ship's muster, HMS *Rinaldo* 3 May 1861–10 Feb. 1865
ADM 38/9247 Description book of HMS *Vesuvius* 13 May 1862–8 Nov. 1864
ADM 50/284 Journal of Admiral Keppel
ADM 50/317 Journal of Admiral Keppel
ADM 50/329 Journal of Admiral Robert Smart
ADM 53/6261 Ship's log HMS *Illustrious*, 12 July 1857–16 July 1858
ADM 53/6262 Ship's log HMS *Illustrious*, 17 July 1858–31 Dec. 1858
ADM 53/7357 Ship's log HMS *Aboukir* 26 May 1859–28 Nov. 1859
ADM 53/7358 Ship's log HMS *Aboukir* 29 Nov. 1859–26 May 1860
ADM 53/7623 Ship's log HMS *Cadmus* 17 Dec. 1862–6 May 1863
ADM 53/7751 Ship's log HMS *Emerald*, 29 Apr. 1861–5 Dec. 1861
ADM 53/7752 Ship's log HMS *Emerald*, 6 Dec. 1861–27 July 1862
ADM 53/7792 Ship's log HMS *Britannia* 1 Jan. 1859–31 Dec. 1860

ADM 53/7904 Ship's log HMS *Nile* 21 July 1861–7 June 1862
ADM 53/7905 Ship's log HMS *Nile* 8 June 1862–25 Mar. 1863
ADM 53/8005 Ship's log HMS *Forte* from 28 Jan. 1860–31 Oct. 1860
ADM 53/8006 Ship's log HMS *Forte* from 1 Nov. 1860–23 May 1861
ADM 53/8007 Ship's log HMS *Forte* 24 May 1861–6 Mar. 1862
ADM 53/8046 Ship's log HMS *Vesuvius* 13 May 1862–17 Dec. 1862
ADM 53/8149 Ship's log HMS *Rinaldo*, 4 Jan. 1862–6 Sept.1862
ADM 53/8150 Ship's log HMS *Rinaldo*, 7 Sept. 1862–6 June 1863
ADM 53/8223 Ship's log HMS *Revenge* 15 Jan. 1862–9 Oct. 1862
ADM 53/8402 Ship's log HMS *Edgar* 30 May 1863–20 Feb. 1864
ADM 53/8403 Ship's log HMS *Edgar* 21 Feb. 1864–5 Dec. 1864
ADM 53/8760 Ship's log HMS *Victory*, 1 Jan. 1862–3 Jan. 1863
ADM 53/16349 Ship's log HMS Triumph 1 Jan. 1885–25 Apr. 1886
ADM 101/223 Medical journal of HMS *Rinaldo* 1 July–31 Dec. 1862 by Dr Archibald Leslie Archer, surgeon.
ADM 115/1 Ship record and establishment book, HMS *Aboukir* 25 May 1859–25 Aug. 1862
ADM 115/2 Ship record and establishment book, HMS *Aboukir* 25 May 1859–25 Aug. 1862
ADM 115/131 Ship record and establishment book, HMS *Britannia*, 1 Jan. 1859–31 Dec. 1863
ADM 115/132 Ship record and establishment book, HMS *Britannia*, 1 Jan. 1859–31 Dec. 1863
ADM 115/147 Ship record and establishment book, HMS *Cadmus* 7 May 1859–6 May 1863
ADM 115/320 Ship record and establishment book, HMS *Edgar* 11 July 1862–14 Dec. 1865
ADM 115/331 Ship record and establishment book, HMS *Emerald* 12 May 1859–7 Nov. 1863
ADM 115/407 Ship record and establishment book, HMS *Forte* 24 Jan. 1860–8 Sep. 1864
ADM 115/829 Ship record and establishment book, HMS *Rinaldo* 13 May 1861-10 Feb. 1865
ADM 115/1029 Ship record and establishment book, HMS *Victory* 1 Jan. 1862–31 Dec. 1866
ADM 196/15 Naval officers' service records (Queensberry)
ADM 196/37 Naval officers' service records (Queensberry)
ADM 196/43 Naval officers' service records (Percy Sholto Douglas)
B 9/428-9 Bankruptcy papers, Oscar Wilde
CRIM 1/41/6 Trial of Marquess of Queensberry for libel
DPP 1/96 Correspondence concerning possibility of prosecuting Lord Alfred Douglas
HO 45/24516 Correspondence concerning possibility of prosecuting Lord Alfred Douglas
J 77/532/16267 Annulment of Queensberry's marriage with Ethel

National Archives of Scotland

GD164/1942 Letter from Queensberry to Earl of Rosslyn
SC 15/41/11 p.p. 310–324 Testamentary papers of Archibald William Douglas
SC15/41/26 p.p. 1078–1086 Testamentary papers of John Sholto Douglas
SC15/41/28 p.p. 516–518 Additional inventory of John Sholto Douglas
SC15/41/28 p.p. 1262–1264 Additional inventory of John Sholto Douglas
CS116/43/2/1887 Scottish divorce papers

BIBLIOGRAPHY

National Library of Scotland, Rosebery Collection

MS 10075 f. 171 Letter from Queensberry to Earl of Rosebery 1879
MS 10076 f. 30 Letter from Queensberry to Earl of Rosebery May 1880
MS 10079 f. 122 Letter from Queensberry to Earl of Rosebery 16 Nov. 1882
MS 10083 f. 300 Letter from Queensberry to Earl of Rosebery 21 Sept. 1885
MS 10084 f. 191 Letter from Queensberry to Earl of Rosebery 23 Nov. 1885
MS 10085 f. 36, Letter from Queensberry to Earl of Rosebery 30 Jan. 1886
MS 10085 f. 69 Letter from Queensberry to Earl of Rosebery 15 Feb. 1886
MS 10065 f. 39 Letter from Queensberry to HM Queen 17 July 1893
MS 10098 f. 117 Copy of letter sent by Queensbery to W. E. Gladstone 20 Oct. 1894
MS10098 ff. 140–141 Letter from Ellis to Earl of Rosebery 22 Oct. 1894
MS 10089 f. 25 Letter from Drumlanrig to Earl of Rosebery 24 Mar. 1891
MS 10097 f. 241 Letter from Drumlanrig to Earl of Rosebery 18 Sept. 1894
MS 10016 f. 129 letter from Prince of Wales to Earl of Rosebery 2 Sept. 1893
MS 10176 ff. 255–259 Earl of Rosebery memorandum Aug. 1893
MS 10176 ff. 260–261 Copies of letters from Queensberry to Earl of Rosebery Aug. 1893
MS 10097 ff. 267–270 Letter from Henry Foley to Earl of Rosebery 21 Sept. 1894
MS 10049 ff. 42–44 Letter from Sir George Murray to Earl of Rosebery 19 Oct. 1894
MS 10049 ff. 45–48 Letter from Sir George Murray to Earl of Rosebery 22 Oct. 1894
MS 10098 ff. 183–6 Letter from Neville Waterfield to Earl of Rosebery 27 Oct. 1894

National Museum of the Royal Navy, Portsmouth

Item 303/79 Log HMS *Aboukir*, kept by C. A. Browne, Master's Mate June 1859–Oct. 1862

Royal Archives Windsor

PPTP/PP/QV/MAIN/1894/10728 Letter from Queensberry to Queen Victoria, 22 Oct. 1894
VIC/MAIN/A/25/117 Letter from Lord Palmerston to Queen Victoria, 8 July 1856
VIC/MAIN/C/28/58 Letter from Lord Aberdeen to Queen Victoria submitting Archibald Lord Drumlanrig's name as comptroller, 26 Dec. 1852
VIC/MAIN/D/42/104 Letter from Lord Rosebery to Queen Victoria, 12 June 1893
VIC/MAIN/L/21/83, 84, 86, 87, 87A Correspondence concerning the Drumlanrig peerage, 1893
VIC/MAIN/Y/60/234 Letter from Rosebery's secretary to the Queen from Bad Homburg, 29 Aug. 1893
VIC/ADDA5/423, 438 Letters from the Prince of Wales to Alfred Montgomery, possibly 1884 and 1886

Senate House Library, University of London

Herbert Spencer Archives undated letters 791/332

Southampton University, Palmerston Archives

RC/F/741/1 Letter to Lord Palmerston from Queen Victoria, 9 July 1856
PP/RC/FF/ 29/1, p. 1 Letter from Lord Palmerston to Queen Victoria, 14 June 1855

University of Tulsa, Oklahoma

Richard Ellmann Papers, Coll. No. 1988–012, Department of Special Collections and University Archives, McFarlin Library

BIBLIOGRAPHY

Published sources

Allen, Grant, *The Woman Who Did*, John Lane, London, 1895

Andrews, Allen, The *Splendid Pauper*, Harrap, London, 1968

Anon., *Echoes of the Eighties. Leaves from the Diary of a Victorian Lady*, Eveleigh Nash, London, 1921

Anon., *Fifty Years of London Society*, Eveleigh Nash, London, 1920

Anon., *The Light of Other Days*, Edinburgh Press, London, 1924

Anon., *Songs by the Wayside of an Agnostic's Life*, W. Stewart, London, 1883

Anon., *The Trial of Oscar Wilde from the shorthand reports*, privately printed, Paris, 1906

Astley, Sir John Dugdale Bt, *Fifty Years of my Life in the World of Sport at Home and Abroad*, 4th edn, Hurst and Blackett, London, 1895

Behrman, S. N., *Portrait of Max: An Intimate Memoir of Sir Max Beerbohm*, Random House, New York, 1960

Benson, E. F., *As We Were*, The Longman's, Green, London, New York, Toronto, 1930

Bloxam, John Francis (ed.), *The Chameleon: a Bazaar of Dangerous and Smiling Chances*, privately printed, Oxford, Dec. 1894

Blyth, Henry, *Old Q, the Rake of Piccadilly*, Weidenfeld & Nicolson, London, 1967

Bonner, Hypatia Bradlaugh, *Charles Bradlaugh*, 2 vols, T. Fisher Unwin, London, 1894

Boon, John, *Victorians, Edwardians and Georgians*, 2 vols, Hutchinson, London, 1928

Booth, William, *In Darkest England*, Salvation Army, London, 1890

Bradley, J., *The Boxing Referee. An Exhaustive Treatise on the Duties of a Referee and an Explanation of the Queensberry Rules, etc*, Queenhythe Printing & Publishing, London, 1910

Burke, John, Esq., *A General and Heraldic Dictionary of the Peerage and Baronetage of the United Kingdom*, Henry Colburn, London, 1826

Carnegie, David W., *Spinifex and Sand*, Arthur Pearson, London, 1898

Chancellor, E. Beresford, *The Lives of the Rakes*, 6 vols, Philip Allan, London, 1925, vol. 5: *Old Q and Barrymore*

Chimmo, William, *Midshipman's Diary: a Few Notes Extracted from the Cockpit Journal of a Man-of-war*, J. D. Potter, London, 1862

Cokayne, George Edward (ed.), *The Complete Baronetage*, 5 vols, *c.* 1900, reprint, Alan Sutton, Gloucester, 1983, vol. 5, p. 72

Crespigny, Sir Claude de Champion, *Forty Years of a Sportsman's Life*, Mills and Boon, London, 1910

Croft-Cooke, Rupert, *Bosie*, W. H. Allen, London, 1963

Crook, J. Mordaunt, 'The New Square Style: Robert Smirke's Scottish Houses', in Ian Gow and Alistair Rowan (eds), *Scottish Country Houses 1600–1914*, Edinburgh University Press, Edinburgh, 1995, pp. 206–16

——, 'Sir Robert Smirke, a Centenary Florilegium', *The Architectural Review*, vol. 142, no. 847 (Sept. 1967), pp. 208–10

Debrett, John, *The Peerage of the United Kingdom of Great Britain and Ireland in two volumes*, J. Moyes, London, 1820, vol. 2 Scotland and Ireland

——, and William Courthope (eds), *Debrett's Complete Peerage of the United Kingdom of Great Britain and Ireland*, J. G. & F. Rivington, London, 1834

Deghy, Guy, *Noble and Manly. The History of the National Sporting Club, incorporating The Posthumous Papers of the Pelican Club*, Hutchinson, London, 1956

Dixie, Lady Florence, *Across Patagonia*, Richard Bentley, London, 1880

——, *The Horrors of Sport*, Humanitarian League, London, 1891

——, *In the Land of Misfortune*, R. Bentley, London, 1882

——, *Isola; or, the Disinherited, a Revolt for Woman and All the Disinherited, with Remarks therein by George Jacob Holyoake, Esq.*, Leadenhall Press, London, *c.* 1902

——, *Izra, a Child of Solitude*, John Long, London, 1906

——, *The Songs of a Child and Other Poems by 'Darling'*, 2nd edn, Leadenhall Press, London, 1901

——, *The Story of Ijain*, Leadenhall Press, London, 1903

Douglas, Lord Alfred Bruce, *The Autobiography of Lord Alfred Douglas*, Martin Secker, London, 1929

——, *The Collected Poems of Lord Alfred Douglas*, Martin Secker, London, 1919

——, *Oscar Wilde and Myself*, John Long, London, 1914

——, *Oscar Wilde, A Plea and a Reminiscence*, Introduced and annotated by Caspar Wintermans, Avalon Press, Woubrugge, 2002

——, *Oscar Wilde, A Summing Up*, Icon Books, London, 1962

——, *Without Apology*, Martin Secker, London, 1938

—— (ed.), *The Spirit Lamp*, James Thornton, Oxford, 1892–3

Douglas, Sir Robert, Bt, *The Peerage of Scotland*, 2 vols, 2nd edn revised by J. P. Wood, Edinburgh, 1813

Eardley-Wilmot, Rear-Admiral Sir Sydney M., *An Admiral's Memories*, Samson Low, Marston, London, 1927

Egremont, Lord, *Wyndham and Children First*, Macmillan, London, 1968

Ellmann, Richard, *Oscar Wilde*, Penguin, London, 1988

Fane, Lady Augusta, *Chit Chat*, Thornton Butterworth, London, 1926

Foote, C. W. *Reminiscences of Charles Bradlaugh*, Progressive Publishing, London, 1891

Gide, André, *If It Die*, Martin Secker & Warburg, London, 1950

Gifford, John (ed.), *The Buildings of Scotland: Dumfries and Galloway*, Penguin, London, 1996

Grant, James, *Old and New Edinburgh*, 6 vols, Cassell, Petter, Galpin, London, Paris and New York, 1880

Gronow, R. H., *Celebrities of London and Paris*, Smith, Elder, London, 1865

——, *Reminiscences and Recollections of Captain Gronow*, 2 vols, J. C. Nimmo, London, 1889

Groome, Francis H., *Ordnance Gazetteer of Scotland*, 6 vols, Thomas C. Jack, Edinburgh, 1885

Gross, Samuel W., *A Practical Treatise on Impotence, Sterility, and Allied Disorders of the Male Sexual Organs*, Henry Kimpton, London, 1881

Harris, Frank, *Oscar Wilde, his Life and Confessions including the hitherto unpublished Full and Final Confession by Lord Alfred Douglas, and My Memories of Oscar Wilde by Bernard Shaw*, 2 vols, Garden City, New York, 1930

Harris, Admiral Sir Robert Hastings, *From Naval Cadet to Admiral*, Cassell, London, 1913

Headingley, Adolphe S., *The Biography of Charles Bradlaugh*, Freethought, London, 1883

H.G.H.C, *Amateur Boxing Association: Its History*, Amateur Boxing Association, London, 1965

Holding, T. H., *Uniforms of the British Army, Navy and Court*, Facsimile edn Frederick Muller, London, 1969; originally published T. H. Holding, London, 1894

Holland, Merlin, *Irish Peacock and Scarlet Marquess: the Real Trial of Oscar Wilde*, Fourth Estate, London, 2003

——, and Rupert Hart-Davis (eds), *The Complete Letters of Oscar Wilde*, Henry Holt, New York, 2000

Hollingshead, John, *Good Old Gaiety*, Gaiety Theatre Co., London, 1903

Holyoake, George Jacob, *The Principles of Secularism Illustrated*, Austin, London, 1871

Hume, David, *The History of the House and Race of Douglas and Angus*, Mortimer and McLeod, London, 1820

Hutchinson, Horace G. (ed.), *Private Diaries of the Rt. Hon. Sir Algernon West, G.C.B.*, E. P. Dutton, New York, 1922

Hyde, H. Montgomery, *Famous Trials 7: Oscar Wilde*, Penguin, London, 1962

——, *Oscar Wilde*, Magnum, London, 1977

——, *The Other Love*, Mayflower, London, 1972

——, *The Trials of Oscar Wilde*, William Hodge, London, 1949

Jackson, Patrick (ed.), *Loulou. Selected Extracts from the Journals of Lewis Harcourt (1880–1895)*, Fairleigh Dickinson University Press, Teaneck, NJ, 2004

Kent, John, *Racing Life of Lord George Cavendish Bentinck MP*, William Blackwood, Edinburgh and London, 1892

Keppel, Sir Henry, *A Sailor's Life*, 3 vols, Macmillan, London, 1899

Knowlton, Charles, MD, *Fruits of Philosophy*, Preface by Charles Bradlaugh and Annie Besant, The Reader's Library, San Francisco, 1891

Lennox, Lord William Pitt, *Drafts on My Memory*, 2 vols, Chapman and Hall, London, 1866

McCabe, Joseph, *Life and Letters of George Jacob Holyoake*, 2 vols, Watts, London, 1908

Macfarlane, Robert, *Mountains of the Mind*, Granta Books, London, 2004

McGee, John Edwin, *A History of the British Secular Movement* (1948) Accessed online, 22 Dec. 2011) http://www.infidels.org/library/historical/john_mcgee/british_secular_movement.html

Mackay, Charles R., *Life of Charles Bradlaugh MP*, D. J. Gunn, London, 1888

McKenna, Neil, *The Secret Life of Oscar Wilde*, Arrow, London, 2004

McKinstry, Leo, *Rosebery: Statesman in Turmoil*, John Murray, London, 2005

Manchester, Duke of, *My Candid Recollections*, Grayson and Grayson, London, 1932

Marjoribanks, Edward, *The Life of Lord Carson*, 3 vols, Victor Gollancz, London, 1932

Mason, Stuart, *Bibliography of Oscar Wilde*, 2 vols, T. Werner Laurie, London, 1914

Maxwell, Sir Herbert, *A History of the House of Douglas*, 2 vols, Freemantle, London, 1902

Menzies, Amy Charlotte, *Further Indiscretions*, Herbert Jenkins, London, 1918

Miles, Henry Downes, *Pugilistica, the History of British Boxing*, 3 vols, John Grant, Edinburgh, 1906

Millard, Christopher Sclater (compiler), *Oscar Wilde: Three Times Tried*, privately printed, Paris, 1915

Montgomery, Fanny Charlotte (née Wyndham), *Mine Own Familiar Friend*, 3 vols, Hurst and Blackett, London, 1872

——, *Truth without Prejudice*, J. G. F. Rivington, London, 1842

Montgomery, Florence, *A Very Simple Story*, R. Bentley, London, 1867

Mosley, Charles (ed.), *Burke's Peerage, Baronetage & Knightage, 107th edn*, 3 vols, Burke's Peerage (Genealogical Books), Wilmington, Delaware, USA, 2003

Moyle, Franny, *Constance: The Tragic and Scandalous Life of Mrs Oscar Wilde*, John Murray, London, 2011

Nares, George S., Lieut. R. N., *The Naval Cadet's Guide; or Seaman's Companion*, Portsea, London, 1860

Navilus, *A few Days in the Life of a Royal Naval Cadet on board HMS 'Britannia'*, George Phillip, London, 1894

Naylor, Leonard E., *The Irrepressible Victorian*, Macdonald, London, 1965

Neale, J. P., *Views of the Seats of Noblemen and Gentlemen in England, Wales, Scotland and Ireland*, J. P. Neale, London, 1823

Nethercot, Arthur H., *The First Five Lives of Annie Besant*, Rupert Hart-Davis, London, 1961

Nevill, Ralph (ed.), *The Reminiscences of Lady Dorothy Nevill*, Edward Arnold, London, 1906

——, *Under Five Reigns by Lady Dorothy Nevill*, Methuen, London, 1910

O'Byrne, W. R., *A Naval Biographical Dictionary*, John Murray, London, 1849

Paget, Lady Walpurga, *In My Tower*, 2 vols, Hutchinson, London, 1924

Paul, Sir James Balfour (ed.), *The Scots Peerage*, 9 vols, David Douglas, Edinburgh, 1904–14

Pearson Hesketh, *Labby (The Life and Character of Henry Labouchère)*, Hamish Hamilton, London 1945

Portland, Duke of, *Men, Women and Things*, Faber and Faber, London, 1937

Queensberry, Marquess of, Francis Archibald Kelhead Douglas, *The Sporting Queensberrys*, Hutchinson, London, 1949

——, and Percy Colson, *Oscar Wilde and the Black Douglas*, Hutchinson, London, 1950

Queensberry, Marquess of, John Sholto Douglas, *Marriage and the Relation of the Sexes, an Address to Women*, Watts, London, 1893

——, *The Spirit of the Matterhorn*, W. Mitchell, London, 1881

Roberts, Brian, *The Mad Bad Line*, Hamish Hamilton, London, 1981

Robertson, J. M., *Charles Bradlaugh*, Watts, London, 1920

——, *A Short History of Freethought Ancient and Modern*, Swan Sonnenschein, London, 1899

Robinson, John Robert, *Old Q: a Memoir of William Douglas, 4th Duke of Queensberry*, Sampson Low, London, 1895

Schroeder, Horst, *Additions and Corrections to Richard Ellmann's Oscar Wilde*, 2nd edn, privately printed, Braunschweig 2002

Sherard Robert H., *The Life of Oscar Wilde*, Mitchell Kennerley, New York, 1906

——, *Oscar Wilde, the Story of an Unhappy Friendship*, Greening, London, 1905

——, *Oscar Wilde Twice Defended from André Gide's Wicked Lies, and Frank Harris' Cruel Libels, to which is added, A Reply to George Bernard Shaw, A Refutation of Dr G. J. Renier's Statements, A Letter to the Author from Lord Alfred Douglas an Interview with Bernard Shaw by Hugh Kingsmill*, The Argus Book Shop, Chicago, 1934

——, *The Real Oscar Wilde*, T. Werner Laurie, London, *c.* 1915

Smalley, G. W., *Society in London by a Foreign Resident*, 8th edn, Chatto & Windus, London, 1885

Smythe, F. S., *Edward Whymper*, Hodder & Stoughton, London, 1940

Spencer, Herbert, *Social Statics; or, the Conditions Essential to Human Happiness Specified, and the First of them Developed*, John Chapman, London, 1851

Stephenson, John (ed.), *A Royal Correspondence*, Macmillian, London, 1938

Stock, Lady Gertrude, *Linked Lives*, Hurst and Blackett, London, 1876

——, *Nature's Nursling, a Romance from Real Life*, 3 vols, Kegan Paul, Trench, London, 1885

——, *A Wasted Life and Marr'd*, Hurst and Blackett, London, 1892

Stone, J. M., *Eleanor Leslie*, Art and Book, London, 1898

Strauss, David Friedrich (trans. M. Blind), *The Old Faith and the New*, 2 vols, Newburgh, New York, 1873

Sutherland, Douglas, *The Yellow Earl. The Life of Hugh Lowther 5th Earl of Lonsdale, KG, GCVO, 1857–1944*, Cassell, London, 1965

Tennyson, Alfred Lord, *The Promise of May*, printed for the author, London, 1882

Thorold, Algar Labouchère, *The Life of Henry Labouchère*, G. P. Putnam's, The Knickerbocker Press, New York and London, 1913

Vincent, William Thomas, *Recollections of Fred Leslie*, 2 vols, Kegan Paul, Trench, Trübner, London, 1894

Walford, Edward, *Hardwicke's Annual Biography for 1857*, Robert Hardwicke, London, 1857

——, *Old and New London; illustrated. A Narrative of its History, its People, and its Places*, 6 vols, Cassell, Petter and Galpin, London, 1873–8

Walker, C. F., Lieut-Commander, R. N. (Retired), *Young Gentlemen. The Story of Midshipmen from the XVIIth Century to the Present Day*, Longmans, Green, London, 1938

Ward, E. M., *Memories of Ninety Years*, Hutchinson, London, 1925

Warwick, Frances Countess of, *Life's Ebb and Flow*, Hutchinson, London, 1929

Watson, R. P., *Memoirs of Robert Patrick Watson*, Smith, Ainslie, London, 1899

West, Sir Algernon, *Contemporary Portraits*, T. Fisher Unwin, London, 1920

——, *Recollections 1832 to 1886*, Harper & Brothers, New York and London, 1900

Whymper, Edward, *The Ascent of the Matterhorn*, John Murray, London, 1880

——, *Scrambles amongst the Alps in the Years 1860–69*, John Murray, London, 1893

——, *The Valley of Zermatt and the Matterhorn, a Guide*, John Murray, London, 1897

Wilde, Oscar, *The Works of Oscar Wilde*, Hamlyn, London, 1977

Wilmot, Admiral Sir Sydney Marow Eardley, *An Admiral's Memories*, Sampson Low, London, 1927

Winton, John, 'Life and Education in a Technically Evolving Navy: 1815–1925', in J. R. Hill (ed.), *Oxford Illustrated History of the Royal Navy*, Oxford University Press, Oxford, 1995

Wolff, Sir Henry Drummond, *Rambling Recollections*, Macmillan, London, 1908

Wyndham, V., *The Sphinx and her Circle*, André Deutsch, London, 1963

Yeats, W. B., *Autobiographies*, Macmillan, London, 1955

BIBLIOGRAPHY

Periodicals

Aberdeen Journal (*Aberdeen Weekly Journal* from 1876)
Agnostic Journal
Bailey's Monthly Magazine of Sports and Pastimes
Bat
Belfast Newsletter
Bells' Life in London, and Sporting Chronicle
Birmingham Daily Post
Bridgwater Independent
Bridgwater Mercury
Bristol Mercury
Bulletin
Caledonian Mercury
Cape Monthly Magazine
Chameleon
Champion and Weekly Herald
Cork Examiner
Court Journal
Daily Alta California
Daily Chronicle
Daily News
Daily Telegraph
Dublin Mail
Dumfries and Galloway Courier
Dumfries and Galloway Standard and Advertiser
Dumfries Standard
Dundee Courier
Eastbourne Gazette
Echo
Edinburgh Evening Courant
Era
Essex County Standard
Evening Herald
Evening News
Examiner
Freeman's Journal
Freethinker
Friend of India (Calcutta)
Fun
Gazetter and London Advertiser
Gentlemen's Magazine
Glasgow Herald
Glasgow Mail
Globe
Graphic
Hampshire Telegraph and Sussex Chronicle
Hobart Tasmania Mercury
Hull Packet
Illustrated London News
Illustrated Police News
Irishman
Johannesburg Star
Land and Water

BIBLIOGRAPHY

Leeds Mercury
Leicester Chronicle and Leicestershire Mercury
Liverpool Mercury
Lloyd's Weekly
London Daily News
London Figaro
Manchester Guardian
Manchester Times
Mercury (Hobart)
Moonshine
Moray and Nairn Express
Morning Chronicle
Morning Post
National Observer
New York Herald (European edn)
New York Herald (US edn)
New York Times
Northampton Mercury
Northern Echo
Northern Star (Australia)
Nottingham Evening Post
Pall Mall Budget
Pall Mall Gazette
Penny Illustrated Paper
Preston Guardian
Racing Times
Reynolds's Newspaper
Royal Cornwall Gazette and Falmouth Packet, Cornish Weekly News & General Advertiser
Sacramento Daily Union
San Francisco Call
San Francisco Chronicle
Satirist
Scotsman
Secular Review
South Australian Advertiser
Sporting Gazette
Sporting Life
Sporting Times
Standard
Star
St James's Gazette
Sun
Telegraph
The Times
Truth
Vanity Fair
Weekly Register
West Australian
Western Mail
Westminster Gazette
Whitehall Review
Worcestershire Chronicle
World
York Herald

BIBLIOGRAPHY

Genealogical Data

Baptismal record of South Bersted 1842 accessed Family History Centre London, film 0918259

Parish Registers of Cummertrees 1733–1855 accessed Family History Centre London, film 1067957

Acts of Parliament and official publications

The Metropolitan Police Act 1839 (2 & 3 Vict. c. 47)

Section 11, The Criminal Law Amendment Act 1885 (48 & 49 Vict. c. 69)

The Libel Act 1843 (6 & 7 Vict. c. 96).

Admiralty Circular No. 288, 23 Feb. 1857

Accessed http://freepagesgenealogy.rootsweb.ancestry.com/~pbtyc/Navy_List_1870/Mid_Exams.html

Online resources

David Wynford Carnegie, in the *Australian Dictionary of Biography* accessed 1 Mar. 2012. http://adb.anu.edu.au/biography/carnegie-david-wynford-5509

Information on St Peter's Church, Zermatt accessed 18 Mar. 2011. http://www.ics-uk.org/churches/Switzerland_Zermatt.shtml

Sinnott, Nigel, 'The Rev. Stewart Headlam and Friends: Anglo-Catholics, Atheists, Actors, Aesthetes and Radical', Talk given to the Existentialist Society Melbourne, 1 Aug. 2006, http://www.hadland.me.uk/sinnott_headlam.pdf accessed 1 Mar. 2012

Index